William Russell

Normal Training

The principles and methods of human culture

William Russell

Normal Training
The principles and methods of human culture

ISBN/EAN: 9783744723541

Printed in Europe, USA, Canada, Australia, Japan

Cover: Foto ©Thomas Meinert / pixelio.de

More available books at **www.hansebooks.com**

THE

PRINCIPLES AND METHODS

OF

HUMAN CULTURE:

A SERIES OF LECTURES ADDRESSED TO YOUNG TEACHERS.

BY WILLIAM RUSSELL,

EDITOR OF THE AMERICAN (BOSTON) JOURNAL OF EDUCATION, 1826 TO 1829, AND PRINCIPAL OF THE NEW ENGLAND NORMAL INSTITUTE, LANCASTER, MASS., ETC., ETC.

PART I. INTELLECTUAL EDUCATION.
PART II. MORAL EDUCATION.

SECOND EDITION.

HARTFORD:
THE AMERICAN JOURNAL OF EDUCATION.
1873.

PREFATORY REMARKS.

THE series of lectures, of which the following are a part, was addressed, originally, to students pursuing a course of professional study, under the author's direction, in the Merrimack (N. H.) Normal Institute, and in the New England Normal Institute, Lancaster, Massachusetts. The course, as delivered, extended to the subjects of physical, moral, and æsthetic culture; including, under the latter heads, remarks on principle as the foundation of character, and suggestions on the cultivation of taste.

In the delivery of the lectures, it was deemed important to avoid the unfavorable influence of formal didactic exposition, in a course of professional lectures to a youthful audience. Equal importance, however, was attached to a strict observance of the systematic connection of topics, and the theoretic unity of the whole subject. The method adopted, therefore, in the routine of the lecture-room, was to treat a given point daily, in a brief oral address on one prominent topic, selected from the notes embodying the plan of the whole course.

At the suggestion of Dr. Henry Barnard, the notes, in their connected form, were transcribed for insertion in his Journal; and the lectures on Intellectual Education were selected for this purpose, rather as an experiment, on the part of the author, in his uncertainty how far it might be advisable to present the whole series. But the unexpectedly favorable reception which the course on intellectual education has met from teachers, both at home and abroad, would have induced the writer to transcribe the other portions of the series, had health and time permitted. The subjects here referred to, however, will be introduced, from time to time, as may be practicable, in future numbers of Dr. Barnard's Journal.

The thoughts presented in the following pages, the author hopes, may serve to attract the attention of teachers who are so situated as to occupy the ground not merely of instructors but of educators, who have it in their power to control, to some extent, the plan and progress of education; and all teachers of the requisite zeal and thoughtfulness, even in the most limited sphere of responsibility, can do much in this way, by their personal endeavors in instruction. It is not in one department only, or in one stage, that the field of education needs resurveying.

PREFATORY REMARKS.

The whole subject, notwithstanding our many valuable recent improvements in processes and methods, physical and moral, as well as intellectual, needs a careful reconsideration as to its true requirements, and a thorough revision of our plan of procedure and modes of culture.

It is true that, in seminaries of education of every grade, we are ceasing from a blind following of prescription imposed by the past. Mental discipline, rather than intellectual acquisition, is now more generally recognized as the true aim of education; and liberal changes and generous allowances, as regards the adaptation of text-books and plans of instruction, have accordingly been made. But, as yet, the point of view selected by most even of our most considerate and genial counselors on the great theme of education, has been far from a commanding one. It has been that of subjects and sciences and departments of knowledge, with their respective demands upon the mind, instead of that of the mind itself, and its divine laws of action and progress, as prescribed by its own constitution and wants, its appetites and instinctive preferences. To attract attention to these, as the true principles of education, is the chief aim of the suggestions embodied in the following pages.

PART I.
INTELLECTUAL EDUCATION.

CONTENTS.

	PAGE.
INTELLECTUAL EDUCATION,	9
The teacher's aim in instruction,	9
Necessity of plan and method,	10
Preliminary analysis,	11
Outline of intellectual instruction,	12
I. THE PERCEPTIVE FACULTIES,	12
1. Classification by modes of action,	12
2. Curiosity,	14
3. Observation,	17
4. Knowledge,	21
5. Appropriate processes for their cultivation,	26
II. THE EXPRESSIVE FACULTIES,	57
Introductory observations,	57
1. Enumeration,	58
2. The actuating principle,	70
3. Tendency or habit of action,	75
4. Result of the action—communication,	76
5. Educational processes for their cultivation,	80
6. Means of correcting prevalent errors,	93
III. THE REFLECTIVE FACULTIES,	101
Introductory observations,	101
1. Enumeration,	102
2. The actuating principle: inquiry,	121
3. Tendency of action,	122
4. Result of the action: truth,	125
5. Educational processes for their development,	127
Concluding explanations,	152
INDEX to the principal topics considered,	155

CULTIVATION OF THE PERCEPTIVE FACULTIES.

INTRODUCTORY OBSERVATIONS.—The circumstances in which the following lectures were delivered, will, it is thought, account for the prominence given in them to many things merely elementary, as regards the science of mind and the philosophy of education. An audience favored with the advantages of high intellectual culture, or of long experience in instruction, would, doubtless, have required a different treatment of many topics discussed in such a course of lectures as the present. But a long series of years occupied in the training of teachers, has proved to the author of the present communication, that the greater number of candidates for the office of instruction, and of those to whom its duties are comparatively new, need nothing so much as an elementary knowledge of intellectual philosophy, and of logic, in their connection with education, as the science which teaches the appropriate development and discipline of the mind.

The Teacher's Aim in Instruction.—Few teachers, at the present day, regard knowledge as the great end even of intellectual education. Few are now unwilling to admit that the chief aim of their daily endeavors, as instructors and educators, should be to train, develop, and discipline the powers by which knowledge is acquired, rather than to attempt the immediate accumulation of knowledge itself. In practice, however, and, more particularly, in the case of young teachers, and of those who follow the occupation as a transient one, and not as the vocation of a life-time, the eagerness for definite and apparent results, or even showy acquirements, too often induces the instructor to confine his attention to the mere mechanism of specific processes, —to the committing to memory, and the repetition of a set task, with or without the aid of explanation. This course he knows will nominally secure a single point in practice or effect. He thinks, perhaps, that, although not fully understood or appreciated now, it will certainly benefit the mind of his pupil at some future day, when his

---

*The series of lectures of which the present forms a part, extended to the departments of physical and moral training. But those on the progress of intellectual culture, are selected as more easily presented in the form of a series of articles for an educational Journal.

mind is more mature. Hence, we still have, in our school routine, too much of mere rule and repetition, detached fact and specific direction, the lesson of the hour and the business of the day, and too little of the searching interrogation, close observation, reflective thought, and penetrating investigation, by which alone the mind can be trained to the acquisition of useful knowledge, or the attainment of valuable truth.

Necessity of Plan and Method.—The master builder, when he goes to oversee his workmen, and watch their progress in the work of raising the edifice, for the construction of which he has entered into contract, never fails to carry with him his plan of erection, and with that in his hand, for constant reference, gives directions for even the minutest details in working. He does nothing but in execution of his plan, and in strict accordance with it. The master builder thus reads a lesson to the master instructor, (inward builder,) who, although he needs not plan in hand, for his peculiar work, needs it no less, ever present to his mind, if he wishes to become "a workman that needeth not to be ashamed;" if, in a word, he would enjoy the conscious pleasure of referring every day's labor to its destined end of building up the mental fabric in strength, and symmetry, and enduring beauty.

The young teacher, as he reviews the business of the day with his pupils,—and would that this were a daily practice in every school!—should ever refer, in his own mind, at least, to the general effect of every exercise, as tending to the great results of education,—to the expansion of the mind, to the formation of habits of observation and inquiry, to control over attention, to the clearing and sharpening of the percipient faculties, to the strengthening of the mind's retentive power, to securing, in a word, intellectual tendency and character, as the basis of moral development and habit. The teacher, not less than the builder, should ever have, in his mind's eye, the plan of his edifice; aud while, during the whole process of erection, he wastes no time on fanciful theory or fantastic ornament, every operation which he conducts should be, to his own consciousness, part of a great whole, tending to a grand consummation. Text-books, processes, exercises, apparatus of every description, are properly, but the pliant tools, or the subject material, in the hands of the skillful teacher, by means of which he does his great work of "building up the being that we are;" and all these aids he arranges, selects, modifies, and applies, according to the system suggested by his plan and purpose.

As the overseer and artificer of the mental fabric of character, the teacher who is worthy of the name, must necessarily possess a knowledge of the material on which he works. It would be well, were this knowledge always profound and philosophical; and, among the happy anticipations suggested by the establishment of normal schools, none is more cheering than the hope that, ere long, society will be furnished with a numerous class of teachers, competent to understand and guide the young mind through all its stages of growth and development, and furnished with all the requisite means of securing the noblest results of human culture.

Meanwhile, the laborers who are already in the field, and who have not enjoyed, perhaps, extensive opportunities of acquiring a scientific knowledge of the chemistry of mental culture, must be content with such aids as their own observation, reading, reflection, or experience, may furnish.

As a slight contribution to the common stock of professional facilities, the author of the present article would submit the following outline to the consideration of his fellow teachers, as an intended aid to the systematizing of their efforts for the mental advancement of their pupils.

The analysis which follows, extends, it will be perceived, no farther than to the limits of intellectual education. The physical and the moral departments of culture, may be discussed at another opportunity, and must be dismissed for the present, with the single remark, that the natural unity of the human being, demands a ceaseless attention to these, in strict conjunction with that more immediately under consideration.

PRELIMINARY ANALYSIS.—Contemplating man's intellectual constitution as subjected to the processes of education, we may conveniently group his mental powers and faculties under the following denominations:—*perceptive, reflective*, and *expressive*. In expression, as a function of man at the period of his maturity, the order, in the preceding classification, may be termed the normal or usual one. Man perceives, reflects, speaks. But in education, whether regarded as a natural process or an artificial one, the order of classification suggested by the experience and the history of the human being, in his early and comparatively immature condition, would present the *expressive* powers as in exercise long before the *reflective*, and, subsequently, as the appointed means of developing these, through the medium of language.

OUTLINE OF INTELLECTUAL CULTURE.—An outline map, or plan of intellectual culture, as aided by the processes of education, may be carried into practical detail, as suggested by the following prominent points of analysis.

§. 1. Classification of the intellectual faculties, by the different modes, or forms of mental action.

2. Statement of the actuating principle, or impelling power of each class or group of faculties.

3. The tendency, or habit of action in each class.

4. The result, or issue of such action.

5. The educational processes adapted to each class of faculties with a view to aid its natural tendency, and secure its results.

From the imperfection of our language, in relation to topics strictly mental, or purely philosophical, the word *faculties* is unavoidably employed to represent the diversities in modes of action of the mind, which, in itself, is, properly speaking, one and indivisible. But if we keep fully before us the etymological signification of the term *faculties*, (resources, means, powers,) we shall regard it but as a figurative expression, suggestive of the indefinitely diversified states, acts, operations, processes, powers, or modes of action, attributable to the mind, —itself a unit.

Adopting the general classification before referred to, we may commence the partial filling up of our outline with

1. THE PERCEPTIVE FACULTIES.

§. 1. Their *modes* or forms of action :

a, sensation ; *b*, perception ; *c*, attention : *d*, observation.

2. *Actuating principle*, or impelling force, *curiosity*,—or the desire of knowledge.

3. *Tendency*, or habit of action,—*observation*.

4. *Result*, or issue of action,—*knowledge*.

5. *Educational process*, forms of exercise, or modes of culture, development, and discipline suggested by the four preceding considerations,—*examination, analysis, inspection, interrogation, direction, information, comparison, classification, induction*. In other words, the appropriate *presentation of objects to the senses*, accompanied by mutual question and answer by teacher and pupil ;—with a view to quicken sensation, awaken perception, give power of prompt and sustained attention, confirm the habit of careful observation, stimulate curiosity, and insure the extensive acquisition of knowledge.

(1.) CLASSIFICATION OF THE PERCEPTIVE FACULTIES, BY THEIR MODES OF ACTION.

§. (*a*,) *Sensation*,—the *organic* action by which objects, facts, and relations are presented to the mind, through the media of the *senses*, and which form the conditions of perception.

§. (*b*,) *Perception*, or cognition,—the *intellectual* action by which the mind *perceives*, (takes notice, or cognizance of,) data presented by the senses.

§. (c,) *Attention*,—the *mental* action by which, under the incitation of *desire* or *volition*, the percipient intellect *tends*, for the purposes of distinct cognizance, towards the object, fact, or relation presented to it.

§. (d,) *Observation*,—*the voluntary, sustained, or continuous exercise of attention*, with which the mind directs itself toward the object of its contemplation, for the purpose of complete intuition and perfect recognition.

All the terms now defined, are but different designations for the various forms in which the intuitive action of the intellectual principle is solicited by objects external to itself. The English language, as the product of mind working chiefly in practical directions, possesses little of the clearness and distinctness in nomenclature which the topics of intellectual analysis so peculiarly require. But the four terms used above are sufficient to comprise the prominent forms of perceptive action, in the various processes of intellection. They all refer significantly enough, to the first efforts of intelligence, when, previous to any introversive or reflective act, of comparatively subtile or intricate character, it obeys the instinct of its appetite, and finds its sustentation by feeding on the aliment tendered to it by its Author, in the objects which environ it. To watch and guide, and coöperate with this instructive principle, is the true office of education, as a process of nurture and development, working not in arbitrary or artificial, but in salutary and successful forms,—forms not devised by the fallible ingenuity of man, but by the unerring wisdom of Supreme intelligence.

Prevalent error in the order of cultivation.—Contrary, however, to the obvious suggestions of fact, education is still too generally regarded as consisting, during its earlier stages, in arbitrary exercises of memory on combinations of printed characters, abstract numbers, or even the metaphysical relations involved in the science of grammar. The excuse offered for a blind following of precedent in this direction. usually is the peculiar susceptibility of memory, during the period of childhood, and the comparative difficulty experienced in attempts to cultivate it at a later stage. Were the educational cultivation of memory directed to the retaining and treasuring up of those stores of knowledge which are naturally accessible to the mind of childhood. within the range of its daily observation, the plea would be justifiable; man's endeavors would be in harmony with the obvious instincts and endowments of the mind, and would tend to its natural expansion and development. But directed to the mechanical and arbitrary results at which these endeavors so generally aim, their influence is detrimental. Their immediate effect is to quench the natural thirst for knowledge, to create a distaste for intellectual activity, and thus to defeat the best purposes of education.

§. The law of true culture lies in the primary craving of the young mind for material on which the understanding may operate; digesting it, in due season, into the regular form of knowledge which memory loves to retain, and which judgment ultimately builds up into the systematic arrangements of science.

(2.) CURIOSITY, THE ACTUATING PRINCIPLE OF THE PERCEPTIVE FACULTIES.

§. The Teacher's proper place.—The teacher who enters intelligently upon his work of cultivating the minds entrusted to his care, knows that his chief duty is to cherish the spontaneous action of their powers, and to make them intelligent and voluntary co-workers in their own development.) He observes, therefore, with careful attention, the natural tendencies and action of the intellectual system, as the physiologist does those of the corporeal, so as to become competent to trace the law of development, and adapt his measures to its requirements. He thus becomes qualified to take his proper place, as an humble but efficient co-worker with the Author of the mind, recognizing and following His plan, in modes suggested by a wisdom higher than human.

The attentive study and observation of the natural workings of the mind, in the successive stages of its progress, from incipient intelligence to maturity of reason, imply, however, not merely a careful analysis of the facts and modes of mental action, but a watchful observation, with a view to detect, in all cases, the moving power or *impelling principle* of action, to aid and regulate which is the educator's chief work. The ceaseless intellectual activity of childhood, maintained through the various media of perception, furnished by the organs of sense, is obviously stimulated by the constitutional principle of *curiosity,* an eager *desire to know* and *understand,* and therefore, *to observe* and *examine.* Hence the irrepressible and searching questions with which children, in the instinct of faith, appeal to whomsoever they think can satisfy their craving for information.

To feed this mental appetite, to select and prepare its proper nutriment, to keep it in healthy and healthful activity, to quicken and strengthen it, to direct and guide it, as a divine instinct, leading to the noblest ends, should be the teacher's constant endeavor. To awaken curiosity is to secure a penetrating and fixed attention,—the prime condition of human knowledge; and even when it leads no further than to wonder, it is preparing the advancing mind for the awe and the reverence with which, in later stages of its progress, it looks up to the knowledge which is "too high for it."

5. The emotion of wonder analogous to the instinct of curiosity.—Curiosity, like the kindred element of wonder, finds its sustenance in whatever is new to sensation or perception; *wonder*, in turn, leads the mind to dwell on whatever is *strange, intricate*, or *remote; astonishment*, arrests it by whatever is *sudden* and *powerful; awe*, commands it by whatever is *vast;* and *amazement* overwhelms it by whatever is *incomprehensible* or *inscrutable.*) Yet all of these effects,— even those which, for the moment, act on the perceptive intellect with a repulsive force that makes it recoil in conscious weakness from the object of contemplation,—are but various forms of stimulating, impelling, or attracting force, acting on the irrepressible vitality of the mind; and no incitements are ultimately more powerful in maintaining the most resolute and persevering activity of its powers.

Mental effects of novelty and variety.—In the great primary school of nature, as established and furnished by the Author of all, we observe, accordingly, that in the multiform variety of objects with which the young human being is surrounded, at the first dawning of intelligence within him, the novelty of the whole scene around him, and of every class of objects which it presents, is forever tempting his susceptible spirit to observe and examine, and explore, by the conscious delight which every new step affords him.

Evils of monotony, and advantages of variety.—Nor is the obvious design of the great Instructor less conspicuous in the feeling of satiety and weariness which is always superinduced by continued sameness of mental action, whether prolonged in the same mode of exercise, or on the same class of objects. The observant teacher thus learns his own lesson of duty,—to avoid undue limitation in the objects and forms of intellectual action, to shun sameness and monotony of routine, and protracted exertions of attention, as all tending to exhaust and enfeeble the mental powers. His endeavors, on the contrary, are all directed to a due diversity in the presentation of objects, and in the mode of mental activity which they call forth; and, in whatever instances frequent repetition is indispensable to exact perception, he is particularly careful to exert his ingenuity to the utmost, in devising new modes of presentation, so as to secure fresh and earnest attention to the same objects or facts, by the renovating effect of the new lights and new aspects in which he causes them to be viewed.

Faults in former modes of education.—It is unnecessary, in our day, to dwell on the obvious faults of the obsolete practice of confining young children within doors at all seasons, compelling them to remain long in one attitude or posture without relief, condemning them to long periods of silence and constraint, and forcing them to con unmeaning and irksome tasks. These injurious practices are now, for the most part renounced; and more genial and rational modes of early education are beginning to prevail. As yet, however, we have only made a beginning. We have reformed our modes of school architecture, and have allowed children the unspeakable benefits of space and air, and more frequent change of place, and posture, and exercise. Objects and pictures are now employed, to some extent, as instruments of mental culture; and the wisdom of all these changes is proved in the greater happiness and better health of our little pupils, and, more particularly, in their greater docility, and their superior intellectual progress, as contrasted with the state of things under the former *regime* of irksome monotony, restraint, weariness, and stupidity. We are very far, yet, however, from approaching the bountiful variety and delightful novelty furnished in the great model school of infancy and childhood, as established by the Divine founder.

Intellectual furniture of school-rooms.—Our primary school-rooms should be so many cabinets of nature and art. Every inch of wall not indispensably required for blackboard exercises, should be secured for educational purposes, by specimens of plants, minerals, shells, birds, and whatever else can be appropriately placed before the eye. The arranging, classifying, and describing of these, should precede any analysis or study of letters or syllables. Pictures representing such objects, should form a second stage of exercises in attention, observation, and description, before any alphabetic drilling whatever. The examination of objects and of pictures, should, in a word, form the natural preparatory training of the perceptive faculties for the more arbitrary and more difficult exercise of studying and recognizing the unmeaning, uninteresting forms of alphabetic characters with their phonetic combinations.

Injurious effects of mere alphabetic drilling.—Curiosity, the natural incitement of intellect, is easily awakened when we obey the law of the Creator, and direct it to His works,—the natural and appropriate stimulants of the perceptive powers of infancy; but when, leaving our proper sphere, and restricting our educational efforts to the mechanical training of eye and ear, we use these organs, and the informing mind, for the limited purpose of recognizing the complicated and irregular geometrical combinations of line and angle, presented in alphabetic characters, and repeating the sounds so arbitrarily associated with these, we take the mind out of its native element; we consequently force and distort its growth, dwarf its stature, and enfeeble its powers.

Effects of the salutary excitement of the feeling of wonder.—But it is not in the first stages only of mental culture, that the influence of novelty and variety is required as an incitement to observation, by the frequent presentation of new and fresh objects of attention, by the agreeable surprises occasioned by new forms and new stages of animal and vegetable life,—all tending to excite a lively curiosity, which leads, in turn, to careful attention, close examination, and successful study. Curiosity should often be awakened by the yet more powerful influence of *wonder*. Objects rare and strange, combinations intricate and even puzzling, should sometimes be called in, to excite a yet more energetic action of the perceptive intellect, in its endeavors to grasp the objects of its contemplation.

Whatever in nature is wonderful,—whether we employ the microscope, in revealing the intricate structure of plant or insect, in the minuter and closer examination of the works of the Creator; or the telescope, in the contemplation of the starry heavens, and the study of the magnitudes and motions of the bodies which people the depths of space,—all should be brought to bear on the young mind, to call forth that sense of wonder which so delights and inspires it, and prepares it, at the same time, for the influence of those sentiments of awe and reverence with which the advancing intellect learns to trace the signatures of Deity.

(3.) OBSERVATION, AS THE TENDENCY OF MENTAL HABIT, UNDER THE INCITING INFLUENCE OF CURIOSITY.

The natural effect of intellectual instinct.—The motive power, or impelling force, by which, in the ordinations of the mind's omniscient Author, its perceptive faculties are incited to activity, and induced to render their tribute to the resources of intelligence, consists in that restless desire to observe, to examine, and to know, which constitutes man a progressively intelligent being. Impelled by this insatiable mental thirst, he is led instinctively to those streams of knowledge which constitute the waters of intellectual life. His perceptive powers thus stimulated, acquire a tendency to ceaseless activity,—a trait which forms the peculiar characteristic of the early stages of his mental progress, and which is greatly quickened by the vividness of sensation in the constitution of childhood. Hence the promptness and versatility of attention at that period, and its remarkable susceptibility to the influences of cultivation and discipline.

These aids, it is true, are, as yet, too scantily furnished in the processes of education; and, even without them, the human being, as he advances under the promptings of instinct, and the guidance of self-intelligence, attains, as in the case even of the savage, to a high degree of perceptive power. The keen, quick, and penetrating glance of his eye, the acuteness and certainty of his ear, the readiness and exactness of his observation of every object within the range of his vision, the searching closeness of inspection with which he examines everything new or uncertain, often furnish an impressive lesson on the value of training, to those whose means and opportunities of intellectual culture are so superior to his own.

Effects of cherishing the habit of observation.—The habit of observation, duly cherished in early years, by the judicious care of the parent and teacher, becomes the security for ample acquisitions in the field of knowledge, and for the daily accumulation of mental resources and of intellectual power. The observant mind, like the close-knit net of the skillful fisherman, encloses and retains the living treasures within its sweep, and deposits them, for use, in their appropriate place. The undisciplined, inattentive, unobservant spectator seizes and retains nothing in his slack and ineffectual grasp.

Suggestive significance of terms in intellectual and educational relations.—The etymology of the word *apprehension*, (seizing, grasping, laying hold of,) suggests an important lesson regarding the value of intellectual training, as dependent on the habit of attentive and close observation. The word *attention*, (tending, reaching, or stretching toward,) is not less instructive in its signification, implying the *tendency*, or the gravitating of the mind's perceptive power toward the object of notice, for the purpose of cognizance, as the first stage of intelligence. The term *observation*, (watching, with a view to obey or follow,) is yet more monitory to the teacher; as it intimates that the true study of external nature demands vigilance, docility, and fidelity; in one word, the devotion of the whole mind to the business of intellectual acquisition. *Perception*, (taking, through a medium,) refers us back to the humble office of sensation, as indispensable to the process of *taking into* the mind the treasures of knowledge offered to the grasp of sense, for the purpose of transmission to the percipient power, the inner principle of intelligence. All of these terms, in the nomenclature of mental science, tend to the same important end, in the uses of practical education: they all point to the appropriate discipline of the perceptive faculties, by means of objects addressed to the senses, as the primary stage of intellectual culture.

Educational errors.—Former modes of education rendered the use of terms such as the preceding, a nullity, or an absurdity. The child shut up within the naked walls of a school-room, seated on his uncomfortable bench, and mechanically conning by rote, the ill-fitting names of alphabetic elements, or trying to piece them into syllables, had little use of the precious gift of *sense*, but a few lines and angles to *perceive*,—unless a friendly fly should happen to alight upon the page of his primer,—no inducement to *attention* but the fear of Solomon's prescription for "minds diseased," nothing half so interesting to *observe* as the little winged being accidentally crawling on the page before him, displaying the curiously constructed mechanism of its form, its gauzy wings, and many-feathered little limbs, or stopping now and then, to dry-rub instead of washing them, and its tiny head, and flexible bit of neck, almost too diminutive to be seen. But woe to the little student of nature, in the genuine act of *observation*, if he should lift his eye from his book, and follow his brisk little visitant flying off to perform the visible miracle of walking up the perpendicular plane of the window pane, or the yet more puzzling feat of walking the ceiling with his head downward.

Rational method.—The child, in the case supposed, indicates the real want of his nature, and mutely, but most eloquently, pleads for a lesson on insect life, (entomology,) before one on the alphabet. Furnished with the data which the lesson on insect life and form, character and motion, would present to his eye, he would be receiving a rational preparatory discipline of attention and observation, in the close and careful examination of all the details of shape and configuration, exhibited in the living and attractive object before him. His recognition of figure and outline, thus secured, he would, in due season, transfer, easily and willingly, to the artificial display of them in the forms of printed characters.

Benefits resulting from the early formation of habits of attentive observation.—The early training of the perceptive faculties, by a varied and genial discipline of the power of attention, so as to render the habit of observation an unfailing characteristic of the man, becomes doubly valuable, as a result of education, when we regard its effects on the intellectual tastes and pursuits of individuals. A taste for the study of nature, early formed, leads to the practice of collecting specimens, and thus furnishing the means of successful study to the person himself, who collects them, and at the same time to all whom he is disposed to aid in such pursuits. Were even the elements of botany, geology, mineralogy, and zoölogy, generally adopted, as they ought to be, as subjects of attention in primary education, a knowledge of natural science, would, ere long, be diffused throughout our community; a taste for the study of nature would become an intellectual trait of our people; the pursuit of agriculture, arboriculture, and horticulture, would be more intelligently and more advantageously followed; the citizen would doubly relish his season of respite in the country; taste and intelligence would extend their influence over all modes of life; and science would be unspeakably a gainer, in its noble purposes and offices, by the multitude of active minds and busy hands called in to collect, and contribute materials for its various forms of investigation. The field of human knowledge might thus be indefinitely enlarged, and its advantages and enjoyments be more extensively diffused.

But it is not merely as a matter of scientific progress, or of taste and enjoyment, that the proper training of the perceptive faculties, by means of objects and observation, rather than by the materials furnished in books, becomes an important consideration in the planning of modes of education, and methods of instruction. Practical utility, also, has its claim to urge in this relation. The larger number of persons, even in the most advanced communities, as regards civilization and refinement, are occupied in some form of active exertion, as the daily vocation of individuals; and while no generous mind can ever look on education as a benefit or a blessing, if it is to be used as a means of training for the occupation of a given caste, it is not less true, that every individual, in whatever class of society, would be vastly benefited by an early course of cultivation on all subjects akin to those which are to form the staple of his mode of life. Botany, geology, chemistry, entomology, for instance, all have their relations to agriculture; and a few hours devoted weekly to the elements of these sciences, will, by their inspiring influence on the young mind, expedite rather than retard the ordinary processes of school education.

Importance of commencing early the study of Nature.—But while no formal or extensive study of these branches can be rationally attempted in primary education, it is most emphatically true, that, in the study of nature, more than in other forms of intellectual action, nothing can be advantageously done but on condition of an early beginning, and the judicious improvement of the opportunity afforded during the period of leisure and susceptibility which occurs to all human beings but once in life. Childhood and youth are, by the Creator's appointment, the period for forming taste and acquiring habits. The most resolute struggles in after years, seldom succeed in effecting a change of mental occupation, or in lending attractive interest to new pursuits. The "pliant hour" must be taken for all processes of mental budding, grafting, or pruning, as well as in those of the orchard. An early dip into the study of nature, will serve to saturate the whole soul with a love for it so strong as to insure the prosecution of such subjects for life. (The season is auspicious; the senses are fresh and susceptible; the mind is awake; the heart is alive; the memory is retentive; nature is yet a scene of novelty and delight; and application is a pleasure). The twig may now be bent in the direction in which the tree is to be inclined.

Universal susceptibility to instruction, drawn from Nature.—In a diversified experience of nearly forty years in the field of education, one teacher, at least, can testify that he has not yet found the mind so dull, or the heart so callous, as to resist the attractive intellectual influence of the analysis of even one plant or one mineral. The mysteries of beauty and awe which hang over such objects, as an investing celestial glory, entrancing the imagination and the heart, and all but translating the intellect itself, have a power of attraction which the dullest, coarsest, and most brutalized boy in a ragged school, cannot resist. But of the moral influence of early education, when directed to the aspects of nature, it will be more appropriate to speak in that special connection.

Effects produced on mental character, by the study of Nature.— *The solidity and the firmness of mental character*, which are acquired by the study of *things*, preceding and accompanying that of words and books, are a natural effect of the early and seasonable cultivation of the habit of observing, analyzing, comparing, and classifying, which even the slight examination of any natural object induces.—A clear, decisive, and discriminating judgment, and a retentive memory, are among the other fruits of that mental training which commences with definite objects, capable of being analyzed and reconstructed by the natural and appropriate action of the young mind, in virtue of its own powers and native tendencies. But these considerations, also belong properly to another and more advanced stage of intellectual discipline, at which *the reflective faculties*, and maturing reason, are beginning to put forth their claims for culture and development, in addition to the preparatory training which they may have received in the blended exercises of sense and intellect, in the action of the perceptive faculties.

(4.) KNOWLEDGE, THE INTELLECTUAL RESULT OF THE ACTION OF THE PERCEPTIVE FACULTIES.

Impelled by the instinct of curiosity, and guided by the habit of observation, the young mind,—whether more or less assisted by education,—advances to the goal designated by creative Wisdom,—*the acquisition of knowledge*, the appointed means for erecting the fabric of character on the scale outlined by the Great Architect, but left to man's industry and intelligence, for the filling up and the symmetry of detail.

The part of education which lies more immediately before us, as the object of our attention, being the cultivation of the intellect, the acquisition of knowledge becomes, in this view, a consideration of primary importance, as, at once, a source of intellectual wealth and power, and a most effective means of mental development. Knowledge, as a result of culture, is undoubtedly of inferior value to discipline. But the efforts put forth in the acquisition of genuine knowledge, are, in themselves, a disciplinary process, and the indispensable instruments of further cultivation. Yet more,—intellectual acquirements are true and durable riches,—valuable for their own sake, not merely from the resources which the accumulation of them places at the mind's command, but from their own intrinsic value, as imperishable because intellectual things, and as the successive steps of mental elevation in the scale of being. In reference to intellect, knowledge is, in one most important sense, an end, not less than a means and a measure of progress. Profound, extensive, and varied knowledge, is one of the crowning glories of man, as an intellectual and progressive being, capable of ceaseless development and acquisition. Most emphatically is this true of him, the soundness, and exactness, and completeness, of whose knowledge, are the assurance that he shall be a safe and competent guide along the path of education.

Actual knowledge.—But what is knowledge? How is it acquired? It—not by the repetition of the words or the processes of others, not by the transfer from one mind to another of the verbal statements of fact or of abstract principles, not by the formation of vague and partial notions, formed on superficial data, and floating loosely in the mind, not by a half perception or half consciousness of something indefinite or supposititious, not by an assent to rash assumptions or confident assertions, not by the recollections of extensive reading, or perhaps, of attentive listening, retailed in fluent expression, not by accumulating the amplest furniture of second-hand theories and systems, whether plausible or absurd, or even logically consistent. (*Knowledge is what we have experienced in our own intellect*, by means of our own observation or reflection, the fruit of personal perception, or of conscious reason, acting on the positive data of sensation.) So narrowly must the term be limited, when we refer to the action of the perceptive faculties, or to their appropriate training and discipline. Knowledge, in these relations, is (*the accurate interpretation of the facts of sense*) in matters, usually, of color, form, number, weight, or sound, and the relations which these bear to one another in the processes of induction and classification. With the other sense of the term, in which it refers whether to truth or to theory, and implies the deductions of reflective *reason*, we have not, at present, to do. It belongs to a subsequent stage of the analysis of the modes of mental action, as subjected to the processes of intellectual cultivation, and occurs in connection with the discipline of the "reflective" faculties.

Literal accuracy of verbal statement, a false test of knowledge.—The acquisition of knowledge, however, is, notwithstanding all our advances, of late years, in the philosophy of education, too generally confounded with the repetition of the verbal statements of definitions, rules, and systems, as contained in books, even in relations so palpable as those of form and numbers. The test of knowledge, accordingly, with some teachers, to this day, is, even in the exact sciences, the fluency with which a definition or a rule is orally repeated, verbatim, from a text-book, and the mechanical accuracy or despatch with which a correspondent problem is solved, or a proposition demonstrated.

True knowledge experimental and personal.— True perceptive knowledge, on the other hand, or that which is actual and personal, implies, in all relations of form and number, that the individual who possesses it, has seen the object in question, or its representative, in palpable shape, in surface or in outline, that he has subjected it to actual measurement and comparison, or has an exact image of its form and configuration before h's mind, that he has actually counted or grouped objects in numbers presented to the eye or to the mind, or that he has compared these with one another, and traced their relations, by strict and exact observation; and the proper office of the text-book is but to confirm and embody the result, and classify it in the exact language and systematic arrangement of formal science, as the specimens are labelled and shelved in a collector's cabinet. The use of scientific method, in the statements of text-books, is but to give logical arrangement to mental acquisitions, not to induce mere assent, whether silent or oral, and not to facilitate the mere repetition or verbal enunciation of propositions.

The proper business of the teacher, as a superintendent of mind.—The true office of the teacher is to see that the pupil is led by his own conscious experience and observation, through the process of perception prescribed in every exercise which he attempts; that the operation is intelligently performed at every step, and the result rendered certain, as far as the limitations of human faculties permit. By frequently repeated performance of the requisite process, the principle in question thus becomes an integral part of personal knowledge with the individual; and his faculties receive, at the same time, a discipline which gives them facility and force in all analogous procedure in which expertness and skill are desirable attainments. In due season, also, he is able to sum up his acquirements in knowledge, in the clear and definite and precise language which science demands, and of which his text-book furnishes a perfect specimen on which he can rely.

At first, however, the young operator may need even the palpable aid of actual objects; and the judicious teacher knows well when to give, and when to withhold such help, when to appeal to the blackboard, and when to have his pupil rely on the mind's eye, during the successive stages of intellectual training. He is careful, however, not to slight or hurry over the business of the rudimental course, in which the reference to actual objects is the main reliance for a sure personal knowledge of the facts of form and number. The collateral discipline, also, arising from the attentive observation and careful study of plants, minerals, leaves, insects, and other natural objects, the intelligent teacher values highly, from the power of attention, and the habit of exact observation, which it tends to secure, by the definiteness which it gives to the action of the mind, and the certainty which it stamps on knowledge.

Contrasted examples of neglect and culture.—True education has no more striking proof of its good effect than may be observed, when the apathy and ignorance of young persons who have been allowed to neglect the observation and study of nature in childhood, and afterwards to go through a class-drill on a given branch, by means of a text-book, are contrasted with the intelligent personal interest and intimate knowledge of those who have been wisely induced to turn an early attention on the productions of nature, and thus to acquire an early love for such studies, and a life-long enjoyment of the pleasures which they afford. Adults of the former class take little interest in the " floral apostles " of the poet, who are ceaselessly preaching the perfection of their Source, or in the pebble at their feet, which, to the intelligent eye, is the medallion struck by the Creator's hand, in commemoration of one of the epochs in His reign. These eloquent monitions of a perpetual Divine presence, are, to such minds, the dead letter of a handwriting which they have not been accustomed to trace, and on which their listless eye falls, as does that of the sceptic, on the page of written revelation. The mind, on the other hand, which has been early trained to an intelligent personal interest in the productions of Creative wisdom and power, enjoys a personal property, and a personal reference, in every object in nature, finds, in "the meanest flower that blows, thoughts that do often lie too deep for tears," and ultimately to it,

> "The delicate forest flower,
> With fragrant breath, and look so like a smile,
> Seems, as it issues from the shapeless mould,
> An emanation of the indwelling Life,
> A visible token of the upholding Love,
> Which are the soul of this wide universe."

The definiteness and the certainty, however, which give conscious life and power to all such knowledge, depend, to a great extent, on the faithful training which the perceptive power has undergone in the nurturing stage of education. The poet whose words of truth and love convince us that he has attained to the rank of an inspired seer, set out on his career from the common starting place of infancy, in blank ignorance of every object and of every fact around him; and his brother bard whose office it is to announce, in the language of astronomy, the harmony of the spheres, and read to mankind the legislation of the heavens, had no vantage ground at his outset on those excursions which ultimately extend beyond Orion and the Pleiades. Nor was there any special dispensation antecedent to the slow but sure processes of culture, in favor of the electrician who, in the maturity of his acquirements, became competent to transmit and diffuse intelligence with the literal rapidity of lightning; and what shall we say of the barefooted mason's boy, who commences his career of "glory and of joy," plodding over the stone which he has broken with his unpracticed apprentice hammer, and, at length, reads, from that same fragment, to the delight and astonishment of mankind, the facts of an antediluvian world? All the treasures which such minds have brought from their various explorations, as tributes to the treasury of science, and to man's dominion in the sphere of knowledge, are but the varied fruits of unwearied, progressive observation, accumulating fact upon fact by the patient process of attentive examination of objects, and by the skillful exercise of well disciplined perceptive faculties. Such noble efforts of mental power we contemplate with a delight mingled with reverence and gratitude to their authors, as benefactors of the race. The worship which human ignorance, in its wondering admiration, extended, of old, to the mythic demi-god and hero, might, we think, have been pardoned had it been offered to our venerated contemporary Humboldt, who, at an age rarely attained by modern man, withdraws, at intervals, from the onerous duties of a councilor of state, to record the acquisitions of a mind which, from early years, has been exploring the wonders of nature, and now, year after year, pours forth another and another book of the great epic of creation, to which he has so appropriately given the sublime title, "Cosmos."

The written life of this truly great man, however, only enables us to trace the progress of another watchful observer of nature, as, step by step, he observes, examines, compares, classifies, aggregates, and accumulates, till he stands before us an intellectual Atlas, upholding the sphere of human knowledge. Liberal education, favorable opportunities faithfully improved, an insatiable thirst for knowledge, and devoted application to the acquisition of it, explain the wonder. Let us inquire then, for a moment, into the processes by which human culture achieves the miracle of such results, $\frac{1}{25} \cdot 7\textit{?}$

(5.) THE APPROPRIATE EDUCATIONAL PROCESSES FOR THE EXERCISE, DEVELOPMENT, AND DISCIPLINE, OF THE PERCEPTIVE FACULTIES.

The law of progressive intellection.—Watching the successive steps of man's intellectual development, as he advances, consciously or unconsciously, in pliancy and power of mind, we see him first incited by an irrepressible principle of *curiosity*, stimulating him to watchful attention, *close observation*, and *minute inspection*, for the purpose of acquiring a satisfactory *knowledge* of things around him; that he may, in due season, be prepared to enter upon a new and higher cycle of his ceaseless progress, and from the materials of *perception*, feed the *reflective* faculties of *judgment* and *reason*, which lead to the higher goal of *truth*, where alone the cravings of intellect can find rest and satisfaction.

Provision of educational apparatus.—The first care of the watchful and intelligent teacher, as the guide and director of the intellect, is obviously, in compliance with the law of intellectual progress, as traced above, to make liberal provision of the palpable material of *perception*, by which the instinctive appetite of curiosity is at once fed and stimulated, attention awakened, observation secured, and knowledge attained. Objects abundant in number, and varied in character, form and aspect, but chiefly those furnished by nature, and, more particularly, those which occur most frequently within the range of the child's actual observation, are the true and appropriate apparatus of his education. To the examination and inspection of these his mind naturally tends; to the process of extracting knowledge from these, his perceptive powers are expressly adapted; in such occupation he takes delight; working on such material, he is inspired by the consciousness of progress and of perpetually augmenting vigor; and thus he becomes a willing and efficient, because an intelligent agent in his own development.

DISCIPLINE OF THE SENSES.—*Sight; color.*—Sensation, though the humblest form of mental action, being the first in the natural order of intellectual development, suggests to the parent and teacher the great importance of a due attention to the early cultivation of the senses, especially of those whose action is so distinctly intellectual in character and result as is that of *sight* and *hearing*. The proper organic training of the eye implies, what is too often overlooked, an attentive regard to *color*, as well as *form;* the former of these being very early developed, and evidently, in all normal cases, a source of peculiar delight in infancy, not less than of high æsthetic gratification in subsequent appreciation of beauty, both in nature and art. Long before the infant shows any distinctive recognition or appreciation of form, it manifests a keen perception and intense pleasure in the observation of all objects of brilliant color.

Under the management of the judicious mother, balls of the three grand primary colors of the painter,—blue, red, and yellow,—form an inexhaustible source of pleasure to the infant eye; while they give an unconscious exercise and discipline to the perceptive faculty, and prepare the way for the subsequent, definite, and intelligent recognition of the great lines of distinction drawn on the field of vision by the Hand which has blended color with light. Field or garden flowers, or even wayside weeds, placed within the range of the eye, serve a similar purpose. Subsequently, the principal intermediate *gradations* of color, as they occur in objects of nature or of art, in varied tints and hues, may be presented to the sight, in due succession, as a pleasing exercise for the faculties of childhood, in its progress. For this purpose, flowers, the prism, the tints and half tints of the clouds, the glow, or the hue of evening and morning skies, throughout the year; the ever-varying colors of autumn, from their fullest flush to their gradual waning and decay; all are admirable materials for the intellectual and æsthetic cultivation of the human being, along the successive stages of his development. The mind early trained to a sense of the beauty of color, can hardly be withheld, in after years, from the profoundest application to the study of light, as "a feast of nectared sweets, where no crude surfeit reigns." Purity and perfection of taste in art, are another sure result of early cultivation, in this respect. How much intelligence, and how much intensity of pure and even sacred gratification, may thus be superadded to the sentiment of reverential delight in the works of the Creator, it would be difficult for even the most skillful master of expression to say.

Form.—The early cultivation of a discriminating perception of the distinctive characters of *form*, through a carefully conducted, progressive discipline on objects submitted to the eye, is one of the most purely intellectual processes to which the mind of childhood can be subjected. The cube, the sphere, the cylinder, the cone, the pyramid, when judiciously introduced among the playthings of early childhood, as was strikingly exemplified in the schools of Pestalozzi, become unconsciously, but most surely, a basis and standard in all the relations of form; and, under the guiding suggestions of the teacher, they tend to give the mind definiteness and certainty in its action, on whatever relates to geometrical details of figure in nature, art, or mechanism. The primary truths of solid, superficial, and linear geometry, are thus imbedded in the mind, identified with its action on all visible objects, and help to constitute the observer an intelligent spectator, through life, of the grand elemental forms of the universe.

Measure.—Convenience and utility, too, have their claims to urge in favor of an early discipline of the eye on all details of *measurement*. An exact appreciation of measure, for in-door purposes, should be laid in permanent inch, and half and quarter inch marks, on the school-room wall; and to these should be added those of the foot and the yard. A mile, with its subdivision into halves, and quarters, should be measured off, as a permanent standard for the young eye, as it approaches or leaves the threshold of the school-room. The acre and the rod, and all other details of land measure, should be made familiar to the eye of boyhood, by express measurement, in the nearest accessible field or square.

Number.—Veritable ideas of number belong, also, to the early discipline of the eye, and are greatly dependent on the actual presentation of objects, for this special purpose. We read, in the accounts of one English exploring voyage, that the inhabitants of one group of islands in the Pacific, had do definite ideas of any number over five; and experienced teachers are well aware that, in the case of pupils accustomed to depend on the mere verbal memory of the words which represent numbers, and unprovided with a firm basis of actual observation of palpable objects, and the personal knowledge which such experience gives, there is an obstinate difficulty in forming definite and distinct conceptions of numbers, which resembles, too nearly, the confusion and helplessness of mind felt by those unfortunate islanders, in their attempts to transcend the limits of their terminal number, five.

Most of the early arithmetical operations of very young pupils, should consist in handling and counting visible objects, in enumerating marks, in grouping objects and marks, in numbers gradually progressive, from the smallest to the largest in amount; so as to secure expertness and promptness in the process of addition, in varied forms. Successive exercises should follow in multiplication, in subtraction, and division, all performed, day after day, on visible objects handled, and on marks expressly made for such purposes of training, before the purely mental processes of arithmetic are attempted on abstract numbers, even of the smallest groups. A prevalent error with teachers still continues to be that of merely exemplifying true teaching in such forms as have been mentioned, for a limited period, too limited to tell upon the habits of the mind. Long continued training alone, is adequate to the proper purposes of discipline, certainty and skill, namely, in forming combinations which must sometimes be both extensive and complicated. It is unreasonable to expect rapidity and expertness in the processes of mental arithmetic, without the preparatory discipline which results from the actual observation of the facts of number and combination, in objects presented to the senses. Such discipline alone, can yield that personal knowledge, and that conscious grasp of mind, which give clearness and certainty to the action of the intellect in arithmetical operations.

Natural objects: animated forms.—But it is not merely the contemplation of inanimate objects which the mind, in childhood, requires as a foundation for true perception and exact observation, or as a means of securing prompt and sustained attention. The liberal training of the senses, as a primary step in intellectual cultivation, extends the study of color, form, number, and sound, to the rich domain of animated nature, in the animal as well as the vegetable kingdom, and thus brings the vivid sympathy of the young heart with kindred life and motion to the aid of the opening intellect. From the *pebble*, the *shell*, the *flower*, and the *leaf*, the judicious mother and teacher will pass to the *insect*, the *bird*, the *quadruped*, and the *fish ;* and as their individualities and diversities are successively enumerated and dwelt upon, the details of color, form, and number, arrest and fix the volatile attention of the child, and win him to habits of close, minute, and exact observation.

Analysis and *classification*, the two great master powers for the acquisition of knowledge, in whatever direction, are also thus called in to aid the progress of the young observer in his study of nature.

The tendency of the mind to *observe, compare, examine,* and *classify* whatever is submitted to its action, thus early encouraged and stimulated, becomes an habitual trait of the mental character, and tells, with powerful effect, on the intellectual progress of the individual, in the more abstract relations of *language* and of *mathematics*. It is a great error to suppose that, because of the intense pleasure which attends the study of natural objects, there is not a profound and rigorous discipline of mind attending the equally intense intellectual action which accompanies the pleasure. *Analytic examination* is one and the same process, whether it is directed to the component parts of a *plant* or of a *word*. Keen and penetrating attention, close, minute, and thoughtful observation, exhaustive analysis, systematic arrangement, and methodical classification, are equally indispensable in the one case as in the other. But in giving precedence to the study of the object, and postponing that of the word, we are obeying the ordination of the Creator, who has furnished the apparatus of the first stages of human development, in the natural objects which first solicit the attention of the child, by the attractions of beauty and pleasure.

Pictorial art.—Nor is it only by means of natural objects that the sense of sight contributes to the exercise and discipline of the perceptive intellect. Art, too, renders here a rich tribute to the resources of education. Models and pictures, and the humblest attempts to produce these, as repetitions of the mental impressions received from nature, give inexpressible delight to the susceptible and imitative spirit of childhood. Their effect is invaluable, in training the perceptive faculties to the keenest, closest, long-sustained action, without the sense of weariness or fatigue; and their inspiring and refreshing influence gives vivacity and force to the whole mind. The clear perception, fixed attention, watchful observation, and active exertion, which they both require and cherish, particularly when the child is permitted to attempt to produce imitative efforts of his own, in drawing or modelling, meet so successfully the craving of the young spirit for action and endeavor, that they become powerful aids to mental development. The working hand is thus brought to the aid of the active eye, as a test, at the same time, of its correctness of vision, which is proved by the degree of truthfulness in the delineation. This productive method of exercising the perceptive and executive faculties, yields to the child the peculiar delight of having achieved something palpable, as a proof of power, and is, meanwhile, working in his mind the silent effect which is to appear, in due season, in the symmetry and gracefulness of his handwriting, and the neatness of whatever he attempts, whether in plan or execution.

The ear: music.—The varied world of sound, comprising *music* and *speech*, is another wide field of culture to the intelligent mother and the elementary teacher. The extent to which the sense of sight may be cultivated, as regards precision and certainty and truth of action, is indicated in the perfection which is attained by the sculptor and the painter, whose copies of nature are, in some instances, so faithful, and so beautifully perfect, as to confer an immortality of fame upon their authors. But little notice, comparatively, is taken of the delicate susceptibility of the *ear*, in relation to the offices of culture. Yet no sense, not even that of sight itself, is capable of attaining to so high perfection by the aids of training and discipline. The innumerable minute distinctions of sound, which the performance of even a single piece of music, by a single performer, often requires; but, still more, the multitude which the composer of one of the master-pieces of harmony must be capable of recognizing, discriminating, and combining, with a measured exactness transcending all other efforts of perceptive intellect: these remind us, most impressively, of the extent and value of cultivation, when we recall the fact, that the performer and the composer commenced their artistic training on the common footing of all human beings, a percipient mind, and an organ capable of telegraphing to it the notes of the singing bird, the song of the mother or the nurse, or the artless strains of some juvenile performer on pipe or flute.

Speech.—We have yet another proof of the susceptibility of the ear to the influences of cultivation, when "the well trod stage," in the exhibition of a play of the 'myriad-minded' Shakspeare, displays in the voice of the skillful actor, the whole world of human passion, with its ever-varying tones, uttered in the language of poetic inspiration, now moulded by the serene influence of heavenly contemplation, as when Lorenzo speaks to Jessica, while they sit on the moon-lit bank, of the "smallest orb which she beholds, still quiring to the young-eyed cherubim;" now breathing the deep tones of Hamlet, solemnly musing on the mysteries of life, and death, and destiny; now the hollow mutterings of conscious guilt from Macbeth, while meditating the murder from which he yet recoils; now the hoarse accents of remorse wrung from the bosom of him whose "offence is rank" with the blood of "a brother's murder;" now the scarce articulate horror of "false, fleeting, purjured Clarence;" the maddened scream of mingling grief and rage from the injured mother, Constance; the love raptures of the empassioned Romeo; the ringing laughter of Mercutio; or the torture of Othello, as he fluctuates from the ecstacies of overflowing love and joy, to the curses of hatred, the outbursts of grief, and the agonies of despair.

In all these forms the well trained actor, by the mastery of his artistic skill, exerts a power over the sympathies of his audience which far transcends the highest achievements of representative art in any other form. The arduous training to which the histrionic artist subjects his voice, in order to produce such effects, shows to what extent the cultivation of the ear may be carried. It is by the indications of this faithful, prompting monitor, that he guides every step of his vocal efforts, till he attains to those consummate effects of genius which, in some instances, have conferred on the individual a fame coëxtensive with the civilized world. Yet he who is, perhaps, thus renowned, commenced his early efforts, with the usual stumbling utterance of a school-boy.

Enunciation.—Passing from the higher sphere of music and poetry, in their influence on the cultivation of the intellect, through the medium of sense, we come to one of the most important stages of education, in the discipline of the voice for the useful purposes of speech, as dependent on accuracy of ear,—the only reliable guide to correct results. The unconscious freedom with which we utter thoughts in our native tongue, leaves all persons who are not advantageously trained by precept or example, exposed to the evils of incorrect habit, in utterance. The extensive prevalence, also, of corrupted usage, in the negligent practice of general society, increases the liability to error in the style of the individual. There was wisdom in the Roman maxim, that the nurses of children ought to be persons of correct habit, in enunciation. The influence of early example, is the most binding rule of speech, as the baffled and disappointed teacher, after all his endeavors, is often made to feel.

One early begun and long continued daily practice, in primary training, should consist in the careful, correct, and distinct *articulation* of the component elements of speech, as accomplished in our own language. These should, at first, be practiced with reference to *the exact sound of every letter of the alphabet*, singly and separately; afterwards they should be enunciated in the groups which constitute *syllables*, on a graduated progressive scale of difficulty, till every variety of combination can be uttered with perfect distinctness and perfect fluency; finally, *the pronunciation of words* should be practiced in a similar manner, till the style of the young learner is freed from all corrupt and local mannerism, and he is prepared to take his place among the cultivated in speech as well as thought, and, by his personal manner of expression, to evince the style of educated habit as preferable to that of vulgar negligence.

Elocution.—In the secondary and in the more advanced stages of education, the discipline of the ear should be extended, so as to embrace all the refining and highly intellectual influences of music and poetry, as combined in *elocution.*

Intellect, feeling, and imagination, are all inseparably united in the appropriate expression of sentiment, as embodied in the language of *oratory* and *poetry;* and their finest effects in utterance depend on a nice susceptibility of ear, which culture only can secure to full extent. Music and elocution, the most humanizing of all arts, prescribe the apparatus and the forms of training to which the ear should be subjected, through the whole course of education. In the analysis and the discrimination which vocal discipline demands, in the recognition which it secures of the almost infinitely diversified and ever varying character of tones, in their expression of intelligence or of emotion, there is an admirable discipline of intellect implied, which, though less formally displayed than in other modes of exercise, is not, on that account, the less effectual. Of the high *moral* value of the susceptibility which such training tends to cherish, it is not now the appropriate time to speak. We may advert to it under a subsequent head.

The subject of *healthful physical training* is not now under consideration; yet sensation, and consequent perception, are dependent on the condition of the organs of sense, and therefore of the whole corporeal frame, which must be in a healthy condition to secure the natural and true action of nerve and brain,—the apparatus of perceptive action in the intellect. The attentive and efficient cultivation of health should be regarded, not merely as a condition of intellectual life, but as the first step in the formation of intellectual character. The clear eye and the quick ear of health are highly intellectual in their tendencies, and are for ever detecting and offering material for the intellect to examine or explore. The dull organs of a morbid frame, on the contrary, are too torpid to respond to the awakening touch or beckoning invitation of nature, and leave the clouded intellect to sleep or to dream.

PROGRESSIVE CHARACTER OF THE PROPER DISCIPLINE OF THE PERCEPTIVE FACULTIES.

The varied exercises of eye and ear, as organs of sentient mind, should always, under the guiding management of the teacher, advance in intellectual character from stage to stage, so as to secure the benefits of a progressive discipline, commencing, indeed, at the threshold of sense, but ever tending more and more inward, till they become nearly inseparable from the action and character of pure intellect. They thus render the keen eye and the quick ear prompters to clear perception, fixed attention, penetrating observation, careful comparison, and discriminating judgment, and so conduct to consummate intelligence.

The teacher who works in intelligent coöperation with the constitution of the beings whose character it is his office to mould, is content to labor patiently in the field of *sensation*, as, at first, forming the sole ground on which he can rationally meet the dawning mind, with the hope to exert a genial and effectual influence on its development. He dwells long, accordingly, on the prominent outward characteristics of objects, as most accessible to the unpracticed faculties of infancy, as best adapted to elicit their activity, and tempt them forth to more and more energetic effort. He furnishes, with no sparing hand, the opportunities of intuition, in the abundance and variety of the objects which he presents to the senses. He selects these, however, with such judgment and skill that the young mind shall be incapable of regarding them with a mere vacant aspection or listless intuition, but, on the contrary, shall be made to feel that there is within them a soliciting power, a magnetic attraction, to which its own nature responds, and by which it is led on, from stage to stage, till it finds itself in possession of the mental treasures of clear perception and definite knowledge.

VOLUNTARY EXERCISE OF THE PERCEPTIVE FACULTIES, A CONDITION OF INTELLECTUAL DEVELOPMENT.

Attention as a voluntary act.—The teacher who recognizes the law of intellectual growth, is aware that, in adopting measures to aid the progressive unfolding of the perceptive faculties, he may trust largely to the mind's own instinctive and spontaneous tendencies to action, if only due provision is made for mental activity, by supplying the objects of sense which naturally invite and stimulate perception. But regarding the mind as a voluntary and self-directing agent, he knows that unless its own efficient coöperation is secured in the processes on which its energies are exerted, its activity will be ever tending to subside, or to degenerate into mechanical and unmeaning routine. The result, he is aware, must, in such circumstances, be a morbid intellectual inertness of habit, or a deceptive show of forced organic action, instead of the movements of mental life. His great endeavor, therefore, will be to succeed in evoking ATTENTION,—that power of the mind which brings into vigorous and efficient activity the percipient intellect,—that power which, by its own innate force, impels and sustains perception, in whatever direction it is called to act, or in whatever process it is employed.

The customary definition of this power, or faculty, as *voluntary per-*

ception, suggests to the educator his true office in cultivating and developing it. It implies that he no longer restricts his efforts to presenting such objects as solicit and secure the mind's notice, by the law of natural instinct, but that, addressing himself to the principle of *volition*, he calls it forth, as a moving force, impelling the mental machinery from within, and enabling it to arrive at knowledge, by its own action. The true teacher never commits the error of resorting to the exercise of his own will, instead of that of his pupil, as the propelling power. He is aware that his success, as an educator, is to be measured, not by the force with which he can bring his own power of compulsion to bear on the faculties of his pupils, but by the intensity with which he can bring their mental energies into voluntary play, in processes which leave a *residuum* of living force, as a result on mental character. He knows well that no degree of exertion can command attention, by a mere act of will, at the moment; that, by the law of the mental constitution, a train of circumstances must be laid before the desired result can be ensured; that an exercise of will is not, in the natural analogies of mental action, a merely arbitrary act of self-determination; but that, on the contrary, *will* is solicited by *desire*; a feeling or affection of the mind being the natural and necessary preliminary to volition; and that the intelligent guide of the intellectual powers must, therefore, appeal to *feeling*, as the natural and reliable prompter of the will. In other words, the educational process, rightly conducted, is so contrived as to create a desire to arrive at the given result, and proceeds upon that security for the action of will in determining the direction of the mind, and sustaining the exertion of its powers.

Trained under such influences, a disciplined attention is the sure fruit of culture; and power of attention is not unjustly termed the key which unlocks all the gates of knowledge, and secures an entrance to its innermost secrets of intelligence.

Attention, as a power or mode of intellectual action, regarded in connection with the cultivation of the perceptive faculties, requires the application of the various expedients by which it may be rendered *prompt, earnest, close,* and *continuous,* as the exigencies of subjects and of the mind may demand.

Promptness of attention.—Such results imply that the educator, as a skillful gymnasiarch in the arena of mind, trains it through every variety of evolution by which it may be rendered *quick* in movement, ever ready for instantaneous action, so as to secure that pliancy and versatility by which it can at once direct itself to its object, or relinquish one object or train of thought for another, when the moment for change has arrived, and pursue the object of its aim with whatever velocity of motion may be requisite to reach it, in due season.

Speed and despatch, however, not haste and hurry, should be the ends at which the teacher aims in all drilling processes. A wakeful and lively attention, ever on the alert for action, implies sound and healthful and invigorating training. A harassed and exhausted mind, dragged or driven along the path of exercise too arduous, or too long continued, can never yield the results of genuine discipline.

With very young pupils, especially, the obvious indication of nature is, make free use of *striking* and *attractive* objects, illustrations, and remarks. One object at a time; words few and well chosen; no lagging or drawling on the part of either pupil or teacher, yet no hurry, no impatience, no impetuosity; proceeding smoothly and swiftly, but quietly and gently in all movements; yet sometimes, for the purpose of arresting attention, adopting the grateful surprise of a sudden change, briskly executed:—these are the characteristics of skillful and genial training, such as quickens the life power of intellect.

Earnestness of attention.—The power of *earnest* attention is another trait of mental habit to which the successful teacher directs his endeavors, as an invaluable attainment to be secured, through his agency, by his pupils. To this end, he avoids carefully all exercises not interesting or inviting to the young mind. *Objects, pictures, penetrating questions, vigorous exertion,* in varied forms, for mind and body,—strenuous endeavor called forth, at intervals, to cope with *difficulties, interesting facts* stated, or stories told,—the wonders of nature and of art exhibited, interesting *conversation* maintained, in which the pupils interchange thoughts with the teacher, *word-pictures* of peculiar power and beauty, selected from the poets, early attempts at *drawing*, exercises in *planning* and *building*, tangible illustrations in architecture, masonry, carpentry, or joiner-work, in juvenile style, for hours of recreation, the *analysis of plants*, the tracing of the *anatomy* of animal forms, in specimens of *insect* organization, in the osseous construction of *birds, fishes, reptiles*, &c.; all lessons made, as far as practicable, matter of *active work*, rather than merely passive attention; the ceaseless use of the *slate*, the *pencil*, and the *blackboard*, in recording, repeating, and illustrating every thing which admits of such forms of expression; these, and every other resort which ingenuity can invent, are all required in the exigencies of actual teaching.

Earnest attention and strenuous application, on the part of pupils, are the natural result and unfailing reward of the teacher's own facility and skill in devising and executing inspiring models of whatever he would have his pupils execute. The efficacy of his own ear, eye, and hand, secured by his own self-culture, is the only guaranty of his success, as a faithful trainer of the perceptive faculties. The general introduction of music and drawing, now in progress in all well-taught schools, together with the increasing attention given to elementary lessons in botany and mineralogy, is opening a highly beneficial course of discipline for the young mind, in whatever concerns the power of earnest and effective attention, as an attribute of intellectual character.

Closeness of attention.—The thorough discipline of attention, however, as the directing force of the perceptive faculties, implies that it is not only rendered prompt and earnest in action, but *close* and *minute* in its application. A faithful *analysis* is conditioned, in all departments of study, on a clear and distinct perception of *every particular*. Nothing must be suffered to escape notice. No analysis can be complete that is not exhaustive, to the extent of its object. Close and minute inspection is indispensable for the exact observation of many of the most instructive and the most beautiful of the details of nature, in the forms of animal and vegetable life,—for the successful watching of the processes of chemistry,—for forming exact estimations of quantity and number,—for tracing the diversities of even inanimate form, the delicate gradations of color, the minutest difference of sound and form, in the details of language, together with all the nicer distinctions, and discriminations of thought, when embodied in words, for the purposes of communication.

To secure these results, we are again directed to the early and effectual training of the perceptive faculties on the objects of nature, as the first step in the true education of the mind. The minutest point of form in the structure of leaf or blossom, the child traces with delight; and this native tendency of mental action, extended in its range of objects, and confirmed by the law of habit, becomes not only a source of intellectual enjoyment, but of conscious power and ultimate success, in all investigations, not merely of nature and external objects, but, by the inevitable law of analogy, in every department of research on which the intellect is competent to enter. The power of close attention, sharpened by judicious early training of the perceptive faculties, attains in due season, to consummate certainty and success in those processes of minute analysis which are, in many instances, the crowning glories of science.

No contrast can be more striking than that exhibited in the two cases of neglect and culture, in this relation of mental action. On the one hand, we have the loose, superficial, imperfect attention, which glides listlessly over the surface of things, without note, and consequently without knowledge; on the other we see an acute, keen, penetrating, searching inspection, which nothing escapes,—a mind whose knowledge is exact and complete, whose information is the result of narrowly examined and well ascertained particulars.

The intelligent teacher, knowing that the keenest exercises of discriminating judgment are, by the law of mental constitution and habit, not unfrequently dependent on the close examination of details, on the power of tracing and detecting the minutest shades of difference in objects and their component parts, leads his pupils, by the closeness of his questioning, to follow the minutest ramifications of diversity, amid apparent similarity, in the objects which he uses as instruments for sharpening their perceptions to the keenest inspection of every feature which is accessible to the discernment of sense. Beyond this point he passes to the use of the microscope, one of the most valuable implements ever devised as an aid to the processes of human culture. A cheap instrument of this description, in the hands of an attentive teacher, has a power which no degree of mental inertia can resist. It has been known to convert, in a few days, a whole school of uncultivated, thoughtless, turbulent children into an attentive, thoughtful, inquiring, docile, and orderly company of little students of nature.

A few minutes occupied daily in observing and tracing the forms of objects, in detail, is, in addition to its ultimate effects on mental habit, of the greatest service in the humble relations of alphabetic teaching. A ground work is thus laid for the accurate recognition of the elements of form combined in the visible shapes of printed and written characters, and a surer and more rapid, because a more intelligent, progress secured, as regards the accuracy of the eye in recognizing, or of the hand in repeating the lines, angles, and curves, which constitute the complex forms of letters. Accustomed to the close and minute analysis of form on visible objects of different sorts, the child, if permitted to treat his alphabetic characters in a similar way, takes delight in detecting and naming their constituent parts; and, particularly, when he is permitted to try to delineate them for himself, and thus, as it were, bring them under a kind of ideal subjection to his power.

The discipline of particular observation and searching attention, early secured, becomes, in due season, a complete guaranty for the correct and successful performance of the various gradations of mathematical problems in which a well trained and exact attention is required, whether for the relations of form or those of numbers; and throughout the successive stages of education, in all its departments.

The well trained mind becomes ultimately like the thoroughly magnetized instrument, which leaves no stray particles of the steel-filings scattered abroad, but agglomerates them every one to itself; with a certainty which renders the act no unfitting analogy for illustrating the universal law of gravitation.

Tenacity of attention.—Having used his best endeavors to render the faculty of attention prompt, earnest, and close, in its action, as the guide of the perceptive faculties, the teacher has yet another character to stamp upon it. He would have it not only quick and vivid, and searching, but *tenacious* and *persistent*. From an element volatile, fluctuating, and superficial, in its first manifestations, he would have it become, at length, a power fixed, and steadfast, and unfailing. Patiently training it through its incipient stage of short, feeble flights, he inures it to lengthened excursions and sustained exertions, such as all valuable mental attainments demand. Here, again, Nature comes to his aid, furnishing him liberally not only with numerous instruments of discipline in her manifold forms, as objects, individually, attractive and interesting, but with those *complexities* of shape, and color, and number, those *organic relations*, and *organic contrivances*, those *compound bodies*, those *intricate combinations of elements and processes*, which all require not only an earnest and close, but a long-sustained, unflagging attention, as the only condition of faithful and exact observation and accurate knowledge.

The intelligent teacher watches carefully the progressive development of his pupil's power of attention, and exercises it according to the increasing force and firmness of its grasp, so as to secure a perpetually *growing power of retention*, through all the successive exercises which he contrives for its discipline, on *natural and artificial forms*, their various *combinations, numbers, powers, and characteristics*, of whatever denomination in the vocabularies of science and art.

Regarding attention as the master power in the grasp of the perceptive faculties, he values, most of all, its strength and retentiveness, its ability to maintain an unbroken sequence of activity, such as not unfrequently demands the incitement of the most earnest desire to arrive at the wished for result, and produce, in turn, the most resolute determination of the will to persevere in action till the result is mastered.

Here, again, the teacher finds his best resort in the objects and processes of nature; unwearied attention is in no way so effectually secured, without undue or fatiguing exertion, as in analyzing and inspecting the various *parts* of *plants*, or the *anatomical mechanism* of animal forms, and, more particularly, of insects. While no humane or enlightened teacher would ever propose even one half hour of unbroken attention, on the part of very young pupils, twice that time may safely and advantageously pass in the suggestive questions of the teacher, and the ready answers of the pupils, during the examination of a single specimen of the productions of nature. In such circumstances, instruction takes its best form,—that of interesting *conversation;* and time flies only too fast for both parties in the exercise. Another sustained effort of attention may, by a judicious change in the form of mental action, be as easily secured by permitting the pupil to make such attempt as he can at *delineating,* in detail, the parts of the object which he has been contemplating; still another may be obtained by permitting him to describe in *words,* and at full length, what he has observed; and even the giant Despair of "composition" may be conquered by allowing the pupil to write his description.

Such processes prepare the young student in due season, for those arduous and unflagging exertions of attention by which he ultimately succeeds in solving lengthened and complicated problems in mathematics, disentangling long and inverted sentences by tracing the grammatical relations of their parts, and following, with patient assiduity, every step in extended and abstruse processes of reasoning on subjects more purely mental in their character.

The teacher who would merit the rank of an educator, and who would render all his processes of instruction not merely didactic but disciplinary, can never be too careful to accustom himself to survey the whole field of human culture in its completeness; to keep ever before his own mind the strict unity of the principle of intelligence, the analogy and cotendency of its various modes of action, and the identity of their results in the enlarging and quickening of its powers, and the strengthening of its grasp, on whatever subject it may be called to fasten. Philosophical writers, of high repute, have, sometimes, in their zealous advocacy of the value of their special studies, as instruments of mental discipline, been led greatly to underrate the disciplinary influence of all intellectual training connected with the observation and study of nature. They seem to have overlooked the fact that quick, acute, penetrating. close, persevering attention is one and the same priceless attainment, whether exhibited in the examination of an external object or in the investigation of the most abstruse of subjects that can be submitted to the action of human intellect.

The experienced and observing teacher knows well that his students who excel in the exercises prescribed in the departments of logic and metaphysics are those whose faculties have been most thoroughly disciplined in the processes of analysis, comparison, and classification, of induction and deduction, applied to the study of natural objects, under the guidance of mathematical and physical science. The materials on which the mind works in each of these great groups of subjects are undoubtedly wholly different; but its action is virtually the same in both—attention leading to discernment, discernment to fact or to truth.

The student who is thus trained in the true unity of his intellectual being, issues from the preparatory sphere of education well prepared to meet the exigences of actual life, whether these present themselves in the form of intelligent and prompt activity, or in that of rigid investigation and profound research.

NATURAL CONNECTION OF THE PERCEPTIVE AND THE REFLECTIVE FACULTIES.

To enable his pupils to extend the exercise of *attention* into that of continued *observation*, is the great aim of the teacher, who works intelligently on the material of mind, with a view to elicit power of thought. As far as the discipline of the perceptive faculties extends, the end of culture is to create an *observing* mind; from which, in the beautifully perfect arrangements of the great Author of intelligence, spring, in succession, a *reasoning* and a *reflecting* mind. The latter, however, can never be obtained without due obedience to the Creator's law of succession, in the development of intellect. The materials of reason and reflection lie, to a great extent, though not exclusively, in the field of observation; and, a regard to the law of natural and healthy development, therefore, induces the teacher to look carefully to the first steps of his procedure in the processes of cultivation. Having used his best endeavors to vivify and invigorate the power of attention, by all appropriate means and appliances, he proceeds to the use of every genial method of confirming the tendency of the mind to maintain that faculty in *habitual action ;* to stamp on the intellect, as a characteristic trait, an inquisitive and appropriating spirit, which examines and searches into all things within its sphere, aggregates their riches to itself, and ever comes home laden with results for the exercise of powers and faculties yet greater than itself; and, to which it is ordained to minister. It is thus that the mind becomes the delighted and conscious agent in its own advancement.

PROCESSES BY WHICH THE HABIT OF OBSERVATION IS SECURED.

The frequent solicitation of attention, by the presentation of attractive objects, would, of itself, as we see in Nature's unaided training of the savage, provoke a tendency to observe and to inquire. But, the action of the intelligent teacher, in aid of Nature, and in obedience to her dictation, is founded on a law of moral certainty, derived from the study of the laws of mental action. Understanding and relying on the susceptibility of the mind to the influence of the objects by which it is surrounded, and the perfect adaptation of these objects to that end; and, aided, no less effectually, by that inward thirst for knowledge, that burning desire to observe and understand, which actuates the young mind itself, the enlightened teacher knows he has but to attract *attention* to the object which he wishes to employ as a material in the fabric of knowledge. Attention gained, secures *perception;* if the object is properly selected, and skillfully handled.

The volatility of attention in the immature mind, which, if unguarded, tends to mental dissipation and superficial observation, the teacher counteracts by genial measures, adapted to arrest and fix this subtle element of mental power, and carry it successfully forward, from step to step in observation, till the end in view in investigation is attained. The successive steps of the mind's progress, under the guidance of a skillful instructor, in endeavoring to arrive at the result of true perception, exact observation, and complete knowledge, are suggestively indicated in the process of investigating the structure of any visible object, and naturally present themselves in the following order: *examination, analysis, inspection;* aided by *interrogation, direction,* and *information,* and extended successively to the more complex processes of *comparison* and *classification.*

Examination, as a Process in Intellectual Training.—In the absence of the prompting and directing power of genial culture, it is true, perhaps, that most of our race are permitted to fill the measure of their days without one definite or quickening thought of the objects by which they are surrounded for a life-time. The peasant boy, who, of all human beings, is the most favorably situated for the contemplation and intelligent study of nature, seldom experiences the friendly aid of a suggestive question, that might lead him to appreciate the elements of intellectual wealth, in which the field of his daily labor abounds. Education has given him the ability to compute his wages, to read, or to sign a receipt; and, thus to meet the humble demands of his animal subsistence. It may even have afforded him some formal instruction in grammar or geography. But, it has not even hinted to him that, in "herb, tree, fruit, flower, glistering with dew," there are wonders of skill, and beauty, and power, fitted to fill his soul with delight, and to exalt him to a higher intelligence; that, in the bud, as it opens in spring, in the expanded blossom of summer, in the tinted leaf of autumn, in the shell which he picks up from the sand of the brook, in the very pebble which he "turns with his share, and treads upon," there are offered to his mind whole volumes of the richest knowledge, which the study of a life-time cannot exhaust.

An eloquent American writer, speaking of the advancement of education, says: "The time may come when the teacher will take his pupil by the hand, and lead him by the running streams, and teach him all the principles of Science, as she comes from her Maker." The teacher is here rightfully represented as fulfilling, in his humble sphere of duty, the highest offices of philanthropy and of religion. Such is the teacher's noble and beneficent function, in favoring circumstances; yet, not less when, yielding to the exigencies of life, he is confined within the walls of his school-room, but brings in Nature's apparatus from without, to give life, and meaning, and efficacy to his instructions, and win the young mind to the earnest and devoted study of the works of the Creator.

Intellectual Effects Resulting from the Examination of Objects.— The zealous teacher, working with such light shed upon his labors, knows that, in presenting a product of Nature to the eye, he is presenting a germ of thought to the mind, which, under his skillful management, shall duly unfold, in leaf, and blossom, and ultimate fruit. He knows that, in the absence of a guiding suggestion, his young pupil may have looked a thousand times on that leaf, as a thing which did not concern him; on the shell, as only something queer; on the pebble, as an unintelligible intruder, perhaps, on his personal comfort; on the flower, as something pretty, that his sisters are fond of; on the fruit, as a sufficiently satisfactory morsel for his palate; and, that thus, in the great universal hall of learning, stored with library and apparatus, the orphaned mind may have sauntered away the precious hours of early life, without having been induced to study a single lesson, or engage in a single exercise. All this the teacher is well aware of; but, he knows, too, the hidden life and power that lie wrapped up in the little object with which, as a specimen from Nature's cabinet, he proceeds to magnetize the sentient intellects before him. He knows that, as surely as these susceptible beings are brought near enough to come within the range of action, they fall under the spell of its power, are charmed to rapt attention, and carried on, in wondering and delighted observation, till they are finally arrested by the grateful surprise of conscious knowledge, and advanced intelligence.

Is it a plant which forms the subject of the lesson he would give? He has but, by a striking question, to break the crust of habituation, which has blunted the perception of his pupils, and hinders their mental vision. He has but to ask them to *describe* its parts, in detail, as he holds it up before them, and he has gained the grand preliminary condition of effective perception,—attentive *examination*. As the description extends its ramifications, the weed, which had been a thousand times trodden under foot, without a thought of its nature or construction, becomes an eloquent expositor of Creative mechanism and life; its parts become organs and channels of vitality,—a wondrous laboratory of chemical elements and action; the individual object becomes a member of a family, each of whom has his life and his history, his birth, growth, maturity, and decay; leaving, as the moral of his story, the parting suggestive question, riveted in the wondering mind, "Am I not wonderfully made?"

One such result,—and the more common the object which secures it the better,—one such result is sufficient to ensure a repetition of itself, in a thousand other instances. The ice of indifference is broken; and the observer may now see clearly, through the transparant water, the many-formed beautiful pebbles on the sandy bed of the stream. The time and trouble of examination, it is now found, are amply repaid in the conscious pleasure of intelligent observation; and, they are no longer begrudged. The mind has now become desirous to observe, examine, and explore. It has already set out on a career which, were all educators intelligent agents, would be ceaseless to all to whose advancement it is their part to minister.

Example of a Successful Teacher.—A most striking exemplification, in this respect, of successful instruction, was often exhibited in the devoted labors of the late Josiah Holbrook, who, although the very extent of some of his plans for the advancement of popular education may have rendered their execution difficult for the endeavors of an individual, yet was uniformly successful in his attempts to introduce the study of natural objects, as a part of early education in all schools. Trusting to the power of attraction and development latent within a stone, picked up by the wayside, he would enter a school, with no other apparatus of instruction provided; and, holding up the familiar object, would succeed, by means of a few simple but skillfully-put questions, in creating an earnest desire in his young audience to be permitted to look more closely at the object. He would then hand it to them, and have it passed from one to another.

Having thus secured the preliminary advantage of *earnest attention*, his next step would be, by a few more brief questions, to lead his little class to a close and *careful examination* of the specimen submitted to their notice; and, to their surprise and delight, to enable them to see that the bit of granite in their hands,—although but one stone to the eye, at first sight,—actually contained portions of three different kinds of rock. He would then give his pupils an unpretending but thoroughly effective exercise in *analysis*, by inducing them to point out distinctly each component element, apart, and to describe, at the moment of doing so, its points of difference from the others, by which the eye might recognize and the mind distinguish it.

Another stage, in the well-planned lessons of this true teacher, would lead to a yet closer *inspection* of the component elements in the object of observation, by the presentation of separate specimens of each, in *comparison* with the smaller portions of them perceptible in the stone. The transparency of the *mica*, its laminated form, its beauty to the eye, would all come up in turn, for due notice and remark; nor would its peculiar adaptation to several of the uses and conveniences of life be overlooked. The *quartz* element, with its beautiful crystalline aspect and forms, its value as a gem, its wide diffusion in the granular condition, its presence and its effects in the composition of rocks and soils,—all briefly exemplified and enumerated,—would form a copious subject of instruction and delight. The *feldspar*, too, with its creamy tint and block-like configuration, and its valuable uses in the hands of the potter and the dentist, would come in for its share of delighted attention and studious observation.

Here was the true office of instruction faithfully exemplified. Here was genuine mental activity, on the part of the pupil; and, here were its natural effects,—vigorous, healthy expansion and development, together with the pure, natural, and salutary pleasure of intellectual exercise,—more dear to the child than even his favorite play. Here, too, were effectually secured the moral influences of culture, docility, order, regularity, voluntary attention and application, gratitude to the instructor for personal favor and benefit consciously received, an earnest desire implanted for the true and enduring pleasures which spring from knowledge, and the first steps taken in the life-long pursuit of science. The teacher, having put himself into a true living relation to the mental constitution of his pupils, could, without delaying for formal calls to order or attention, proceed, at once, to the benign office of his vocation, as the guide of the young mind. By a wise preventive method,—not by authority, rule, or penalty,—he secured the devoted attention and good order of his pupils, and, not less, their own happiness, their sympathy with him, at the moment, and their habitual reverence for him, as the living source of knowledge.

After one lesson, such as has been described, the substantial and durable effect resulting from it was usually perceptible in the fact that, on the dismission of the school, the juvenile members of Mr. Holbrook's audience would be found resorting to whatever place they thought likely to furnish them with specimens such as he had exhibited in his lesson. This was almost universally the case when the lesson happened to be given in a rural region, where objects of the kind in question were easily obtained. But, not less zeal for collecting specimens for juvenile cabinets, would sometimes be manifested in the more confined sphere of city life, an instance of which it would be difficult for the writer to forget.

An eager group of little collectors were scrambling for specimens around the temporary shed of the stone-masons occupied in the erection of a public building. They were busily replenishing their pockets with such pieces as struck their fancy, and stopping now and then to compare specimens, or each to examine his own more closely. Drawing near to the juvenile company of geologists, as their heads were clubbed together in earnest inspection of a specimen, the observer heard one exclaim, "Well, I do not think it is the right kind. For, you know, Mr. Holbrook said the way to spell granite was not *g-r-a-n-i-t-e*, but '*mica, quartz,* and *feldspar*.' Now, there is not a bit of mica in any of these stones." The observer happened to know of Mr. Holbrook's visits to the school to which the boys belonged; and, as he saw that the little students had just found their way to the exact spot in investigation where Mr. H. would be glad to meet them, so as, by means of a little closer analysis, to enable them to detect the difference between granite and "sienite," he relieved their anxiety by telling them that they had better not throw away the pieces they had picked up, but carry them to the school-room, next morning, and ask Mr. Holbrook to tell them why there was no mica in their specimens, and what those black specks were. One of the little explorers returned to his home, on the following day, to tell, with a face all radiant with intelligence, about the quarries of Syene, in Egypt, the quarries of Quincy, and those of the "Granite" State, and even to go into some details, in which neither of his parents was sufficiently versed in science to follow him satisfactorily.

Analysis, in its Connection with the Discipline of the Perceptive Faculties.—An eminent writer has truly said that a dwarf, behind his steam-engine, may remove mountains. Analysis is the correspondent power of the intellect. It is the grand instrument in all the operations of the perceptive faculties. It is observation working scientifically; and, of all the implements of science, it is the keenest in its edge, the truest in its action, and the surest in the results which it attains. It is the key to knowledge, in all departments of intelligence; and, perfection in its processes is the crown of glory on the head of him who stands foremost in the field of scientific research. Education, as the power which trains and forms the mental habits, has no higher boon which it can confer, as the result of years of practice and discipline.

Valuable, however, as this process is, education, in the history of the past, could lay but slight claims to the merit of having formed the mental habits which it implies; since the means and opportunities of analytic intellection were withheld or neglected, to a very great extent, in consequence of the omission to provide the requisite objects and exercises for the discipline of the perceptive faculties. Education, while it consisted chiefly in arbitrary forms of exercise on abstract principles, connected with formulas in language and in number, drawn from the sciences of grammar and arithmetic, precluded the exercise of perception, by causing the learner to assume, instead of investigating, the primary facts of language and of number. At the present day, we obey the law of inductive procedure, and substitute personal observation and distinct perception for wide assumption and broad assertion. This is true of, at least, the modes and methods of all who profess to teach philosophically, as not mere instructors, but educators of the mind. Still, there remains much to be done with reference to the early direction and training of the intellectual faculties, so as to ensure the selection and presentation of the proper materials on which the intellect should be exercised in the first stages of its course of discipline.

Analysis, as a process of observant mind, implies the presence of objects which, by its solvent power, it is to reduce to component elements; and, as the real object, the fact, the actual relation, precede, in the order of nature and development, the ideal image, the intellectual abstraction, the logical deduction, early education in its primary operations, should conform to this law of order and of progress, and, in prescribing its first forms of exercise and discipline, should obviously draw its materials from the external universe of palpable realities, and not from the internal world of pure thought, in which the young mind possesses so little conscious power. Nor is it well for the mind that the habit of analytical observation and study, so indispensable to its successful action, in all forms of acquisitive exercise, should be deferred to the later stages of intellectual culture. Facility in analysis, acquired by practice on the accessible forms and relations of external objects, is easily transferred, by analogy, to the arithmetical exercise of resolving complicated numbers into their simpler constituent groups; or, the grammatical one of reducing a perplexing period to its primary elements, and these, in turn, to their component parts.

Progress in mathematical science and linguistic study, would be much surer and more rapid, if, instead of being demanded of the earlier stages of mental progress, it were postponed to a period subsequent to that of analytical exercise, practised, for years, on objects perceptible to the senses.

Analysis, as the systematic process of examination, is one and the same thing, in whatever direction it is applied; its power as an instrument of discipline, is as fully felt in investigating the structure of a plant as that of a sentence; and, the intelligent teacher, while superintending such a process, will feel the same weight of obligation resting on him in the one case as in the other. He will, accordingly, be watchful over the manner in which the process is conducted, that it be not superficial, or hasty, or partial, but thorough-going, deliberate, and exhaustive, as far as it ought to extend; and, that it be furnished with faithful expression, or record, at every step of its progress. It is thus only that the indispensable broad line of distinction can be drawn, which gives certainty to knowledge, by separating what has been examined from what has not been, and measures what is known by what has been done.

Inspection, as a Disciplinary Process for the Perceptive Faculties.—When analysis has faithfully performed its peculiar task, and singled out for observation the very last component element in the object of investigation, there remains yet, to the attentive teacher, another stage of perceptive progress to be accomplished by his pupil, under the suggestive direction of a mind which has already traveled the path of knowledge. The searching *inspection of the individual elements* which compose a complex whole,—an inspection so minute, that each element may be described and defined in its distinctive unity of constitution and character, and, in the clearly traced relation which it bears to the whole, as well as in each of its own chief characteristics, or prominent features,—becomes, perhaps, in turn, an element in some wide-sweeping induction, for purposes of comparison and classification.

Elementary botany,—that which a young child is perfectly competent to study, and which requires but the seeing eye and the attentive mind, to examine and describe the different parts of a plant, or even a root, a stem, a bud, or a leaf,—abounds in the best of materials for exercise in close and minute examination of details. To render this process a tendency and a habit of his pupil's mind, is here the office of the educator. Yet, this is but one of the numerous resources of nature on which he may draw for the cultivation of the highest traits of intellectual skill and expertness, as attributes of the young minds, which it is his business to train to the highest pitch of mental power to which he can raise them.

In the examination of a plant, for example, he does not limit the attention of his pupils to the mere analysis of the whole into its parts. Every part, separately, he makes an object of distinct inspection and investigation, in every light in which observation or science enables him to hold it up. No feature of individual character is suffered to escape notice,—no detail, how minute soever it may be, in which it differs from, or resembles, a correspondent point of form or function, in another specimen of kindred character.

In lessons on animal life,—to use another example,—the juvenile student, under the charge of the watchful teacher, is directed to observe the fact, which minute inspection discloses, that, in one instance, where he would naturally, at first glance, think that he has seen two *feet*; he will actually discover, on closer inspection, two *hands*; that, in observing the figure of the chimpanzee, he has been contemplating neither biped nor quadruped, but a quadrumanous (four-handed) animal; and, that this distinction is founded chiefly on the careful examination of the member which he had been accustomed to call a *toe*, but which is, in reality, a *thumb*, designed to aid in the actions of grasping and climbing, which are so important to the animal's mode of life. The close inspection of one member thus becomes, for the time, the turning point on which the young student depends for the recognition of a grand distinction in nature, and for the true understanding and proper appreciation of the scientific term in which this distinction is recorded. √

Interrogation, as an Instrument of Intellectual Discipline.—In the language of general writers on subjects connected with the experimental and tentative processes of science, man is said to *interrogate* nature. The figure is a most suggestive one to the teacher, with reference to his business and duties. It presents man in his appropriate attitude of an attentive and docile child of Nature, inquiring trustfully of her concerning the causes which lie too deep for mere intuition, but which her maternal spirit is ever ready to reveal to earnest desire and faithful endeavor. The human parent and the teacher stand, to the young mind, in the same oracular relation, as expounders and interpreters of the great volume of creation. But, how seldom is the inquiring spirit of childhood encouraged to avail itself of its lawful provision for the furnishing of that knowledge which it consciously craves, as the sustenance of its life! How seldom does the teacher feel the full force of the obligation which the inquisitive habits of childhood lay upon him, to encourage the spirit of curiosity which prompts the many questions of the child! How seldom does he feel that his business is to incite, and stimulate, and prompt, and enliven, in every way possible to him, this primary instinct, which impels the mind toward the goal of knowledge! How seldom does he enter into the spirit of the wise suggestion of the poet; and, even when in the very act of feeding the intellectual appetite, so contrive as "by giving" to "make it ask!"

Book Questions.—The teacher is not usually so remiss in regard to the importance of interrogation, as a stimulus to intelligence, so far as concerns his own resort to that process. Far from it! He knows its value, as a pointer or guide-post, to definite results. Nor are there wanting instructors so reliant on interrogatory forms, and so distrustful of their own power to devise them, that they conduct the whole business of a lesson, following literally the numerous questions printed on the page of the text-book. Such questions, it is true, are not to be despised and rejected in the wholesale style in which they are sometimes disposed of by the young and sanguine teacher, who has just begun to see their inadequacy to the purposes and wants of personal instruction. The printed question, even when extended to minutiæ, may be rendered very serviceable to the formation of habits of faithful application and close study, as well as accurate recapitulation; if the young student is directed to make use of it as a test, in regard to the exactness of his preparation for a personal examination on the subject of his lesson; if he is duly trained not to regard the printed question as merely the teacher's part in a verbatim mechanical dialogue between the master and himself, in which the last word in the sentence of the one speaker forms the literal "cue" to the first word in that of the other, but, as a criterion of his knowledge of the subjects, as a friendly intimation that, if he can not furnish an answer to the question before him, he is so far deficient in his preparation to give intelligently an account of the part of the subject to which the question refers.

Children's Questions.—But, it would be more to the purpose of the young teacher's business, if,—instead of the printed aid offered to him in what should be his own part of a lesson, and which, if he respects his own mind, he will draw only from his own resources, according to the needs of the pupil,—the page of the text-book abounded, rather, in the questions which *children* would like to ask, for their personal information. The judicious instructor will always make free use of interrogation, as a means of ascertaining or aiding the degree of his pupil's intelligence. But, he will not overlook the fact that this process, like that of the printer, in taking his proof impression, is to certify a result,—not to create it. The questions which the child is permitted or encouraged to put to his teacher, are, often, the sole means by which the former is enabled to "set up" accurately in his mind the facts of the lesson required. The number and the closeness of these questions become, further, the expression and evidence of the interest which the pupil takes in the lesson. To the teacher who possesses the patient and sympathizing spirit of his office, these questionings come gratefully to his ear, even when they betray the "blank misgivings of a creature wandering in worlds not realized." It is then that he is most impressively reminded of the true nature of his work, as an intellectual guide and conductor. He is ever careful, therefore, to provoke, rather than repress, interrogation; and, even so to frame his own questions that they shall serve to call forth fresh inquiries from his pupils.

The appropriate discipline of the perceptive faculties, depending, as it does, on the frequent presentation of objects of sense, with a view to win attention, and secure exact observation, implies that the teacher resorts, on all occasions, to close questioning, as the suggestive process by which the pupil is induced to use his own perceptive power, to rely on the fidelity of his own observation, and thus to acquire a knowledge which is substantial and thorough-going. But, it is not less true that, in proportion to the pupil's interest in the efforts which he makes, and the progressive steps which he takes in every process, his very attainments will be suggesting and prompting further inquiries, for his future guidance. The spirit and intelligence, as well as the pleasure, therefore, with which he proceeds in his work, will depend, to a great extent, on the consciousness that he is not working in the dark.

Mode of Answering Questions.—The answer to the pupil's questions, however, the true teacher is well aware, is not always to come from the lips of the instructor. It is often left intentionally to be the fruit of the learner's further efforts and closer examination. To withhold an answer to the most eager question, is sometimes a truer kindness than to give it. The ripe and perfect fruit of knowledge must sometimes, like that of the tree, be patiently waited for, and wrought for.

Leading Questions.—The wise teacher, however, will know as well when to put the skillful leading question, which does not supersede, but rather calls forth the activity of the pupil's mind. The leading question, though unlawful at the bar, is, under the management of the prudent teacher, the very turning point, in some cases, which decides whether he is "apt to teach," as an intelligent guide to the results of actual knowledge and true discipline.

Direction and Information, as Didactic Processes Connected with the Exercise and Discipline of the Perceptive Faculties.—The answers given by a judicious teacher to the questions of his pupils will often consist in references to the sources of information, rather than in direct replies. In the study of natural objects, it is peculiarly important that the pupil should see, and think, and judge, and discover, for himself. To such training in self-reliance and self-help, the exercise of the perceptive faculties on the details of form in animal, plant, and mineral, is preëminently adapted. The embarrassing complexity and intricacy, and the baffling abstruseness, and the perplexing obscurity, which sometimes characterize other subjects of investigation, and which call so loudly for the teacher's frequent aid to his pupil, do not exist here. The simplicity and the beauty of nature's products, invite and attract attention; and, every successive stage of examination leads unconsciously to another. The teacher has but to indicate and to prompt, and thus leave the mind the rich satisfaction of achieving its own progress. He is not tempted to fall into the besetting sin of instruction,—that of anticipating, and assuming, and asserting, and so quenching the mind's healthful thirst by the lukewarm distillations of precept and rule, instead of leaving it to refresh itself by drinking at the cool, vivifying fountain-head of original observation.

An eminent naturalist once gave a very impressive lesson in the art of teaching to one who is himself, professionally, an instructor. The question proposed to the savant was, "How may we distinguish snakes which are venomous from those which are not?" "Come into my study," was the answer, "and I will place before you some of each kind; and, then, by examining, you can see for yourself." It is thus the true teacher proceeds with his pupils: it is thus he gives certainty to knowledge, and clearness and vigor to the mental faculties.

As a guide and director of the mind, the intelligent instructor points his pupils to the sources from which he himself obtained information, and thus admits them to the honor of partnership with him in investigation and accumulation. Teacher and student thus become allied by friendly participation in the same pursuits; and, a high, though unostentatious, moral effect is blended with the cultivation and enjoyment of intellect.

The teacher, however, who thus wisely throws his pupils, as far as practicable on their own resources, does not thereby preclude the ample furnishing of all needed information, which intelligent appreciation and successful application may require. He will, on the contrary, take pleasure in disclosing facts, in tracing analogies, and furnishing explanations, when these serve to give additional value and attraction to the theme of his instructions. He will thus contrive, at once, to satisfy and to stimulate the mind's natural craving for knowledge, and make every step of progress the foothold and the impulse to yet another. He will still be careful, however, even when imparting direct information, to confine it within those limits which shall leave a wide and inviting field for the pupil's own investigations, and secure his personal interest in future explorations, which may subserve the important purposes of acquisition, as connected with attainments in the various departments of education, or with those advances in science which may form a large part of his own conscious happiness, and contribute, ultimately, to the general diffusion of knowledge.

Comparison, as a Disciplinary Exercise of the Perceptive Faculties.—The unity of the intellect, as a principle in the human constitution, forbids any attempt at literal or exhaustive analysis, in the study of its diversified character and modes of action. In educational relations, more particularly, all attempts at the analytic observation of mental phenomena, for purposes of intelligent and healthful culture, must ever be regarded as merely analogical presentations and figurative expositions. The successive stages of mental development and discipline, in like manner, are incapable of being cut apart and separated by any dividing line of demarcation. On the contrary, they naturally blend into one another, with a closeness of connection, and a delicacy of shading, which does not admit of precise distinctions, or marked discriminations.

When we group, therefore, the various modes in which intellect manifests itself in action, and designate one of these groups by the term "perceptive," and another by the term "reflective," we recognize a distinction, with regard to which, even a superficial observer of the mind's activity, would not venture to say that it is not founded on an actual difference. Still, we should find it extremely difficult to lay down a precise line of demarcation, and say with certainty, in every instance, here terminates the perceptive, and here commences the reflective action of intellect. Thus, in assigning its place to the master faculty of intelligence, we should feel no hesitation in ranking *reason* among the reflective faculties. But, when this noble power descends, as has been so happily expressed, to the humble office of "judging according to sense," it necessarily partakes of the character of the class of faculties with which it mingles in action. It constitutes, thus, an element and a condition in *perception* itself; as is verified by the consequences of its absence, in the intellectual action of the insane person, who distinctly enough *perceives* the form of his friend, but, in the inexplicable aberration of reason, salutes him as a foreign ambassador, come to do him the honor of a visit, in consideration of his world-renowned skill in disentangling complicated questions in state policy.

Comparison combines, usually, an act of volition with the process of observation, directed to two or more objects, for the purpose of recognizing their unity or diversity of character; and, hence, is properly regarded as but the preliminary or introductory step to the act of *judgment*, which pronounces the case one of analogy or anomaly. It is not unusual, therefore, to class comparison as purely an act of judgment, or decisive reason; and, by its office, a *reflective* faculty. As a process of intellection, however, it obviously commences with the perceptive act of attentive *observation;* and, as a disciplinary and developing operation in mental culture, it falls under the special care of the educator, as an exercise in the early training and forming of intellectual habit.

Proper Rank of Comparison, as an Intellectual Process.—Regarded in connection with the study of natural objects, the act of comparison, is an exercise of the perceptive faculties, which, in the order of intelligence, is the immediate sequel to the processes of examination, analysis, and inspection. These, indeed, are but the legitimate preparatory stages for its wider mode of action, and higher offices in the sphere of intelligence. Yet, in its turn, it is but the humble ministration of intellect to the yet higher offices of *classification*, under the guidance of the master function of *induction*, which presides over all the varied forms of intellectual activity, connected with the observation and study of nature.

Intellectual Effects of the Discipline Resulting from the Exercise of Comparison.—Comparison, as a process of intelligence, commenced under the watchful eye of the teacher, on the objects of perception,—the only sure and firm ground of early mental development,—gives a certainty and a skill to the perceptive action of the mind, which tell, with sure effect, on all analogous operations of a more purely intellectual or even an abstract character, in later stages of education. The influence of the habit of careful and exact comparison, extends, with full effect, to the highest efforts of mature mind, in the most complicated and intricate relations of thought, in mathematics, in logic, and in language. Comparison, as the first step in the higher progress of the mind, when making its transition from the study of single objects to that of numbers, and grouping them, by their *analogies*, in *classes*, brings the intellect under the dominion of *order*, introduces it to the discipline of *method*, and ultimately rewards it by the recognition of *law*. Principle and rule then take charge of the intelligent mind; and, as "strong siding champions," beat down every barrier to its progress toward consummate knowledge.

Natural Objects peculiarly adapted to the purposes of Comparison, as a Disciplinary Exercise.—As means of discipline for the perceptive faculties, in various modes of comparison, the materials for practice, furnished in the different departments of nature, are peculiarly adapted to the great ends of education. Their mutual resemblances and contrasts, the prominent features of their correspondent forms, seem to solicit comparison and classification, as destined results of man's mental adaptation to the scene in which he moves, and which so abounds in objects of attractive interest,—the germs of intelligence, enveloped in consummate beauty, that they may lead to the conscious delights of knowledge.

By the introductory discipline resulting from the humble exercise of carefully comparing objects and their characteristic parts, the young mind receives its preparation for the scientific intelligence and the conscious pleasure with which it subsequently enters on the wide range of action afforded by the inviting analogies revealed in the study of comparative physiology and anatomy, and in all investigations to which science conducts, wherever exact classification and consummate knowledge are dependent on attentive and faithful comparison,—a condition equally indispensable, whether in collating the vestiges of past eras in the physical history of our globe, or those of language and of intellect, as revealed in the investigations of philology.

Classification, as an Exercise for the Discipline of the Perceptive Faculties.—This form of intellectual action,—which, in its various aspects, may be said to constitute and to consummate human knowledge, in whatever department we contemplate,—is the immediate sequel of the preceding act of mind, in collating the objects of observation, or their peculiar features and characteristics. The resemblances which comparison recognizes in objects, become the leading titles and significant designations of groups and classes. Intellect is thus freed from the burden of the endless and unsatisfactory task of wandering from object to object, in detail, without any conscious thread of connection or guidance, and without any suggestion of a definite end in view, in its wearisome mode of action. By the aid of classification, the chaos of disconnected individualities is converted into an orderly creation, where everything, as of old, is seen to exist "after his kind." Knowledge thus becomes a series of aggregated accumulations, arranged and labelled to the intellectual eye; and, investigation is rendered a rational and inviting pursuit,—directed by definite aims, and leading to satisfactory results.

Benefits of Classification, as an Intellectual Exercise.—By the process of classification, man is enabled to trace the successive footsteps of the Creator in the outward world, to recognize the grand law of universal order, and yield obedience to its dictates in his modes of mental action. The student of nature, pursuing his investigations in this spirit, is prepared, by successive illustrations of fact, to amplify his classifications into those wide inductions which are the glory of science, and which aid the intellect in accomplishing the vast generalizations for which its powers of comprehension and its ceaseless aspirations seem equally adapted.

The exercise of classification tends to create in the young mind the love of order and method. It is, in fact, a strictly logical discipline, resulting in the highest mental benefits, and preparing the heart for the influence of the most exalted moral principle. It belongs, however, as a process of mental culture, to a very early stage of intellectual progress, and begins appropriately with the first conscious steps of advancement in the observation and study of nature. The child, in Nature's great school, finds himself placed in a vast cabinet of specimens, which he takes a peculiar pleasure in examining, and from which, even when little aided by formal education, he draws, with delight, stores of personal knowledge, and the pure pleasure of the conscious activity which his spirit craves.

The objects of nature, as the results of a designing Mind, seem peculiarly adapted to the end of drawing forth the action of intellect and building up intellectual character in the human being. In no respect is this more true than with reference to the facilities furnished in the three great kingdoms of nature, for the purely intellectual processes of arranging and classifying the objects of observation. The young mind here finds itself placed in a sphere of order, in which every thing is arranged for the correspondent action of thought; in which every object invites to observation, and every group solicits a recognition of the principle of classification.

Early Training in Classification.—Furnished with such an apparatus for the purposes of instruction, the teacher has but to point suggestively to the successive classes of objects most easily accessible to the young learner in the great classified receptacles of earth, air, and water. He has but to encourage his pupil to collect, compare, and classify the various forms of mineral, plant, and animal, which lie within the range of his daily walks; or, even to deposit, in any convenient and suitable receptacle, groups of leaves of similar form, and to define the shape or the feature which, in his distribution of them, is made the ground of classification. The learner thus obtains a measure and a record of his progress in knowledge; and, the knowledge which he acquires, possesses a true and substantial character, which, in turn, affects that of his mind, giving it a taste for solid acquirements and genuine pleasures.

CULTIVATION OF THE EXPRESSIVE FACULTIES.

INTRODUCTORY OBSERVATIONS.—The classification of the mental faculties under the designations of "perceptive," "expressive," and "reflective," was adopted in the preceding lecture of this series, as a convenient one for a survey of the human mind, with reference to the purposes of education. This classification, it was mentioned, could not be regarded as founded on lines of distinction which could be assumed as rigorously or literally exact; since its terms are properly but so many names for various states, acts, or operations of the mind,—itself one and the same in all.

Imperfect as such a classification must necessarily be, however, it enables us, by its distinctions, to trace more clearly and definitely the forms of mental action, and the power which the mind possesses of exerting itself in different modes; and it affords to the educator, when contemplating the intellectual capabilities of man with reference to the processes and effects of culture, the advantages of analysis and systematic examination, as aids to the prosecution of his inquiries.

Following the order of nature and of fact, when we trace the succession of action in the exercise of man's intellectual powers, as these are designated in the classification which we have adopted, we observe that, in the mature and deliberate use of the mental faculties, the habitual and normal succession is, (1.) *Observation*, (2.) *Reflection*, (3.) *Expression*. In the immature and susceptible condition of childhood and youth, however, the spontaneous activity and development of the communicative tendencies of the mind cause the action of the expressive faculties to precede that of the reflective; and to this law the order of education will properly correspond.

The perfect action and discipline of the power of expression, require, no doubt, all the aid derived from the maturity of reason and reflection, and, consequently, an advanced stage of intellectual culture. But, in the history of man's mental progress, under the guidance of natural laws, the educator perceives and recognizes in the young mind, an early necessity of utterance, or of expression in some form, as one of the divinely implanted instincts by which it is actuated, and which therefore becomes an indication to be obeyed in the plan and progress of culture.

The phenomena of the external world irresistibly impel the child to utter the emotions which they excite; and the judicious educator will always encourage the young observer to record them, long before the era of experience in which they become subjects of reflective thought or profound cogitation. To give consistency and effect, however, to the forms of expression,—whether for purposes of record or of discipline,—a certain degree of progress must have been attained in the exercise and development not only of the perceptive, but also of the reflective faculties;—a result inseparable, indeed,—as was mentioned in the preceding lecture,—from the right direction of the perceptive powers themselves. In this and in every other attempt to trace the order of mental development, we are always brought back to the grand primal truth that the mind is properly *one*, in all its action; we are reminded that this great fact is the basis of all true culture, and that the different intellectual *faculties*, as we term them, are but the varied phases or modes of action of the same subtle power.

As an introduction, accordingly, to the discussion of the principles which regulate the cultivation of the expressive faculties, as a department of intellectual education, our last lecture followed, to some extent, the necessary connection existing between the discipline of the perceptive faculties and the primary action of the reflective. With this preliminary preparation, we will now proceed, on the plan indicated in the first lecture of this series, to the study of the various forms of mental action which, in the figurative language unavoidable in all intellectual analysis and classification, may be termed the *expressive* faculties.

The plan proposed embraced, it will be recollected, the following prominent features :—(1.) an *enumeration* of each group of faculties, by its *modes*, or forms, *of action;* (2.) *the actuating principle*, or impelling force, of each group; (3.) the *tendency*, or habit, of action in each; (4.) the *result*, or issue, of such action; (5.) the *educational processes*, forms of exercise, or modes of culture, suggested by the four preceding considerations.

Following the order here mentioned, we commence with the

  (I.) ENUMERATION OF THE EXPRESSIVE FACULTIES.

These may be grouped under the following designations :—Emotion, Imagination, Fancy, Imitation, Personation, Representation, Language, Taste.

Explanatory Remark.—To ascertain, with precision, what powers or attributes of the human being should be regarded as properly comprehended under the above denomination, the educator would do well, here as elsewhere, to advert to the primitive signification of the term which is employed to designate the class of faculties to which it is applied. At every step of his progress in the study of man as a being capable of systematic development, the teacher finds a guiding light perpetually emanating from the primary sense of the terms which constitute the nomenclature of intellectual philosophy, in its nalysis of the human faculties. These terms are often highly figurative, and hence peculiarly suggestive with reference whether to distinctness of classification, or to purposes of culture and development. In no case does this remark apply more forcibly than in the present. The term "expression," (*pressing out*,) implies, in the first instance, the existence of something *within*, which, under the action of a force, working whether from within or from without, is *pressed out*, and thus rendered external, palpable, or perceptible.

Referring this term to the phenomena of human experience, we derive, from its primary and figurative sense, the inference, or implication, that man is endued with the power of giving an external manifestation to his internal conditions of thought or feeling. The form of this manifestation may be that of attitudes and actions of the body, changes in the aspect of the countenance, effects on the tones of the voice, or efforts in the organs of articulation, and modifications of the accents of speech; it may appear in imitative acts, in suggestive graphic delineations, or in intelligible written characters. But in all cases, it is the *re*presentative *ex*pression (pressing *out*,) of what has been *im*pressed, or is *present, within*.—The inward working may be that of a feeling, an affection, an emotion, or a passion: it may be that of an impressive idea, or of a thought, an opinion, or a sentiment. But the result is invariably an outward effect, audible or visible.

Whatever power or faculty, therefore, has an agency in the process of thus giving an external manifestation to an internal mental condition, will be appropriately comprehended under the designation "expressive;" and the classification will be exhaustive and complete, if it include all those mental states, acts, or operations which give *form* to thought or feeling. The preceding enumeration of the expressive faculties, however, is intended to present only those which are prominently active in the ordinary conditions of humanity, and which are the principal subjects of disciplinary training, in the processes of education.

1. EMOTION: *its Offices in Expression.*—Emotion is the natural language of that *sensibility* which tends to render man conscious of

himself, which serves to unite him, by a law of sympathy, with other beings as well as with those of his own race, and which, as a stimulus to his power of will, impels him to the various forms of salutary and pleasurable, or injurious and destructive action. Without this power, ("emotion,"—*moving outward*,) man might, indeed, possess the profoundest capacity of feeling, the utmost depth of thought, the grandest or the most beautiful forms of imagination. His whole inner world might be consciously a scene of ideal glory. But, to his fellow man, he would be mute and unintelligible. Self-contained and solitary, the individual would be as destitute of sympathy as of expression, and live unappreciated and uninterpreted, because incommunicative and unintelligible.

Emotion, therefore, we find is not left wholly at the discretion or the control of man, as a purely voluntary power. Its first and all its strongest manifestations are spontaneous and involuntary. It is the natural and irrepressible language of that wondrous capacity of pleasure and pain with which the human being is invested, in consequence of the susceptive sensibility with which his Creator has seen fit to enliven and to protect his nature.

Emotion, as the natural expression of sympathy, renders feeling legible and audible, and thus enables man instinctively to utter or to interpret the language of the heart; as an intimation of the will, it enables him to read the disposition and intentions, friendly or hostile, of his fellow beings. It is an early instrument of power to the helplessness or the sufferings of infancy, while it proclaims the presence of pain, and brings to the little patient the ready sympathy and remedial aid of the mother. It expresses and attracts the sympathetic affections of childhood and youth. (It gives eloquence to the speech of man, warmth to the cordial welcome of friendship, or fire to the hostility of hatred. It melts in pity and compassion for suffering; it glows with indignation at oppression and wrong; it bends in humility and adoration before Infinite majesty, and in reverence to human worth; or it looks haughtily down on the lowly, spurns the petitioner for mercy, and tramples on the weak and the unresisting. Its power for good or evil is unspeakable in all that involves the moral or the intellectual character of human utterance.)

The Forms of Emotion.—These are as various as the mental relations of man. It is Love, in the instincts of *affection;* Wonder, in those of the *intellect;* Awe, in those of the *spirit;* Admiration, in those of *sentiment;* Joy and Grief, to the *heart;* Hatred and Revenge, in the *malignant* passions; Ardor and Enthusiasm, in the aspirations of the *soul;* Courage and Exultation, in *conflict;* Fear and

Terror, in *danger ;* Embarrassment, Confusion, and Shame, in *failure* or *defeat ;* Anguish, in *pain ;* Contrition or Remorse, in conscious *guilt ;* Agony and Despair, in utter *ruin ;* Serenity, Tranquillity, and Peace, in conscious *rectitude ;* Calmness and Composure, in *self-control ;* Sorrow and Gladness, in *sympathy ;* Laughter, in *mirth ;* Caricature, in *humor ;* Gloom, in *melancholy.*

Effects of Emotion.—Its aspects and its traits are as numerous as the ever-changing moods of the "many-sided mind ;" and its power of expression ranges through all degrees of force, from the gentle half-whisper of confiding love, or the accents of a mother's tenderness, to the scream of madness and the burst of rage. It moves to deeds of gentleness and mercy, as consciously pleasing acts dictated by the principle of duty; and it prompts to the perpetration of crimes at the thought of which humanity shudders. In all circumstances it becomes an expressive language of indescribable power,—a power for the exercise of which man is laid under responsibleness the most appalling. Its genial effects carry man beyond the limits of his nature, and enable him to approximate to the benignity of an angel; and its malignant workings invest him with the character of a fiend.

Emotion, the Inspiration of Language.—Emotion, as the natural, involuntary, or irrepressible manifestation of feeling, is, in itself, the primary form as well as cause of expression. The writhings and the outcries of pain, the tears and the wailings of sorrow, the smiles and the sweet tones of pleasure, the leaping and the laughter of exuberant joy, the exultant attitudes and shouts of triumph, the frown, the harsh tone, and the blow of anger, are all a universally intelligible language. But emotion is also the power which gives life, and force, and effect to *voluntary* and *deliberate* utterance, not only in the tones of spoken language but in the burning words which the glowing heart prompts to the pen of the eloquent writer, and which, when read from the mouldering parchment or the crumbling tablet, ages after they were written, have still the power to stir men's blood, "as with the sound of a trumpet." It inspires the modern youth with the eloquence of Demosthenes, in the words with which he "fulmined over Greece ;" it kindles the heart of the student in his "still removed place," with the fire and the shout and the fierceness of the battle scenes of Homer; it appalls him with the spectacle of the victims of inexorable fate, in the defiant appeals of the suffering Prometheus, as he writhes on his rock of torture,—in the superhuman agonies of the doomed Orestes,—in the wailings of the guiltless Œdipus, when he is awakened to the complicated horrors which he has unwittingly drawn down upon himself and upon the very authors of his being.

It is the same expressive power, in its more genial forms, which lulls the youthful reader into the dreamy repose of the pastoral scenes of the eclogue, where

> "Every shepherd tells his tale
> Under the hawthorn in the dale."

It is the same power, in its ecstatic moods, which lights up the soul with the brilliant fire of the lyric ode, whose burning words have immortalized equally the bard and the hero of the antique world of gods and godlike men; and it is still the same magic power over sympathy which holds us entranced over "what, though rare, of later age," we feel to possess the same sway over the heart as that which was written of old for all time.

2. IMAGINATION: *its Office in Expression.*—Emotion endows man with the *power* of expression: his ability to give force and effect to expression, is as his capability of emotion; and the vividness of emotion is dependent on his susceptibility of feeling. But the utmost intensity of feeling might exist in internal consciousness merely; the most vehement excitement of emotion might find no definite or intelligible manifestation; it might be but the idiot's "sound and fury, signifying nothing;" the noblest sentiments of the human soul might find no adequate expression; were it not for the action of another faculty,—that whose office it is to give *form* to the vague effects of feeling, to embody the evanescent phenomena of emotion, and to give to the abstractions of thought and the generalizations of sentiment a definite shape and the durability of a permanent record.

Consciousness and introversion might enable the individual man to hold communion with his own inner conditions of thought and feeling; and memory might enable him to recall them. But, as it is not given to man, by any act of mere direct introspection, to read the heart or mind of his fellow man, sympathetic and intelligent human intercommunication requires, as a condition, the aid of some power or faculty by which feeling may be distinctly manifested, not merely in its stronger and involuntary excitements, but also in its quietest moods, in its gentlest movements and most delicate effects. The communication of pure thought, apart entirely from excited emotion, is also a necessity of man's mental character and relations. Intellect, not less than feeling, has its claims on utterance, that the individual may become consciously a progressive being, and that mutual intelligence and benefit may be ensured to society. Some means, in a word, are needed to *represent* what is present to the mind, to suggest the idea or the thought which, by a law of his nature impelling him, man desires to communicate to his fellow being.

Analogy, the Medium of Expression.—Taught by a wisdom above his own, man finds, in the analogies of the outward universe, correspondences to his own inward states of thought and feeling. These analogous forms he refers to as interpreters, in his acts of expression; he transfers them, by a heaven-taught instinct, from their original places in the visible outward sphere to his own inner and invisible world of thought and feeling. These borrowed forms, addressing themselves to a common nature in common circumstances, become the suggestive language of emotion and intelligence between man and man; and, as intellectual skill and expertness are developed, these forms are at length multiplied and complicated so as to assume all the varied shapes of the current coin of speech, even in its most arbitrary modes;—just as, in the history of human intercourse, traffic, which commenced with the interchange and barter of commodities, gradually becomes a process of purchase and sale, by the adoption of convenient forms representing value and price.

Significance of the term "Imagination."—The power by which man recognizes the analogies of form presented in the external world, the power by which he *represents* these, the power by which he transfers these to his own internal world, and thus *images,* by analogy, his invisible, impalpable, feelings and conceptions; the power which thus embodies sentiment, and gives shape to language and all other modes of expression, is suggestively named " Imagination,"—the *imaging* faculty.

The Sphere of Imagination.—The office of this faculty, as an expressive power, is one of vast extent and of immense value; and its domain, like that of emotion, is indefinite. Intellect, in its widest excursions and its highest aims, is definite and limited. Its outward sphere is that of sense, as comprehended by the understanding, and measured by the rule of judgment ; its inner sphere is that of reason acting on data of definite thought, even in its purest abstractions and widest generalizations. Intellect, in its judicial and critical capacity, may justly assume the authority of deciding on the symmetry and proportion of expression as the form of thought. But it has no creative, no inventive power by which to call up form ; it may interpret or explain feeling ; but it can not, without the aid of imagination, embody it. Imagination extends its dominion alike over feeling and intellect : it possesses, exclusively, the power of investing them with form. As a sovereign in the vast world of analogy, it reaches, in one direction, to the farthest limits of the outward universe, wherever form exists, in conditions known or unknown ; in another direction, it penetrates the deepest secrets of human feeling, and brings them up from their darkest regions of half-unconscious being to the world of form and light, endues them with conscious life and speech, and sends them abroad as ministering angels of good or evil ; in still another direction, it explores the ethereal world of thought, and, by its creative energy, gives imagery, and form, and recognized character to impalpable ideas, clothes the naked conceptions of intellect with the garb of symmetrical expression, forges the golden links of language for the continuous processes of reason, invests sentiment with the living majesty and power of utterance, and crowns the inspired productions of the artist and the poet with the consummate beauty of form and the music of immortal verse.

3. FANCY: *its Effects on Expression.*—This faculty, although it possesses a character so peculiarly marked by external tendencies, and proneness to a lower sphere of action than that of imagination, can hardly claim, with justice, the dignity of a separate and independent existence. The term "Fancy," (*fantasy*,) is, strictly speaking, but another name for *imagination*, when that faculty, as an expressive power, assumes, occasionally, a lower than its wonted office, and, not content with the creation of *form*, descends to the addition of minute detail, in the shape, or figure, or color of its embodiments. Fancy, considered as a separate faculty, may be regarded as the servant and laborer of imagination, employed to take charge of all the merely outward effects of expressive art, but whose ambition sometimes leads it to aim at higher offices than it is, in itself, competent to fill. Attempting the creation of visible beauty, it assumes the office of a presiding deity over the fleeting, fluctuating phenomena of fashion and other manifestations of arbitrary taste. Uniting itself with humor and burlesque, it displays the whole world of fantastic oddity, drollery, and grotesque effects, of every species. It handles, with peculiar skill, the pencil of the caricaturist, and delights, sometimes, in the most hideous exaggerations. It contrives, occasionally, to lay mischievous hands on Taste, and with perverting influence to make her play all manner of antics, quite unconscious, all the while, how infinitely absurd and ridiculous she is making herself appear. Hence the whole world of absurd form and combinations in modes of dress and decoration, in incongruous architecture, deformed sculpture, distorted drawing, tawdry coloring, paltry novel-writing, fugitive (and vagabond) verses, agonistic orations, and nondescript lectures.

Fancy, however, has also her own becoming and proper part to play, when, in strictest unison with true Taste, and in filial obedience to her parent, Imagination, she gives symmetry to our dwellings and to our garments, genuine grace to manners, true beauty to our gardens, happy touches to the details of artistic execution, chaste style to writing, and manly plainness to speech.

4. IMITATION: *its Tendencies.*—The faculty of Imitation and the tendency to its exercise, which,—in the earlier stages of life, more particularly,—man possesses in common with many other of the animal tribes, form, in whatever regards expression, a peculiar source of power. It ensures, when judiciously developed, as a salutary instinct, all the advantages arising from native facility, as contrasted with the comparatively slow acquirements and laborious endeavors of mere artificial or mechanical training. The long non-age required for the comparatively slow development and maturing of the human being, implies a large dependence on the fostering care of parental guardianship and example; and the innate propensity to imitation, on the part of the child, coincides, in the effect of rendering more ample the opportunity of a long course of model training and practical lessons in the appropriate accomplishments of humanity. Among these, Speech, as the consummation of the expressive faculties, thus becomes the inheritance which one generation transmits to another,—a possession unconsciously acquired, although actually the result of long-continued training, and sometimes, of painful efforts in detail.

Drawing, as an Imitative Art.—The imitative tendency of the young, leading, as it does, to the perfecting of utterance, as an exercise in which practice begets skill, extends its influence, by the law of analogy, far and wide, over every branch of art which involves expression as a result. Nor is there one of all these branches which does not, by the habitual practice of it, under the same law, serve to discipline and perfect the power of expression in every other.

The feelings, the imagination, the conceptive power, the taste, and even the critical judgment of the young mind, are all called into as active exercise, in every earnest attempt to draw in outline, to shade, or to color the form of any external object, as in any endeavor to describe it by tongue or pen. Indeed, the extreme fixedness of attention demanded for exact and faithful delineation by the pencil, ensures a yet higher degree of mental activity, than does any other form of descriptive execution, and contributes more effectually to the development of graphic power of expression in language, than can any direct exercise in speech or writing; because the same powers are exerted in the one case as in the other, but with much more care and closeness of application.

Music, as an Imitative Art.—Another of the poetic and purely beneficent forms of the divinely implanted faculty of imitation, by which man attains the development of his powers of expression and communication, is that of Music, in the form of *song*. The young ear drinks in, instinctively and intuitively, the beauty of sound, as the eye takes in that of form and color. The laws of melodic variation of tone seem to be inscribed on the human ear, with few exceptions, as the laws of graceful form and expansion are stamped on the plant. But the musical sense is not a merely dry perception or recognition, or a mechanical obedience to law. It is one of the most delightful forms in which man becomes conscious of the pleasure of feeling or the power of emotion; and, as his culture extends, he recognizes it as the intelligent utterance of sentiment, in the noblest expressions of social sympathy, or even of devotional aspiration.

The imitative practice of music, accordingly, in all its forms, from the humblest lullaby of the nursery to the most exalted strains of the perfect vocalist, becomes a powerful discipline of the ear, because of the heart, the intellect, and the imagination. It prepares them to receive more fully the impressions of the melody of speech, and, in due season, to give forth their effects in appropriate expression. The child imbibes from the mother's song the theme of its own imitative efforts, and from the simple beauty of the natural model, catches, at the same time, unconsciously, the emotion of which it is the utterance, and thus early learns to unite expression with feeling. At a later stage of his musical culture and development, he acquires more consciously and more distinctly, a perception of the inspiration which marks the tones of the empassioned eloquence of the orator and the poet, and learns to appreciate the delicious melody of the "numerous verse" which "clothes the poet's thought in fitting sound."

The great masters in musical science and art, abundantly prove, by the transcendent delight which their efforts yield to universal man, the power and value of music as an expressive art, independently of its relation to the cultivation of the power of language. But the intensity of pleasure derived from the perfection of musical composition and execution combined, suggests instructively to the educator the power which even the elementary practice of this imitative art exerts on the character of expression, when embodied in the forms of language,—the ability which it gives to touch the heart, or to kindle emotion, and to throw the whole soul of the speaker and the writer into the mould of utterance.

5. PERSONATION: *its Tendency and Effects, as a Mode of Expression.*—The faculty of *imitation* with which man is endowed, as a form of expressive power, leading him to the acquisition of language, is early manifested in the passion of childhood for Personation; the living, actual representation of what he sees going on in the human

world around him. The lively feelings of the child are not satisfied with the mere verbal presentation of thought and feeling in the arbitrary and conventional forms of language. He has an instinctive desire to impersonate the being of others in himself, and thus to enter more fully into their feelings, and acquire a truer power of expressing them. To his fresh sympathies and ever active imagination, life around him is a drama: "all the world's a stage, and all the men and women are but players," each performing his part.

The child, the primitive man, the poet, all tend to dramatize human life, and to present it in living impersonation. The boy struts the mimic soldier, to his own mimic music; he drags his little wagon as an imaginary fire-engine, or mounts a chair and plays the orator to his little mates. In his puerile sports, he enacts a character or an incident, in dumb show, and requires that his juvenile companions shall express it in words. He personates a hero in history, or makes one in a group in a tableau, in which, as an Indian brave, he is about to dash out the brains of Captain Smith with his war-club, when his sister, as the compassionate princess Pocahontas, rushes in, and rescues the hero. At the academy exhibition, he personifies Mark Antony weeping over the murdered Cæsar, and with words of fire rousing the Romans to mutiny, "crying havoc! and letting slip the dogs of war;" or he resorts, in preference, to the pen, and dramatizes a scene from his country's history, which he and his class-mates enact to the life, according to their power. In the maturity of his intellect, and amid the grave duties of professional life, he pauses, perhaps, to recreate himself, and delight the world with the production of a Comus or a Hamlet, in which, besides furnishing the composition, he still takes an active part in the business of representation, and, true to the dramatic instinct of his nature, sustains a character himself. It is thus that he completes the educational training by which he attains to the height of eloquence and expressive power in word and action; and this dramatic faculty of personation, while it gives vividness and intensity to his utterance, proclaims the meaning and intention of the self-discipline to which he was early impelled, by unconscious instinct.

6. REPRESENTATION : *The Language of Signs.*—In addition to the more imaginative and, sometimes, physical or corporeal manifestations of expressive power, which the human being exhibits in imitative acts, he possesses, as his special attribute, in virtue of his intellectual endowments, working in unison with the instinctive elements of his nature, that peculiar faculty of Representation, by which he is enabled to suggest his thoughts or feelings to the mind of his fellow man, by substituting for graphic or mimetic, or other forms of delineation, con-

ventional *signs*, audible or visible, devised by his imaginative faculties of invention and combination. These signs are recognized and defined by his conceptive intellect; they are interpreted by the understanding, acting on a law of arbitrary association, established by mutual agreement or common consent, and ultimately sanctioned by prevalent usage. Furnished with this primitive telegraphic apparatus of audible and visible signs, man is enabled to put himself in communication with his sympathetic, intelligent, and rational fellow-beings,—to reveal to them the workings of his mind, and disclose the inmost secrets of his heart.

Speech and Writing.—Disciplined and perfected by art and skill, and aided by ingenious and asiduous educational cultivation, man's primitive power of utterance and expression, ultimately manifests itself in the consummated forms of *spoken* and *written language*, regulated by the laws of thought, as dictated by the sciences of *logic* and *grammar*, and adorned by the graces of *rhetoric*.

Language, a measure of Power.—The feeble but persevering endeavors of childhood to conquer the difficulties of articulation, and to compass the power of oral expression, indicate, by the successive years which the task demands, how arduous is its accomplishment, and how thoroughly it puts to proof the ability which the young human being possesses to direct and develop his own powers of execution. Yet more striking is the magnitude of the task and the triumph, in the progress achieved by the student of written language, from the date of his first attempt, in boyhood, to pen a letter or compose a theme, to the time when, in the maturity of his intellectual manhood, he rises to address assembled multitudes of his fellow men, and to sway them by the potency of triumphant eloquence; or when he issues from his poetic privacy a work which shall live for ages, as an object of wonder and admiration.

Pictured and Written Characters.—Somewhat similar, indeed, have been the difficulty and the progress in the attainment of a mastery over the merely external part of written language; as we perceive when tracing the process from its primal rude attempts in the form of graphic delineations, through its advancement to symbolic representation, and, ultimately, to phonetic characters and alphabetic letters. Of the width of this vast field of human labor, and of the toil which its cultivation has cost, we have no adequate conception, till we look at the graphic delineations which form the historical records of Nineveh, or at the symbolic hieroglyphics and the clumsy phonetic characters inscribed on the temples of Egypt, and then contrast with these the simple and symmetrical letters of the Greek or

Roman alphabet, known and read alike throughout the ancient and modern world of civilization.

The Value of Language.—Man's expressive power seems to have consummated itself in the representative phenomena of language. In this form his whole nature, animal, intellectual, and moral, finds effectual utterance; and by this instrumentality, does he become preëminently a progressive being. Language is the channel in which the ceaseless stream of mental action flows onward to its great results. Without this outlet, his soul, imprisoned within itself, would stagnate, and all its wondrous powers perish from inaction. As the medium of communication between mind and mind, language renders education practicable, and brings to the aid of the individual the accumulated thoughts of all times and of all men. Language is the peculiar and chosen province of education. Every process of human culture is conducted through its agency; every result attained in human progress is recorded in its terms; and in every civilized and cultivated community language is justly taken as the measure of individual and social attainment.

7. TASTE: *The Signification of the Term.*—The word "Taste," employed to designate one of the expressive faculties, might seem, from its primary signification, (*relish,*) to be one appropriately applied rather to a passive and receptive condition of mind, than to one so active or energetic as are all those which are properly termed "expressive." But, in the affairs of the mental world, not less than in those of the political, *influence* is often more efficient than *power.* So it is with Taste.—The office of this faculty in relation to expression, is to retain, in the selection and use of language, the *relish* for appropriateness, symmetry, and grace, which the soul has imbibed from the primitive beauty of the forms and the effects—in other words, the language—of nature,—that other name for life and truth.

Character of True Taste.—As true taste secures genuine beauty of effect, it is not a merely passive power. It rejects every false savor; for it relishes only the true. It refuses to inhale the flavor of the artificial perfume; because it prefers the aroma of nature. It detests the ugly, and shuns the ungraceful; but it loves the truly beautiful, and builds the fabric of noble thought "after the pattern shown it on the mount," as a chaste harmonious whole, conceived in pure ideal perfection, and executed with faultless skill, like that structure which

> "Rose like an exhalation, with the sound
> Of dulcet symphonies and voices sweet;
> Built like a temple, where pilasters round
> Were set, and Doric pillars overlaid
> With golden architrave; nor did there want
> Cornice or frieze with bossy sculpture graven;
> The roof was fretted gold."

Taste is not a quality merely negative in its influence: it is, in language, a positive power. It suggests and prescribes beauty; and, in all expression, beauty is power. Taste virtually decides and ordains the forms of language. It is therefore justly classed as an expressive faculty. It blends its effects, undoubtedly, with those of imagination and fancy, and with those of sentiment and emotion; controlling and directing and modifying these by its intuitive recognition of the eternal laws of beauty and proportion, and instinctively rejecting every blemish. If it is sometimes lost, to appearance, in the effects produced by the more obvious working of other expressive forces; its actual presence and power are not less deeply felt in the pervading harmony which, in such circumstances, it has established, and the genuine beauty which it has diffused. Its influence extends over every form of expressive art; and its results are equally legible in all. It guides the pencil of the painter, the chisel of the sculptor, the tool of the artizan, the hand of the musician, the pen of the poet, the voice and action of the speaker. It reigns over every form of language; and it moulds alike habit, character, and manners; for all of these are but varied modes of expression.

Taste, under the Influence of Culture.—Of all the faculties with which man is endued, none, perhaps, is more susceptible of cultivation than taste; and none yields larger results to the process. Trained under the fresh aspects of nature, and the strict discipline of truth, it becomes one of the most healthful influences that a liberal culture infuses into the human soul. It leads to the true, the pure, and the beautiful, in every relation of thought and feeling. Next to the hallowing influence of religious principle, it elevates and refines the whole being, and confers pure and lasting enjoyment on its possessor. It forms one of the most attractive graces of character, and breathes a genuine charm over the aspect of social life. But neglected, corrupted, or perverted, deprived of the healthful air of nature, abandoned to coarse and low association, vitiated by the influence of false custom, distorted by conventional regulations, or tainted by the impure atmosphere of vice, taste becomes depraved, and morbidly craves deformity instead of beauty, and prefers falsehood to truth.

(II.) THE ACTUATING PRINCIPLE, OR IMPELLING FORCE, OF THE EXPRESSIVE FACULTIES.

FEELING: *its Office in Expression.*—The Sensibility with which the constitution of man, as a sentient animal and as a self-conscious moral being, is invested, and by which he is stimulated to action and to utterance, may, for our present purpose, be defined as that element in his nature, which,—whether manifesting itself in temporary *sympathy*, in permanent *affections*,—in vivid *emotion*, or intense *passion* has, for its office, the excitation of his being. As the stimulus of his constitution, it impels man to the function of expression, as a result indispensable to sympathy and communication,—the necessary condition of his social and moral life. It originates in that sensibility to pleasure and pain by which the Creator has enhanced to man the enjoyment and the value of his organized and conscious existence, and secured it, at the same time, by a law of instinctive dread, from exposure to peril and to destruction.

Feeling, as an Incitement to Sympathy.—The effect of sensibility, in this relation, is three-fold; producing in man, (1.) a sympathy with the conditions and aspects of the surrounding external world, whether pleasurable or painful, attractive or repulsive; (2.) the mutual sympathy, conscious correlation, and consentaneous action of the two component elements of his constitution,—body and mind; (3.) a sympathy with his fellow men, which makes him a partaker of their pleasures and pains, causes him to desire a return of their sympathies to himself, and consequently leads him to expression and communication, as the means of exciting and attracting it.

Feeling, as an Involuntary or Empassioned Instigation.—The sentient and susceptible nature of man, his capacity and his experience of pleasure and pain, affected by causes whether external or internal in their operation, render him liable to unconscious and involuntary excitement, rising, sometimes, to the height of passion. This excitement manifesting itself in emotion,—the main spring of expression, —becomes, in some circumstances, itself a language sufficiently definite, intelligible, and expressive; as may be observed in the laughter and the crying of the infant, in the sympathizing countenance of the compassionate mother, in the ruffled features and angry temper of impatient youth, in the ghastly face of the terrified child, in the glare of the hostile savage, or in the glad smiles of the emancipated schoolboy at his holiday sport.

Feeling, influenced by Imagination and Volition.—The beings and forms of his own ideal world of imagination and fancy, or of creative thought, have also their exciting power over the internal sense of pleasure or of pain, and impel man, more or less voluntarily, to exhibit emotion, and to find its natural or customary form of expression in the articulate words of speech,—in the simpler eloquence of mere vocal tone, uttered or suppressed,—or in the silent but more enduring form of the written word.

Influence of Feeling on the Artist.—Even language itself, however, in its most distinct and definite forms, is not always sufficiently expressive for empassioned emotion. The admiration of grandeur or beauty may be strong enough and deep enough to demand some more palpable and durable shape in which to express itself. The intense delight in beauty impels the Artist to devote himself to days and nights of toil over the image which alone can satisfy the longing of his soul, for the visible presence of the loveliness which his fancy has conceived in his inner world of life and form.

On the Actions of the Child and of the Adult.—It is the untaught, unconscious working of the emotion of love which makes the child find expression for his sympathy in the act of imitating the gait and actions, and the characteristic expressions of those whom he admires. Nor does adult man always escape the effects of this tendency, when maturity of mind and habits of grave research seem sometimes to render the result ridiculous.

On the Actor and his Audience.—The natural delight in sympathy and communication, is the incitement which impels the actor on the stage to assume and exhibit, in his plastic frame and features, the agonies of dramatic passion, in all their terrific extremes, while he personates the ravings of Lear, the frenzy of Othello, or the remorse of Macbeth; and it is the same cause which attracts, night after night, to the crowded theatre, the audience who thus acknowledge the force of the great element of sympathy in human nature, and the power which vivid expression exercises over the heart, when it has even the well sustained semblance of coming from the heart.

On the Eloquence of the Orator.—It is from sympathy with the very passions which he delights to excite, that the orator devotes his days of seclusion and nights of application to the study of every art by which expression may be heightened and emotion aroused, when the decisive moment is come, and the interests of the state are at hazard, and men are to feel that their welfare or their safety is to depend on adopting the views of an eloquent and competent leader.

On the soul of the Poet.—It is sympathy with the highest sentiments and emotions of his race, and the conscious delight in giving these a noble utterance, that inspires the poet with the assurance of immortality, while he meditates his great theme, and touches and retouches his artistic work, till it stands forth complete in the majestic beauty and perfection after which his soul has, for years, aspired.

Universality of Feeling, as the Actuating Principle of Expression.— In all the above and similar instances, the sympathetic feeling which thirsts for expression, and impels to the utterance or the recording of sentiment, is one and the same. It may assume the definiteness and the depth of a personal affection, or the intensity and the comparative excess of a passion, to whatever extent the instigation of feeling may excite the sentient agent. But it is still the same element of sensibility, only working in deeper channels, and with a stronger tide, and therefore doing its work more effectually and impressively. In whatever form, it is still but an act of obedience to the law of his constitution, by which man, as a sympathetic being, is impelled to expression, that he may attain to the power and the habit of communication; and thus fulfill the conditions of his social and moral nature.

Influence of Feeling on Moral Character, as a Form of Expression.— The extent to which the element of feeling exerts its power over expression, and the degree to which its development in this relation may be carried, under the influence of educational culture, can be appropriately measured only when we trace it to its effects on the tendencies, the character, and the will of human beings individually, or in their aggregations in society. In either case, we see it in the gentle, the peaceful, and affectionate spirit of the genuine disciple of Him whom we reverence as the "meek and the lowly," and in the genial intercourse of communities governed by the influence of His law of universal love; or we read it in the arrogance, the violence, and the hatred, of which perverted humanity is so fatally capable. As "out of the abundance of the heart the mouth speaketh," the prevalent emotions and expression, the manners, and the habitual language of man, in these opposite conditions of individual and social life, will depict themselves on character and action.

*Influence of Feeling on the Character of Art.—*In the visible language of graphic art, we read the same lesson of the power of feeling as an element of expression. We see it in the appalling force with which the sculptor has presented the agony of pain and struggle, in the writhing frame and contorted features of Laocoon, or the perfect placidity and repose with which he has invested the face and form of Antinöus. Nor is the lesson less impressive when we turn from the superhuman fierceness of expression in attitude and features, which characterizes the delineations of passion and penal torture, in some of the figures depicted by the hand of Angelo, to the serenity, the sanctity, and the unutterable loveliness, beaming from the half-divine forms in which innocence or holiness is pictured by the pencil of Raphael.

*Its power in Music.—*The ear drinks in the same lesson of the power of empassioned expression, while it listens to the great masters of musical art, and feels the majesty of its utterance, as conceived in the soul of Handel, and worthily executed by the skillful hand of the accomplished performer. From such effects of sublimity and force and solemn grandeur, down to the breathings of tenderness in a plaintive strain of pastoral melody, the thrill, responding to the stirring air of the soldier's march, or the wild gayety of the peasant's dance, we have but the varied forms in which emotion evinces its sway over this most expressive of arts, by the inspiration which it breathes into its numberless moods.

Its Effect on Language.—To the emotive force of feeling, Language owes all its sublimest and most beautiful forms of cultivated utterance, whether in expressing the depth of affection or the intensity of passion; and the remark is equally true of the literature of the elder world and that of modern times. In no record of humanity is the fact more strikingly exhibited than in the pages of the Sacred volume, where the heart of man is laid open in all its workings, in the primitive language of poetic imagination and Divine truth combined, and where the human soul pours itself forth in every mood; now wondering at the vastness of the creation, or adoring the infinite majesty of the Creator; now humbled to the dust, under the sense of man's insignificance, or, in the tones of contrition and penitence, imploring the boon of pardon; uttering thanks for boundless goodness and mercy; rejoicing in the conscious favor of God; sympathizing in the gladness and beauty of nature; touched by the paternal tenderness and compassion of Jehovah, or joining in the denunciations of "indignation and wrath, tribulation and anguish," threatened to his enemies.

In all the uninspired delineations of thought which have come down to us from ancient times, it is the same pervading element of feeling which has given them their lasting life and their sway over the mind. To some prominent passages of this character we have already alluded; and, for the present, the allusion must suffice. Nor have we time now to dwell on corresponding examples drawn from modern literature, the peculiar charm of which, in one word, is the power with which it calls forth the natural emotions of the heart. In every form which literature assumes, as a power or an influence over the soul, exerted through the medium of expressive language, the main spring of effect, the grand motive power, is feeling. The life of expression, in all its cultivated forms of language or of art, is emotion.

Feeling, under the Guidance of Education.—Recognizing the fact last mentioned, the intelligent superintendent of education will direct his endeavors to the due cherishing, strengthening, and developing, as well as to the moulding, guiding, and governing of this great element of intellectual and moral power. With his eye fixed on this momentous issue, he will watch the natural tendency and direction of the instinct whose action he is to guide, so as intelligently to coöperate with its spontaneous working, and aid in the accomplishments of its peculiar office.

The teacher is, to a certain extent, or, at least, so far as he is a teacher of language, bound to furnish his pupil with the invaluable advantage resulting from a ready command of correct expression, one of the surest passports to usefulness and success in life. But the life-spark of expression can not be struck from a dull mind. The latent fire of feeling must be kindled, must be brought to the surface, that it may glow in the living look and audible tone of emotion, or beam forth in the burning words of eloquence, whether flowing from tongue or pen. The judicious instructor will resort to every expedient suggested by the life and beauty of nature and of art, as sources of inspiration, whence corresponding life, and beauty, and expressive power may be breathed into the soul of his pupil, and live in his utterance.

III. THE TENDENCY OR HABIT OF ACTION, IN THE EXPRESSIVE FACULTIES, AS IT IS MANIFESTED IN UTTERANCE.

Utterance an Instinct.—When we contemplate man as a being capable of education, he may, for our immediate purpose, be regarded as furnished by his Creator, with what may be termed the *apparatus* of expression, in the gift of the various faculties which we have been hitherto considering. We perceive him further provided with an adequate *motive power*, by which this apparatus is propelled, in the involuntary or voluntary action of feeling. The indication next to be observed by the educator, as the suggestion for his guidance, in his endeavors to coöperate with Nature's tendency to development, is, In what direction does the action of the expressive faculties naturally tend ? What, in this instance, is the instinct of spontaneity ? What, under the guidance of his own inward promptings, does the child incline to do or to become ? What habit or attribute of character does he thus acquire ? The answer furnished by observation, in this case, plainly is,—Man, as a sentient, intellectual, and sympathizing being, acting under the primary impulse of instinct, and without any interference of human culture, obviously inclines to Utterance, (throwing himself *out*,) or, in other words, to *self-revelation*, as an ordained function of his nature, verifying and crowning his intelligence, and constituting him a social and moral being, capable of progress and of culture. He craves and finds expression, accordingly, in many and various forms : he makes himself felt and understood, in some way or other, by his fellows. Under the guidance of education, he but learns to do this more definitely and successfully, through language and expressive art. From a sentient and intelligent, he develops thus into a communicative being,—the result, so far, of the combination of unconscious and voluntary education, and, at the same time, the condition and the pledge of subsequent intellectual and moral progress.

Repression a Common Error of Educational Training.—The attentive observation—not to say the systematic study—of man, to which the educator and teacher should ever feel himself bound, as the only security for the intelligent and successful discharge of his duties, suggests, at this stage of our subject, the fact, that a prominent feature of error, in the too prevalent arbitrary modes of education, has been the *repression* rather than the development of the natural desire of utterance in childhood.

From the very first steps of his mental and moral progress, man is not a merely selfish and receptive being. He longs to impart his feelings, and to communicate his observations: he wishes to give, as well as to receive: he feels impelled to utter himself that he may impart and confer, not less than receive. His impulse, as a sympathetic one, is unselfish, generous, noble. When the child exclaims to his playmate on the beauty of the flower which they see, he does not merely call for sympathy in the delight which he feels: he would, by his instinctive expression of pleasure, suggest and impart that delight.

Utterance, under the benign guardianship of Nature, as its Author's interpreter, is thus, essentially and substantially, a moral process, not less than a merely sympathetic and intellectual one. Nor, in education, should it ever be forgotten that, by the Creator's ordination, every utterance of a feeling or an emotion, gives it additional strength and life; and that, obeying the divinely instituted law of speech and communication, we are aiding in the process of building up, day by day, and hour by hour, the fabric of human character.

Arbitrary education, however, is, in no feature of its meddling mismanagement more conspicuous than in the *restriction*, the *reserve*, and the *silence*, which it is ever so prone to impose, and on which it is so apt to plume itself, with reference even to the very first stages of its repellent sway.

The five years' probationary and preparatory silence which Pythagoras is said to have exacted of his disciples, might be an excellent discipline for mature minds, as an introduction to the "metaphysic bog profound," into which he meant thereafter to plunge them. But one of the first and most urgent wants of childhood is utterance. The innocent little human being is ever thus holding out his petty link in the golden chain which binds heart to heart, mind to mind, and man to God: he is ever ready to join his link to that of his neighbor. But the mechanical educationist, with his "look at your book, and not at me!" frowns the infant volunteer back to his seat, to his individuality, and his isolation; and the chain by which the little petitioner for sympathy and knowledge, might have been lifted with the conjoined force of the mental world, is of no avail to him: his link of connection with it is yet detached. His turn has not yet come, in the great game of opportunity; and he must bide his time as best he may.

Appropriate Training.—Under the unerring and genial guidance of the mother, the child is not perpetually immured within doors, or confined to one spot, or fixed in one posture: he is allowed, occasionally, at least, to behold the outward world, to range the fields, to walk on the road, to observe the objects around him, to feel their attractive force, to admire their beauty, to wonder and to inquire about what is new to him, to utter his exclamations of pleasure, to examine, and to name whatever strikes his attention. He thus enjoys his own nature in the free exercise of his faculties; he is consciously progressive in intelligence and in speech, as in feeling, and, so far, is effectually and successfully preparing to become, in due season, eloquently expressive.

Disadvantages of City Education.—The worst, perhaps, of all the many evils attending the supposed necessity of congregating in cities, and adopting artificial modes of life, is one but little thought of. The parent who relinquishes his rural home in the open village street or in the field, flatters himself, perhaps, that he is securing better educational advantages for his children, when he takes up his abode in one of the confined dwellings of the close-crowded city. He may find, by the exchange, a teacher more expert in turning the machinery of instruction, and a more ample supply of the learning to be had from books. But the nobler, the truly liberal part of his childrens' education, he has foregone forever. The free scope, the pure, bracing air, the rich variety of nature,—the healthful influence of these on the growing frame and the expanding mind, on the susceptible heart, on the plastic imagination, on the whole soul and character; these are sacrificed, and with them, the best capabilities of culture.

Educational Benefits of Rural Life.—In no respect are the losses just mentioned greater than in regard to the part of education which we are now contemplating. To the child reared in the freedom and the beauty of nature, everything around him becomes a language, expressing the happiness which he unconsciously enjoys. His vocabulary is furnished in the forms, the colors, the life, the sounds and motion, amid which he finds himself. The half-conscious awe which he feels, under the deep shade and the sweeping boughs of the great elm, through which he looks up, with a pleasing dread and wonder to the over-arching sky, the beautiful wild-flower which waves and nods to him as he passes, the brook which runs bubbling and gurgling through the meadow, the majesty of the flowing river, the roaring of the winter wind through the bare trees, the whirling of the snow-flakes, the glittering garment of the ice-storm, the opening of the spring buds, the fluttering of the summer leaves, and the sailing of the falling leaf in autumn, the enlivening voices of the domestic animals, the entrancing music of the birds;—these, and a thousand other unpaid teachers, have all been training him in a language true, copious, perfect, and inspiring,—compared to which, book-learning is but as the dry husk to the rich nutritious grain.

Genial Culture.—To favor and cherish, not to check, utterance—to elicit, not to repress expression,—to multiply, and deepen, and expand, and fill, not to dry up, the sources and reservoirs of language;—these are the true offices of education. The cultivation of the young mind, taking a suggestive hint from the cultivation of the young tree, should allow a liberal scope of nutrition, of growth and expansion, before calling in the aid of the pruning knife. A large part of early education should consist in conversation, in which the pupil should freely partake, as the natural means of acquiring accuracy and expertness, as well as freedom, in expression. The tendency to write and to draw, should have full scope and ample encouragement. Care should be taken to render interesting and attractive every form of exercise by which the student may ultimately attain to the free, forcible, and correct expression of thought. To the various modes of securing such fruits of culture, in detail, we shall have occasion to advert in the sequel.

IV. Result of the Action of the Expressive Faculties:— Communication.

The Power of Communication.—In the previous stages of our present inquiries, we have been occupied with the *classification* of the powers of expression, their *springs of action*, and the *habitual tendency* and direction of their current, under the guidance of unassisted nature and of education. The next step in the progress of investigation preliminary and introductory to the actual work of express culture, is the consideration of the Results at which, whether by the law of natural development or that of educational cultivation, the human being arrives, in consequence of the exercise of his powers of expression.

The immediate result of utterance is Communication,—the impartation and interchange of sympathy or sentiment, by which man inspires his fellow man with the same feeling, affection, emotion, passion, thought, or sentiment, which actuates himself; and which, as the circle of kindred minds is enlarged by the aggregation of numbers, extends his personal mood or mental condition throughout the sphere of the community of which he is a member.

Intellectual and Moral Effects of Communication.—The views, the will, and the power of an individual, acquire, through communication, an ascendency, it may be, over a nation, or even over the whole civilized race, for successive ages; while, on the other hand, the intellectual acquisitions, the moral and spiritual attainments, the sympathies and the accumulated resources of nations and of ages, may be brought to the aid of the individual, through the magic power of language.

For good or for evil, man's power of communication with his fellows, gives to the aggregated multitudes of a whole people, or even of the race, the unity of purpose, the singleness of aim, the directness, the personal efficiency, the ease and the certainty of action of a single agent; while it equally arms the individual with the intellectual, the physical, and the moral force of millions. The sage, the orator, the poet, the artist, the statesman, the warrior, thus become the recognized representatives of a people or of mankind, to whom communities and nations bow in submission or in homage, and to whose ascendant genius they render the tribute of heart and hand, of treasure, or of life. Thus, too, the youth, in his studious endeavors to advance his intellectual and moral condition, has the aid arising from the experience, the counsels, the guidance, and the sympathies of the intelligent and the virtuous of every age and nation which possesses an accessible record of its progress; and the student whose days have been spent in strictest seclusion and unremitting investigation, enjoys the assurance that the fruits of his solitary research and strenuous application shall be gathered not by himself alone, but by whatever enlightened and sympathizing minds, throughout the world, and in all subsequent time, shall come within his sphere of communication by living voice or written word.

Value of Communication.—Communication, as the boon of language, is not to be measured by its immediate results merely, as a telegraphic convenience for the impartation of feeling or the conveyance of thought,—great as its uses, in this relation, are to the whole race. Language is the vehicle of all knowledge. Like the noble ship, costly and valuable in itself, but yet more valuable in the treasure with which it is fraught, it comes laden with the accumulations of countless minds and boundless wealth. To measure its full value, we should have to compute the number and the worth of every acquisition which the mind has garnered up in the records of every department of science and literature, and thus rendered capable of conveyance from man to man, and from generation to generation, throughout the world.

V. Educational Processes for the Cultivation of the Expressive Faculties.

These may be classed under the following heads: The Attentive Observation and the Love of Nature; the Study and the Practice of Art; the Study of Language; the Practice of Exercises in Oral and Written Expression.

OMISSIONS AND DEFECTS IN MODES OF CULTURE.—*Language.*—The plan of education generally adopted for the exercise and discipline of the expressive faculties, indicates little philosophical design, logical consistency, generous spirit, or liberal scope, in the course which it prescribes. It is founded on views too narrow and exclusive; and its execution has been too mechanical. The mother's and the teacher's eye has been fastened too exclusively on the facts of *language* alone, as so many detached points to be mastered in detail. Hence the injury sometimes done to the organs of speech, by premature attempts to conquer some of the difficulties of articulation, in the mother's zeal for the precocious development of the faculties of her child; and hence, also, the mechanical and arbitrary processes of alphabetic training, in its customary forms. The eager desire for immediate definite results, has caused the teacher, too generally, to overlook the great facts that language is but one of the forms in which the expressive faculties are exerted, or in which expressive power is to be developed, and that the successful cultivation of language is inseparable from due exercise in all the kindred forms of expression to which the mind naturally tends.

The general plan of education is limited to instruction and practice in the oral and written forms of language, in the school routine of *reading* and *grammar*, and what is termed *composition*. The forms of exercise and the methods of training, also, in these departments of education, have too generally been literal and mechanical; and the poverty and imperfection of the results have betrayed the defects of the plan which prescribed them.

Methods too exclusively Passive and Receptive.—The great importance of a full and generous development of the whole mental constitution, as indispensable to the right action of any of its elements, having been overlooked in the plan of education, due allowance has too seldom been made, in the training of the mind, for the adequate exercise and discipline of the active nature and of the expressive powers of the human being. The general prescription of the processes of instruction, has evidently been directed to the *receptive* action of the *understanding* and the *impleting* of the *memory*. The mind of the pupil has been too uniformly kept in a comparatively *passive* condition. He has not been permitted and invited to use sufficiently even those materials of expression which he has, from the earliest steps of his progress, in the routine of education, been so laboriously employed in accumulating. Expression, neglected in early training, becomes difficult in later stages; and conscious failure incurred in attempting it, renders it distasteful. Effort, under such circumstances, is reluctantly made, frequently intermitted, and ere long discontinued.

Neglect of our own Language.—No remark is more common or more true, than that even our highest and best courses of culture do not result in furnishing accomplished men, as regards the actual use, in speech or writing, of our own language. Ample time, comparatively, is usually allowed for the study of the ancient languages, and even for that of some of the modern; but little is expressly assigned for the thorough acquisition of our own, which, to ensure to the student a perfect command of it, should be the groundwork of daily exercises, thoughtfully planned and carefully executed; from the first steps in education onward to the last day of professional preparation for the business of life.

Faults of Unconscious Teaching.—Some of the many causes of imperfect teaching, in the department of language, may be found in the fact, that the true nature and actual character of early training are not recognized by those whose office it is to superintend the first steps of childhood in the path of development. The mother and the primary teacher too often overlook the vast influence of *example*, which, to the imitative nature of childhood, always becomes a model. Hence the imperfect articulation, incorrect pronunciation, mechanical monotony, and lifeless tone, which are so generally prevalent in school reading. These faults are, too often, faithful copies of the style which the ear of the young learner has unconsciously caught from his mother, his teacher, or his class-mates, and which habit rivets on his voice, for life.

Error in Alphabetic Instruction.—The mechanical manner in which the child's first lessons in reading are sometimes conducted, is another cause of failure, in the department of instruction to which we now refer. In many schools, the young pupil never has his attention called, definitely or consciously, to the fact that the letters of the alphabet are *phonetic* characters, the whole value of which con-

1 F

sists in the *sounds* which they represent: in many, he may pass through the whole course of instruction without being once called to practice the constituent elementary sounds of his own language: in very many, there is no attempt made to exercise and develop, modify, or cultivate, in any form, the voice itself. Hence the prevalence of the errors which have been already mentioned as fruits of unconscious imitation, and which careful, early cultivation can alone prevent.

Neglect of the Meaning of Words.—An obvious defect in prevalent modes of education, as regards adequate preparation for the free and correct use of our native language, is the yet too common neglect of early and progressive *etymological training* in the analysis of words, and the tracing of the significant value of their component syllables, so as to ascertain and fix in the mind their exact meaning and full power, and to follow their transitions from a primary to a secondary sense, or from one which is figurative and imaginative to one which is purely intellectual or merely practical. It is such intimate knowledge, and such only,—the fruit of daily exercise and careful training,—that can give, at length, to the mature scholar, or the professional speaker, that mastery of words, which now so often, when almost too late, he feels that he needs for the full and perfect expression of his thoughts.

Defective Forms of Reading Exercises.—A common and marked failure of education, as regards the course of instruction in reading, is partly attributable to the cause last mentioned,—the unintelligent enunciation of words,—but largely, also, to the mechanical perusal and unmeaning pronunciation of sentences, as merely so many successions of audible sounds. Such exercises deaden rather than enliven the powers of expression, as they blunt rather than sharpen the understanding, for the intelligent conception of meaning. Yet, in not a few schools is it the fact, that even quite young pupils are never asked, in performing a reading exercise, to point out, previous to the pronouncing of a sentence, those words in it which are most significant or expressive, and accordingly require that special force or turn of utterance, which alone can render them *emphatic*, so as to convey their full sense, or bring out the whole sentiment which the sentence was framed to express. A similar neglect is too prevalent as regards the effect of proper *pauses* in reading, which should always suggest to the ear an intelligent analysis of a sentence into its constituent portions of sense, not, as is very frequently the case, a mechanical analysis, servilely following the grammatical punctuation with measured uniformity of utterance, whatever be the depth of thought, or the force of feeling, implied in the language of the composition. As the syntactical punctuation, although it may often coincide with the expressive and significant rhetorical pausing, does not necessarily do so, but, on the contrary, is sometimes directly at variance with it, the effect of uniformly following the points, must, in such cases, be a positive hindrance rather than a help to intelligible or appropriate reading, as an exercise of voice. The utterance of the common phrases, "Yes, sir," or "No, sir," will furnish sufficient illustration here. The comma preceding the word "sir," is due to the eye, on the score of syntax, but not to the ear or the voice, on that of sense.

It is in the audible reading of *poetry*, however, that the defects of current education are most strikingly exhibited, as regards the discipline of the expressive faculties. Poetry, as the language of imagination and feeling, speaking to the heart, properly requires a mode of reading obviously quite different from that of the usual forms of plain didactic prose, addressed to the understanding merely. The word-pictures of the poet paint their imagery on the imagination; the intellect interprets their forms; the heart beats in response to the graphic delineation; and the voice gives expression to a correspondent melody of tone, while it utters the words of the verse. To read poetry aright, therefore, implies the poet's inspiration, imparted to the soul and voice of the reader,—an exalted state of imagination, a sympathetic vividness of feeling, unconscious quickness and acuteness of intellectual conception, a plastic voice and expressive tone. An appropriate course of preparatory discipline of feeling and imagination, is obviously, then, as indispensable to poetic utterance, as the right understanding of the intellectual sense of a sentence, is to the ordinary reading of prose. For this purpose, every grand or beautiful form of nature or of expressive art to which he can resort, with a view to give susceptibility to feeling and imagination or pleasure to taste, now becomes, in the hands of the intelligent teacher, an instrument of power, to aid him in the processes of culture. Now is the time when he feels how deeply he must ever be indebted to the vivifying influence of music, painting, and sculpture, and every chaste form of decorative art, as the effective means of opening the eye of the soul to the vision of grandeur or of beauty, firing the heart with the ardor of inspiration, touching it with the sense of tenderness and love, and refining the taste by the display of true elegance and grace.

The dry, prosaic, lifeless style in which poetry is too generally read in our schools, is more injurious than beneficial, not merely to the faculties more immediately concerned in the conception or utterance of poetic composition, but to the action and influence of all those powers, mental and moral, which tend to elevate and refine the soul, and mould the character to the highest forms of excellence. There is something akin to the barrenness of spirit with which the sceptic peruses a page of sacred scripture, in the utterly mechanical manner in which the well-drilled pupil in mathematics or in grammar, is sometimes permitted to read strains of the purest poetry, embodying the sublimest sentiments, and calling for tones of the deepest and most vivid emotion, or even of the most exalted passion.

The general neglect of appropriate means for cherishing sensibility and cultivating taste, in the relation now referred to, is the more to be regretted that it prevails most in that form of education and in that class of schools in which it tells with the deepest effect:—I refer to our common modes of mental cultivation, and to those seminaries in which the mass of our people are trained. The recuperative influences of classical culture, in our higher literary institutions, does something to redeem, in this respect, the omissions and the defects of earlier training. But it is much to be feared that, even in our boasted New England education, as generally conducted, the young who are to receive no such remedial aid for disproportioned and defective cultivation, close their school course without the benefit of a single effort, on the part of instructors, to render their pupils capable of appreciating or expressing the sentiments embodied in the best passages of our own literature and that of the parent land,—a literature which contains confessedly more of the inspiring elements of pure morality and noble character, as well as genuine beauty, than any that has yet appeared on earth; not excepting even the model languages of classic antiquity.

Instruction in Grammar.—It is but of late that those who prescribe the forms of education or the modes of instruction, have furnished the working teacher with the means of rational and philosophic training for his pupils, in another department of culture professedly occupied with the discipline of the expressive faculties, but, in past years, so formally conducted, for the most part, as to embarrass and retard rather than aid the progress of development. A great change, unquestionably, has taken place in the character of text-books on Grammar; and in this branch of instruction we have recently been provided with valuable facilities for improvement, in several excellent treatises, well suited to the true uses of a text-book,—not a synthetic synopsis of the science as it lies in the mind of the consummate grammarian, but a gradually progressive and practical presentation of the subject, from its simplest elements upward, in a course, at the same time, so strictly logical, that every step leads, by a law of thought, to another, and so thoroughly practical, that,—to use the not inapt expression of a German instructor visiting one of our American schools,—the pupil is made, at every step, to "*experience* grammar."

Defective Methods.—Still, too many of our teachers cling to the narrow practice of following, in every grammar lesson, the order of a *synthetic* text-book, in which the subject is admirably arranged for a systematic and philosophic review of the science, but by no means for the successive steps of progress to the young mind commencing the study of it. The method of such text-books is precisely that which must be *inverted* in all true, living, oral instruction, or in any rational attempt to introduce a learner to a knowledge of the subject, and to guide him in his first endeavors to reduce it to practice in illustrative forms of exercise. The logic of instruction requires that the whole science of grammar should be first subjected to a rigorous *analysis* in the teacher's own mind, that its elements may be exhibited individually and successively to that of the pupil, and so become the groundwork of his *inductive* and intelligent progress from the recognition of facts to that of principles and laws. The practical part of the instructor's business, requires, in this, as in all other branches, a strict compliance with the rule of presenting one element only at a time, but in such succession as to develop the whole subject in easy steps of connected progress,—each perfectly understood and thoroughly exemplified; nothing assumed, but everything proved; nothing merely defined without being reduced to practice.

The Practice of Composition.—Till very recently, in comparison, no branch of education connected so immediately with the discipline of the expressive faculties, has been more faultily conducted than this. Without waiting for the development and efficient action of the reflective faculties, or the power of abstract conception and general thought, the teacher, when he has conducted his pupils through a very imperfect course of grammar and mechanical "parsing," and, perhaps, a little technical rhetoric, proceeds to prescribe a task in composition, on some *general* theme requiring the thoughts of a mature and capacious mind, besides the command of a skillful pen, for its proper treatment.

Results of Defective Methods of Teaching.—Called thus, without means, to perform a task which leads him entirely away from the region in which his mind naturally and habitually works,—the *concrete* world of actual observation and of clear conception or conscious feeling,—the pupil finds himself unable to do what is required of him as a personal effort. In these circumstances, if he does not actually shirk the task imposed on him, he has no resort but to repeat the commonplace thoughts and sayings of others, in which he feels no interest, and which, to his consciousness, have no truth. The precious moments of youth are thus worse than wasted; the expressive faculties are withered and dried up; and education, thus misdirected, destroys the powers which it was employed to cherish.

Advantages of Seasonable Training.—Teachers who take the pains to observe well, know that there is a stage in the life of childhood, when expression is a spontaneous tendency and a delight,—when to construct a sentence on his slate, or pencil a little note on paper, is to the miniature " ambitious student," a conscious achievement and a triumph of power. Then is the happy moment for beginning the work of practice, which, if neglected at that stage, will never be easily, naturally, or effectively done afterward. The attempt may be made at a later period, under the influence of a sense of duty, or a feeling of shame, or the consciousness of compulsion. But, by this time, the plastic suppleness and pliancy of the mind is gone; and the whole endeavor proves an affair of difficulty and dislike. The teacher's policy is never to let the moment come when composition, whether in the form of note or letter, or narrative, or description, is felt to be anything else than a pleasure and a privilege. The expression of sentiment, and the argument for an opinion, will then, become as easy, as natural, and as pleasurable employment, as the first steps of conscious progress, in the penning of a juvenile note or letter.

Rhetoric.—The great defect in conducting this branch of education,—a defect which is still very prevalent,—consists in the fact that the study of it is so much a matter of theoretic speculation on principles of taste, or is limited to the mere committing of rules to memory. Rhetoric, to become a useful branch of modern education, should embrace a gradually progressive course of exercises, embodying successively the facts of language, in the use of words and the construction of sentences; it should include the practice of daily writing, for successive years; frequent exercises in the logical arranging of thought for the purposes of expression, and the adapting of the forms and character of expression to thought; and it should be accompanied by the close study and critical analysis of the works of distinguished writers, with a view to acquire a perfect mastery over every form of style.

Elocution: Errors in Modes of Instruction.—Few branches of education are so little understood or rightly practiced as this. We have, in our current modes of instruction, little choice between the faults of style arising from what the indolent incline to term "a generous neglect," through fear of "spoiling" what they claim as "nature," and those faults, on the other hand, which are attributable to literal and mechanical modes of cultivation, and consist in the obtrusion of arbitrary details and artificial forms. Hence the results which characterize the one, in the gross errors of slovenly and low habit, coarse and disgusting manner, uncouth effect, bawling vehemence, and gesticulating violence, of what is sometimes dignified with the name of "popular oratory;" and hence the opposite traits of finical taste, affected elegance, false refinement, and studied contrivances of effect, which belong to perverted culture.

Errors in Theory.—With the advocates of neglect, the true teacher, as a believer in the value of cultivation, can have little sympathy, further than in the condemnation of false and artificial manner. Neglect of culture, he knows well, produces, in regard to all expressive art, the same obvious faults of rawness and inappropriateness, awkwardness and error. It is much to be regretted, however, that the language of some eminent writers, in their anxiety to protest against the errors of mechanical and literal training, gives countenance to the claims of ignorance on this subject, and seems to sanction the utter neglect of cultivation. Prominent among these it is to be regretted that we find an authority otherwise so justly eminent as Dr. Whately, whose own brilliant talents and ready power of expression, while they tend to give him an ascendency over the minds of students and teachers, are perhaps the very circumstances which disqualify him to form a true judgment on the modes of cultivation best adapted to the great majority of minds which fall under the care of the teacher, in the common routine of education. The error,—if one may be pardoned the term,—by which ingenious minds are, on this subject sometimes entirely misled by superficial observation and hasty conclusions, is that of overlooking the great fact that, in the cultivation of any branch of expressive art, education is properly charged with a double duty,—that of aiding, by every favoring influence, the inward power of conception, and that of watching over the outward form of expression. In the former function, education is spiritual, genial, inspiring, intellectual, in its suggestions: in the latter, its office is formative and exterior; it watches, with the nicety of a musician's ear and a painter's eye, over every point of detail, and assiduously trains every organ of the pupil to exactness, as the law of truth, extending to the minutest effect of vocal utterance and visible action. True culture, in this relation, aims at a perfect result, and descends, therefore, to the moulding of every detail.

The necessary Union of Theory and Practice in Teaching.—It is a great error to suppose that, in doing its practical work, education must do it in a narrow and servile spirit, or in a merely mechanical form. Genuine instruction, in its minutest direction, recognizes and impresses a principle which prompts the preference of one form of expression to another; and it takes care to deepen the impression of the principle by means of the associated art in practice. Faithful teaching must always extend to details. There is no slighting or slovening in its work. The difference between true and false instruction, in all art, is simply this: the former in prescribing a rule, refers to the parent principle from which it is derived, and thus makes instruction *logical*; the latter lays down the rule as a detached and arbitrary fact of mere inculcation, and thus renders instruction *empirical* and *mechanical*. The skillful teacher knows how, in inculcating the closest application to detail, to keep the mind intent on the principle which suggests it. No error in educational training can be greater than that of shrinking from or shunning particulars, under the plea of generalizing. In all matters of expressive art, principle must be developed and applied in practice.

Necessity of Detail.—The right expression of a sentiment by voice and action, like every other external act of mind and organ, has necessarily a mode and a form, coëxtensive with the words in which it is embodied; and neither teacher nor student can afford to dispense with one element of the true effect. The attention, therefore, must be directed to the study and observation, "analytically, of the emphasis, tones, pauses, &c.," unless we are willing to neglect the proper effect of these on speech. If we can not communicate sentiment without a due observance of these, they must evidently be studied, more or less, according to their value and importance; and the very office of instruction is, in all such cases, patiently to descend to the study and practice of detail.

Yet Dr. Whately, in his Elements of Rhetoric, asserts that the analytic study of detail, in such matters, "must vitiate every system of instruction founded upon it." For this conclusion, fortunately, however, he gives no reason but what is contained in the brief phrase, "according to my views," and adds, further, the saving clause, "if those views be correct." A true and efficient friend of education, in other respects, thus sides with the opponents of culture, by speaking from the preferences of personal taste and arbitrary opinion, instead of the laws of analogy and universal truth.

In most Anglo-Saxon communities, the teacher of elocution receives his pupils encrusted,—one might say,—with the errors of neglected or corrupted habit, unconsciously contracted from the current faults of his home, his early school, the street, the local style of his vicinity, or that of some popular public speaker. The eradication of these errors is obviously the first duty of an instructor. But, according to the views of Dr. Whately, the instructor must not put forth his hand to touch such faults; for this could not be done without incurring the evil of entering into "analytic details of emphasis, tones, pauses, &c." The fabric of education, in this as in all other departments, resembles the well constructed edifice, liberally and scientifically planned, symmetrically proportioned, and thoroughly finished in detail. The outside observers of the processes of instruction,—among whom Dr. Whately, for the time, takes his position,—are quite willing that the intellectual structure should be a goodly mansion, on the whole, but insist on the notion that it shall be built without any detail of wood, stone, or brick, in particular.

"*Natural Advantages.*"—In the act of utterance, the glance of genius may suffice, at times, for the intuitive recognition of a principle; and the empassioned impulse of artistic temperament, may prompt to instantaneous and perfect expression. The possessor of such attributes may, on exciting occasions, dispense with reflective thought and studious application as securities for success in utterance. But the majority of mankind, whether in youth or maturity, consciously and habitually need all the aids of analysis and study, and are successful in proportion to the closeness of their application and the thoroughness of their practice. The aid, in such circumstances, to be rendered by the intelligent and faithful teacher, is precisely that work of detail to which Dr. Whately objects. The student, through inadvertency, overlooks, for example, the true and appropriate manner of expression in solemn emotion; and, in the utterance of a passage of that character, runs on, through the influence of neglected habit, in a *high*, *loud*, and *rapid* voice. Here, the mechanical teacher will, of course, rectify the error, for the moment, by merely exemplifying the proper style, and making the pupil repeat in imitation of the model, but with no explanation, and with no reference of any point to a fixed principle which might be a guide in future practice. The true teacher, —who never can rest satisfied with anything merely mimetic or parrot-like,—when he indicates errors, endeavors to correct them by referring his pupil to the principle from which they deviate. He interrogates him in this case as to the true and natural style of voice in which solemn emotion is uttered, and directs his attention successively to the facts that it is characterized by tones which are comparatively *low*, *soft*, and *slow*,—as heard in the natural and appropriate utterance of devotional feeling. Teacher and pupil have thus a defi nite aim and an intelligent course before them in the reiterated practice which may be required for the correction of error, and a guiding light to direct them in all similar difficulties which may occur in subsequent exercises. In this department of education, as well as in others, true instruction is nothing else than the exposition of a *principle* along with an *analytical application* of it. Yet this is the very mode of procedure which Dr. Whately condemns, when he objects so decidedly to that method of elocutionary training which calls the attention of the student first to the prominent vocal effects of an emotion, and then descends to the particulars of expression in "emphasis, pauses, &c."

The errors of theory, regarding this department of education, have been dwelt on longer than might have otherwise been necessary, were it not for the proneness of those who superintend and control the forms of instruction, to defer to the authority of distinguished names, and to discourage the well directed efforts of the teacher. The mode in which reading is taught, or elocution practiced, in the successive stages of education, has a greater effect on mental and moral development, than any other branch of instruction: it affects not only the intelligence, but the taste, the habits, and the whole character of the mind. To the young teacher, therefore, it is exceedingly important that his views on the subject be clear and correct.

The practice of Gesture.—The visible part of elocution,—expressive action,—is another subject on which the errors of theory and practice are numerous and great. They consist chiefly, however, in intentional or unconscious *neglect*, on the one hand, and *mechanical cultivation*, on the other. The former cause of faulty habit appears in inexpressive, unmeaning, and inappropriate forms of bodily action, in insignificant tricks of personal habit, or in excessive and violent gesticulation, accompanied by awkward and uncouth attitudes: the latter shows itself in unnatural, affected, or fantastic gestures and positions. The expressive actions which naturally and properly belong to public address on subjects which call forth emotion, being larger and more forcible than those which belong to the habitual style of private conversation, it is of great service, in the training of youth, that, in addition to all the healthful aids arising from manly exercises and enlivening sports, there should be a daily course of training on the principal forms of oratorical action, with a view to ensure force, and freedom, and propriety of manner, as regards the natural language of attitude and action. This language has its principles for the guidance of the teacher and the student as well as the artist. The attentive investigation of these principles is the only source of true and liberal instruction or useful study. From these principles rules for application necessarily flow; and it depends on the teacher and the student whether the latter shall be well and skillfully trained, neglected, or superficially taught.

Artistic Cultivation of Taste.—Provision is formally made, in many seminaries, for a more liberal allowance of cultivation for the expressive faculties, than is afforded in the mere learning to read, in the study of grammar and rhetoric, or in the practice of composition and elocution. The demands of Taste are recognized and complied with, so far as regards a certain measure of instruction in *music* and *drawing*. But, in very many seminaries, the little arbitrary and imperfect instruction which is given in these branches, is too frequently much worse than none; unless we are willing to recognize the forming of bad taste in either art as an admissible service of education.

Lessons in Drawing: Common Mistake.—Many parents and teachers never bestow a thought on the true character or proper uses of art, as a means of mental culture, or as a practical accomplishment, but labor under the false notion that a little dabbling in it, under a very ordinary instructor, is at least something gained toward refinement of taste and graceful habit. There can not be a greater error committed in education than this. Every attempt to copy an imperfect model, brings down the tone of taste, and does something to hinder the attainment of excellence. Neglect is wholesome, when compared with perversion or with false instruction.

"My daughter," says an affectionate mother, "wishes to learn drawing; and Mr. Blank is getting up a class; and I think I shall let her join. Mr. Blank's drawing is no great things, to be sure. But a little notion of drawing can do my daughter no harm, at least; and, perhaps, she may take a liking for it; and then she can find a better teacher, when it will be worth while to have one." Here are the common errors,—that there is any benefit in a little *poor* or *bad* art, or that any speck of it is not a positive blemish; that the elements of art can be taught by an incompetent teacher; and that, after having taste thus perverted, the pupil can rally, acquire new principles, and form new habits. The actual experience of most pupils thus misdirected, is the painful conviction that, without a perfect command of elements, nothing whatever can be done in art, and that every neglected false line or touch, in rudimental lessons, is sure to injure the habits of eye and hand, in all subsequent execution, besides lowering the standard of excellence, and degrading the taste of the student.

Music: Singing.—An error similar to that just mentioned, prevails with regard to instruction and practice in *music*,—more particularly, in instrumental music. The vocal department, however, is not without its many evils of erroneous conception and faulty instruction. Singing, by the formal manner in which it is sometimes taught, becomes one of the listless tasks which the juvenile pupil is compelled to perform in the routine of school duty, instead of being one of the natural enjoyments and welcome recreations of daily life, in which intellectual activity is accompanied by pleasing emotion and free expression. The young learner, who should be permitted to enter at once on the pleasure of listening to pure and perfect strains of actual music, and then to join in the attempt to execute them, in the natural training of ear and voice, is commonly detained for a long course of drilling on technical terms and arbitrary rules. Music is thus rendered a tasteless, irksome, artificial exercise to the pupil, and fails of accomplishing its main objects of quickening the ear, enlivening the feelings, moulding the voice, and cultivating the taste, by the influence of pure and beautiful examples of vocal sound, in the expression of feeling and sentiment.

Demoralizing Influence of Low Taste.—The result is still more injurious when low taste is permitted to obtrude its degrading influences on the sacred sphere of music; when song is treated as merely a form of amusement or of sport, and when the corrupting effects of gross humor and ridiculous caricature, are intentionally introduced in the lessons of an art designed to purify and elevate the soul. When to such influences there is added the express utterance of degrading and demoralizing sentiment, in the words of a piece of music selected for a school exercise, the work of the enemy who sows tares in the field, is fully accomplished; and education lends its hand to the act of helping the young mind not upward but positively downward.

Deficient and Faulty Instruction.—When the grosser evils which have been mentioned, are avoided, there are not unfrequently others, quite serious in effect, arising from the influence of imperfect cultivation and false taste in the teacher, or in the community of which the pupil is a member. Inaccurate, slovenly, and heedless execution defeats all the purposes of musical cultivation, and renders the absence of culture preferable to the possession of it. Every repetition of a fault confirms an error of perception, a perversion of feeling, or a corruption of taste, and deepens it into a vice of habit and a defect in mental character.

Instrumental Music.—The more laborious forms of culture which are indispensable to success in the performance of *instrumental* music, strike yet deeper into the taste and tendencies of the mind, as regards the character and effects of expression. Faults in this department of musical instruction, are, it is true, not so widely diffused as those which are so often displayed in the teaching of vocal music. But they are not less prejudicial to the pupil individually. The incessant and arduous application which is required of all who wish to perform successfully on any instrument, exhausts and discourages pupils who have not a true and deep love of music, together with the enduring physical vigor and muscular power which consummate execution demands. The attempt to continue practice, under such disadvantages, is more injurious than beneficial; and when the pupil is dragged through the daily infliction, the whole course ends in that miserable failure over whose multitude of sins the false charity of society is so often called to throw its mantle. In music, as in every other form of expressive art, no culture is greatly to be preferred to that which entails error and imperfection.

False Models.—The evils of defective cultivation are not less conspicuous when the pupil possesses both taste and diligence and good ability, but is misled in style, by the influence of a false model in instruction. Of late years, the facility of obtaining instruction of the best order, is greatly increased. But a fatal error is still quite current among parents, that elementary lessons do not require a high standard of perfection in the teacher, and that therefore the rudiments of music may be acquired under any supervision. In this way, vast numbers of pupils are rendered imperfect performers, for life, by wrong habits acquired in the earliest stages of instruction and practice,—habits which no subsequent reformatory training is capable of correcting.

Means of Correcting Prevalent Errors in the Cultivation of the Expressive Faculties.

Remedial Effects of Good Instruction.—The remedy for existing evils in this as in other departments of education, lies partly, it must be acknowledged, with parents and the official guardians of public instruction; and some of the evils adverted to are confessedly beyond the sphere of the teacher's action. Still, in the actual business of teaching, even under all the impediments arising from false views of education and false plans of established procedure in instruction, much may be effected in the way of beneficial reformation, by intelligent and judicious measures on the part of the teacher, in his mode of conducting the daily lessons and exercises in those branches of instruction which are recognized and demanded by general opinion or by legislative enactment.

Examples.—Referring to the utterly deficient provision which the general plan of current education makes for the cultivation and development of the *perceptive* faculties, an enterprising and vigilant teacher will find no difficulty in inducing his pupils to take a short walk with him, for a few minutes daily, at a suitable season of the year, with a view to a little familiar conversation with them about the form and character of a *plant*,—even though but a weed on the road-side. The conversation can be easily so managed as to lead to the attentive observation and close examination of every part of the plant, as designated, first, by the name in ordinary use, and, afterward, if convenient, by the more exact term of scientific nomenclature. A microscope, such as may be easily obtained for a few dollars, will be an infallible attraction to observation and inspection, in such excursions, and will prove a most efficient assistant teacher. Curiosity, and wonder, and inquiry, once excited in this way, will cause the young mind to drink in, with delight, every item of information which falls from the lips of the teacher. Actual knowledge will thus be obtained, and its pleasure consciously felt. Feeling and emotion, the main springs of expression, are now brought into play ; imagination is awakened, and, under the guidance of intelligence, will recognize the traces of beauty and skill in the handiwork of Nature. To record, in writing, what the eye has seen, and the ear heard, and the mind conceived, during such a lesson, will be no hardship of Egyptian task-work, but a pleasure and a privilege. Many a faithful teacher in our New England States, has, in this way,—without waiting for an educational millennium, in which *botany, composition,* and *natural theology* shall all be introduced into our common schools, by legislative authority,— "taken the responsibility," personally, and given an excellent elementary lesson in all three.

First Lessons in Spelling and Reading.—The unphilosophical and arbitrary manner in which many branches of education are actually taught, admits obviously of a remedy at the teacher's will. There is no necessity of blindly following the practice of making the child commit to memory the names of all the letters of the alphabet before he is asked to join the sounds of two, so as to read the words *he* or *me.* There is abundance of rhyme, but very little reason, in making the child read a whole column of rarely occurring and even of unintelligible words, because they all happen to have the same or similar combination of letters ; while his bright eyes would sparkle with intelligence and delight, to see, in the column, a single word whose familiar sound would soon render its face as familiar. To the young learner in *the primer, the spelling-book,* or *the school dictionary,* the whole volume arranges itself in three classes of words: (1,) those which children of his age *understand and use*; (2,) those which they *understand*, when they hear them from the lips of older children or of adults, but which they do *not use* themselves; (3,) those which they *neither use nor understand*, but which with the aid of teacher and book, they are, in due season, to learn to understand and use aright. To follow the true order of teaching, in such circumstances, will cost the teacher no more trouble than the simple act of dotting with the pencil point, on the column of the given page of the pupil's book, those words which he finds adapted to the class-lesson of the hour, according to the intelligence and advancement of his scholars.

Phonetic and Empirical Methods.—Another expedient for the removal of impediments to successful elementary instruction, and one which the teacher can easily adopt, after having made the selection of words, as suggested above, would consist in the subdivision of each of the classes mentioned into analogous and anomalous subclasses. All the words of the first class, for example,—those which are familiar to the child's ear and mind, by daily personal use,—are either regular or irregular, as to the combination of their letters in name and sound. The former of these sub-classes may be easily learned by the process of spelling them by the *sounds* of the letters which compose the words. Thus, in the word "page," the names of the first three letters very readily suggest their sounds, the combination of which constitutes the reading of the word. But not so with the word "gag," in which not one of all the letters suggests its own sound by the name given to it. By the principle of analogy, therefore, all words in which the name of the letter prompts the sound to the ear, may be advantageously taught by the *phonetic* method of merely articulating the sounds of the letters successively. The simplicity of this method enables children to make rapid progress in syllabication and in reading; and on the principle of allowing children the pleasure of helping themselves forward in an intelligent, conscious progress, this part of early training should never be neglected. But, even in those words which are familiar, in sense and in use, to the ears and minds of young children, there are very many in which there is little or no analogy between the names of the letters and the sounds which they receive in the pronunciation of a word or the enunciation of a syllable. The *orthography* of such words is no reliable guide to their *orthoëpy*. To name their component letters, therefore, can effect nothing further than to satisfy the teacher that the eye of the child has taken in every letter of the word before him. So far well. But, after all, the child's eye actually learns to take in such words by the letters in mass, and depends on an arbitrary effort of memory, in pronouncing them. The sooner, therefore, that the little learner acquires the habit of reading such words at sight, without puzzling himself with the confusion arising from the discrepancy between the names and the sounds of their component letters, the more easy and the more sure will be his progress.

Each of these methods of teaching, in the elementary processes of spelling and reading, is good for its own purpose;—the phonetic for the analogies of orthoëpy, and the empirical, as it may be called, for its anomalies. But the error in teaching has been the indiscriminate and exclusive use of the one or the other; in consequence of which, the learner's progress has been rendered unnecessarily difficult and tedious. The inherent difficulties of a language so irregular as the English, render the closest attention, on the part of the teacher, to every means of overcoming them, doubly important in early training.

Orthoëpy.—In this branch of instruction everything depends on the living teacher,—on the correctness of his own exemplifications and the diligence of his endeavors. Indeed, there is, commonly, no reason, but neglect on the part of the instructor, why every child at school is not daily and thoroughly trained in the exact articulation of all the elementary sounds of the English language, and in the distinct enunciation of their principal radical combinations; nor any other reason why an obsolete, awkward, or inappropriate manner of pronouncing common words should be tolerated in any stage of education.

"*School Reading.*"—A similar remark may be made, as regards the unmeaning and inexpressive style of reading, which is so current, not only in schools, but in higher seminaries and professional exercises. This fault, so commonly remarked, would not exist at any stage of education, or in any form of life, private or public, if our primary teachers were only attentive to accustom their pupils, in their very first exercises in the reading of sentences, to repeat them carefully, with a view to *the expression of sense* and not the mere pronouncing of words.

Academic Elocution.—This department of instruction is another in which the appropriate cultivation of the expressive faculties is not dependent on any change in the prescribed forms of education, so much as on the personal endeavors of the teacher. Our public speakers would not so generally utter their words in the formal tones of arbitrary pulpit style, were teachers duly attentive to point out to young *academic declaimers* the natural and appropriate vocal expression of feeling and sentiment; nor should we ever see those frenzied extravagances of passion and grotesque gesticulation, which so frequently degrade the style of popular oratory, were teachers careful to cultivate, in academic declamation, purity of taste, and true force of effect, in the utterance of emotion.

Grammatical Instruction.—Even in the teaching of *grammar*, where less scope, perhaps, is given to the discretion of the teacher, it still depends on himself whether he shall follow the precise order of topics in an ill-arranged text-book, or use his own judgment, and present the subject to the minds of his pupils in the order which he feels that an intelligent and practical study of the subject, and a rational progress in its application, demand. Nothing lies more properly within the province of the teacher, than the duty of seeing to it that his pupils thoroughly understand every word of their various lessons, and thus reap the benefit of grammar, in the perfect interpretation and right use of the current words of their own communications by speech and writing, and in the perusal of the useful productions of the press. The faithful use of an etymological spelling-book, and of the dictionary, is all the cost of an aid so valuable to the teacher, and of an attainment so valuable to the pupil.

Practical Rhetoric: School Exercises.—Training in the appropriate use of the English language, ought not to be limited to the mere grammatical exercise of composing sentences. Even in our common schools, it should extend to that cultivation of taste by which neat as well as correct expression is acquired as a habit. To cultivate, in his pupils, the power of appreciating excellence in language, it is not necessary that the teacher should refer them to a systematic treatise on rhetoric. The school reading book usually furnishes abundance of the best materials for culture, in the presentation of the best modes of composition, as exemplified in the language of the pieces prescribed as reading lessons. The very best training for the acquisition of sound judgment and good taste in expression, may easily be had, if the teacher will but secure the intelligent and voluntary action of his pupils, in frequently *analysing* portions of some of the best of such passages, in occasionally *transcribing* them, and even *committing them to memory*. The exercise of careful transcription, is, perhaps, the best practical expedient that can be found for securing that literal and mechanical correctness in the details of the written forms of language, as to orthography and punctuation, which though, indeed, but minor matters, are yet so important, as indispensable to the decencies and proprieties of style. How ineffectual, for such purposes, the common routine of education proves, none can know but persons whose business brings them into extensive observation of such particulars.

Rhetorical Exercises in higher Seminaries.—To remedy the evils arising from the narrow and artificial character of our higher forms of rhetorical culture, we need a wider scope of discipline not only in rhetoric itself, but in logic, and in the principles of taste as embodied in the æsthetics of every form of expressive art. We need, yet more, however, a special course of practical training, for which the rhetorical teacher ought justly to be held responsible,—a course which should consist in the careful and close analysis of distinguished models of successful composition, so as to trace their order and method in the arrangement of thought, the artistic character of their æsthetic light and shade and coloring, the mechanism of their sentential structure, and the aptness of their verbal expression in detail. A long and rigorous course of disciplinary exercise in such forms, would not only furnish the pen of the ready writer for the varied demands of actual life, but the requisite preparatory training for the office of public speaking, in which a ready command of well digested thought and fit expression is so important to successful effort. The student would, by such training, effectually learn the value of clear consecutive thinking, of genuine taste, of manly plainness of diction and simplicity of expression: he would be thoroughly secured from falling into the "bald, disjointed chat," the pompous harangue, the insane extravagance of emotion, and the fantastic verbiage, which are so often palmed on our popular assemblies, and lauded in our transient vehicles of criticism, as wonderful displays of original genius or oratorical power.

The Study of Language.—One very important aid to the generous culture and full development of the expressive faculties, is, as yet, very imperfectly furnished by our higher forms of liberal education. While the study of the ancient languages is formally acknowledged as one of the most efficacious methods of training the mind to a distinct perception of whatever constitutes power or perfection of expression; and while liberal provision of time and means is carefully made, with a view to secure the full benefit to be derived from the contemplation and analytical examination of these faultless models; too little attention is paid to the invaluable advantages which might be gained from a corresponding rigor of study and analysis, directed to the great authors who constitute the classics of modern literature, in foreign languages, and in our own.

The perfunctory perusal and verbal recitation of a few passages from such authors, which usually form a part of academic exercises, in this department of education, can never be seriously proposed as effecting the purposes of critical appreciation and thorough discipline.

In our highest seminaries, little is attempted beyond the processes of grammatical analysis and interpretation, in a course of literal and mechanical routine, even with regard to the ancient classics; a mere modicum of the same species of attention is usually given to the very noblest writers of Germany, France or Italy. The Spanish and the Portuguese languages are given up, for the most part, to those persons who happen to have occasion for the use of them, as a convenience in mercantile operations. The languages of the North of Europe, whose ancestral affinities with the English render them so richly instructive, as regards the full and true understanding and expert use of the most significant and expressive part of our own native language;—these, as yet, are left to an adventurous few, comparatively, —the solitary explorers and pioneers in the study of modern literature.

America, in its peculiar national position, which brings to its open homes men of all countries and of every tongue, possesses unequaled facilities for the extensive acquisition of all the benefits resulting from the study of language in its various forms; and a wide range of advantages, in this relation of culture, should be justly held as the birthright of our children, and as the characteristic distinction of our educated youth and mature scholars. Not that we would have American teachers pursue the course, which is unfortunately yet too common, of giving a superficial attention, for a few months, or a few weeks, perhaps, to one or more of the languages of modern Europe, and then attempting the task of teaching them. But, generally speaking, American teachers who wish to enjoy the advantage of teaching more intelligently and effectually their native language, in consequence of the opportunity of better understanding its character, by their ability to compare it with others,—an advantage beyond price;—most, if not all, of such teachers have easy resort to a living instructor in whatever language they desire to study, and may, in due time, become possessed in this way, of a vast amount of intellectual wealth, the benefit of which is sure to be felt, not only in their own mental action, but in the attainments of their pupils.

In the department of language, however, there is no acquirement of which teachers and pupils stand in more urgent need than that of a perfect command of correct, clear, strong, expressive English. The attention paid to this most important attainment is, as yet, utterly inadequate to the demands of a generous cultivation or those of actual life and its daily duties. Nothing is more common than this humiliating admission. Yet little is done to do away with the necessity for it. We have, it is true, of late years, made some advances toward a better state of things, in our educational provision of better modes of teaching grammar, synthetically as well as analytically; and, in some schools, the practical study of etymology receives a commendable degree of attention. Yet it is rare to find in any seminary that thorough analytical investigation of the words of our language which every student is expected to exemplify in his exercises on a page of the ancient classics.

The study of English words, if faithfully pursued in the daily lessons of our schools, with any thing like the application exhibited in the examination, and classifying, and arranging, and labeling of the specimens of even a very ordinary cabinet, would enrich the intellectual stores of the young and even of the mature mind, to an extent of which we can, at present, hardly form a conception. Nothing, however, short of such diligence will serve any effectual purpose. The student of his own vernacular tongue must be content to employ the same close, minute inspection, the same careful examination, the same correct designation, the same exact location and scrupulous conservation of every word that he would intelligently appreciate or skillfully use, as the mineralogist adopts in the selection and arrangement of his specimens.

Our prevalent modes of education have been so defective, as regards the means or opportunities of acquiring a proper knowledge of the English language, that the humble attainment of perfect orthography is comparatively rare, even among the "liberally" educated. Few students, even in our higher seminaries of learning, are trained to recognize and appreciate the value of an English root or primitive word, to trace a secondary to a primary sense, or a primary to its secondary, to translate a passage of Latinized English into its Saxon equivalent words of the mother-tongue, to draw the line of discrimination between present and obsolete usage in expression, to detect the nice shades of meaning in words regarded as synonymous,—to use, in fact, their own language expertly.

It is universally admitted that no language needs such processes to be applied to it so much as our own. Its vast copiousness, in consequence of its many sources, the conflicting character of these themselves, the comparatively small number of English writers who have been willing to take the pains to write correctly, so far as to merit the name of models, the contradictory usage which has, from this cause, prevailed, even among distinguished authors—all have conspired to render careful study and extensive practice indispensable to the student who would do justice to the great language which it is his birthright to inherit, for all of life's best purposes.

CULTIVATION OF THE REFLECTIVE FACULTIES.

INTRODUCTORY OBSERVATIONS.—In the preceding lectures of this series, we were occupied with the consideration of the *perceptive* and the *expressive* faculties, with a view to the plan and purposes of education. Following the historical order of development in the different classes in which the mental powers may, for such purposes, be grouped, we enter now on the study of the various modes of intellectual action which may be classed under the denomination of
REFLECTIVE FACULTIES.

Here we are met anew by a difficulty inherent in our native language, in the paucity and indefiniteness of the terms which it employs to designate the phenomena of mind. The vagueness of the phrase "reflective faculties," is a serious impediment to clearness and distinctness of conception, as regards any attempt at exact definition or satisfactory classification of intellectual acts or conditions. The term "reflective," however, if we resort once more to the serviceable aid of etymology, as a key to the interpretation of language, will prove strikingly suggestive of meaning; and, by its figurative force and peculiar significance, will atone, to some extent, for its deficiency in philosophic precision.

The term "perceptive," (literally, *taking through*,) suggests the intellectual condition in which the mind is in the act of *taking*, receiving, or forming, ideas *through* the medium of the senses. The term "expression" implies a state in which the mind is undergoing a process of *pressing*, or *being pressed, from within outward*. But the term "reflection," (*bending back*,) suggests, figuratively, that state or act of the mind in which it reflects, repeats, or *gives back, inwardly*, the images impressed upon itself,—the effects of which it is conscious, —whether produced from without or from within, whether occasioned by perception, imagination, conception, or emotion. In this condition is is implied that attention turns inward, and dwells, more or less consciously, on its internal subjects, rather than on the objects by which they may have been occasioned.

The history,—so to term it,—of intellectual action implied in the application of the word "reflective," represents the mind, as in the act of going forth from its inner self, meeting the forms of the external world, and, by the impression which these produce upon it, "reflecting," (turning back or inward,) upon itself, to contemplate and deliberately consider what it there consciously beholds. Nor does the term lose aught of its significance, when it is applied to the inward action of the mind on the phenomena of its own consciousness, when the forms of imagination, or even of pure thought itself, become so forcible as to attract and absorb the attention. The figurative word then represents the mind as turning back upon itself, to look inward, so as to ascertain and define, or consider more fully, the objects of its own creation, and to follow the trains of thought which these suggest. In either of the supposed cases,—whether the objective or the subjective world furnish the data of thought,—the result is an ultimate inward movement, which, although it may, in given instances, lead to the anticipation of external action, as a consequence, is, so far, a purely mental condition, sanctioning the popular usage which applies the term "reflection" to all modes of intellectual action which are of a strictly internal character.

Recognizing this fact of language, and pursuing our analysis of the human faculties as subjects of disciplinary culture, we now, therefore, change our field of observation, and pass from the outward spheres of perceptive observation and expressive communication to the silent, inner, invisible, spiritual, and purely intellectual region of *Thought*. We now contemplate man as made in the image of his Maker, as an intelligent and rational being; and we trace the working of those powers which ally him to "things unseen and eternal."

Following, as before, the method of observing (1,) the *forms* of mental action grouped under a given classification; (2,) their *actuating principle*, or motive force; (3,) their natural and habitual *tendency;* (4,) the *results* of their action; and (5,) the *educational processes* consequently required for their development and discipline, we proceed to a summary

(I.) ENUMERATION OF THE REFLECTIVE FACULTIES.

Memory, Conception, Consciousness, Reason, Understanding, Judgment.

Explanatory Remark.—This classification is presented not as one philosophically complete or exhaustive, but merely as a suggestive outline, for educational purposes. It is intentionally limited to the chief of those forms of mental action which may be regarded as acts or powers not only strictly interior, but *purely intellectual*, as contradistinguished from those which are concerned with the external objects and facts of *perception*, from those which consist in inward or outward movements of *feeling*, and from those which are conversant with the ideal forms and creations of the *imagination*. A more extensive classification, including the subdivisions and subordinate details of reflective intellection, will necessarily present itself at a later stage of our analysis, when we come to the consideration of the various forms of exercise to which this group of faculties is subjected in the processes of education.

(1.) MEMORY: *the Basis of Reflective Power.*—This faculty naturally claims our first attention, when we contemplate man as a being endowed with the power of reflective intelligence. It is this faculty which enables him to take the first step from the exterior and objective world into the interior and subjective. Its exercise empowers him, even in the absence of the objects of sense, to retain or to recall, for indefinite periods, and at indefinite intervals, the ideas which he derived from them. He can thus, at pleasure, dispense with the actual presence of external objects, and yet, by dwelling on them mentally, after he has withdrawn from them outwardly, pursue the trains of thought to which they give rise. As a result, he thus acquires a more intimate knowledge of their relations to his own interior being, and converts the pabulum of intelligence, furnished in the data of the outward world, into the pure elements of intellectual sustenance. The activity of this power is, in fact, the measure of his growth in mental stature and strength. It is the condition of all intelligent progress, whether we regard memory as the grand receptacle and depository of all those elements of knowledge which are at once the rudiments of intellectual life, the springs mental of action, and the material of thought, or as the chain which links the past to the present, and retains every acquisition as a foothold for the next step forward in the processes of reason and the investigation of truth.

Remembrance.—The faculty of memory, even in its comparatively passive and quiescent form of mere retention, or *remembrance*, gives man the power of holding with a firm grasp all the treasures which observation enables him to accumulate from without, and to carry them with him into that internal region of thought where they are to be assimilated to his own mental being, and become component parts of it, in transfigured forms of living power and beauty. Not only so: but even the involuntary susceptibility of this vast capacity preserves in the mind the imprint of every passing thought, every form of imagination, and every mood of feeling, which has character enough to excite his attention and recall him to himself, in the exercise of consciousness and reflection.

Intellectual and Moral Offices of Memory.—This benign retentive power gives unity to man's intellectual and moral life. It is the sure and steadfast anchor by which he grapples the present to the past, and is saved from the fluctuation and fragmentary tossing of "the ignorant present." In the wide field of culture, memory makes the mind the seed plot and garden ground of all the knowledge which human care and kindness have the skill or the power to drop into it. Fertilized by the genial influences of well directed education, the retentive capacity of memory becomes rich in every precious and noble product of mind by which the intellectual life of the world is nourished and sustained.

But it is as an element of intellectual and moral power in human *character*, that this faculty reveals its chief value. Its very nature and tendency is to constitute man a *reflective* being, by withdrawing him from the influence of a too exclusive regard to the present and the external; by soliciting his attention to the profoundest verities of his own intelligent and immortal being; and by balancing the stern realities of experience against the sometimes fallacious solicitations of hope, or the grave actualities of the past against the doubtful promises of the future. It prompts to *thought*, and leads to security amidst uncertainty and distraction. It invites to reflective *meditation*, by the suggestive materials in which it abounds. It cherishes *contemplation*, by opening to the mind's eye the long vista of the past with its fast-linked trains of scene and incident and action, and the ineffaceable impressions which all these have graven upon the heart. It tends to make man a considerate and thoughtful being, by the faithful monitions which it furnishes to the lips of wisdom warning against the errors of judgment or of will, by reminding of their penalties formerly incurred.

Remembrance saves from the domineering ascendency and absorbing attractions of the sensuous and the transient, by intermingling with the fluidity and evanescence of the present the solidity and permanence of the past. It thus tends to give gravity and weight to character; and if its influence is sometimes a shade too sombre for gayety, it contributes a not undesirable element to the sternness of manhood, as a safeguard to the firmness of will. Its office is, in this respect, a preventive one,—to save man from the instability which the exclusive influence of things present and things outward might induce; and, by attracting him inward to himself, it favors the acquisition of that self-knowledge which is the anchor of his safety.

Recollection.—This term is but another name for the faculty of memory, and merely intimates that the impressions made on the mind by a given object, scene, or event, may have been, for a time, effaced, or its elements dispersed, by the intervention of other agencies; and that, with or without an effort of the will to that effect, but by the operation of some law of mental association, the idea recurs or returns, as it were, and, perhaps, unexpectedly and suddenly, to the mind. We are then said to "recollect," (*gather again*,) or recall what had, for a season, escaped the retentive hold of memory.

The very abruptness and suddenness of the transition of thought, in such instances, exerts a peculiar power on the reflective action of the mind, and makes it more striking, more impressive, and more effectual. Recollection may thus light up the soul with the instantaneous gleam of a rekindled thought, or plunge it into the depths of a past grief; or it may arrest the will on the very brink of remembered evil. A long train of profound reflections may thus be suggested, which may exert an influence on the character of a whole life.

A mere flash of reflection has sometimes sufficed, by the instant recalling of scenes of childhood's innocent enjoyment, or the injunctions of parental wisdom and love to reinstate conscience on its rightful throne, and bring back the tempted to himself, or to restrain him from the first steps of a career of ruin. A remembered promise, pledging honor and truth, has sometimes risen up as a barrier against an approaching tide of overwhelming guilt. A verse of sacred Scripture, darting across the mind, has checked the hand already stretched out to do the deed of wickedness which no after tears of penitence could have sufficed to wash out.

But not as a *preventive* only does memory thus subserve man's highest interests: its recurring suggestions are not less frequently inspiring *prompters* to every form of virtue. To the dispirited traveler on the pathway of life, it comes, sometimes, as an inspiring angel, with messages of cheering and encouragement drawn from the remembered virtues of the struggling great and good who have gone before. It points him to "their footprints on the sands of time," and bids him "take heart again." It reminds him that his great reliance is not on the outward and the material, but on that " hidden strength" of which our greatest poet speaks so eloquently. The maxim or the motto which the guardian care of the mother or the teacher had engraven as a watchword on the tablet of the heart, in early years, recurs, sometimes, to incite to noble deeds or noble enduring, the man encompassed by difficulties and dangers before which he would otherwise have staggered. The "one, last, best effort, more," which wins the crown of victory, is that, not unfrequently, which follows the backward glance of memory to the parting scene, and farewell words of a parent's blessing.

Memory as a Subject of Cultivation.—In either form, whether that of retentive remembrance or momentary recollection, memory furnishes the material, and solicits the action, of the whole class of reflective faculties. To the educator, therefore, the judicious cultivation and development of this capacity, in the minds committed to his care, becomes a matter of vital moment, that the impressible memory of the young may be rich in valuable resources, and strong for the aid of every good purpose, sound and healthy in its action, firm in its grasp, and prompt to yield up its acquisitions when in demand for intellectual emergencies.

The true teacher will be careful that this indispensable servant of the mind be not exhausted by overwork, that its strength be not expended on worthless material, that its receptive capacity be not crammed to unhealthful and unprofitable repletion, at the expense of inaction and inanity to all the other capacities of the mind. But of the appropriate modes of exercise for the cultivation of this faculty, we shall have occasion to speak more fully under the head of educational processes.

(2.) CONCEPTION: *Etymological Sense of the Word.*—The primitive signification of this term implies that the mind has the power of "taking" (*receiving*, or *forming*,) ideas "with," (*within*,) itself, whether on data furnished from without, and by the alchemy of mind, transmuted into intellectual forms, or on materials found within itself, originating in feeling or in thought, partaking of its own character, and wearing forms purely ideal. In the process of intelligence, *conception* presents itself as the counterpart of *perception*, performing, in the interior world of thought, an office similar to that of the latter in the domain of exterior observation.

Its Proper Acceptation.—The term "conception," in its full and proper acceptation, comprehends the action of the mind in the intelligent contemplation or cognition of any object or subject in the whole range of the ideal world. It applies to the recognition or creation of the forms of imagination and the figures of fancy, not less than to the ideas of pure intellection. In the former relation, it stands connected with the action of the expressive faculties, as discussed in a previous lecture; but it is in the latter sense, as a contemplative and reflective faculty, that we now regard it. In this connection, it approaches, sometimes to the sphere of memory, and draws from that source the materials on which it acts,—whether these were originally external or internal in their origin.

Different Views of this Faculty.—Contemplated in the light last mentioned, the faculty of conception has, by some eminent writers on intellectual philosophy, been considered as identical with *memory;* while, by others, its definite action on forms furnished by *imagination*, has been regarded as identifying it with that faculty. Hence, we read of the "conceptions of memory," and the "conceptions of imagination." A third class of authors treating of intellectual topics, evidently regard conception as simply an act of the understanding.

The unsatisfactory character of popular usage in our own tongue, as regards the application of language to mental phenomena, is strikingly exhibited in the several arbitrary senses in which the term "conception" is used, as suggesting imperfection, dimness, or remoteness in the objects or subjects of contemplation. We can not, therefore, rely on any consentaneous use of nomenclature as a guide to the character or action of the faculty in question. Adverting, however, to the highly suggestive etymological sense of the term "conception," as it has been employed in the metaphysical vocabulary of all nations, for successive ages, we find the susceptive intellect figuratively represented by it as—when in the act of forming ideas—*impregnated*, or fertilized, not only from the various sources of intelligence furnished by the external world of perception and the interior spheres of feeling and imagination, but as possessing a *self-vivifying* power of creating and contemplating an inner world of its own, more or less analogous to that without, though formed of materials purely intellectual and spiritual;—a condition which is exemplified in the exercises of its own conscious intuition, in the sequences of thought, and in the processes of reasoning. Nor is the independent power of this faculty in any case more distinctly perceptible than when, borrowing the congenial aid of reason, it inspires with intelligence, and moulds into symmetry the fluctuating forms of imagination which hover in the ideal atmosphere.

This strictly interior power of the mind may be regarded as the first step in its consciously reflective action, in which,—not as in the partly involuntary condition of mere remembrance or recollection, it is comparatively passive, or works under a law of necessity,—but voluntarily and deliberately coöperates with impressions received from without, with a consciousness of their tendencies and of its own action. It is this power which virtually confers on man a world of his own, —an intelligent sphere of activity, independent, for the time, of the external universe in which he moves,—a sphere in which his higher intellectual and moral nature has its appropriate scope. The strength, the clearness, and the precision with which this faculty acts, determine his rank in the scale of intelligence and moral power.

Its Susceptibility of Cultivation.—In the relations of educational culture, the exercise of this faculty becomes a subject of deepest interest to those whose office it is to train the mind to true and effective habits of action. Nothing, indeed, can give a more impressive view of the benefits of proper cultivation, or of the susceptibility of this faculty to the influence of culture, than the contrast between the feeble and futile efforts of the child to form an adequate conception of the causes of the most ordinary phenomena of daily life, and the comprehensive grasp of conceptive intelligence with which the mature mind of man reads the great volume of facts and their relations, and interprets their most hidden laws. A similar contrast is exhibited to us in the wondering ignorance of the savage, contemplating the varying aspects of nature, and the man of science, to whom they present themselves as necessary results, thoroughly understood, and as verifications of philosophic theory.

The mere perceptions of the child or of the savage may often be more exact than those of the philosopher, because these depend on the freshness and vividness of sensation. But the *conceptive* power of the mind is, to a great extent, the result of the force of processes purely mental, and the skill and exactness with which these are conducted. In such operations, practice and discipline alone can yield perfection as a result; and for success in them the candidate must look to the sustaining aid and the crowning hand of education.

If we would form even the humblest idea of the mental value of the power of conception, we must refer to all that man has achieved in the acquisition of knowledge or the attainment of truth; we must advert to all the relations which he sustains to things lying beyond the sphere of sense, in the wide regions of opinion, of theory, and of sentiment; we must include his views of his own position in the universe, his views of the character of Deity, of the immortality of the soul, of the obligations of duty, of his social and civil life, and of all the institutions to which his conceptions of these various relations have given origin.

It is in these wider and higher references that conception, as a power of reflective intelligence, indicates its peculiar rank and office. Working by the blended lights of reason and of consciousness, it enables man to construct the fabrics of science and of character, by a consecutive progress of attainments in which every deposit becomes but a substratum for another in the series of an indefinite succession.

(3.) CONSCIOUSNESS: *Etymology of the Term.*—The etymological signification of this term invites our attention for a moment, to the peculiar suggestive value of the first element in the composition of the word. Primitively, the meaning of this element is fully given by the equivalent term *together*, always implying a reference to *duality* or *plurality*. It ranges, accordingly, over the whole class of synonyms which may be grouped under the terms, "collation," "apposition," "union." In the use, therefore, of the term "consciousness,"—since the *root* of the word signifies *knowledge*, or intelligence,—the mind is represented as acting *together* with, or in *union* with, itself—that is, with *self-intelligence*. The prefix of the term, in this instance, accordingly, as in that of the word "conception," has the virtual significance of *inner*, *inward*, or *interior*, and suggests the idea of the mind acting on itself, on the objects of its own creation, or on the subjects of its own reflective conceptions.

Fitness of its Application.—There is a striking appropriateness, in this view, of the term "consciousness" as a designation for that power by which the mind becomes capable of momentarily detaching, as it were, from itself the idea of its contemplation, and working as a two-fold power; one effort of which is to hold up the ideal object, and the other to direct a wakeful and conscious attention to it, for some purpose of examination or reflective inquiry. The intelligent principle thus works—according to the interpretation of the term—*together* with, or in union with itself, in the compound or two-fold action of *conception*, and *attention ;* the latter being introverted, so that the mind is aware of its own condition.

The peculiar fitness of the term in question becomes yet more distinctly apparent, when we advert to the common fact of experience, that, in the outward tendencies of the faculty of perception, the attraction of external objects is often so powerful and absorbing as to cause the mind to "lose its consciousness" in the contemplation of what it beholds, and to forget, for a time, its own existence, in the force of the attraction by which it is evoked, or the intensity of the excitement to which it is subjected, and which it temporarily identifies with the object of its attention. In the state of consciousness, on the other hand, the mind is *self-possessed ;* it is *aware* of its own state of thought or feeling, and *voluntarily* dwells on the fact of introversion.

Different Opinions on the Nature of this Faculty.—Consciousness, as a term applied to the designation of a mental faculty of the reflective class, is, like many other terms in the nomenclature of intellectual analysis, a confessedly imperfect yet significant attempt to suggest a perfect recoginition of an act or state purely internal. The imperfection here felt, attends more or less obviously, yet unavoidably, every attempt to define the action of mind,—that transcendent power whose subtle agency often proves too fine for the grasp of its human representative, language, an interpreter whose terms are all, in consequence of the limitations of humanity, "of the earth, earthy."

The diversity of opinion among intellectual philosophers, therefore, on the nature of this power, is not surprising. Some would ignore its existence as a cognizable faculty, and identify it with the mere reflex act of attention; others elaborate its action in detail, so as to identify it with voluntary and prolonged reflection. Both these classes of observers evidently take the ground that it is dependent on the exercise, more or less active, of the will. But the painful act of consciousness in the experience of corporal or mental suffering, is often altogether involuntary, and resists, sometimes, the strongest efforts of the will, even in the loftiest moods of heroism itself; and the intellectual attraction of a mathematical problem, or a metaphysical question, will fascinate the conscious thinker, and draw him on involuntarily, from stage to stage of its processes, till, in the poet's language, he "forgets himself to marble."

Other authorities on topics of intellectual philosophy, have deemed it more rational to assume that consciousness is an inseparable attribute of intelligence,—necessary to its very existence. They represent it as the element which constitutes the dividing line between thought and mere reverie, between judgment and imagination, or, sometimes, between reason and insanity.

Educational View of this Faculty.—For the preliminary analysis which the intelligent conductor of education requires as his guide in the planning of his procedure, it is sufficient, perhaps, to take the acknowledged ground that consciousness is that state, act, or operation of the mind in which it is aware of its own activity. He will, from this view of the subject, derive two most important conclusions: (1,) that the vividness and distinctness of consciousness must always be in proportion to the clearness, exactness, and force of the ideas which are, so to speak, impressed on the mind from without, and solicit its conscious action as subjects of thought; and (2,) that the definiteness, the fullness, and the depth of consciousness, must always be in proportion to the power of directing and controlling the attention of the mind with reference to its own inward acts and conditions.

Intellectual and Moral Offices of Consciousness.—It is thus that consciousness assumes its true place as a reflective faculty, in the relations of intellect, as the power by which the mind learns to see clearly with its own inner eye, to define with accuracy the ideas which conception creates, to interpret nature's innermost secrets of causation, to follow the lengthening processes of reason, in the profoundest depths of investigation, and so to construct the magnificent fabrics of pure science. The reflective power of consciousness becomes yet more impressive to us, when we regard its vast influence on the moral relations of mental action. It then reveals itself as an agent but a little lower than the divine element of *conscience*, and as the very condition of the paramount influence of that power over heart, will, action, and character. In the unconscious condition of childhood, and in the immaturity of experience, conscience moves with the light step, and the gentle hand and the soft accents of the guiding angel of Innocence. But it watches with a jealous eye, restrains with a firm hand, controls with the tone of command, or rebukes with the voice of reproach, the conscious agent who, in maturity of years, departs from the path of rectitude. But not in the stern monitions or the agonizing inflictions of remorse alone, does conscience act on consciousness. The sting and the lash are not its only implements of discipline. Conscience appeals to man's conscious power for good, when it uses "the spur which the clear spirit doth raise," and reminds him of his position "but a little lower than the angels," his resources of intellect, his moral ability, his relations of duty, his capacity of ceaseless progress, his desire to win the crown of excellence, his obligations to the Author of his being, and his aspirations after an immortality of glory.

Educational Culture of this Faculty.—The educator, therefore, while he would guard his pupils against that selfish and morbid consciousness which dwells exclusively on the condition of the individual, and keeps him forever in the abstracted mood of introspection and introversion, shut up in the cell of self, and withdrawn from usefulness to others, will use all salutary measures to give vigor and life and full activity to this powerful element of mental action and character.

(4.) REASON: *Explanatory Remark.*—The successive changes which, in the progress of time, are produced on the original meanings of words, will sometimes render a literal adoption of the primitive sense of any term an uncertain guide in metaphysical investigations connected with the action and phenomena of mind. A due regard, however, to the etymological structure of terms employed to designate the intellectual faculties, will always serve to suggest useful ideas for the guidance and direction of education. Such terms, it is not to be forgotten, had their origin in simple and primitive states of human life and character, and are therefore exempt from the uncertainty and ambiguity resulting from the mental condition of more advanced stages of society, in which opinion is refined, by false as well as true culture, into more subtle and more sceptical forms, and sometimes falls into the entangling web of sophistry and false judgment. The primitive uses of language betray, it must be acknowledged, the historical childhood of man; but they possess, also, the truthfulness, the simplicity, and the directness of that stage; and their vivacious and figurative character always render them strikingly suggestive. In philosophic investigations connected with the analytic study of mind and the adaptation of modes of culture to mental discipline and development, the primitive signification of terms, whether it be literal or figurative, becomes, at least, an index to analysis, which, if faithfully traced, may lead to true and satisfactory conclusions on topics otherwise obscure and uncertain.

Etymology of the Term.—To apply this remark to the instance before us. Clearer conceptions and juster views of the faculty which we designate by the term "reason," would generally prevail, and would exert a corresponding influence on modes of mental culture, were the original meaning of the word adverted to in discussions connected with these subjects. The word "reason" is but the Latin scientific term "*ratio*," so familiar to the ear and mind of every teacher and every student of mathematics. It has merely undergone some slight modifications in passing from the Latin language, through the French, into our own. Its original sense, therefore, suggests the idea of *rate, measure, or computation*, as a conscious application, or act, of intelligence; and if we would trace the simplest and purest form of reason, we thus find it in the act of recognizing or constituting *rate*, or *ratio*, which in complicated processes, becomes *proportion*, or *symmetry*.

Reason characterized by the Definiteness and Certainty of its Action.—The idea suggested by the primary application of the term "reason," is that of *definiteness* and *exactness* of observation, carried even to the extent of examination by actual *measurement* or computation. No certainty of knowledge can be greater than what is thus intimated, when the inner action of intellect is verified by a direct appeal to objective reality attested by sense; and, in the legitimate uses of language, the measured exactness of verified observation is figuratively transferred to the decisions of judgment and the deductions of reason, in the comparison and examination of ideas and conceptions begun, continued, and ended, within the mind itself.

The processes of thought conducted on this firm ground, possess a definiteness which places the conclusions of reason in striking contrast with the comparatively vague and indefinite intimations of *feeling*, around which the boundary line of distinction can not with certainty be drawn, even in the most vivid states of consciousness. The ideas of reason stand thus contrasted, also, with those of *imagination*, which are often shadowy and indefinite, inexact, or inadequate, and always comparatively fleeting and uncertain;—sometimes, unreal and false, the mere flitting phantoms of fancy. The purely intellectual conceptions of reason, as subjects of the mind's own inner *consciousness*, are, yet further, distinguished from the merely *perceptive* action of sense and understanding, in the relations of intelligence directed to the *external* world. Reason, working on data strictly mental, ever partakes of the certainty of *personal* knowledge and *conviction*, which, to the individual,—whatever it may be to others,—is, in its proper relations, the surest of all the grounds of mental action. Our senses, we are aware, may misinform us: our conscious experience can not.

Offices of Reason in Definition and Discrimination.—This faculty, by the measured accuracy of its action, becomes the means of *defining* our ideas and *discriminating* them in differential detail. It groups them in the *genera* and *species* of orderly *classification*, and *analyses* the complex into the simple, even to the minutest individual element of the compound. It thus enables the mind to search and scrutinize the obscure or the uncertain, till every object is brought out into the light of certainty and conscious knowledege. In these, as in all other forms in which this faculty is exerted, the appropriateness of the primary application of the term by which it is designated, is distinctly perceived. In all its operations, it is stable, sure, exact, to absolute certainty. It was in virtue of its authority that the great modern philosopher " carried," as has been happily said, " the measuring line to the boundary of creation;" and all its inward and conscious exercises partake of the same exactitude.

Reason, an Authoritative Power.—When this faculty condescends to its humbler offices of recognizing the intimations of sense, and accumulating the deposits of knowledge, and maintains a comparatively quiescent, receptive, or passive condition, it bears the unassuming designation of " understanding ;" as it is then regarded as merely furnishing the *groundwork*, or under stratum, of intelligence. But when it assumes the higher office of deciding on and determining the exact relations of thought, it is honored by the highly figurative appellation of "judgment"—a term the etymology of which implies the enunciation of *right*, or *justice*, and hence, whatever, also, is implied in its synonyms, *decree*, *sentence*, or *decision*. Reason, when thus occupied in comparing, measuring. or exactly estimating things or their relations, is, by the use of language, personified as the *judge*, whose office it is *to scrutinize*, *compare*, and *balance evidence*, so as ultimately to *decide* or *determine*, and give *judgment*, *sentence*, or *decree*, according to the usage of ancient times, when it was that officer's prerogative to discharge the office assigned to our modern juries, as well as

1 H

that still recognized as proper to him who presides in the court of justice.

When this master faculty of human intelligence soars to a yet higher pitch, and its action, whether "intuitive or discursive," embraces great and *general principles*, sees or traces the relations of *necessary* and *universal truths*, and announces the majesty of *causation* and of *law*, it resumes its wonted designation of *reason*,—a term too limited for the scope and grandeur of its action, and the dignity of its office, as man's highest functions, in the relations of intellect.

True, it fails whenever it would usurp the appointed place of *conscience*, and *reason* man into perfect rectitude, or when it presumes to supersede the guardian office of *faith*, and offers man the guidance of mere intellection to the recognition of a paternal God. But, limited as it is, by the conditions of humanity, it still is, within the sphere of pure intelligence, that which reflects in man the image of God, and to which, in healthy and normal conditions, all his other intellectual powers pay homage.

Reason as cognizant of Relations.—Reverting to the primitive sense of the term "reason," as recognized in the application of the word "ratio" to processes of measurement connected with time and space, and figuratively transferred to operations purely intellectual, we are reminded that, in all such processes, one object or subject is *referred* to another, with a view to determine or define a *connection* of some sort or other between them. This fact accounts for the usage in language by which reason is represented as the faculty which takes cognizance of, or traces, *relations* in general, or, in other words, refers one thing to another, for purposes of *examination, comparison*, or *investigation*, with a view to ascertain their *connection*, or their *independence* of each other, as an element of thought essential to the acquisition of knowledge or to the discovery of truth. The mind is thus introduced into a sphere of action coextensive with all the outward objects and inward subjects of thought, and expatiates, with the delight of conscious freedom and power, in the two great domains with which it is endowed as its heritage and birth-right; for reason, not less than imagination is an *excursive* faculty, designed to give amplitude and expansion to the being of man; and many of the grandest creations of the latter, are those which it achieves when following the sure and firm steps of the former, in its excursions into the unexplored.

Reason as an Inventive Faculty.—The reference of one object or idea to another, the comparison of one with another, or the discovered relation of one to another, yields within the mind itself, as a result, a

CULTIVATION OF THE REFLECTIVE FACULTIES. 115

third idea, or conception, a creation of its own. Reason thus becomes a combining, creative, and inventive, (*finding*,) faculty, not less than imagination is, in its peculiar sphere; and, by following its well ascertained discoveries through their long and complicated successions of ever fresh-springing truth, attains, at length, the conscious power to move in new spheres of knowledge, created by its own activity, and in which it furnishes its own material, and erects its own structures. It is thus that it empowers man to fulfill the poet's condition of "erecting himself above himself." Reason, not less than its noble kindred powers, Faith and Imagination, is then justly said to " soar."

In the processes of investigation in which the mind pursues its quest of knowledge as the guide to truth, reason becomes the master key of intelligence, the paramount authority of intellect, the law which gives order and unity to man's intellectual being, the crown and glory of humanity in its distinctive supremacy over the lower tribes of partially intelligent nature.

Aberration of Reason.—When disease or passion has beclouded, or disturbed, or deranged this power, which heaven has ordained as the *executive* of its own first law of *order*, in the gradations of intelligence, man is then dethroned and discrowned; and, with the eye of his mind extinguished, wanders, like the blind champion of old, seeking some one to lead him by the hand.

Reason in the processes of Analysis and Abstraction.—When this faculty is occupied with the processes of collating and comparing, for purposes of discrimination, its action assumes the form of "analysis," (*loosening, detaching,* or *resolving,*) so as to simplify the objects or subjects of contemplation, and scan their utmost details of individuality, in character, that the component elements of the concrete may be distinctly recognized, in all their differential relations. Subjected to this process, the *genus*, or general class, is reduced to its component *species*, and these, in turn, to the *varieties* or the *individuals* of which they consist. Last of all, the scrutiny must be extended to the difference between individual and individual, or where still more minute examination is required, to the distinctive elements which may be found comprised within the unity of the individual.

Such, in our previous discussion of subjects involved in the theory of education, we found to be the requisite action of the mind in the exercise of the *perceptive* faculties, when observation descends to the minutiæ of difference on which true distinctions are founded. A similar operation goes on in the interior world of conception, when the *reflective* faculties are called into their peculiar province, when the complex ideas or thoughts of the mind are subjected to the processes of scrutiny and analysis, and the qualities of objects, or of ideas, are, by an act of *abstraction*, (*taking away, withdrawing*,) considered separately, as if they had for the moment, an independent existence. One quality of an object, one attribute of a subject, is, by this concentrated and exclusive act of attention, "abstracted," (*drawn away*,) or detached, mentally, from the object itself, and from all the other qualities of which it is possessed. The mind is, in consequence of this act of "abstraction," enabled to contemplate more distinctly, or to examine more closely and discriminate more exactly, the given quality. The quality so discriminated may, in turn, become the groundwork of classification, or the commencement of a train of abstract reasoning on broad and general principles connected with the laws of nature and the truths of science.

Intuition.—The immediate action of reason by which it assents to self-evident and necessary truths, on mere "intuition," (*inspection or sight*,) without the aid of any intermediate or intervening thought for the discovery of sameness or difference, might, at first view, seem to be improperly introduced in a survey of the reflective faculties or of educational processes for development. But, the *intuitive* exercise of reason is, not unfrequently, the basis of its *reflective* action, and, sometimes, is the *authority* to which it appeals, when prosecuting examination and inquiry to the profoundest depths of research.

Processes of Inference and Deduction.—Reason, as the faculty by which one object or idea is referred to another, in virtue of some real or supposed connection existing between them, takes cognizance of *antecedence* and *consequence;* and, when this relation is, in given circumstances, observed to be uniform, reason, working by the great law of *analogy*, "infers," (*brings in*,) the *continuance* of this uniformity as a necessary principle or law of *order*. In such instances, this "inference," supported by the undeviating testimony of personal or accredited experience, becomes a firm *belief*, which identifies uniformity of antecedence with the power of *causation*, and uniformity of sequence with the character of *effect*. *Sequence* thus becomes the law of rational *connection*, and a security for the attainment of *truth* in matters of *theory* referring to the *external* universe.

In the consecutive *internal* acts of mind, reason gives "sequence" to the relations of *thought*, in exercises purely *discursive* and *intellectual*, by recognizing the dependence of one idea or conception on another, in the relation of *effect* to *cause*. From one defined antecedent idea the mind is authorized to "infer" another, as a *consequence;* from "premises," (*thoughts antecedent*,) to "deduce," (*draw down, derive*,) "conclusions," (*closes*,) results, or final consequences; and thus, by giving *certainty* to *opinion* and *assurance* to *belief*, in relations purely *mental*, it forges the successive links of that golden chain of *intellectual necessity* which binds together the elements of the *moral* world.

Reason, in its processes of Generalization and Induction.—In the wider action of this sovereign power, it takes that highest course of which human intellect is capable; and, in tracing the relations of *causation*, aspires, by its power of *generalization* and its processes of *induction*, to announce and interpret the *laws* of the universe, and to read the evidences of a First ordaining Cause.

In these excursions, reason gathers in, from the vast field of analogy, *corresponding* facts and relations; and, in virtue of that pervading *unity* which comparison has enabled it to discover as existing among them, recognizes that spacious principle of *generality* coextensive with its own capacities of thought, by which it rises above the limits of the concrete and the particular to the contemplation of those abstract ideas and comprehensive principles which constitute the prime elements of intellectual and moral truth, and which bear the stamp of supremacy and the inscription of Law, human or Divine.

Not less impressive or sublime is the action of this august faculty of the human soul, when it puts forth its *constructive* power, and, aided by the scrutiny of patient experiment, it verifies the analogies of phenomena and of fact, "inducts" them, (*leads* them,) into their appropriate groups of *affinity* and *correlation*, plies them with its tentative, magnetic, aggregating power of "hypothesis," (*theoretic, interrogative assumption,*) and, by careful *induction*, at last consummates the vast fabric of "theory," (*intellectual vision,*) whose foundations are laid in the certainty of *knowledge*, and whose walls rise, in the symmetry of *truth*, to heights which inspire the mind with awe.

Ratiocination.—In the dimness of abstract conceptions, in the obscurity of abstruse relations of thought, or in the apparent conflict of contrasted truths, when the eviction of hidden causes, or when the detection of intermediate and reconciling principles, becomes essential to the conscious recognition of ideas, to the distinct conception of relations, or to the firm conviction of truth, reason comes to the mind laboring under *uncertainty*, and brings the aid of its *discursive* processes of *ratiocination*, in the form of *dissertation, argument, discussion*, and *debate*. Assuming the seat of *judgment*, it thus institutes *inquiry*, conducts *examination*, prosecutes *investigation, discriminates terms, scrutinizes allegations, compares* conflicting *arguments, weighs* opposing *evidence, judges* of *facts, rejects assumptions, exposes error, detects truth* or *falsehood*, and pronounces its authoritive and final *decision*, as the inevitable *law* of intellection.

Reason, as cognizant of Truth.—Reason, in its judicial capacity, traces, or recognizes and announces, the correspondence or the discrepance of idea with object, thought with fact, conception with conception, principle with principle, proposition with proposition, sentiment with sentiment, opinion and statement with fact, language with thought, argument with argument, effect with cause. It thus, by the eviction of *truth*, produces in the mind the result of *conviction;* and *truth*, as the consummated and perfect result of the action of *reason*, in its cognizance of the ascertained relations of *knowledge*, demands, in virtue of the supremacy and authority of the faculty by whose agency it is discovered, the assent of the mind, in the form which we term *belief*,—not a bare comprehension or merely passive reception by the *understanding*, not the mere negative acquiescence or silent admission of the *judgment*, but the consentaneous recognition and adoption which come from the *voluntary* action of *reason*, uniting itself with the subject of its contemplation, and identifying with it all its own consequent action. Reason, therefore, has to do with all the preliminary processes by which truth is established; and in the moral not less than in the intellectual relations of thought, has, for its office, the sifting of *evidence*, the scrutiny of *testimony*, the weighing of *proof;* on the validity of all which, *belief*, as the normal and healthy tendency of the mind, is conditioned. In the yet higher sphere of Sacred truth, belief becomes subsidiary to the Faith which *trusts.*

Reason, as susceptible of Cultivation.—As the subject of disciplinary culture, this faculty presents itself to the educator as that to which his chief attention is due, in the relations of intellect, not only from its supremacy in the class of faculties to which it belongs, and the fact of its being the very constituent of intelligence, but from its peculiar susceptibility of development and training, and the extent to which it may be rendered clear, decisive, vigorous, and comprehensive, by appropriate exercise. No faculty reveals more distinctly than this the progressive character of man, as an intelligent agent, if we advert to its dim, uncertain, and feeble action in childhood, and its ceaseless growth in soundness, clearness, and vigor, as life advances to its maturity. But when we contrast the reasoning powers of such individuals as Newton, Locke, Butler, or Edwards, in manhood, with the mere germ of latent capability which they possessed in infancy, we perceive yet more distinctly what education may accomplish for the eduction and strengthening of this powerful element in the mental constitution of man.

The cultivation of this faculty becomes yet more important in its results, when we advert to its value in the relation of morals. Reason is naturally the firm ally of *conscience*, in discriminating between *right* and *wrong*, and in instituting those reflective trains of thought by which man is arrested in the pursuit of sensual gratification, and called home to himself, in the conscious exercise of higher faculties, in the enjoyment of truer satisfactions, and in obedience to the rectitude which he feels to be the great law of his being. Reason, in coöperation with conscience, then becomes the regulating principle of his actions; raising them from mere obedience to *prudence* and *judgment*, and conservative *propriety*, to the higher influences of *self-intelligence, consentaneous action*, and *rational conformity* with the *laws* and *conditions* of *his own nature*, and of the Power by which those laws were ordained. Reason is the eye by which he learns to read the volume of revelation,—whether that written in the language of the "elder Scripture," which speaks of the "eternal power and godhead of the Creator," or that of the recorded Word which makes man "wise unto salvation."

(5. and 6.) JUDGMENT AND UNDERSTANDING : *their Identity with Reason.*—It has been justly remarked by an eminent writer on intellectual philosophy, that, in arbitrarily multiplying the number of faculties attributed to the mind, we confuse our own views of mental action, and lose rather than gain by such uses of analysis. In the prosecution of our present inquiries, it will be recollected, that it has been uniformly our endeavor to keep in mind the absolute *unity* of intellection, under whatever apparent diversity of processes it conducts its action; and the preceding observations on *reason*, as a reflective faculty, have, it may have been perceived, presented the operations of *judgment* and *understanding* as virtually but different functions of *reason.* To venture on a figure drawn from the sciences of observation : *Reason* may be regarded as bearing the relation of "genus" to *judgment* and *understanding* as "species." Reason surveys the whole ground of intellection, whether directed outward or inward ; it works in the great field of *analogy*, and on the common ground of *correlation, cotendency* and *consistency*, in the universal sphere of thought. In its comprehensive action, it proclaims the *harmonies* of the universe. It has the power, therefore, of *investigating* and *proving analogies*, and, consequently, of *rejecting discordant elements.* Descending to this task, reason becomes, in the vocabulary of intellection, "judgment." Stooping yet lower, to *trace* and *verify relations* of *humbler value*, or of *exterior character*, or processes of *passive reception* of *knowledge* or of *truth*, it assumes the lower office and familiar name of "understanding."

Maintaining the justness of this definition of the faculty of reason, we would not, however, overlook the fact, so important to the right management of education, that the more closely we watch the operations of intellect, the more searching the investigation, and the more minute our analysis, we shall be the better prepared to minister to the manifold wants of the mind, and to its healthful development. The subdivision of *reason* into "judgment" and "understanding," if taken as merely a temporary assumption of *theory*, with a view to fuller provision for mental action and discipline, can not be objected to; and, indeed, the common branches of useful knowledge and of scientific acquirement which constitute the material and media of intellectual education, address themselves distinctively to that classification of the mental faculties which is commonly adopted or recognized. Of these we shall have occasion to speak, when discussing the modes and processes of culture. Nor can any detriment to a just view of mind as subjected to invigorating discipline, arise from adopting, for the time, that more comprehensive classification of the forms of mental action, which is now proposed.

An extensive course of study in every department of mental philosophy, can not be too earnestly urged on the attention of all teachers who are so situated as to exert a controlling or directing influence on the plan of education, or to enjoy adequate opportunities of pursuing a full course of professional reading. No serious evil will in this way be incurred, even if the teacher become, in consequence of his studies, the disciple of a particular school of metaphysics or psychology; provided he do not lose sight of the great fact that, as a teacher, he is called to work as a personal and original observer of the actual workings and tendencies of the young mind itself, and, as its guide and director, to proceed according to his own personal observation and convictions, independently of all theories and speculations of a merely abstract character.

One of the greatest metaphysicians of modern times[*]—who, more than any writer or teacher on his class of subjects, is entitled to the rank of an authority—who, to a depth of research and a profoundness of learning which man has seldom attained, adds the simplicity, the docility, and the candor of a child in the attitude of inquiry—has most justly said to the student of mental philosophy: "If he only effectively pursue the method of observation and analysis, he may even dispense with the study of philosophical systems. This is, at best, only useful as a mean toward a deeper and more varied study of himself, and is often only a tribute paid by philosophy to erudi-

---

[*] Sir William Hamilton.

tion." With the same characteristic frankness he remarks, in another connection, that psychology (the direct study of mind) is yet incomplete as a science; since the phenomena of which it takes cognizance have not yet been exhaustively enumerated or defined, and speaks, at the same time, of the service which, in this respect, might be rendered to philosophy by adequate investigation and faithful reporting.

To so noble an office no candidate can more justly aspire than the intelligent teacher. His occupation renders him conversant with mind in its purest and truest states, its primal tendencies and aspirations, its incipient endeavors, and forming habits.

II. THE ACTUATING PRINCIPLE OF THE REFLECTIVE FACULTIES: INQUIRY.

Its analogy to Curiosity.—When we trace the natural development of the human faculties, in their first stage of *perceptive* action, we observe them working by a law of incitement manifesting itself in the restless principle of *curiosity,*—the desire of knowledge. It is this feeling which prompts the child's appealing question, as he points to a new object that has attracted his attention,—" What is this ?" But, as his reflective power developes, and his capacity of knowledge enlarges, his desire of information pierces deeper; and his interrogation takes a shape which indicates a more profound exercise of thought. He now inquires not " *What* is this ?"—but *"How,"* or " *Why* is this ?"

Reason, as the principle of intelligence which gleans and assorts the contributions of knowledge, has helped him to *understand* the exterior character of the object of his attention, and by the due exercise of *judgment,* in analytic observation, to distinguish, and classify, and denominate it accordingly. But a deeper thirst than mere curiosity as to external phenomena and characteristics, now actuates him: a more powerful instinct is at work within him. Reason has reached a maturer stage of development, and, prompted by inquiry, sets out the young explorer in quest not of mere facts, but of *relations* and *causes.* He thus learns to trace the successive links of *connected* phenomena and facts,—to investigate the *connection* itself, and determine its character, to search for interior and hidden springs of *sequence,* to arrive at *principles* and *causes,* to read and interpret *laws,* and, ultimately, to reach the certainty and the completeness of *science.*

The appetite of *curiosity* is satisfied with the knowledge of phenomena and of facts *individually,* or even as *detached* matters of observation : *inquiry* is restless till it arrives at their *connections* and *dependencies,* and the mind is thus put in possession of those relations of knowledge which constitute *principles* and establish *truth.* As an impelling and actuating force, *inquiry,* or inquisition, performs for the intellectual powers, in their comparative maturity, the same genial office which was discharged by the awakening influence of *curiosity* at an earlier stage of mental activity. It is, in fact, but the same instinctive law of the irrepressible desire to *know*, only working in a higher sphere, and for a higher end. Curiosity, working on the *perceptive* faculties, induces a tendency to *observation*, and forms the habit of wakeful attention to external *phenomena*, as the elements of KNOWLEDGE: *inquiry*, as the expressed desire to ascertain *relations*, *principles*, and *laws*, awakens the *reflective* faculties, and impels to *investigation*, with a view to the discovery of TRUTH. In the development and formation of mental character, *curiosity*, as the desire of *knowledge*, tends to create an *attentive* and *observing* mind, characterized by *intelligence*: *inquiry*, as the quest of *truth*, produces a *contemplative, thoughtful, reflective, reasoning* mind, addicted to *exploration* and *research*, and delighting in the attainments of *science*.

But in this higher sphere of intellectual activity, the human being is still acting under the guidance of an implanted *instinct*;—no longer, indeed, a mere unconscious stimulus, but a conscious and recognized impulse of progression toward a definite end and a satisfying consummation. The tendency, however, proves itself equally irresistible in the one form as in the other. For, while the child is sometimes so absorbed in the contemplation of the visible attractions of objects of beauty or of curiosity, as to forego even the calls of appetite for the sustenance of his body, in obedience to the more imperious claims of the wants of his intellectual nature; the adult man may lose himself yet more profoundly, when inquiry compels him to investigation, and plunges him into depths of thought in which he becomes lost to all surrounding objects and relations, and, like Newton, meditates on the fall of an apple, with an intensity and concentration of reflective attention which beguile him of needed sleep, and render him unaware of the presence of food or of the fact of his having omitted its use.

III. THE TENDENCY OF ACTION IN THE REFLECTIVE FACULTIES.
INVESTIGATION.

Its manifold directions.—Inquiry, as the grand prompter of the reflective faculties, impels to habits of investigation and research. It not only leads to the scrutiny of the present, in quest of causes and of truth, but ransacks the records of the past, and penetrates into the probabilities of the future. It impels reason to explore the inmost recesses of nature, in pursuit of latent causes. It prompts man to conduct the experiments by which he interrogates nature of her processes, and wins, as the reward of his faithful inquest, the answers which he records in the archives of science. In the relations of moral truth, it compels the investigation of evidence, the verifying of proofs, the sifting of testimony, for the attaining of certainty and the confirmation of belief. But for its influence, the world would be to man a mass of unconnected objects or facts : he would be to himself a mere embodiment of inconsistent elements, unintelligible and destitute of purpose.

Examples of the spirit of Investigation.—Incited by this principle, the *naturalist* explores the remotest regions of earth, to contemplate' the productions of nature, to survey the great features of the globe, its various aspects of scenery, its mountains and rivers, its atmospheric phenomena, its mineral, vegetable, and animal products, and the mutual relations of cause and effect which all these bear to each other.

The *scientific voyager* and *traveler*, impelled by the irrepressible desire to prosecute his favorite researches, patiently endures fatigue, and sickness, and exhaustion, through every extreme of heat or cold ; he exiles himself from society, for months and years, to pursue his solitary investigations ; regardless of danger and difficulty, he bravely encounters every obstacle, and patiently endures every form of pain and privation. He goes forth with the spirit and hardihood of an invader, to extend the domain of science, and returns laden with the trophies of victory, in discoveries which enlighten and enrich the human race.

In the same spirit of investigation, the *astronomer* secludes himself, for successive months and years, to contemplate and record the phenomena of the heavens, and to immure himself in those labyrinths of computation by which the sublime truths of his noble science are investigated and revealed.

Actuated by the same principle, the *historian* pursues his laborious researches in the records of remotest time, in the half-effaced carving on the crumbling monument, or the dim characters on the decaying parchment,—in the obscure tradition or superstitious myth,—whereever a gleam or a spark of truth is to be found regarding the past life of man on earth. From his devotion to such investigations, no fresh charm of nature, or invitation of social delight, can induce him to withdraw, till he has sifted every alledged fact, verified every event, dispersed the clouds of fable, and let in the pure light of *truth* upon the historic page.

The *philologist*, in quest of a particle of meaning or significant value in the component elements of a word, is another impressive example of the spirit of inquiry leading to profoundest research. Whole years, nay, a long life, are joyfully devoted by him to such pursuits. Language after language, by his slow but sure processes of mining and sapping, is forced to give way to his irresistible energy and persevering toil. Nothing can divert his attention, or turn him from his course of persistent indagation. A syllable or a letter, he feels assured, contains a secreted gem of meaning, the investigation of which will put him in possession of wealth untold; and that element he will trace, at whatever cost of persevering investigation, through libraries and through languages, till the lustre of the intellectual diamond beams full upon his mind. His personal acquisition, purchased at such a price, becomes, in due season, through the instrumentality of his devoted labors, the common property of the intellectual world.

The investigations of the *mechanician* into the laws and forces of nature, again exemplify the power which the spirit of inquiry exerts over the human mind, and the value of the results to which it leads. The long and complicated processes of computation by which the devoted servant of science pursues his study of its principles, when occupied with the intricate combinations involved in the invention of some device of mechanism, by which the well-being of mankind may be promoted for ages; the unabating ardor with which, in spite of every discouragement, he continues to consume fortune and life in the prosecution of his purpose;—all indicate the moving force of the mental principle by which his own interior world of invention and contrivance is actuated; and the results ultimately obtained reveal the value of the intellectual habits which are concerned in the processes of investigation.

The *chemist*, interrogating nature, as he investigates the constitution of her elements, is yet another forcible example of the same spirit. At the risk, sometimes, of life itself, he pursues his inquest of hidden relations, perplexing facts, and hitherto undiscovered elements and undeveloped forces, till he is enabled to enlighten the world by the revelation of a new material in the construction of the physical universe, and an invaluable aid to the welfare of man.

Investigation, in all the relations of mental action, is, in brief, the just price of labor, which man is doomed to pay for value received. The noblest of all intellectual acquirements, the grandest discoveries and most useful inventions, are due alike to this process by which the mind is enabled to read, whether in the world of matter or that of spirit, the laws instituted by the Creator; coöperating with which, man becomes possessed of a portion of divine power, and unaided by which, every attempt of human force or skill must be baffled. The tendency and the ability to penetrate into the depths of causation, constitute the mental prerogatives of man; they lift him up to the rank of nobility, in the orders of intelligence, and make his mind the well-spring of a stream which is destined to flow on forever,—not with the mere casual or limited contributions of *observation,* but ever enlarging itself by the broad and deep affluents of profoundest thought and reflective reason, and richly laden with all the treasures of discovery, which have been accumulated by laborious and successful *investigation.*

IV. THE RESULT OF THE ACTION OF THE REFLECTIVE FACULTIES: TRUTH.

The successive stages of intellectual progress.—Furnished with the interior principle of *intelligence,* invested with the organized apparatus of *sensation,* and provided with the physical *material* for the exercise of his powers, the child, under the guidance of Creative wisdom, sets out on the career of intellectual progress, actuated by the impulse of *curiosity,* whose tendency is to insure the habit of *observation* and that discipline of his perceptive faculties by which he is ultimately enabled to win the prize of KNOWLEDGE. He thus accomplishes his first *curriculum* in the great school established by the benignant universal Providence which careth for humanity, and under whose discipline the law of progressive intellection secures, to a given extent, the welfare of man, whether more or less favored by intelligent human culture. To this first stage of development gradually succeeds that other, in which, through the inward action of the divinely-implanted principle of intelligence, man's own inner, mental world of conscious condition, act, cause, effects, tendency, and power,—of memory, reason, imagination, feeling, and will, is revealed and explored, as a theatre of comparatively unlimited expansion and ceaseless action. Within himself, he finds, at once, the power, the springs, the scope, the materials of this new career of activity, in which he is impelled by the same earnest irrepressible desire to discover and to know, as before, but now working in a higher sphere, and with a higher aim. Prompted by *inquiry,* and impelled to *investigation,* he is thus led onward to that higher goal of intellectual progress, where, by the disciplined action of the *reflective faculties, knowledge* is consummated in TRUTH, and where man discovers, and learns to reverence and obey, the highest law of his being,— subordination to the sway of the Reason which reigns supreme in the universe of thought.

Appropriate application of the term Truth.—The sense in which the word "truth" is properly used in general discussions connected with mental processes, is, of course, wider than that in which it is employed in relations strictly or exclusively pertaining to the science of logic. In the latter case, it implies no more than the exact conformity of the terms of a proposition to the fact which it is obviously meant to announce. But, in well-sanctioned forms of expression on general topics, *truth* is, with equal justice, predicated of the correspondence of language to thought, of art to nature, of action to intention, of antitype to type,—in any relation whatever.

In the working of the mind, the term applies, with not less propriety, to the correspondence of perception to object, of conception to idea, of word to thing, of language to relation, of action to conscience, of habit to character, of aim to end, of opinion to sentiment or statement to fact, of expression or representation to reality or actuality. The word "truth," in brief, covers, properly, the whole ground of intellectual, æsthetic, or moral conformity of thought, expression, or action, to an exact and recognized standard, sanctioned by the canons of criticism or of conscience. It stands opposed, therefore, equally to falsity of conception, of expression, or of action. As a quality, it characterizes alike the habits of the correct thinker, of the exact artist, whether in the use of pencil, pen, or tongue, and those of the sincere and honest man. It secures the individual from the unintentional defects of error, and guards him against the voluntary deviations of design.

In relation, however, to the subject of human culture, and, in particular, to the discipline of the mental powers, truth is regarded as a result of voluntary and studious application,—as a product of the exercise of the reflective faculties, in the quest of ultimate principles in science, physical, intellectual, or moral. Examples in point are furnished in the process of tracing the great laws of physics, in the demonstrations of geometry, in the verification of history, in logical ratiocination, in the discussion of moral obligations, in the scrutiny of evidence. In such investigations, the quest of truth, conducted by well-disciplined reflective faculties, is steadily, skillfully, and successfully pushed onward to the grand crowning result of *certainty* and *conviction*. Unaided by the skill which culture and discipline insure, the mind has no security against the involuntary illusions of error, or the intentional misrepresentations of deceit; it discovers no stability in the outward universe, has no confidence in its own conclusions, no just reliance on itself, no firm conviction of duty, no enlightened faith in testimony; but blown about by every plausible assumption of theory, and every shifting phase of circumstance,—a prey to every reigning delusion, unsettled on any sure foundation of moral principle,—skeptical as to every vital truth, plunging into every approaching fog-bank of error, and drifting, without chart or compass, on the great ocean of uncertainty,—suffers, at length, an intellectual and moral wreck.

Most justly, as well as beautifully, has Bacon said, "truth, which only doth judge itself, teacheth that the inquiry of truth, which is the love-making, or wooing, of it,—the knowledge of truth, which is the presence of it,—and the belief of truth, which is the enjoying of it,— is the sovereign good of human nature."

Guided by his own unassisted reflective reason, man does unquestionably attain to great results, both intellectual and moral. But, enlightened by the knowledge which science and education shed on every relation of his being, what a vast expansion, what a wondrous elevation is he capable of attaining ;—all resulting from the faithful application and skillful exercise of the reason with which his Creator has crowned his intellectual faculties! How noble, in this view, becomes the office of the educator, whose daily endeavor it is to cherish, and strengthen, and vivify this master principle of all intelligence!

V. EDUCATIONAL PROCESSES FOR THE DEVELOPMENT AND DISCIPLINE OF THE REFLECTIVE FACULTIES.

Defective Methods.—If we look at what is professedly and formally done, in our common modes of education, for the exercise and discipline of the reflective faculties; and if we found our estimate on the number of branches of knowledge or of science, and the number and variety of books nominally employed for the purpose, we might be inclined to suppose that, in this important part of culture, much is effected. But, on examining the actual state of things, errors and oversights, in this respect, are found to be numerous, and methods comparatively ineffectual.

Exclusive reliance on exactness of recollection.—*Memory*, the appointed servant of the reflective faculties, whose office it is to collect and keep and furnish the materials for their action, is, indeed, amply laden with the semblance and show of matter ;—but most of it in the form of Hamlet's book of " words, words, words." The too exclusive use of *manuals*, the mere records of knowledge, instead of the actual study of *objects*, *facts* and *relations*, the observation and the understanding of which constitute knowledge *itself*, leads to the cultivation of a verbal and mechanical memory, instead of a living and intelligent one. The fact is still too generally overlooked, that memory is not so much a separate faculty, which can be trained and disciplined by itself, as the mind,—in virtue of its spiritual nature and exemption from limits of time and space,—retaining or recalling what it has once observed or conceived ; that the vigor of this retention, or the force of this recurrence, must always be as that of the original impression , and that the only rational reliance for the healthy and effective action of *memory*, must therefore be the freshness, the force, and the depth of *attention*. But, obviously, no impression made on the mind through the medium of language,—no matter how exact may be the definition, or how true the description,—can ever be so complete or so effectual as that of direct observation through the senses, personal experience, or distinct conciousness. Here, again, we are referred to two great educational principles : that the study of things should precede the study of words, and should always be resorted to, in preference, whereever there is a choice of modes of instruction ; and that, to awaken and develope the reflective faculties, the true course is, in obedience to the Creator's appointment, to use the objects of nature as the apparatus which His wisdom has provided, not only for the exercise and training of the mind's perceptive faculties, with a view to the acquisition of *knowledge*, but for the expanding and deepening of its capacities of discovering *truth*. Observation naturally prompts to thought and reflection. There is, in such circumstances, a conscious, living transition from one sphere of intelligence to another,—from one comparatively lower and more limited to one higher and more spacious. But in the mere contemplation or repetition of the words which describe an object, record a fact, or state a principle, the condition of mind is that of abstraction ; and the mental associations, in such conditions, are always less vivid, forcible and distinct, than in the observation of concrete realities ; and, when the former of these conditions is recalled, its impress is necessarily dim and obscure, compared to that of the latter, which, by the experience of actual perception, has become a comparatively inseparable part of the mental life and history of the agent.

The difference in these two cases will be rendered yet more strikingly apparent, if we suppose,—what is commonly true in verbatim processes of committing to memory,—that the mind of the learner, in his anxiety to retain and repeat with exactness the phraseology of the book which he studies, often glances aside from the contemplation of the *fact* or the principle which he is enunciating, to the literal succession of the *words* in which it is expressed. The mind's power of abstraction becomes, in this way, the very means of its deterioration ; and the memory, abused by this arbitrary and mechanical mode of exercise, loses its healthy power of retention and recollection ; and unfortunately, most of all, in those reflective processes of earnest thought which demand its most vigorous exertion.

The prevalent methods of teaching, moreover, are still too exclusively directed to the exercise of memory, at the expense of neglecting the other faculties,—an evil inseparable from the false views which still usurp the seats of instruction, and make education consist in processes of passive reception, on the part of the pupil ; as if his mind were a capacity to be filled, rather than a capability to be developed, or a life-power to be awakened.

Reading.—The greater number of the subjects which are introduced in early education, as means of exercise and discipline for the mind, are still too commonly treated under the influence of these erroneous views of the character and objects of mental culture. Hence the wearisome experience of the child, when compelled to drudge through the task of committing to memory the *names* of all the alphabetic characters of the language, before, or perhaps without ever, acquiring a knowledge of the *power*, or actual *sound*, of any one of the whole group. Every day, he is giving two or three of these sounds in every one of the short and easy words which he uses in conversation. But he is not allowed the satisfaction of recognizing the fact, that these troublesome and perplexing marks before his eye, are little graphic characters to suggest, phonetically to eye and ear, the very words which he is constantly uttering. When the alphabetic task is accomplished, there follows, usually, in the child's experience, that of hewing his way through whole columns of words, to him unmeaning, because lying out of his sphere in the understanding and use of language; and to this useless toil too often succeeds that of reading multitudes of unintelligible- sentences of a character corresponding to the words which baffled him. But we need not dwell on this topic now, having entered into it at length, in former connections of this part of our subject.

Arithmetic.—In arithmetical instruction, which might be so effective an aid to the development of the mind's reflective power, the same evil still too generally prevails, as in the rudimental stages of spelling and reading. The very first step taken, in some instances, is to prescribe and enforce the committing to memory of elementary tables of numbers, by arbitrary repetition of the words in which these are expressed. Were the child allowed the fair opportunity of first *seeing*, in concrete form, the facts which he is made to assume and communicate in parrot-like form; and were he allowed to *create* them for himself, in visible or tangible shape, in copious instances, and thus to generalize the facts from his own observation, memory would have an intelligent, living office to perform, would work with freshness and strength, and long retain, or easily recall, what attention had proved. Were it required of the pupil thus to *construct* the given table, instead of merely repeating the words in which it is expressed, the exercise of memory would be as pleasing as it would be invigorating. It would thus be aided by the deepening and strengthening effect of the not less delightful processes of *combining* and *constructing*, in the actua.

work of practical operations. The busy hand would thus help the thinking head to clearer views and deeper impressions; and the true and proper work of memory would be done in accordance with the law of mental action.—"AS IS THE EARNESTNESS OF ATTENTION, SO IS THE DURATION OF REMEMBRANCE, OR THE DISTINCTNESS AND READINESS OF RECOLLECTION."

Geography.—The subject of *geography* furnishes very frequently another example of memoriter lessons, exacted, perhaps, with a well-meaning rigorous fidelity to the language of a text-book, but sacrificing the useful knowledge, the pleasing information, and the invaluable mental training and discipline, which this instructive branch of science might be made to furnish. Detached facts, comparative numerical tables, and assumed definitions, are yet too uniformly imposed as a burden on the memory; while the actual survey of even a limited portion of the earth's surface, within daily view, perhaps, of the learner, would furnish him with the best materials on which to build up the noble and majestic structure of geographical science.

Fortunately, through the labors of Professor Arnold Guyot, in his luminous exposition of the philosophy of instruction in this department of science, a new and better era is begun in American schools; and this branch of education is now, in many seminaries, taught on methods strictly logical. The study of geography thus becomes an admirable intellectual discipline, in addition to the systematic forms in which it embodies the great facts and pervading laws of nature, which are its peculiar province as a science. The student, who is trained on this admirable method, has the great features of the globe, and all their relations of consequent fact, imprinted forever on his memory. The very inequalities of the earth's surface, become to him an intelligible language, by which he reads the laws of design, and traces effects to causes, with the certainty of distinct recognition. Taught in this manner, few sciences are more adapted to the development of the reflective faculties, in their first steps of advancement from the field of perceptive observation to that of contemplative survey and rational inquiry, or to that of profound scientific investigation. The methods which Professor Guyot has transferred from the lessons of his own distinguished instructor, Carl Ritter, and the views of the patriarch of geographical science, Baron Alexander Von Humboldt, will, it is to be hoped, soon find their way not only into our text-books, in which they are beginning to appear, but into all our seminaries in which the young mind is undergoing the formative processes of education.

History.—Of all the sciences which are naturally fitted to invite the mind to the full exercise of its reflective tendencies, none would seem so happily adapted to this end as *history*. Its records, while they are, in one sense, but forms of memory, are still the records of man moving on his amplest stage of action, as a human being, intelligent, rational, and moral; blending the relations of individual character and social life with those of the national and political sphere,—with the founding the government, or the fall of states and empires.

History, as it necessarily exhibits man in his moral relations, ought to be one of the most instructive and suggestive of studies. If any subject can excite reflective thought, it is this. Its analysis and scrutiny of human character; its investigation into the motives of action, in every form and condition of life; the research, to which it invites, into the manners and customs of by-gone ages; the careful examination which it induces of the testimony of conflicting records; the views which it discloses of national character and institutions; the insight which it gives into the policy of nations, and the influence of different forms of government; all bespeak the tendency of historical studies to evoke the most earnest and profound reflection. The study of history should be, in itself, an effective discipline of the mind, in all the noblest relations of its action. But, here, too, the mere imprinting on the memory a naked record of detached facts, of single events, or striking incidents, or of the items of a chronological table, is the too prevalent law of custom in the requisitions of educational establishments. The life of history, its suggestive power, as a reflective and moral instructor, is thus killed; and, instead of the living form, in its natural lineaments and beauty, we have but a meagre outline of the dry bones of what, in the technical language of historic compilation, is most aptly denominated a "skeleton."

To the mature mind, willing to encounter fatiguing effort, and patiently to add stone to stone of the intellectual fabric, the plan too commonly adopted in the instruction of young learners, of beginning the study of history with a mere outline of dates and events and eras, may prove practicable, though not easy or pleasant. But, to the youthful spirit, the great attraction of this study lies in its pictures of life and action, and in the sympathies which these evoke. To the juvenile reader all history is biography. The policy of nations, the intrigues of state, the strategics of war, are unintelligible and uninteresting to him; and he ignores them, if they intrude upon the narrative. But the feeling and the character and actions of individuals, he understands, and admires or hates, according to the promptings of his unperverted heart. He follows the steps of the historic hero, through all his scenes of struggle and trial, of effort and of triumph; imbibing unconsciously, in the successive stages of this ideal progress, inspiring lessons of wisdom and virtue from all, or listening to the warnings which recorded experience gives on the evils of folly or of vice.

A course of judiciously selected *biography*, should be the educational introduction to the study of history. The interest attached to the personal narrative, accompanies the young student into his reading on the broader scale of national movements and their various consequences; and the life breathed into the study from the character of its earliest stage, gives warmth and attraction to all its more extensive views and complicated relations.

Language, as the product of the expressive faculties, and as a discipline for their development, we had occasion to discuss under that head, in a former lecture. But we have still to do with it as a part of education adapted to the strengthening of the mind's power of reflective investigation. Our common error in this department, as in others, is a too exclusive attention to the acquisition of a certain amount of knowledge of the etymological and syntactical forms of words and phrases,—a knowledge depending entirely on the exercise of memory in retaining or recalling these forms. Through the various stages of education, the attention is too exclusively fixed on these minutiæ of language; and, neither in the study of ancient or of modern languages, nor even in that of our own, is the mind duly attracted to the character of the sentiments embodied in the works of the authors which are read in the progress of education, nor to the broad distinctive traits which form the character of the given language,—to the individuality which a successful writer stamps on it, or to the mental value of the forms of expression which he adopts. *Philology*, a pursuit so peculiarly adapted to the cultivation of the mind's reflective and investigating powers, is cut off from the student till the strong bias of personal taste or inclination induces him to open this mental vista for himself. *Criticism*, too, the art which demands the closest application of reflective judgment, in addition to perfect purity of taste, is handed over to the lessons of some meagre text-book, which does not contain matter enough within its boards for the proper discussion or fitting elucidation of a single principle of æsthetics.

Logic is another science belonging to the more advanced stages of education,—the study of which ought to exert a powerful influence on the tendencies and habits of the reflective faculties, but which is sometimes very inadequately taught even in our higher seminaries of learning. In some of these institutions, it is customary to restrict the study of logic to the ancient Aristotelian form of it, and without the advantage of the scholastic, syllogistic disputations, which, although always formal in character, and sometimes frivolous in result, were yet designed to be rigorously exact exemplifications of pure logical reasoning ; and which, with all their faults and failures, secured, at least, one great practical object of education, by giving the mind active exercise in applying principles, instead of leaving it merely to listen, and remember, and record. It is true that, in some educational establishments, a more liberal view of logic is entertained, and that, in these seminaries, the science is regarded not merely as one which teaches the art of reasoning, but as that which investigates and enunciates the laws of thought, and involves, therefore, a knowledge of the elements of intellectual philosophy, together with the application of all the principles of mental science which affect the exercise of any class of the various powers and faculties of the mind.

An instructive exposition of this view of logic, as the first stage of purely intellectual discipline, is given in the "Outlines of Philosophic Education," by the late Professor Jardine, of Glasgow University, who, for fifty years, conducted, with distinguished success, his course of instruction, on the plan delineated in his work. That eminently skillful teacher,—for he regarded the duties of a professor in his department as consisting quite as much in conducting the practical processes of training exercises, as in the didactic routine of lecturing,—regarded the study of the Aristotelian logic but as a very limited part of intellectual discipline, and, while he allowed it its distinct place and full value, justly maintained that, for the purposes of modern education, which imply so wide and varied applications of thought,—in directions so different from those pursued in ancient times,—the sphere of study must be greatly enlarged beyond the narrow limits of the scholastic discipline, and a course of training prescribed which shall prepare the mind for the new demands made upon its powers, in the new modes of action with which modern science is conversant.

This broader view of logical discipline is fortunately taken by several of our own recent writers on the subject; and the course of instruction is, accordingly, in some seminaries, enlarged so as to embrace the elements of intellectual philosophy, as indispensable to clear and satisfactory views of logic itself, and to the purposes for which the study of logic was originally constituted a department of education. But even in such instances, the young student is not trained to apply the principles embodied in his text-book to an extensive course of practical exemplifications and personal discipline. He is not called to perform any series of practical exercises bearing the same relation to the science of logic that analytic parsing and written composition bear to grammar. He is not trained to trace the logic of great arguments exemplified in the productions of eminent metaphysical writers. He is not disciplined in the digesting and methodizing of his own conceptions on prescribed subjects, so as to give sequence or soundness to argument, and certainty to his own conclusions.

In the study of *intellectual philosophy* we see, too often, another instance of the imperfect learning by book, without the contemplation of the thing itself of which the book treats. Our current instruction, in this department, consists in little more than the assigning of so many pages of a text-book to be committed to memory; and the progress made in the study of the science is judged of by the correctness or the fluency with which the terms employed in the nomenclature of a favorite system can be repeated, rather than by any actual knowledge or personal opinions on the subject itself. The student is not invited to put forth his own mind, in actual investigations on the topics which he studies: he is not permitted to enjoy the benefit of those conversational discussions with his instructor, which might create a living interest in the subject prescribed, and induce the student to prosecute with effect those unaided researches of individual application, without which knowledge is not to be acquired, or truth ascertained.

In the department of *moral philosophy*, a subject so peculiarly adapted to the development and discipline of the reflective faculties, we find, usually, the same mechanical routine of book-study and recitation adopted. In this highest relation of human instruction, the mind is still left passive and receptive merely; while there is no subject on which original, vigorous, and personal thought is so important to the acquisition of principle or the formation of character. Here, more than anywhere else, living, eloquent instruction from the man, rather than the book, is indispensable to the production of deep and enduring impressions of truth, and the exciting of hearty sympathy with its applications. Here, too, more than elsewhere, is the active use of the student's own mind necessary to the results of true culture on personal habit and character. His own investigations, and his own record of these, ought to be required of him, as the only rational benefit of the guidance afforded by a text-book or a teacher. Conversation and writing would throw life into these subjects, and make them matters of personal interest and personal conviction to the individual; and the fruits of education would thus be more extensively reaped in the experience of society.

APPROPRIATE METHODS OF DISCIPLINE.—We will now turn from the consideration of the subjects which form the usual material for the education and development of the reflective faculties, to the more immediate contemplation of those faculties themselves, with regard to their natural wants and appropriate aids ; and, first, as regards the faculty of

Memory.—In the fact of *muscular* action, the power to retain depends on the firmness of the original *grasp.* The analogy holds in the exercise of memory : the retentive or repeating power depends on the depth of the impression: concentrated and sustained attention is the condition of remembrance. If we would strengthen the memory, we must cultivate force of attention. The indication of nature to the teacher, in this case, obviously is, Select for the mind's first exercises, striking or attractive objects of attention, or interesting subjects of thought. For more advanced stages of mental progress, when accuracy demands comparative minuteness and multiplicity of uninteresting detail, rely on the moral force of the will and disciplined habit, to give closeness and persistency to attention. In all cases, keep fully in mind the great value of mere *repetition* and frequent *review,* without which all ordinary subjects of past thought are ever tending to sink into dimness and obscurity, and, ultimately, into utter forgetfulness.

Mechanical aids to memory may sometimes appear very plausible ; and they often are very amusing temporary expedients. But they actually destroy memory, by setting it aside, and usurping its place. The physiologist tells us that if we omit the due use of the teeth, we forfeit the possession of them. The fact is strictly so of memory. The juggling tricks of perverted ingenuity may seem to conjure up a substitute for the sound and healthy exercise of this faculty. But the subject of the experiment, in this as in all other forms of charlatanry, finds himself, in the end, the victim of deception.

Memory, when employed on subjects comparatively complex, or intricate in their relations, finds its surest reliance,—next to close and fixed attention,—to consist in the grand universal law of *order.* *Arrangement, classification, system, method,* are powerful auxiliaries to memory, as they all tend, more or less, to give sequence to thought, by the law of causation, in the closest connection of antecedent and consequent. One stage of thought thus suggests another ; and the machinery of memory, so to speak, works smoothly and well. The security for remembrance or for recollection, in such circumstances, lies, of course, in the clearness with which connections and relations are perceived, and the fidelity with which they are observed. A treacherous memory is often but the report of unfaithful observation or dim conception.

Habits of Conception dependent on those of Perception.—*Conception,* as a primary power of reflective intelligence, performing for the relations of pure intellection, the same office with that of *perception*, in the exercise of the understanding on the objects of *sensation*, depends, to a great extent, on the character and habits of the *perceptive* faculty. The *relations* which the *conceptive* power discerns between the objects and facts, presented to it by the ministrations of sense, constitute the condition of *intelligent observation*, as differing from mere *ocular aspection*. But these relations necessarily derive much of their reality and force from the vividness of the sensation and the clearness of the understanding, which have attracted *attention* to the external phenomena, and thus have elicited the conceptive acts of mind by which the relations perceived and understood become the ground-work of *reflection* and *meditation*, leading in turn to farther processes of thought, inductive or deductive, as investigation may require.

Clear, forcible and true *perceptions*, therefore, are requisite antecedents of corresponding qualities in *conception* ; and a sound and active condition of the latter depends on similar conditions and habits of the former;—just as healthy *sensation* is, in turn, the pre-requisite of distinct *perception*. We are thus again referred, in adopting educational measures for strengthening and developing the mind's conceptive power, to the attentive observation of external nature, as the proper commencement of early mental training; as the only security, also, for the vigor of all those faculties which aid the mind in digesting and assimilating to itself, by purely internal operations, the materials of knowledge acquired through the action of sense, for the purpose of being incorporated into the mental fabric. We are, at the same time, reminded of the great fact, of which education should never lose sight, that, whatever be the number of faculties into which the intellectual philosopher may, in his scientific analysis, subdivide the action of the mind, or whatever may be the personified individuality which the figurative language of popular usage may arbitrarily confer on any one mode of mental action,—to distinguish it from others,—the principle of intelligence is strictly a *unit;* that it is the *same* agent, whether contemplating the external world through the windows of sense, or looking inward upon itself, and interpreting its own action. In both circumstances, we recognize a voluntary act of attention, followed by an apprehensive or a comprehensive act of understanding. In either case, *intelligence* is the power at work; *knowledge* is the *immediate*, and *truth* the *final* result.

Conception as dependent on Memory and Imagination.—Under the term. " conception," however, in the vague usage to which the English language is unfortunately prone, in all subjects purely intellectual, we usually include states or acts of *memory* and of *imagination*. Nor is it to be denied that the conceptive faculty is often called into action on data furnished by *memory*, as well as on those presented by *sense* or by *reason*. To vivify and invigorate the power of conception, therefore, in such relations, we are admonished to pursue the same course of exercise and discipline by which that faculty is rendered prompt and retentive. Whatever we succeed in doing to improve the *memory*, becomes thus a gain to the power of *conception*.

Again, the prevalent use of language refers many of our conceptive acts to forms of *imagination*. The astronomer, speaking of the sun, tells us of its dark, central body,—of its first layer or substratum of cloudy atmosphere,—of its photosphere, or luminous atmosphere, and of yet a third rarer element, ethereal and slightly colored,—as to the character of which, science is somewhat perplexed with uncertainty. The conceptive power of the mind enables us, in this case, to follow the entrancing description as the scientific observer, aided by the many appliances which modern instruments provide, proceeds with his verified observations; and, with wondering attention, we draw on the tablet of imagination the successive images which his graphic but exact expressions suggest: we see, with the mind's eye, the sun-world, and its enfolding atmospheres, as distinctly in our consciousness as if we surveyed them with eye or "optic tube."

Correctness of Conception.—Even in such cases, however, the truthfulness and the distinctness of the mental picture depend, to a great extent, on the exactness of its correspondence to fact, as regards not only the forms but the character of objects, and the relations existing between them. Here, again, we are referred to the working of the intelligent principle in the modes which we denominate *understanding* and *judgment*, without which the whole structure erected in the mind would be as the poet's "baseless fabric of a vision."

In educational training, therefore, while every endeavor should be used to vivify and incite *imagination*, and to awaken it to its utmost activity by appropriate exercise, with a view to the vast power which that faculty confers on conception, as a creative energy of mind; and while all the aids which nature, art, and poetry, offer to this end, should be fully employed; there remains yet a task for education to perform, in inuring the conceptive faculty to the discipline of *reason* and *judgment*, so as to render it exact, and truthful, and symmetrical, in all its work.

The means by which the mind is to be formed to such habits in its conceptive action, are evidently the same which we would employ for developing and strengthening the reasoning powers: first, *the interesting presentation* of the objects and facts of the *natural* world,—so as to elicit thought and reflection on their character and relations; secondly, the *teacher's* skillful *suggestion*, designed to aid the observer in tracing those relations to principles and laws of logical science; and, thirdly, the careful training of the mind to *the contemplation of its own action*, to the critical inspection and exact *discrimination of the results* of its action, and to the thorough *investigation of the laws of thought*, applied to the quest of truth.

CONSCIOUSNESS :—*as an aid to Reflective Reason*.—Of the reflective conditions of mind which tend to give accuracy to knowledge, or certainty to truth, none is more conducive to such results than that of *consciousness*. Not that it necessarily constitutes a separate power or faculty; (since it is plainly but an act of introverted attention, by which the mind becomes aware of its existing states, acts, or processes;) but rather that it is a mental condition distinctly recognized in all the languages of civilized man, and implies the power which the intelligent principle possesses of holding up, in distinct vision to itself, its own acts and operations;—whether these refer to the external world of perception or the interior world of thought. This power of self-observation, when the attention is directed to relations purely intellectual, is necessarily the condition and the measure of force with which the mind pursues its trains of reflection, traces the invisible relations of sequence, or follows the continuous processes of meditation, in the prosecution of those profound researches which the depth and intricacy of scientific or moral truth not unfrequently require.

Its Susceptibility of Culture.—In the relations of moral culture, this faculty,—so to term it,—works in so close and intimate union with the great master principle of *conscience*, that its importance as a fact of mind demanding the earnest attention of the educator, in his capacity of moral guardian, is, at once, apparent. On that department of our subject we do not, at present, dwell, as it will invite our attention hereafter, in its proper place. But, as an intellectual condition, subject, to some extent, to the action of the will, and to the influence of disciplinary exercise, it is obvious that conciousness or self-observation, may, like any other power which the mind possesses, be rendered vivid, prompt, and operative, by repeated action.

Man commences his intellectual and moral life an *unconscious* agent, in the unknown and wonderful world around him, in childhood. He is as utterly unconscious of the influences exerted on himself as he is ignorant of the true character and relations of the objects by which he is surrounded. Absorbed in the contemplation of the broad field of the external world, or in the observation of its objects individually, he is lost alike to the consciousness of his own being, and to that of

CULTIVATION OF THE REFLECTIVE FACULTIES. 139

the effects which are wrought within him by these very objects. Drawn onward by an unconscious power of attraction, he follows the study of nature, in obedience to an instinct of which he is not yet aware, but which, by leading him out of himself, conducts him to the school of *observation*, where knowledge commences, and from which he, in due season, returns, empowered by the instruction he has received to *observe* and *understand himself*.

As his nobler powers mature, they begin to work on the data which observation has furnished; and, as he examines, he thinks, he compares, he reflects, he reasons; he becomes aware of a more powerful influence and a deeper satisfaction than that of mere observation, while he consciously follows his successive conceptions, and meditates not only on the relations of object to object, and of effect to cause, in the outward universe, but on the yet more wonderful and mysterious action of his own inward being, to the conciousness of which he is now fully awakened. This newly-discovered world attracts his attention with a yet greater force and intensity of interest than that of the external sphere, in which he has hitherto moved; and the growing strength of his intellect, he finds, is more fully exerted and more decidedly proved in this inner region of its action, than in the outer field of sense and perception. He delights, accordingly, in this conscious exercise of a higher power, and recognizes the nobility of reason.

Such is man's progress, even when little assisted by the formal aids of education. But we see thus more clearly how judicious and skillful training may render conciousness comparatively *vivid*, *definite*, and *distinct*, by aiding, with appropriate appliances of exercise and discipline, this capability of reflective contemplation, of self-intelligence, and of self-development, which grows with the growth, and strengthens with the strength of the maturing mind. If this power is permitted to lie neglected and undeveloped, the result is uniformly a characteristic dullness, obscurity, and vagueness in the mind's habitual action. This fact we recognize, in full exemplification, when we contrast the uncultivated, half-conscious child, youth, or man, with the well-educated and the self-intelligent.

Mode of Culture.—Subjected to processes of cultivation, however, this faculty, like memory, can not be brought under the law of direct action. *Memory* is to be reached through *attention*; to enliven and strengthen the former, we must work upon the latter. We have no more power over it, separately, than we have over the reflection of an object in a mirror. Memory is the reflection of attention. We can not render the image distinct, unless the object is so. The same is true of *consciousness*. It has no separate or independent existence

It is, so to speak, the mind's reflection of itself; it is but an act of attention directed inward. The vividness, the definiteness, and the distinctness of consciousness, are,—as the corresponding properties in the act of attention,—blended with the consentaneous force of will coöperating in the act. In this latter circumstance, its action differs from that of memory, which is often, even in its most vivid delineations, wholly involuntary. But the depth and fullness of consciousness are always dependent, more or less, on the force of the will which directs the act of attention inward. It is thus rendered more perceptibly a subject of culture by educational training.

Morbid Unconsciousness.—To some minds the intellectual and moral value of habits of wakeful consciousness, is very great from, perhaps, some defect of organization or fault of habit, inclining the individual to a half-dreamy condition of *reverie*, in which the mind loses power over its own action, and becomes lost amid the scenes of memory or of imagination. To the artist and the poet, an intensity of abstracted attention is, in some relations, the condition of imaginative power of conception and of living expression. But, in such cases, the mind is healthy, vigorous, and voluntary, in its action: it is obeying one of its own highest laws, which demands this almost superhuman power of abstracted and concentrated attention, for the contemplation and embodiment of ideal images of perfection. The abstractedness and "absence of mind," on the other hand, which become habitual from neglect, are nothing else than a *morbid unconsciousness* indulged,—a result of organic or mental *weakness*, and a habit utterly destructive of voluntary power of attention or depth of thought. In some mournful instances, it is the sure precursor of insanity.

In all circumstances, the tendency of such habits is to cherish a morbid preponderance of imagination over reason and judgment, and to create a dreamy twilight of thought, in preference to the clear light of intellectual day. Listlessness of attention, and dullness of understanding, and every other evil of mental torpor, are thus entailed on the intellectual character.

Cultivation of the Reasoning Faculty.—The principle of reflective intelligence assumes, in the language of recognized usage, the various forms of action implied in the terms *understanding, judgment, reason;* and this triple denomination suggests also the progressive measures adopted in education, for the cultivation of this master power of intellect.

Understanding, as the primary act and condition of intelligence, is involved in every instance of *perception,* even in the cognizance of the mere form and character of outward objects; in the contemplation of facts, its aid is indispensable to the *apprehension* of their connections and relations; and, in the tracing of these, its assistance is requisite to enable the mind to arrive at the *comprehension* of principles and causes. When the mind is unable to put forth this prehensile, (*seizing, grasping, holding,*) power, we say, in current phrase, the connection, the principle, the cause, or the relation, is "not understood." Reverting to the etymological signification of the term, by which this faculty is designated, we observed that the action of the "understanding" was represented as a necessary *ground*, or *foundation*, without which, of course, there could be no superstructure of thought or knowledge. In the terms now introduced, which denote the two chief forms of action in the process of understanding, the figurative suggestion is not less forcible or appropriate, than in the former instance. The uninformed understanding, is, in the latter case, represented as the *powerless hand*, which is not put forth, which does not lay hold on its object, or which lets it slip.

Natural Development of the Understanding.—The appropriate training of this fundamental faculty of the mind is distinctly indicated to the educator in the first natural workings of intellect in childhood. The inciting principle of curiosity impels the child to observe and to learn. But he is not satisfied with the mere knowledge of the external character of objects; he is eagerly desirous to understand their internal construction, and hence he tears open, and pulls to pieces, even the flower which delights him; and the indulgent father knows that it needs a sharp eye to keep the little investigator from practicing a similar experiment on a gold watch.

Educational Development.—That spirit of inquisition which is implanted in the mind, to secure its progressive development, renders the examination and inspection of objects, for the discovery of their internal structure and character, an exercise still more attractive and inviting to a child than that of the perception even of beauty in form or color; and the investigation of the connection and relations of phenomena and of facts, yields him a deeper gratification than the delight arising from the recognition of any merely exterior trait of character in outward objects. Here, then, is the proper place where to commence the training of the understanding to the exercise of true apprehension and full comprehension, in the acquisition of a thorough knowledge of the objects by which the child is naturally surrounded, and of their relations to one another, in mutual adaptation, or in cause and effect. Perception is thus transmuted into knowledge; without which transition there is no intellectual progress. The understanding of relations is the mediating process by which object is linked to object, fact to fact, and relation to relation ; till knowledge, in its turn, becomes the completed chain of principle and truth, in the relations of system and science.

Practical Exercises.—One of the most hopeful indications of the general progress of opinion on the subject of education, is afforded in the comparatively recent introduction into primary schools of lessons on *objects,*—not merely the productions of nature in animal and vegetable and mineral form, but the common objects of observation in the child's daily notice at home and in school, in the street, and in the workshop. The young mind is thus strengthened, while it is gratified, by the exercise of tracing design and adaptation in the various contrivances of mechanical ingenuity. The conscious understanding of relations and processes, becomes to the mind what the expanding and enlivening influence of light is to the plant; while the self-intelligent agent enjoys the double pleasure of growth and the consciousness of it. Understanding, as the mind's prehensile and digestive power, appropriates to itself the material of its own life and strength, and quickens and expands with every acquisition, till it reaches the culminating point of the full maturity and vigor of a well-developed capacity.

Observation of the processes of Nature.—Next to the study of the elementary principles and application of mechanics, as a means of enlightening and invigorating the understanding by disciplinary exercises in tracing combination and operations to their causes, should come appropriate exercises in watching and tracing *the great processes of nature, daily* passing before the learner's observation, and inviting him to the study of those larger displays of power and intelligence, which are exhibited in the mechanism of the worlds moving in space, and obeying the laws of time.

The *chemistry* of nature, too, should be made to furnish ample employment for the exercise of the understanding, in tracing the curious relations which that vast department of knowledge discloses. No science has more power than chemistry to stimulate curiosity, and provoke inquiry, and thus invite the mind to penetrate the mysteries of nature, and evolve the hidden causes and secret influences at work in phenomena, which the mind can not contemplate without the feeling of wonder, and which, at first, seem to baffle the power of intelligence ; but through which the prying eye of the understanding learns, ere long, to penetrate, in the inquest of relations by which mystery is solved and difficulty explained. A simple elementary course of experiments, in this department of science, by the light which it sheds on common phenomena, exerts a great power over the young mind;—suggesting inquiries and leading to investigations which call the understanding into wakeful and vigorous action on all facts accessible to observation. The teacher, who is true to his office, as guardian of the young mind, and who takes pleasure in aiding the formation of habits of intelligence and inquiry, will spare neither time, nor trouble, nor expense, in his endeavors to secure to his pupils the benefit of such aids to their intellectual culture.

Combined Exercises of Understanding and Judgment: Arithmetic. In the department of mathematical science, there is no lack of attention to the study of *arithmetic*, as an important branch of exercise and discipline for the reflective faculties, in the relations of the understanding operating on numbers. In this branch of culture, the purely mental processes first introduced by Pestalozzi, and transferred to American schools by the late Warren Colburn, have let in a flood of light not only on the subject of arithmetic, as an instrument of intellectual discipline, but on the whole field of education, and on all the details of methods of instruction, as regards the principles of rational and genial development applied to the human mind. Whatever may be the case elsewhere, there are few schools, in New England at least, in which arithmetic is not philosophically and successfully taught; and the vast improvement, or rather the entire renovation of the character of our primary schools, since the introduction of Colburn's method, may well suggest to the thoughtful teacher the immense amount of benefit which would certainly follow corresponding changes in other departments of education.

Geometry.—Another branch of mathematics admirably adapted to the cultivation of the mind's reflective and reasoning powers, when applied to external relations, and one which forms, by its very nature, the vestibule to all the other apartments of the great temple of knowledge, has not commonly met with that attention or that place which its importance requires. Geometry is too commonly deferred till a late stage, comparatively, in the progress of education; and it is, for the most part, taught abstractly, commencing with its *linear* forms. But the few teachers who have ventured to break away from the trammels of routine and prescription, and who have taken their suggestion from the obvious fact that, even in early childhood, the mind is delighted with the observation of definite forms in all their simple varieties, and that, at this stage of progress, form exists only in the visible and tangible concrete, and not in the abstract,—the few teachers who have here followed nature's course, and allowed the young learner to commence an easy elementary and practical study of geometry in its relation to *solid* objects, have found no difficulty arising from permitting children to commence their attention to this branch of knowledge at a very early age, and to unspeakable advantage, as regards the exactness of mental habit which this mode of discipline so peculiarly tends to form.

From the observation and study of the *solid*, the transition is rational, natural and easy to the consideration and examination of its *surface;* and here another wide field of thought is opened to the mind of the juvenile learner,—yet one which is perfectly practicable to his faculties, and which he can always submit to actual survey and ocular measurement. With the solid body in his hand, the little student finds it an easy and a pleasing step to proceed from the contemplation of the *surface*, to that of its "*edges,*" as he calls the boundary *lines* of the surface; and here still another delightful scope of observation opens to his mind, as he proceeds to compare line with line, and, applying the definite and exact relations of number, learns to *measure*, and thus to give certainty and precision to his observations, and accuracy to his conceptions.

General Effects of Mathematical Discipline.—In the more advanced stages of education, the modes of instruction in the department of mathematics, are, from the nature of the subject, of a character so definite and comparatively immutable as to suggest methods and forms of exercise uniform and sure. Hence, the admirable results secured by the discipline to which the reasoning powers are subjected in the prosecution of these studies. The value of mathematical training consists, chiefly, in the exactness of attention and discrimination, and in the orderly procedure of thought required in the processes which it prescribes, and, consequently, in the correctness of conception and accuracy of judgment thus attained in the habits of the mind. Another invaluable advantage of mathematical studies, connected more immediately, however, with their advanced stages of mental application, consists in the extent and scope of their operations, combined with the perfect sequence of every step in their procedure, and the confidence which they serve to create in the mind's own action, by the certainty of its conclusions.

The main duty of the teacher, in this department of education, lies, from the very character of the subject, in watching carefully the mind's first steps in the earliest stages of exercise; so as to see to it that the perfect rigor of intellectual discipline is attained, which mathematical science is designed to produce, that there be no yielding to juvenile impatience, tending to laxity of attention, careless assumption, heedless oversight, and unconscious inaccuracy of mental habit. In more advanced stages of progress, the successive branches of the subject afford, by their own intrinsic character, a comparative security for correctness in the processes of evolution, and especially in the case of all students whose first steps have been carefully watched.

Common Mistake.—There is an opinion somewhat prevalent, even among those who have the control of education, that the certainty of mathematical reasoning, depending on the peculiar character of the grounds on which it rests, has but little effect on the formation of accurate habits of judgment in relations which have no firmer foundation than matters of opinion, or of taste, or of metaphysical inquiry. But, in this view of the question, the inevitable influence of the law of *analogy* on the constitution and habits of the mind is overlooked. The educational effect of any study lies not so much in the specific character of the subject, or the particular exercises of intellect which any one of its processes requires, as in the analogous tendencies and habits which the given exercise contributes to form. The perfect precision of observation, the scrupulous correctness of judgment, and the strict sequence of thought, which mathematical operations demand, are invaluable aids to every process of mind in which the reasoning faculties are employed. A disproportioned excess of attention to mathematics in the assignments of education, may, certainly, be chargeable on the plan of intellectual culture adopted in many seminaries of learning, and, particularly, of such as are devoted to the mental training of the female sex. But this mistake, like that of attempting the exposition of moral truth by mathematical forms of reasoning, does not prove any want of adaptation in mathematics to the design and purpose of intellectual discipline on kindred subjects, or in the results of such discipline in the formation of mental habits and character.

Logical and Critical Discipline.—Of the great importance of a thorough practical logic, for the discipline of the reasoning faculties,—a course comprising processes of strict personal training in the art of thinking,—we have had occasion to speak, under other heads of our present investigation, and on this topic we need not now enlarge.

Another department of higher mental culture, the art of *criticism*, was briefly adverted to, on a former occasion. As one of the highest forms in which reason can be applied, and as the ground-work of all true discipline of imagination and taste, it claims a large share of attention in educational training. But, to render this department of study truly beneficial, it needs a thorough revision and enlargement of its plan. As generally adopted in our seminaries of learning, it is made to consist too much of processes of training by which the mental eye is sharpened for the perception of *error* and the detection of *defect.* This is but the negative part of critical discipline, and is chiefly directed to the faults of others, rather than those of the observer himself; while, as a forming and moulding process, its chief benefit would lie in its efficacy in training the mind to the perception and recognition of *positive beauty* and *perfection*, and in forming the tastes and habits of the individual by a strict but genial *preventive* discipline, which should preclude the tendency to deviation from the principles of beauty and truth. To secure the results of such discipline, a liberal course of early training, directed to the intelligent recognition of beauty in nature and in art,—as was suggested in a former lecture,—becomes an indispensable foundation. The reasoning, on the data thus furnished, would necessarily become positive and practical. The mind would proceed under the sure guidance of ascertained principle; and the canons, so called, of criticism, would have an authority more sure than merely the speculative opinions of an individual, or of a class of theorizers. But, so far are we, as yet, from a truly liberal standard of education, that in all our higher seminaries, scarcely can we find a place assigned to any course of *æsthetic* study or training. Yet no species of discipline could be prescribed so admirably adapted to the generous development of the powers of judgment and reason, as that critical exercise by which the mind, in the analysis and combination of the elements of beauty, learns to interpret to its own consciousness the laws of grace and of harmony.

Philosophical Training.—The principles of *intellectual* and *moral philosophy*, we have already adverted to, as peculiarly adapted to the discipline of the *reflective* faculties. The great facts which the mind recognizes in contemplating the principles of the former of these branches of science, and the vital truths which it evolves in tracing the relations of the latter to the former, call for the exercise of reason and judgment on materials purely mental, and, by their very nature, fitted to train the mind to habits of close investigation and nice discrimination. On these habits is the mind's whole reliance to be placed in tracing the subtle distinctions on which the eviction of the profoundest truths not unfrequently depends.

On such subjects, as also in relation to logic and criticism, it was suggested, in a former connection of our subject, that education should be rendered more personal and practical in its methods; that it should comprise, in its measures for discipline, the mental efforts of the student himself in thought, conversation and discussion, rather than the mere endeavor to retain in memory the definitions and statements of a text-book.

Civic Training.—The study of civil polity, as it comprehends subjects collateral to history and to ethics, forms a theme well-suited to the exercise of the mind's reflective powers, by the trains of thought to which it naturally leads. As a branch of education, it should be extended to an attentive survey of all the political relations of human society, as embodied in forms of government, in national constitutions, in international law, in civil institutions. Independently of the value of such investigations to the intelligent discharge of the duties of life, in all countries favored with constitutional immunities, the class of subjects now mentioned is of the utmost moment in the higher relations of education, as affording large scope and full exercise for the reasoning powers, in the investigations and discussions to which such subjects naturally invite the mind of the student. The discipline, however, resulting from this branch of studies, depends, obviously, on the extent to which it is made a matter of personal thought, of written dissertations, and of oral discussion, on the part of the student. In this, as in other departments of ethical science, our colleges would do well to arrange their exercises on the model of the debating society, or of the moot-courts of professional schools; so as to elicit voluntary mental action and effective coöperation on the part of students in their own education. The random exercises of debating clubs, as they are commonly conducted, in which little or no systematic preparation is made for discussion, do not serve such a purpose. For educational influences, careful premeditation and critical supervision are equally necessary to render discussion an appropriate discipline.

Natural Theology forms another branch of study peculiarly fitted to call forth and improve the reflective and reasoning powers of the mind. Every new advance of science gives additional attractions to this ennobling theme of contemplation. The profound thought to which it leads, the large analogies which it reveals, the great truths which it urges home to the mind, the sublime heights to which it conducts aspiring reason,—all indicate the high value of this branch of philosophic investigation, as an effective means of enlarging and invigorating the noblest faculties with which man is invested.

The subject of natural theology is, by no means, neglected in our customary routine of studies, either in schools or colleges. It is carefully designated on the programme of instruction, and regularly assigned to a definite term of the course. But restricted, as the attention given to these subjects generally is, to recitation from a formal text-book, little of the peculiar effect of personal investigation into them is felt on the mind at the time, or marked on the subsequent mental character of the student. Personal examination, and actual analysis and manipulation, are as much needed in the illustrations which serve to throw light on the subject of natural theology as they are in the study of any other branch of science. The actual, ocular inspection of objects, is felt to be the only means of effective instruction in all other subjects which require the verification of principle by reference to fact. Without the aid of such practical measures, the best of text-books becomes dry or tedious, and, at all events, fails of exciting the earnest attention and personal interest which secure the energetic action of the whole mind, give life and vigor to its habits of action, and insure the further prosecution of inquiry in after stages of life.

To secure an earnest voluntary application to this noble study is not difficult, if the instructor take pains to invite his students to personal investigation of the numberless evidences of Divine power, wisdom, and goodness, which are furnished in every department of nature. The pleasure of observing, recording, and reporting these, is one to which the teacher who will faithfully make the experiment will find few minds so torpid as to be insensible.

Evidences of Christianity.—This subject, too, has its appointed place in our seminaries of learning; and that it is a study required in our higher schools for the female sex, as well as in our colleges, is a happy indication. But, the unintellectual, unmeaning process of reciting merely the paragraphs of a text-book, has the same injurious effect in this as in other departments of education. No subject can be presented to the mind on which the importance of clear and distinct views, or deep impressions and personal convictions of truth, are so important to the student, as on this;—none on which the utmost rigor of deduction, the closest investigation, the most cautious induction, are so imperatively demanded. The mere verbatim committing to memory, or even the careful recapitulation, of the arguments presented in the best of manuals, is a process too passive for any valuable purpose of educational influence on the individual. The second-hand knowledge thus acquired, makes too slight an impression to become a permanent personal possession; as the experienced teacher has sometimes cause to feel most deeply, when he sees a promising youth, who has recited his way successfully through a whole manual of "evidences," so easily caught and entangled in the slight web of superficial and sophistical arguments offered by a fluent fellow-student, inclined to skeptical habits of thought.

The result is quite different when the instructor prescribes, not the mere language or reasoning of a single author, but a careful comparison of several, and a *resumé* prepared by the student himself, together with a full statement of objections, and the arguments by which these are rebutted. A still deeper impression is made on the mind of the individual, when such recapitulations are made, not only in the regular form of writing, but in that also of deliberate, correct, and, if possible, earnest oral expression. It is thus only that great and vital truths can be woven into the texture of his own mind, and become, as it were, inseparable parts of itself.

Practical Exercises.—In conclusion of these suggestions regarding the development and discipline of the reflective faculties, a few other forms of practical exercise may deserve attention, as matters which devolve on the personal action and diligence of the teacher,—in regard to the aid which his living instructions and intelligent supervision ought to furnish, in addition to the customary course prescribed in manuals or text-books; and here we may advert to the great value of

(1.) *Systematic Reading*, as a means of cultivating reflective and thoughtful habits of mind,—reading, I mean, which is *study*, and not mere *perusal;* reading which is attentively done, carefully reviewed, exactly recorded, and, if practicable, orally recounted. Memory, under such discipline, becomes thoroughly retentive, information exact, judgment correct, conception clear, thought copious, and expression ready and appropriate.

(2.) An important aid to systematic reading may be found in the exercise of writing a careful, marginal *synopsis* of valuable works, comprising all their principal *topics*, distinctly presented, and, in addition to this, a penciled *analysis* of every prominent head or paragraph into its constituent subordinate *details*. In the case of standard works of great value and permanent authority, it may be worth while to draught a separate *plan* of the entire *work* under study, in which the synopsis and the analysis are so arranged to the eye, that the advantage of a mental map of the whole subject is secured for distinct and easy recollection, by the union of logical and ocular method.

(3.) As a means of training the faculty of *judgment* to correctness in its decisions, and exactness in discrimination, exercises in *analysis*, on every description of material, are of the greatest value. In the earliest stages of education, these may be performed, to great advantage, on objects in *nature*, particularly on the structure and organization of plants, with the aid, too, of the microscope. At a more advanced stage, the analysis of *language*, successively extending to sentences, clauses, phrases, words, and syllables, in written as well as oral forms, is another exercise of great value for sharpening the power of discrimination and forming habits of correct judgment. Still greater benefit attends the oral analysis of *discourses*, essays, and other didactic compositions, for the purpose of tracing their authors' trains of thought, following these in detail, and afterward recording the analysis, as has been already suggested.

(4.) To cultivate successfully the reasoning faculty, no method more effectual can be adopted than that of training the mind to a perfect observance of the prime law of *Order*. This great principle comes to the aid of the young mind, as creative ordination applied to chaos. The countless multitude and variety of objects soliciting observation, in the early years of childhood, and even at much later stages, often throw the mind into confusion and perplexity, till *order* comes to its aid, and, like the benevolent fairy in the fable, *arranges* the complicated masses and irregular accumulations, and lets in the light of *system* and *method* upon the elements of the mental world. Conflicting objects and relations are thus parted by due *distinction ;* accordant elements and phenomena are grouped together, by their *analogies* and *affinities*, their *connections* and *dependencies*, the *predominance* of some and the *subordination* of others ; till, at length, the authority of *Law* is recognized, and harmony established.

To attain this result, *Reason*, the supreme ordaining faculty, has to exert its power in various modes of operation. *Judgment*, as reason's executive, has to *collate, examine, compare, associate, combine* and *classify* the objects of observation and the subjects of consciousness. For such purposes no exercises can be better adapted than those which commence with the action of the *perceptive* faculties, and yet involve the use of the *reflective*, to a certain extent. Nature's great systems, in her three vast kingdoms, furnish, of course, the best material for such exercise and discipline of the mind, by combining with its perceptive action the aid of reflecting reason, in the contemplation and study of the vast domain of creation. As a noble discipline for the rational faculties, in their ascendancy over those of outward observation, and yet in perfect harmony and coöperation with them, no exercise can be more beneficial than that of surveying, in the light of *science*, the elements and forms of external nature. An illustration in point may be found in the science of *botany*, which is now rendered so generally accessible and so highly attractive, by recent manuals presenting this subject on the "natural" system, as an instructive and interesting branch of knowledge for all minds. Another example occurs in the arrangement of the *animal* kingdom presented by Cuvier, and modified by our great contemporary naturalist, Agassiz. The generous labors of this distinguished instructor, in his endeavors to bring his favorite subject before the minds of teachers, in forms happily adapted to the condition of their schools, have afforded the best suggestions for conducting appropriate exercises in this department of education. And it is to be hoped that many of our seminaries will henceforward enjoy the benefits of the admirable mental discipline resulting from those habits of attentive observation, careful examination, and close analysis, as well as those of orderly arrangement, enlarged contemplation, and systematic classification, which the thorough study of nature is so happily adapted to insure.

But it should never be forgotten by the teacher that it is the extent to which the student is induced to carry the *personal observation* and *actual collection* of natural objects, and the care and fidelity with which he arranges his specimens according to the requirements of scientific classification, which determine how far the higher powers of his mind will be benefited by the study. There are too many seminaries, even now, in which the teacher, far from following the instructive personal example of the eminent authority to whom we have just referred, and joining their students in the actual exploration of nature, in the field exercises of observing and collecting, permit them to stay within doors, and "study" the whole subject by book.

The value of personal observation and actual investigation, as the only sure means of rendering the educational materials furnished in external nature, and in the action of the percipient intellect on these, conducive to the development and discipline of the mind's reflective power, is evinced in all the other relations and departments of physical science. The study of *astronomy*, as commonly conducted in our seminaries of all grades, has been, till recently, a process of mere bookwork, of committing to memory the successive sentences of a manual, and repeating them by word of mouth. The actual observation of the heavens was a thing not thought of but as a matter of occasional gratification to curiosity; while, to render astronomy an effective instrument of mental culture, capable of awakening attention and eliciting reflection, the nightly survey of the varying aspects of the firmament, in conjunction with the passing hours, and the actual positions, or apparent shifting of the planetary bodies, should be continued till the eye finds itself, so to speak, at home in that upper world of wondrous facts, and the observer can literally "call the stars by name."

Many teachers have it easily in their power to render the young mind this noble service, which may stamp a thoughtful character on its habits of action for a whole life-time. Happily, many of our colleges are now enabled to offer to those who enjoy the superior opportunities of study afforded by such seminaries, the facilities for actual observation, which modern science and art so amply provide, in this department of education. But, in most of our higher schools and academies,—even in some which are favored with the possession and occasional use of a telescope,—the actual study of the heavens, even with the naked eye, or the humblest endeavor to note the position and movements of the heavenly bodies, so as to enable the learner intelligently to read the sky, remains, as yet, a thing seldom attempted.

Were early education in this department rightly conducted, the young student would be prepared to receive with delight those sublime revelations of astronomical science which exhibit the laws of order and subordination,—of mutual influence and adjustment,—ruling in the apparent " wilderness of worlds," and indicating the controlling power of that Reason which presides in eternal supremacy over the universe.

Concluding Explanations.

The brief and imperfect survey of the ground and principles of intellectual culture, which is here concluded, was, as has been intimated, originally presented in the form of conversational oral lectures to successive classes of young teachers and of persons intending to enter on the occupation of teaching. The views presented in these lectures were adapted, therefore, to the mental circumstances of students to some of whom any form of systematic investigation on the subject of intellectual discipline was wholly new, and to many of whom the philosophy of education was, as yet, a field unexplored. This fact will serve to explain the strictly elementary character of the preceding discussion, and the familiar style of its illustrations, as well as the frequent iteration of special topics; while the vast importance of the subject itself, in relation to the anticipated office and duties of the teacher, as the educator and guardian of the young mind, together with the acknowledged too general neglect of such considerations, rendered it necessary that the lecturer should endeavor to present the whole work of education in the impressive light of the highest relations and principles of human action.

To some of the readers of this journal, therefore, the whole series of these lectures may have seemed common-place and uninteresting; and to others the course of analysis may have seemed too abstract and philosophical for the ordinary purposes and business of education. The contributor of this and the preceding communications of the series to the pages of this journal can only plead, in answer to both classes of objections, that, for many years, his personal field of observation and of action has made it necessary for him to endeavor to meet the wants of ingenuous minds, conscious of deficiencies in their own course of early training, and earnestly desirous of the guiding light of the simplest, yet the highest, educational principles, to direct their own efforts for the advancement of others. Successive years, occupied in three of our New England States, in endeavoring to aid the noble aspirations of those whose daily labors form the ground of the

CULTIVATION OF THE REFLECTIVE FACULTIES. 153

intellectual and moral hope of the community, have convinced the writer that the teacher's professional wants are most satisfactorily met when elementary principles of education are simply stated and practically illustrated, and the highest relations of human duty are presented as the motives to personal and professional action.—Long may the "plain living and high thinking" of their ancestry continue to characterize the teachers of New England!

The allusions made, in the course of the preceding discussion, to existing defects in "higher" seminaries, might seem uncalled for in a course of remarks addressed to young teachers. To explain this apparent intrusion, it may be sufficient to say, that some of the classes to which these lectures were originally addressed included among their members individuals who, though young both in years and experience, were graduates of the highest class of literary institutions, were anticipating professional employment in such establishments, and were attending the course of lectures with reference to the application, in their personal instructions, of the principles under discussion.

Apart, however, from this relation of circumstances, the consideration of principles of education, and methods of instruction, necessarily extends through the whole educational course of training; and defective methods of teaching are but little less injurious in the higher than in the lower forms of culture. The fact, moreover, is undeniable, that the renovation of the character of instruction, whether at home or abroad, has uniformly commenced in the primary stages of education, and won its way gradually upward;—a circumstance easily accounted for, when we recollect that, in the reformation, now so generally effected in elementary teaching, more regard has been paid to the wants of the *mind*, and less to the demands of *subjects*, than formerly was the case in the management of primary schools, or than is now, in the customary regulation of institutions of the highest nominal order, in most of which the *subject* of study is still too uniformly regarded in preference to the *instrument* of study.

To some readers of the journal, the intellectual philosophy, involved in the principles adopted in the preceding analysis of mental action and development, may not seem satisfactory,—as not according, in express terms, with established authorities on such topics. To objections of this character the author can only suggest that, in the circumstances of many of those to whom his lectures were addressed, it was not practicable to assume the data of a previous course of study in intellectual philosophy; and all that could properly be done, on his part, was to interweave, with his suggestions for the guidance of instructors in their professional endeavors, such elementary views of

1 K

mental action and tendency as might afford intelligible ground for these suggestions.

At the same time, the writer feels free to say that, following the counsels of his own instructor, the venerable Jardine, (a student and successor of Dr. Reid,) he could not adopt any "system" of intellectual philosophy as such. All systems hitherto offered have contributed useful suggestions for the guidance of inquiry. But none, as yet, can be regarded as exhaustive or complete. The *mind*, as a subject of study, has not yet received the humble measure of justice which we yield to a plant or a mineral,—a careful observation and close examination of its own character, apart from the obscuring influence of the conflicting views and metaphysical speculations of great writers and eminent authorities. But, to the teacher, philosophical theory is a doubtful aid, compared to his own daily inspection of the mind itself, in its actual working and obvious tendencies. He is, if he understands his position, himself a primary observer, authority and reporter, in the science of mind, as developed in the processes of education. His work is that of a living philosopher, in act. To his young disciples, he is Plato, and Socrates, and Aristotle, embodied in one person;—opening to their expanding minds the highest spiritual, moral, and intellectual relations of truth.

The ground thus assigned as the field of the teacher's labor, is not too high to be assumed by any instructor, whatever be the nominal rank of the seminary in which he teaches. A mind accustomed to large views, and working on broad principles, will, unconsciously and necessarily, adopt methods correspondent, and will radiate, from its own action, light and truth throughout the sphere of its influence. Nowhere is this statement more strikingly verified than in the case of an intelligent teacher, in the direction and instruction of an elementary school. It is in this sphere that ingenuity, and tact, and originality, and skill are most needed, in endeavors to develop intellectual capabilities, and build up the great fabric of mental power. Nowhere else, in the whole field of education, is the demand so urgent for a thorough insight into the nature and working of the mind, for the light to guide its advances, or the power to mold its expanding character.

INDEX.

Alphabet, mere drilling on, injurious, p. 16; error of omitting the sounds of letters, 81; recognition of the forms of letters, 38.
Analogy, the medium of expression, 63.
Analysis, preliminary of intellectual faculties, 11; as a process, facilitated by training on objects, 29; its disciplinary character and value, 46, 47.
Apparatus, educational, provision of, 26.
Art, pictorial, as a discipline of the perceptive faculties, 30.
Articulation, practice of, 32.
Attention, definition of, 13; as a voluntary act, 34, 35; promptness of, 35; earnestness, 36; closeness, 37; aided by the microscope, conducive to alphabetic instruction, to mathematical attainments, 38; tenacity of, its value, how attained, 39; ultimate effects on mental power, 40.

Classification as a disciplinary process, 55; its appropriate materials for early training, 56.
Communication, the result of the action of the expressive faculties; viewed as a power, 78; its intellectual and moral effects, its value, 79.
Comparison, as a disciplinary exercise for the expressive faculties, its influence on rational and reflective processes, 53; its relations to classification and induction; to order, method, law, principles, rule; proper materials for its exercise, 54.
Composition, practice of; defective methods, 85; seasonable training, 86.
Conception, etymology and acceptation of the term, 106; different views of this faculty, 107; its susceptibility of culture, its intellectual and moral value, 108.
Concluding explanations, 152.
Consciousness, etymology of the term, 108; fitness of its application, different opinions of the nature of this faculty, 109; educational view; intellectual and moral offices of consciousness, 110; its educational culture, 111.
Culture, intellectual, outline of, 11, 12.
Curiosity, the actuating principle of the perceptive faculties, 14.
Deduction, as a process of reason, 116.
Direction, as a didactic process, 51; exemplified, 52.
Drawing, its effects as a discipline of the perceptive faculties, 30; common mistake regarding its relation to the cultivation of taste, 91.
Elocution, as a discipline of the ear; its connections with music, oratory, poetry, 83; errors in instruction, 86; in theory, exemplified by Dr. Whately, 87, 90.
Emotion, its offices in expression; a result of sensibility, 59; naturally spontaneous and involuntary, the language

of sympathy, its various forms, 60; its different effects; its influence on language, 61.
English language, neglect of, 81, 99, 100.
Enunciation, its connection with articulation and pronunciation, 32.
Errors in education,—in the order of cultivation, 13; in school *regime*, 16, 19; in the cultivation of the expressive faculties,—repression, 76; limited exercise in passive forms, 80; incorrect example, false alphabetic training, 81; neglect of the meaning of words, defective reading exercises, 82, 83; arbitrary methods of teaching grammar, composition, 84, 85; rhetoric, elocution, 86—90; drawing, music, vocal and instrumental, 91—93; remedies for these errors, 93—100.
Etymology of terms applied to mental action, and educational relations, 18, 49, 50, 101, 106, 107, 108, 111, 112, 116, 117.
Expressive faculties, cultivation of; their place in the order of action and development, 57; classification of, 58; their actuating principle, 70; their tendency, 75; result of their action, 78; their educational processes, 80, 93—100.

Fancy, its effects on expression, 64.
Feeling, the actuating principle of the expressive faculties, 70; an incitement to sympathy, an instigation; influenced by imagination and volition; its influence on the artist, 71; the child, the adult, the actor and his audience, the orator, the poet, and on all forms of expression, 72; on moral character; on art, as exemplified in music, 73; on language and literature; its subjection to the guidance of education, 74.
Furniture, intellectual, for schoolrooms, 16.

Gesture, a subject of cultivation, 90.
Grammar, methods of instruction, 84, 85.

Holbrook, Josiah, an example to teachers, 44.

Imagination, significance of the term; sphere of the faculty, 64.
Imitation, its tendencies; drawing, as an imitative art; music, 65.
Inference, as a process of reason, 116.
Information, as a guide to observation, 51, 52.
Inquiry, the actuating principle of the reflective faculties; its analogy to curiosity, 121.
Inspection of objects, as a disciplinary exercise; exemplified in botany, 48; in zoölogy, 49.
Interrogation, as an intellectual discipline, 49; book questions, children's questions, 50; leading questions, 51.

Intuition, an act of reason, 116.
Investigation, the tendency of action in the reflective faculties; its directions, 122—exemplified in the scientific traveler, the astronomer, the historian, the philologist, 123—in the mechanician, the chemist; its value in all the higher relations of thought, 124.
Judgment, identical with reason, 119.
Knowledge, the result of the action of the perceptive faculties, 21; actual, 22; verbal accuracy a false test of; true knowledge experimental and personal, 23.
Language, a measure of power, 68; its value, 69; study of languages ancient and modern, of the English language, 98—100.
Memory, the basis of reflective power; remembrance, 103; intellectual and moral offices of memory, recollection, 104; suggestive power of memory, 105; its susceptibility of cultivation, 106.
Method, importance of, to the teacher, 10.
Methods, defective, of instruction, regarding the action of the reflective faculties, 127; exemplified with reference to reading, arithmetic, geography, history, language, logic, intellectual and moral philosophy, 129—134; appropriate methods for the discipline of the reflective faculties, 135—151.
Modeling, its uses in training the perceptive faculties, 30.
Models, false, in music; their injurious effects, 93.
Monotony, evils of, in modes of training, 15.
Music, as a discipline for the ear, 31; errors regarding it, 91—93.
Nature, importance of early study of, 20; universal susceptibility to its influence, effects of on mental character, 21; value of the study and observation of it, as a discipline of intellect, 40.
Novelty, need of in modes of early training, 15.
Objects, study of, with reference to color, form, measure, number, organization, 27—29.
Observation, definition of, 13; its influence as an instinctive intellectual tendency, 17; its effects as a habit, 18; cherished by early attention to elementary botany, geology, mineralogy, zoölogy, 19; habits of attentive observation, how secured and confirmed, 41—46.
· Perception, definition of, 13.
Perceptive faculties, cultivation of, 9; contemplated with reference to their classification, 12, 13; their actuating principle, 14—17; their tendency, 17—21; the result of their action, 21—26; their appropriate educational processes of exercise, development, and discipline, 26—55.

Personation, as a mode of expression, 66; exemplified in the successive stages of life, 67.
Philosophy, mental importance of, to the teacher, 120.
Plan necessary for the guidance of the teacher, 10.
Processes, educational, for the discipline of the perceptive faculties, 12, 26—55; of the expressive, 80, 93—100; of the reflective, 127—151.
Progressive intellection, law of, 26; progressive discipline of the perceptive faculties, 33.
Ratiocination, definition of, 117.
Reason,—explanatory remark, 111; etymology of the term; definiteness and certainty of action in this faculty, 112; its offices in definition and discrimination, its authority, 113; its cognizance of relations; its inventive character, 114; aberration of reason; uses of reason in analysis and abstraction, 115; intuition, inference, deduction, 116; generalization, induction, ratiocination, 117; reason, as cognizant of truth, as susceptible of cultivation, 118; judgment, understanding, 119.
Recollection, definition of, 104, 105.
Reflective faculties, cultivation of; introductory observations; etymology of terms, 101; classification, 102; actuating principle, 121; tendency, 122—124; result, 125, 126; educational processes, 127—151.
Remedies for errors regarding the cultivation of the expressive faculties, 93—100.
Remembrance, definition of, 103.
Representation, a form of expression, 67.
Repression, evils of, 9.
Revision, necessity of in the plan of education, 5, 6.
Rhetoric, methods of teaching, 86.
Sensation, definition of, 12.
Senses, discipline of; sight, color, 27; form, measure, number, 28; natural objects, animated forms, 29; the ear, music, speech, 31.
Speech and writing, results of discipline, 68.
Taste, significance of the term; character of true taste, 69; its positive power; a subject of culture, 70.
Teacher, his true point of view, 6; his aim in instruction, 9; his need of plan and method, 10; his place as an observer of the mind, 14; his proper business as its superintendent, 23.
Truth, the result of the action of the reflective faculties, 125, 126.
Understanding, its identity with reason, 119.
Utterance, the tendency of the expressive faculties, 75—78.
Variety, its importance in modes of culture, 15.
Wonder, its analogy to curiosity, 15; its effects, 17.

II. MORAL EDUCATION.*

LECTURES ADDRESSED TO YOUNG TEACHERS.

BY WILLIAM RUSSELL,

Editor of the American Journal of Education (Boston,) 1826–29.

INTRODUCTORY OBSERVATIONS.

Importance of the Study of Man's Moral Constitution.—The vital part of human culture is not that which makes man what he is intellectually, but that which makes him what he is in heart, life, and character. Intellectual cultivation, however, is a source of moral power to the individual, not merely in the mental aid which it enables him to render to others, but in that which it gives him for the understanding and government of himself. All intellectual training, therefore, is necessarily moral in its influence, so far as regards enlarged opportunity and power of intelligent, voluntary, and efficient action. It is only misguided ignorance, blinding prejudice, or perverted ingenuity, that would ignore or undo, in educational administration, the natural union of morality with intelligence.

A culture exclusively intellectual serves but to exhibit the skeleton of the mental frame, which moral influence is to furnish with the means and the power of action, and into which religious principle is to breathe the breath of life. But when moral culture assumes a separate and formal character, it ceases to be a living spiritual reality, and becomes but a mechanical routine of "the letter" which, we are told, "killeth." No reliance for effective moral influence on disposition or character, can be safely placed on mere didactic inculcation or catechetical instruction. The oracles of Divine truth tell us, that the highest moral training—the spiritual—does not separate "admonition" from "*nurture*"—the life-giving influence—but combines the two in the educational process of "bringing up." The true study of the human being, as a subject of meliorating culture, contemplates the child in the living unity of his whole nature. It regards him as an intelligent self-conscious, self-impelling, self-guiding, self-responsible agent, yet dependent on, and responsible to, the law of a higher power

---

* At the suggestion of Hon. Henry Barnard the following series of lectures has been transcribed from the author's general course on Human Culture. originally addressed to the students of the Merrimack, (N. H.,) and New England, (Lancaster, Mass.,) Normal Institutes. A previous series on Intellectual Education, may be found by referring to Vols. II., III , and IV., of this Journal.

than his own, which has summed up and defined his individuality in a conscious will.

All careful investigation, however, in the mental, not less than in the physical world, implies an examination so close as to constitute a thorough analysis—not, in this instance, for the sake of a mere philosophic solution, but for the purpose of securing a true synthetic construction of life and character, by the better understanding, so obtained, of constituent elements and the influences which may best secure their living union and power. In every process of "instruction," (*inward building*,) the educator, whether parent or teacher, if he would work thoughtfully and successfully—if he would avoid laying upon the mental foundation of created capability a superstructure of "wood, hay, stubble," instead of the "gold, silver, and precious stones" of true worth and value—is in duty bound to see to it that he attentively observe, and carefully study, the nature and constitution of the being, whose fabric of character it is his office to aid in building up. The educator must, in a word, thoroughly understand and appreciate the elements of human character. These must be familiar to him in all their relations, and in all their varied workings, that he may understand more fully the means and sources of healthy action and healthful regimen, which it is his duty to prescribe.

True position of the Teacher as a Moral Educator.—Even to the youngest and least experienced of teachers, who wishes to acquit himself to the moral obligations under which he is professionally laid, equally to his pupils and himself, we would earnestly recommend not the practice of looking into some text-book of moral philosophy, for his own guidance, or for the instruction of his pupils, but—in the true spirit of an earnest, faithful, and intelligent instructor, who is aware that all he daily does or omits is a part of the effectual, living education of the subjects of his influence—the careful study and watchful observation of the moral indications and tendencies of his pupils, as intimating their capabilities and suggesting his measures and resources. It is his part to carry on, in successive stages, the sacred offices of parental love and wisdom, daily transferred to his charge, to be fulfilled in the sphere of the schoolroom, according to the measure of his judgment, his skill, and his benignity. But the proper home influence, though so often missing, is the true ideal of purpose, plan, and work, for the teacher; and, so far as regards moral results, in the schoolroom as at home, the appropriate influence must ever be that of an authoritative, affectionate, living, presence—not that of an inanimate book or a deadening routine.

No one doubts that, to become a skillful cultivator of the intel

INTRODUCTORY OBSERVATIONS. 159

lectual capabilities of his pupils, the instructor must understand the character and action of the intellectual faculties—not merely as these exist in the enumeration of particulars in a text-book of mental philosophy, but as they actually reveal themselves in the personal action and relations of the living pupil, in whatever concerns the use and exercise of his mind. The teacher must take the position not of a student of intellectual philosophy, ruminating in his study, but of a wakeful observer and inquirer into the phenomena of an actual, living specimen of the human mind, whose course is to be, in part, dependent on the fidelity of his observation, and the genial character of his influence. Our previous course of suggestions on the cultivation of the intellectual faculties, it will be recollected, assumed this ground as the appropriate and peculiar one of the teacher, and the only one on which he could justly be regarded as doing aright his professional work. The same ground we would claim for the teacher, when surveying the field of moral culture.

ARRANGEMENT OF TOPICS.

Recapitulation of Method.—The plan which we propose to adopt in the following series of lectures, will still be, as in the former series, that which places the teacher as a responsible personal observer and reporter on phenomena and facts; watching and aiding the progress of human development. Our survey of the field of intellectual cultivation, as founded on the nature and constitution of the human being, presented, (1.) it will be recollected, *a given class of the mental powers and faculties,* themselves, as subjects of examination; (2.) *the actuating principle,* or moving spring, *of these powers;* (3.) their perceptible *natural tendency,* or course of action; (4.) *the results* of their action; and, (5.) *the educational processes* designed for their appropriate development.

Following this plan, we avoid all mere theoretic speculation, and stand on the sure ground of observed fact—the only point of view for the discovery and recognition of truth, or the direction and guidance of the teacher. We thus, moreover, place the work of education in the teacher's own hands, as a charge devolving on him, not merely professionally, but personally, and laying him under his just responsibility, as an agent for others, and as one intrusted, in the capacity of temporary guardian, with the dearest of all human interests, and the best of all hopes—hopes extending even to a never-dying life.

I. CLASSIFICATION OF THE MORAL CAPABILITIES.

Unity of Man's Moral Constitution.—Adopting the above method for our course of suggestions on moral education, we should proceed to enumerate, as a class, the most prominent of the peculiar powers and faculties which constitute man a moral being, capable of moral influence, instruction, and development. But as every moral act involves the whole man—not merely the executive organ of muscle or nerve, intellect, heart or will, but all, in their living unity and active coöperation, we can not, as when examining the intellectual faculties, select any class or group of powers as exclusively constituting the moral capabilities of the human being. We must take into view his whole nature, comprehending, as it does, the vast range of his physical, intellectual, emotional, and voluntary attributes, in the personal constitution and organization of the individual.

1. HEALTH *as an element of Moral Life.*—Man's moral condition, and his capability of moral development, depend, in no slight degree, on that intimate connection which the Creator has ordained between soul and body. As a necessary condition of the unity of man's complex nature, wholeness of being is essential to whole and true, that is, normal action, whether of body, or of mind, or of both. Physical disorder, by its reactionary character, disintegrates its subject as a moral agent, by withdrawing the executive organism from coöperation and consentaneous action, in subordination whether to the dictates of reason and conscience, the solicitations of feeling, or the normal activity of the will. Physical suffering, and its attendant involuntary irritation, are sufficient to overcast the clear healthy action of the judgment, to stifle the monitions of conscience, to change the natural current of affection, to generate angry passion, and propagate moral evil, to any extent—from the petty ebullitions of peevish temper, to the outbreaks of the fiercest anger, or of raving and furious insanity. Health, then, the educator must ever be careful to enumerate among the conditions of morality, whether the healthy state of the agent be owing to the normal sanity of mere bodily condition, or to that health of the higher nature, conscience, which, in man's fallen state, must so often be invoked, to rule the turbulent and rebellious tendencies of a morbid physical organization, and which, when enlightened, and strengthened, and purified, by supernal aid, is a surer reliance than the happiest condition of the best normal animal life.—To this branch of our subject we shall have occasion to refer more distinctly, under other heads, in the discussion of parental and educational influences.

2. INTELLECT, *and its culture, important elements of Moral Life.*— The vital fact of man's moral unity of constitution, involves the condition of his intellectual nature, as sound and true, or otherwise. The unhealthy condition of the bodily organism, is sufficient to subvert, as we have seen, the whole moral character of the human being,

in seasons of excessive morbid reäction. *Sanity and vigor of mind*, not less than health of body, and conditions of moral life and action; as is sadly manifest when we advert to those unhappy cases in which there has been an overthrow or obscuration of the god-like power of reason itself. Insanity, whether in the form of mental aberration or delusion, is competent not only to impair, but to obliterate, the distinctive mental and moral attributes of man.

The enlightened humanity of our day mitigates by genial, and sometimes, successful treatment, the sufferings of our nature, when reduced to such deplorable conditions; and its kind offices are crowned with yet more marked success, in its endeavors to raise the idiotic and the feeble minded to a comparatively healthy intellectual and moral level. It is one of the highest tributes paid to moral culture—we may observe in passing—that such replacements of depressed human nature are generally recognized as owing their success to the purely moral measures adopted in effecting them, whether in cases of insanity or of idiocy.

Culture essential to Intelligence, and therefore, to Moral Elevation.— Gross ignorance, and utter absence of mental culture, are proved to be, in general, fruitful sources of crime, and of moral evil in every shape. It is not enough that a sane mind and sound judgment be taken into the account, as, indispensable elements in the production of legitimate moral results in action and character. The intellect beclouded and darkened by ignorance and its attendant hosts of error and prejudice, or benumbed by neglect and disuse, is incapable of the clearness and activity which belong to the normal states and conditions of the human mind. A pure, intelligent, and loyal adherence to principle and to conscience, can not, in such circumstances, be expected to exist. The character indicated in sacred scripture, "a brutish man" who "doth not know," may not have chosen his condition; but, while in it, he is disqualified for every proper exercise of man's reflective and moral nature. The density of ignorance to which some classes of the population of European cities, and the majority of the slave population of our own country, are sunk, shows, in its deplorable depression, and its nearly hopeless extinction or absence of conscience, how important the daylight of knowledge is to a pure atmosphere in the human soul.

Evils of excessive Cultivation.—Morality necessarily implies a certain degree of intelligence and of culture. But, unhappily, there is, as is too plainly apparent in the forms of civilized and city life, a condition in which a moral inefficiency of mind is attributable not to the absence, but to the injudicious excess of cultivation; and the pale and emaciated features of school children and students, too generally indicate the incompatibility of sedentary life and close, studious application, daily sustained, with a natural, healthy condition of body. The parental complaints against schools, as undermining the temper and vivacity of childhood, confirm the truth that the "much study" which "is a weariness of the flesh," impairs, also, the healthy vigor and freshness of the spirit.

Genial influence of appropriate early Culture.—Were early education what it should be, a course of invigorating, life-giving observation of nature and its products, and a succession of healthful, inspiring exercises, alternating with soothing relaxation and cheering recreation, and a strictly limited and very moderate exercise of pure intellection; culture and intelligence would cease to be, as now, too often purchased at the expense of a healthy tone of mind and habit. But, as we must recur to this branch of our subject when we come to the discussion of educational methods, we must leave it, for the present, with this postulate, that a sound, clear, vigorous, and well trained *understanding*, capable of correct and decisive *judgments*, is as important as the possession of *reason* itself, to constitute man a responsible, moral agent. In other words, that his *rational faculty* is a *moral power*.

3. ÆSTHETIC CULTURE: *its Moral Influence on Imagination and Taste.*—Among the intellectual sources of moral life and power, a prominent place must ever be assigned by the judicious educator to the moulding and directing efficacy of imagination and taste. If these influential faculties are untrue or impure in their action and character, the tendency of the whole moral being is "only evil, and that continually." If they are sound, healthy, pure, and vigorous, they become sure safeguards, faithful guides, and genial companions of the youthful spirit. They, also, rise to the rank of powers in the moral domain of humanity.

Moral influence of the impressions of Sublimity and Beauty.—In that commingling of intuition, feeling, and imagination, and, sometimes, even of reflective judgment, by which the soul is at once overawed, and delighted, and exalted, in the contemplation of the vast, the sublime, the majestic in nature or in thought, or in that only less elevating influence which is inspired by the blending effects of greatness and grace in the grandeur of nature or of noble art, or even in that delighted and admiring love which is elicited by the presence of beauty in the myriad forms and hues with which the Creator has invested the living and ever-varying aspects of nature, which man delights to imitate in art;—in all these relations of mind is involved a moral element of power, by which man's nature is ennobled and purified, and prepared, as in the vestibule of a sanctuary, for those yet higher and more effective influences which lift awe into adoration, and attract the soul to the beauty of holiness. Such at least, we know, is the natural tendency of unperverted mind, and the experience of every soul on which the true Light shineth.

The mind which, under the purifying influence of genial culture, enjoys the refining emotions and clear perceptions of a true "taste," (*relish*,) for those pursuits which lead to the admiring contemplation of nature, and to the practice of those arts which enable man to express his admiration of nature—possesses, in its love of the beautiful, a natural preparation for the reception of all those salutary impressions which, in a higher relation, are stamped upon the heart by the irresistible power of every trait of loveliness of disposition and character embodied in the daily beauty of a pure and amiable life.

The Graphic Arts which embody and repeat and perpetuate such impressions, are not to be overlooked in an enumeration of man's capabilities of refining and elevating culture, even in its strictly moral and spiritual relation. The dumb statue, by its perfect symmetry and grace, or its touching beauty, makes the heart eloquent inwardly with delight and love, with admiration, or with tenderness and sympathy. The portrait which recalls the image of the lost and lovely, the good and the true, the noble and the worthy, speaks most touchingly to us, from the spirit of the departed, in the language of the heart. The landscape which skillful art presents as a microcosm of glorious nature, conjured from dead, material means and implements, by a concentration of man's inventive genius and educated hand, deepens, at once, our love of this our earthly home of palatial grandeur and finished beauty, benignantly assigned us by the great Father, for our preparatory abode, and our admiration of the powers with which He has endowed the beings created in his image. The art which at once refines and elevates, does a noble preparatory work in rendering more vividly susceptible those faculties by which the soul, when awakened to the consciousness of its highest relations, is yet more effectually purified and ennobled.

But *Music*—that art which God has been pleased to consecrate for His own special service in the offices of human devotion, and which may be employed in the humble station of a peculiar minister to man's enjoyment, as a sentient being, capable of ever new and ever pure gratification from the concord of sweet sounds, is, in its influence on the soul, an element of singular moral efficacy, in its power to inspire with reverence, with joy, with ecstatic delight, to calm and soothe the agitated spirit, to touch the heart with sympathy for sorrow, or to mingle the humanizing emotions of brotherhood and companionship. Rightly cultivated and rightly practiced, it affects with a pure and benign influence both mind and heart; and happily, of late years, has it taken its appropriate place in schools, among the effective means of moral culture not less than æsthetic.

It is no undue enlargement in the enumeration of the moral capabilities of humanity, to include within its sphere the whole range of those arts by which man's conceptions of grandeur and beauty are rendered more definite in themselves, and more effective in their influence on his character.

4. SENSIBILITY, *as an element of Moral Life.*—In our preceding observations, we have adverted to health of body and mind, and to intellectual and æsthetic culture, as determining, in degree, man's moral capabilities; since a normal physical and intellectual state is the natural condition of normal moral action. Proceeding to the further consideration of the moral capacities and powers, the next element in our enumeration will be that *Sensibility* which, by Creative ordination, links man, by the sense of *pleasure* and *pain*, to the outward world, establishes a sentient world within himself, and gives birth to the vital elements of *love* and *aversion*, in all the varied forms of *appetite, instinct, desire, feeling, affection, passion,* and *emotion,* by which man is attracted or repelled, by which he is prompted to action and expression, and which consequently determine his *morality,* (*manner* of action.)

5. THE INSTINCTIVE TENDENCIES, *as Moral Incitements.*—(1.) *Appetite,* the natural primal craving for satisfaction, which implies a sense of want and a desire of gratification, more or less definite according to the degree of intellectual development and definite consciousness, secures, by Divine appointment, the perpetual renovation of vigor, health, and life, of comfort and complacency. In the natural sympathy of mind and body, it tends, also, to generate the genial dispositions and emotions, and to diffuse the moral element of happiness. The intelligent educator recognizes it as a moral power, in its influence on habit and character. He well knows that, in its pure and healthy conditions, it is an effective promoter of serenity and tranquillity and cheerfulness, and favors the exercise of the benevolent affections; that, when neglected, it brings on an irritative reäction, too strong, if extreme, for the control of the guardian power of conscience; and that, when glutted by excess, it imbrutes the whole being, and leads to those degrading habits by which humanity is desecrated or ruined.

(2.) *The natural Love of Activity.*—One of the earliest manifestations of instinct is the restless desire of action, which is seen even in the involuntary and spontaneous motions of the muscular frame in infancy, in the insatiable thirst for exercise in childhood, in the irrepressible tendency of boyhood and youth to active exertion, in the indefatigable industry of adult man; and not less in the instinctive craving for intellectual action, and the inextinguishable curiosity of the young mind, in the eager appetite for knowledge on all accessible subjects, and the earnest desire to investigate the problems of our being and destination, which impel the maturer mind, at every stage of life. The same desire of activity is marked in the child's natural craving for sympathy and affection, and in that desire for esteem and approbation which mark the dispositions of youth and manhood. All these impelling powers, as they tend to enlarge the sphere of life to the individual, and prompt him to fill it by corresponding exertion, become vital elements of moral life and character.

(3.) *The natural Aversion to Pain.*—This instinctive principle, which makes the sentient nature a provisional guardian of the safety and welfare of infancy, and, in degree, of humanity, throughout the course of life, operates, at first, with more obvious reference to the protection of organic life and health. But, as the mental powers progressively unfold themselves, and conscious sympathy becomes a source of pleasure or of pain, the instinct becomes a moral sentiment, and leads its subject to avoid whatever seems fitted to excite painful or disagreeable emotions in the consciousness of his fellow beings. It advances as self-consciousness becomes more fully developed, to that moral rank which places it in alliance with conscience, and warns us to shun the foreseen pain of evil doing, and the reproaches of that faithful monitor which Divine wisdom has implanted in the bosom of man to represent its own jurisdiction. It rises, at length, to that fear of God which deters from sin, under the dread of His sovereignty or the apprehension of his displeasure, and which, in its truest and most genial form of filial awe, forbids the very thought of offense. The power of this instinct is most impressively shown when, as in some deplorable instances, its first monitory warnings have been disregarded, and its terrific reaction drives reason from the throne of intellect, or haunts a death-bed with horrors.

(4.) *The desire of Enjoyment*—which, in infancy and childhood, tends to seek for gratification in the sphere of the sentient nature in its animal relations, rises to intellectual and moral action, with progressive development, in subsequent stages of life and character, till it becomes the conscious pursuit of even the highest happiness of humanity, exalts successively the aims and endeavors of man to his utmost elevation of moral action and character, and stamps itself as one of the most powerful agents in the advancement of his being.

(5.) *The desire of Power.*—No attribute of his nature more distinctly marks the character of man as a progressive being, than that love of power which actuates the very infant in his attempts to stand, to walk, to speak, to put forth efforts of muscular force. The child, the boy, and the youth, all evince the activity of this principle, in the conscious ambition for progress and advancement by which they are impelled to earnest endeavor and arduous exertion, physical, intellectual, and moral. The sense of power is, in every stage of human life, one of the strongest feelings of pleasure of which man is conscious. In the maturity of his powers, it crowns his endeavors to explore the worlds of nature and of thought, to achieve the miracles of perfect art, to attain to positions of affluence or of rank, to enjoy, in whatever form, the splendor of greatness. It prompts man, at every stage of his being, from childhood onward, to aim at the relative manifestation of power which is exhibited in superiority over others, in the ability to control, direct, and sway the minds and actions of his fellow-men. This instinct of his nature becomes an element of immense productive force for evil, when perverted; although, when prompted by benevolence, and restrained by justice and rectitude, it has occasionally made men the benefactors of their race.

(6.) *The desire of Estimation.*—This principle which, in childhood, is manifested in the desire of love and approbation, becomes, in the adult, a love of esteem and respect, and, so far, is unquestionably a worthy motive power, and one which, subordinated to conscientious integrity and honor, elevates the character and prompts to benevolent action. When it degenerates to mere love of fame and applause, or sinks to the miserable desire for distinction or mere notoriety, its effects are, of course, as degrading as in its purer forms, it is ennobling. In any form, it is an element of peculiar power in man's moral constitution.

(7.) *The desire of Society.*—This principle man partakes with the gregarious races of animal life. It manifests itself in the clinging desire for sympathy and association, characteristic alike of infancy, childhood, and youth. It becomes, in manhood, the foundation of social and civil life, widens the sphere of the individual, and amplifies his being by the sympathy, the intelligence, the material and moral aid of a whole community of his fellow men. As an element of human progress and power, it ranks among the strongest and the most ample of man's moral resources.

(8.) *The desire of Freedom.*—In the stages of infancy and childhood, and of immature life generally, the instinctive desire to throw off restraint, and to enjoy liberty of action, is the natural expression of that native desire of development which impels the progressive human being in every direction that promises the pleasure of conscious effort and power. Partaking, however, of the partial blindness attributable to all forms of mere instinct, it needs the direction and guidance of faculties higher than itself, to constitute it a uniformly safe element in activity. But as it is capable of employment in the service of man's best rights and interests, and, in that capacity, has achieved some of his noblest triumphs for intelligence, virtue, and happiness, it takes justly a high rank among his moral capabilities, as an indispensable condition of development and progress.

6. THE PRIMARY EMOTIONS, *as Moral Powers.*—Sensibility, the susceptibility of feeling, the great source of moral life, presents its numerous family of emotions as constituent members of the group of moral powers and faculties by which man is rendered capable of meliorating culture and spiritual growth. Emotion, as the manifestation or expression of feeling and affection, is not merely the natural language of the heart, rendered visible or audible, but in virtue of the law of sympathy and mutual incitement, existing in the various faculties of the soul, it is itself a vital moral element reäcting with a powerful augmenting force on the source whence it springs. As an inner movement of the soul rendered legible, it has, in many cases, become, by universal consent and usage, a synonym for the interior condition whence it originates, whether in the quiet moods of serenity or the turbulence of passion.

(1.) *Joy.*—One of the earliest feelings manifested by look and action, in the infant stage of life, is that joyous emotion which constitutes, so largely, the happiness of animal existence, in all its earlier conditions. The genial nature of this emotion is indicated in the intense gratification which it evidently yields to its immediate subject, and which, by the law of sympathy, it diffuses to all sentient natures within its sphere. From its lowest forms of serene *complacency,* to its more positively marked degrees of *animation* and *cheerfulness,* its higher expressions of *delight,* of *gladness,* and *hilarity,* or its more sedate and lasting satisfactions, in the mature sense of *happiness* which attends true enjoyment, its influence on life and health, on conscious feeling, on temper and disposition, on the whole intellectual and moral nature, is, in the highest degree, salutary; while undue devotion to its influence precludes the possibility of benefit from those deeper and more lasting pleasures which flow from serious thought and earnest purposes. Mirth, habitually indulged, leads to habitual levity and frivolity, and foregoes the distinctive dignity of man. The healthy and genial inspiration of joy, however, even intelligent educators are sometimes prone to forget, is, in all the relations of moral condition and moral cultivation, one of the strongest influences to which the young mind, by the law of its constitution, is peculiarly subjected as a vital element—the oxygen, of its spiritual atmosphere.

(2.) *Sorrow, grief, regret, repentence, remorse.*—These emotions, diametrically opposed, in all their effects, to the genial influence of the preceding, are to be eschewed as permanent educational elements in any normal plan of early training; yet they have their salutary office in abnormal instances, in softening obdurate hearts, and subduing obstinate wills, or in awakening torpid and dormant intellects. Their office, in the business of education, is that of exceptional remedies for exceptional evils: they are punitive and reformatory in their character, rather than genial and preventive. They belong not to the primary stage of nurture, but rather to the secondary one of discipline. Still they are sometimes of the greatest value, when they spring from ingenuous feelings of regret for conscious error, or self-reprehension for conscious faults. It was once most happily said, "The tear of contrition serves to wash the mote of sin out of the eye." The hour of grief is that which enhances the value of consolation. The blameless sadness of the young heart calls for the gentle soothing of the voice of affection. Sorrow for deplorable losses blesses the voice which can say, in genuine sympathy and cheering kindness, "Let not your heart be troubled!" The moment of "the heaviness of the countenance" is sometimes that in which "the heart is made better," by detaching it from the burden of conscious evil, and preparing the will for the better course of a new life. In such circumstances, the judicious aid of the attentive educator may assist in the inauguration of a new moral era in the personal history of the pupil. Even the rougher and severer discipline of repentance and remorse becomes, to the hardened adult, a minister of mercy, when it wrenches the sinner from the thraldom of evil habit, and sets him free from the "bondage of iniquity."

The moral power of this whole class of emotions—from the unaccountable cloud of depression which sometimes steals over the sunshine of the young heart, to the deepest plunge into the darkness of remorse—is peculiarly marked for its efficacy in the renovation of feeling, and even of disposition and character. In the sphere of the family and the school, it sometimes marks the record of the day's history with the beginning of a salutary reformation of temper and deportment. But, in the imperfections of human management, it sometimes is permitted to mark the commencement of a reactive sense of wrong, when the feeling is unjustly caused by arbitrary or erring authority. It then becomes a power for lasting evil.

(3.) *Timidity, fear, terror.*—Like the natural aversion to pain, these instinctive emotions, which are so easily excited in childhood, bespeak the guardian care of the Creator, in his gracious provision against danger, and consequent destruction to the organic frame, or to the mental constitution. They are the swift preventives of evil, the safeguards of humanity in peril. But the vividness of childhood's emotions needs the aid of the guardian auspices of education to prevent a salutary instinct from degenerating into unreasoning excess, and to protect the mental and moral nature from the paralyzing effect, which, in unhappy instances, has extended to the overthrow of reason itself. The timidity of childhood may, if not watched over, become habitual self-distrust, embarrassment, confusion of thought, or even moral cowardice. Wisely guarded, it may be converted into a protection from rashness, presumption, and foolhardiness. Fear may be sometimes needed as a restraining influence on forwardness and impudence, or as a check upon daring hardihood, in resistance to authority. But its influence is unfriendly to the healthy development of disposition and character. It never rises to the dignity of an aid to the development of principle. It may aid in producing a vivid apprehension of coercive and compulsory measures, and so lead to obviate their necessity. But its low rank among instincts, its semi-brutal character, at best, place it among the motives which a generous educator would ever despise. If called in, for a moment, to quell resistance to authority, it yet can never attain to the dignity of a genuine moral influence. Expediency may sometimes sanction the appeal to its effect, as a matter of necessity. But, if admitted at all into the circle of moral relations, it can not be ranked higher than among the abnormal. As for its extreme form, terror—humanity, at the present day, forbids any resort to it, as a moral expedient. The peril of insanity lies too close at hand to permit any human being to adopt it, even as a means of deterring from evil. Its only salutary use is its instinctive office to prompt the instant flight from peril to life itself. So, and so only, does it prove a benefit.

(4.) *Indignation as a moral sentiment.*—The intelligent moral instructor will, of course, carefully guard his pupils from confounding this principle with the mere animal emotion or passion of anger. Anger is the mere personal reäction of maddened feeling and blinded reason, which man is capable of in common with the brutes, and which vents itself in violence on the agent of injury. Indignation is that impersonal sentiment which regards not the agent but the act, which makes the young heart glow at the sense of wrong, when the teacher is relating an instance of oppression or cruelty, which occurred, perhaps, ages ago, and in some distant land. This species of resentment is a purely mental thing, a salutary and ennobling emotion of reäctive sympathy, which belongs to man as a being consciously endowed with free agency, and equally abhorring a condition of unjust subjection, and the oppression which causes it—

as a being instinctively impelled to oppose and overthrow every palpable form of evil which besets the condition of humanity. Indignation has inspired many of those peaceful revolutions which have renovated the social and moral condition of communities, more frequently than it has originated those bloody revolutions which have sometimes been the birth-throes of national life and liberty.

(5.) *Wonder.*—Among the first indications of mental life, in childhood, is the emotion of wonder, which, at that stage of human progress, is so often called forth by the novelties of observation and experience. The freshness of feeling which it indicates, and the manifest delight attending it, show plainly its power as an element of mental life and moral activity. This emotion, judiciously evoked and skillfully cherished by the watchful educator, becomes not only a genial and a powerful incentive to intellectual exertion, but the tribute of the young heart on the altar of the yet "unknown God," who is waiting to be, in due season, revealed to intelligent faith. The wonder which the novelty of all created things raises in the dawning consciousness of childhood, is the preparatory stage of the intelligence and reverence which are afterward to blend in the soul, as it rises to the recognition of the Author of life and the Giver of its law of duty.

(6.) *Awe.*—This emotion transcends that of mere wonder, and thrills the soul with a profounder sense of power, whether exhibited in the tremendous forces of nature, in its astounding aspects of elemental commotion, as in the heaving fire of the volcano, the dashing billows of ocean, the rush of the cataract, the blinding flash of the lightning, the roar of the thunder, or the fury of the tornado, or in the calmer majesty of mountain forms, the overwhelming vastness of impenetrable forests, or the immeasurable depths of space. As a moral inspiration, it aids the feeble faculties of man in his attempts to dwell upon the conception of almighty power and eternal duration; and while he must ever sink consciously baffled in all his attempts to comprehend Him "whose greatness is unsearchable, and whose ways are past finding out," yet he never feels more vividly the greatness of his own nature, limited though it is, than when losing his human littleness in the contemplation of the great and marvellous works which bespeak the majesty of Him who is "the same yesterday, to-day, and forever."

This overwhelming and yet ennobling emotion, education has it for one of its special offices to deepen and expand by all the aids which nature and science furnish to the inquiring mind of man. Its influence is doubly salutary, as it prostrates the human being in conscious insignificence before his Creator, and, at the same time, exalts Him who is the "Majesty of heaven and earth."

(7.) *Hope.*—As an intelligent inspiration, of intellect, heart, and will, in activity connected with the sense of duty, hope, the expectation of success, becomes an element of high moral value and power.

It is congenial with the conscious happiness of being which naturally belongs to the joyous associations of early childhood, and, indeed, of young life in all its various stages. It inspires and sustains the aspirations of boyhood and youth, and invigorates the exertions of manhood. It is a silent tribute from the heart of man to Divine benignity; and when elevated and hallowed by faith, it rejoices in the anticipation of a future life of perfect felicity. Its rank, and its efficacy as a moral influence, constitute it one of the highest powers by which man's moral nature is actuated.

7. THE BENIGNANT AFFECTIONS, *as elements of moral life and power.*—(1.) *Love.*—By the great pervading attribute of sensibility, inherent in his constitution, man learns to feel his condition before he knows it, and to sympathize with his fellow-beings before he is capable of understanding them. The law of *Sympathy*, written on his whole nature, as a primary element of his being, which ultimately developed into every form of social and benevolent feeling, brings him, unconsciously, at first, under the dominion of the paramount law of *Love*, which attracts him toward his fellow-beings by a genial and kindly influence which he delights to feel, and which, as his conscious intelligence gradually unfolds itself, he learns to understand as mutual and reciprocal. This mysterious power ties the heart of the infant to that of the mother, and that of the mother to the infant with an affection stronger than life. In the little community of home, it links the souls of brothers and sisters in fraternal union of affection. It is the sacred law of parental and filial duty, and moves the whole moral machinery of human life in its hallowed and blessed sphere of privacy.

There virtue has its purest forms and dearest aspects, its genuine, spontaneous amenities; and though unknown beyond its own quiet sphere, has its own unseen record of generous self-sacrifice, and of fortitude more than heroic. Among the noblest motive powers of moral action, the affections of home are those to which the enlightened educator will ever assign the highest place, as regards the capabilities of the human heart for living development.

(2.) *Gratitude.*—This peculiar benignant reäction of love, in view of favor or kindness experienced, mingles largely with the exercise of filial and fraternal affection, and enters into every emotion called forth by the consciousness of benefit conferred, in whatever degree—from the ordinary acts of human kindness and courtesy, to those greater expressions of benevolence, which bestow safety or comfort and happiness, in valuable and lasting forms of beneficent action. This generous emotion is not always accompanied with the satisfaction of being able to remunerate a benefactor by any adequate return. The service or the favor which calls it forth, is sometimes greater than language or action, or any form of external expression, can equal. It may be sometimes so great as to prompt the devotion of a whole life to the friend or benefactor toward whom it is directed. Such is true filial attachment. Such is man's position toward his Creator.

The promptings of this generous emotion lead, sometimes, to the noblest manifestations of true sensibility and self-renouncing devotion. Some of the brightest passages on the page of history are those which record the heroic actions to which this feeling has given birth.

In the relations of education, its influence on the ingenuous mind and heart of youth, forms one of the most sacred attachments of human life. A grateful feeling of returning love for the guardian mental care which, in our early years, watched over, and served to form and mould within us, the ideal image of excellence at which we were taught to aspire, the filial reverence which the heart, in such circumstances, so gladly pays as a tribute to wisdom and worth, insure the inspiration of the noblest aims in all subsequent life, to the heart which is conscious of them.

8. THE GENEROUS AFFECTIONS, *as Moral Powers.*—(1.) *Friendship.*—The cordialities of disinterested friendship, and the mutual good offices of human kindness and reciprocal obligation are but expansions of fraternal feeling from the primary sphere of home; and their efficacy in promoting human well-being, on a broad scale, render them powerful instruments of good, as well as rich elements of moral life in the heart.

(2.) *Patriotism.*—On a yet wider field, patriotic attachment and principle, as they cherish the generous spirit of self-devotion, give ample scope for the cultivation of the virtues which adorn and dignify human life. The noblest pages of history are those which exhibit the magnanimity of genuine patriotism. As a feeling of the heart, or a principle of duty, this sentiment possesses peculiar power in inspiring man to noble deeds; and as a spring of development to personal character, it must ever rank high among the moral capabilities of man.

(3.) *Philanthropy.*—The expansive feeling which embraces the whole human family in the wide open arms of brotherhood, is a virtue yet more disinterested, and more true to God and man, than even the truest and the warmest patriotism. It is eminently the Christian's virtue, so far as he is true to the teachings and example of Him who came to proclaim "good will to men," and charged his followers with a message of love to "the whole world." The history of genuine Christianity is chiefly the record of those who went forth on this errand, "with their life in their hand," and who were ever cheerfully ready to deposit it in pledge of their devotion to the well-being of "Barbarian, Scythian, bond, or free."

Among the powers which characterize man as a moral being capable of culture, and of advancement in the scale of excellence, no trait of disposition gives larger promise than this; and on none does humanizing culture produce larger effects.

(4.) *Humanity toward Animal Nature.*—As the offspring of Divine love, the human spirit, though its lustre has been dimmed by the breath of sin, yet retains something of the characteristic benignity of its Source; and the range of its benevolent sympathy is not limited to the circle of its fellow beings, but flows forth, if not unnaturally diverted from its channel, to the wider sphere of universal being. In its relation even to the humbler races of the creation, which have been subjected to its dominion, by the appointed gradations in the scale of life, it manifests itself capable of a beneficence for which the designation of "*humanity*" has been suggestively chosen.

The universal law of Love, if obeyed, expands and elevates the soul of man to that moral comprehensiveness of being which ranks him "but little lower than the angels;" and while he is thus permitted to see "all earthly things put under his feet," his crown of royalty is indeed one of "glory and honor," because it invests him with the conscious responsibility of an intelligent and moral sovereign. This true majesty of man is the source at once of his just self-respect, and of some of his noblest regal attributes and virtues, to cherish and confirm which is among the special offices of appropriate human culture.

9. RELIGIOUS PRINCIPLE, *as a Moral Power.*—(1.) *Reverence.*— The feeling of which the young mind is conscious, as one of the dawning intimations of the development of its own reflective powers, when contemplating the dignity, the authority, the wisdom, and the benignity of the parental character on which it consciously depends for being and happiness—is although not yet fully or distinctly developed to its own consciousness, one of the profoundest emotions of which it is susceptible; and to the unperverted heart it is one of the strongest cords of sacred obligation by which it is bound to all filial duty.

The emotion thus experienced is naturally transferred, by the mind's law of association to all forms of venerable human worth and dignity. It is called forth by the wisdom of age, by nobility of character in exalted station, and, in degree, by all authority justly exercised. It marks alike, in such circumstances, the deportment of ingenuous youth and of true manliness. Its indications in the intercourse of life are the assurance of that susceptibility by which judicious cultivation, and the inspiration of a genuine faith, are enabled to lift the human soul in reverence to the Father of spirits, and to create a sacred regard for all that Divine truth reveals as duty. Its value as an element in moral cultivation, is beyond expression, great, as regards its influence, whether in securing the respect and obedience due to parents and teachers, to seniority in years, and to eminence in attainments, or in conferring on education itself, its true character as a sacred relation in the business and duties of life, and as a connecting link in the chain which gives unity to man's being in its extension to a higher sphere of mental and spiritual existence.

(2.) *Faith.*—Another element of the highest power in moral relations is the Faith which believes and trusts, and thus unites man to his fellow man, and man to the Author of his being. A great writer has denominated this principle as that " which holds the moral elements of the world together." Without it, man is an isolated, helpless, hopeless outcast, wandering on the shores of being without aim and without direction, ready to be "swallowed up and lost," at the end of his brief career of earthly life.

Faith is the source and spring of all moral life, and, as a capability in the relations of culture, its productive power is comparatively inexhaustible, or limited only by the measure of endeavor. It lifts man above himself, and supplies him with a power beyond his own. It gives the parent and the teacher an influence nearly unbounded. In its highest form, it solves, with light from above, the great Christian paradox, " When I am weak, then am I strong."

(3.) *Conscience.*—The primordial moral element which holds sway over all man's powers and faculties, is Conscience. This great regulator of the springs of action no competent educator can ever permit himself to regard in the merely popular light of a reporter and penal officer, following the acts of which it takes cognizance only after they have been committed, or irretrievably determined. As the sense of duty, it presides over the whole mental being. As an intelligent agent, it partakes in the work of consciousness and reason. It knows and judges. It remembers, indeed, with fearful exactness, the deeds of the past. But, it has also the eyes of intuition and of inference for the present, and the power of prospection, prediction, and suggestion for the future. In feeling—unless blunted or extinguished—it is sensitive, to the utmost degree of acuteness; and it pierces to the very "joints and marrow" of the moral organism. Its cautery is terrible in its unsparing intensity. By Creative ordination it is paramount to the will. It prompts, and threatens, and remonstrates, and commands, and forbids, and impels or deters, with absolute authority;—irresponsible to any higher power within the whole domain of humanity, and acknowledging none without, but the one supreme authority of God and duty.

As an intelligent sentiment, and determining principle, it sums up man's moral capacities and powers in their whole extent of life and action. It constitutes him what he is in the sight of God, and in his own consciousness—a responsible moral agent, whose motto, written on his inmost being, is "*Be perfect.*"

Under the prompting influence of conscience, as the law of duty, appointed by the supreme lawgiver, a devout regard to His authority, and a grateful sense of His benignant care, the young mind, enlightened by the teachings of "the wisdom which cometh from above," is betimes elevated to that *piety* toward the Father of all, which raises the personal worth and virtues of the human being, in his aspirations, to the height of sanctity, carries up all questions of moral action to the highest of all tribunals, and breathes into all his endeavors of duty the inspiring breath of a spiritual life and a divine power. Most justly did the fathers of New England require of the teacher of youth that he should regard himself as specially set apart for the "nurturing" of childhood in "piety," as the security for all those virtues which insure the safety of a community and are the adornment of humanity.

10. THE WILL, *as a Moral Power.*—Man's ability to determine the moral course of his actions, to choose the right and avoid the wrong, can never be made clearer to himself by the light of "science falsely so called," than it is in his own inmost convictions. It never is obscured to his consciousness till, wandering from his limited sphere of possible conception, he bedims it by some cloud of metaphysical speculation, and perplexing casuistry—"darkening counsel" by "skeptical doubts" and "words without knowledge." Conscience, the only competent court, adjudges him free, innocent or guilty, commendable or culpable, in every act within the limits of his power, yet—for that very reason, not independent of the authority which pronounces sentence on his actions, and which involves the existence of an authority higher than itself, to which he is strictly responsible, here and hereafter, though at liberty now to follow the bent of his individual will. To the doings of this determining and executive power, which directs and moves the arm, whether it is stretched forth to succor or to kill, attaches, then, a moral character of fearful power; and to influence it for good, and not for evil, to guide it in the path

of rectitude and benevolence, is the appropriate work of education, as the guardian of human welfare.

11. THE PRACTICAL VIRTUES, *as Moral Powers.*—High among these attributes stands *Rectitude*—that power of self-adjustment by which man corresponds to the dictates of conscience, as the sense of right, which keeps him true to his position in the moral universe—true in thought, word, and deed, to the posture in which his Creator placed him when He " made man upright." This principle confers on the human being that noble power of self-poise, which bespeaks his dignity, as a free agent, endowed with the ability, to maintain his moral identity and stability, amid all the fluctuations of circumstance, or the plausible solicitations of evil. It tends to render him sacredly regardful of *truth* in all his communications with his fellow-beings, and of *equity* and *justice* in all his transactions. It stamps his character with *integrity* and *honor*, in every station of power—with *fidelity, honesty,* and *punctuality* in the discharge of every obligation of duty. Truthfulness, is, in a word, the one sure and firm foundation of every personal virtue, and the only ground of reliance between man and man. Without the security which it affords, the whole fabric of human society would be but a hollow structure of falsehood and hypocrisy, and life but a degrading scene of deceit, imposition, and intrigue, issuing in universal corruption and misery.

A sacred regard to truth, in all its relations of communication, whether in expression or action, while it is an element so indispensable to the existence of human virtue, in any form, is one which more than most others, is a growth of culture in the soul, and peculiarly needs the genial guardianship of watchful care, mature wisdom, and consummate skill, on the part of the cultivator. The fertile imagination and artistic fancy of childhood, are prone to create a world of unreality around the unconscious spirit, in its immaturity of knowledge and experience; and a guiding mind is ever needed to lead it onward to a distinct perception of the sacred beauty which invests the simplicity and severity of truth, and which renders any conscious violation of it a desecration. The force of truthfulness, as a moral principle, when so directed and matured, is seen in that loyal and devoted adherence to its dictates, which is exhibited in the constancy and genuine heroism of the martyr. In his estimation, it is held dearer than life, no intensity of pain or suffering has the power to wrest it from him.

12. THE HUMANE AND GENTLE VIRTUES, *as Moral Powers.*—Under this designation may be properly included those traits of disposition and character which soften the heart of man to his fellow man—

the *sympathy* which is not a mere passive condition of feeling or organic susceptibility, but a living, active participation in the emotions evinced by our fellow creatures; leading us to *rejoice* in the happiness of others, to *compassionate* them in conditions of want and distress, to *commiserate* sorrow and suffering, in every form—ignorance, error, degradation, vice, and every pressure of evil which afflicts or depresses humanity;—to cherish the catholic spirit of universal *charity, tolerance* for the sentiments which differ from our own, uniform *tenderness* toward woman and childhood, *calmness* under irritating treatment, *meekness* under a sense of wrong, *quietness* and *mildness* with the violent, *patience* and *forbearance* with waywardness and opposition and injury, *pity* for the erring, *mercy* for the evil-doer. All these godlike traits of disposition are the features which characterize the peculiar spirit of true Christian culture; none of them the mere fortuitous products of a happy constitution of body or of mind, but all earned by ceaseless watchfulness, and diligent endeavor, and, sometimes, by arduous struggles, and none of them perfected without aid from on high.

13. PERSONAL QUALITIES, *in their Moral Influence: The Self-asserting and Self-sustaining Virtues of the Individual Man.*—(1.) *Self-respect.*—As a being created in the high sphere of intelligent and moral existence, and possessed of an immortal nature, man enjoys, in a just self-respect, a security against degradation by any influence which he feels to be unworthy of the rank assigned him in the universe. Consciously noble in origin and destination, he tends, if not perverted or degraded by habit, to noble action; and if, in the plenitude of Divine favor, he is consciously recovered from a fallen condition, he feels it his immunity, as "a new creature," to have been liberated from a state of bondage—set free for the enjoyment of a "glorious liberty," and impelled to run a new and noble career. Respect for his own nature and personal condition—when kept pure from the senseless interminglings of pride, or haughtiness, or arrogance, of overweening self-esteem, or exclusive self-regard—insures to man the proper dignity of his being, and tends to elevate all his aims and actions. It is an element of high moral power; and the judicious cultivation of its influence is a prominent duty of all whose office, as educators, constitutes them the guardians of humanity.

(2.) *Ambition.*—Feeling the nobility of his nature, man, when not hopelessly degraded, instinctively seeks to act in harmony with his conscious position, and, under the influence of ambition, to aspire after advancement, in every stage and relation of his life. This desire may, it is true, be suffered to center on merely selfish purposes—on the personal aggrandizement of an individual, to the exclusion or depression of others, and to the violation of their rights. In such cases, it sinks to the level of that brutal greed which prompts one of the inferior animals to usurp the better place at the trough, and monopolize its advantages, to the exclusion of the weaker members of the herd.

But the desire of advancement, as that of progress and attainment, is utterly free from all considerations of relative superiority or advantage. It is obedience to an ennobling instinct, pure in its character, and beneficial in its results, not merely to the individual whom it elevates, but to all whom it enables him to aid from the higher sphere of ability to which he has been raised. To the student it is a most powerful incitement to application and exertion; and in the relations of moral attainment, its influence is a salutary inspiration of the highest order. It is not incompatible with the purest spirit of benevolence, in the largeness of the plans on which it delights to work, and the inestimable value of the benefits which it delights to bestow. It urges the Christian aspirant to "press toward the mark," "for the prize of his high calling," and incites him by the promise of a "crown of life."

(3.) *Magnanimity.*—Ambition naturally tends to generate another personal quality of noble character and influence—that magnanimity which lifts man above the littleness that would limit the scope of life, and fritter away its purposes in paltry pursuits, in trivial employments, or low gratifications, in snatching at mean advantages, or mingling in petty strifes. This ennobling virtue incites its possessor to high aims in all his plans and purposes, and to an utter disregard of meanness in motive or action, as manifested by others toward himself. It overlooks malice and injury, or forgives their results. It disdains revenge. It is a sure preventive of that sordid narrowness of soul which induces man to drudge, throughout life, for the mere purpose of accumulating wealth, or to practice the degrading shifts of a niggardly parsimony in expenditure, through fear of diminishing his hoards. A magnanimous spirit scorns the selfish littleness which thus wraps the individual in himself, and shuts the door of his heart against the natural claims of human brotherhood. It gives a generous breadth to measures of usefulness and benevolence, and raises human activity to a higher sphere and ampler scope in all directions.

(4.) *Resolution.*—This attribute, so important in all the practical relations of life, implies the clearness of perception and readiness of judgment in consequence of which the will is empowered instantaneously to decide the course of action. Hence the certainty and the swiftness with which execution follows purpose, the invaluable habit of promptness and dispatch in business, and of punctuality and efficiency in performance, as contrasted with the lagging irresolution, and halting, unavailing endeavor, which invariably issue in failure and disappointment.

The power of energetic and decisive resolve determines, at once, the practical value of an individual, and the reliance which may be placed on him by others. It determines, in fact, the mental health and moral life of the man, the efficacy of his action, and the estimation of his character.

Many constitutions are so formed that even this trait of mental freshness and vigor, so natural to early life, in general, needs diligent cultivation to secure its due development in particular cases. The dreamy indolence, the languid inactivity, the tendency to aimless reverie and absence of mind, which proceed from organic feebleness, wear the same aspect with the profound abstraction of deep and earnest thought, and thus excite, perhaps, in the mind of the parent or the teacher, the expectation of the fruits of close thinking and severe application—an expectation sure to be disappointed. The irresolute youth is prone to sink into habitual vacancy of mind, indecision of purpose, vacillation and feebleness of judgment, sluggishness and utter inefficiency of will.

(5.) *Courage.*—A kindred quality of soul to power and promptness of resolution, is that genuine courage which man, as a self-reliant and independent agent, is naturally called to exert; and which, as a being of conscious energy and power, by his very constitution, is one of the primary instincts of his nature. It enables him to assert his place in the creation, as an agent intrusted with dominion, to a vast extent, over nature and circumstance, and destined to a high position by the exercise of his peculiar endowments. It protects him, at the same time, from any undue ascendency usurped over him by a fellow-man. It prompts him to oppose and resist every encroachment on his rights, and to imperil life itself in defense of his natural liberty of action. It nerves him to encounter danger, to triumph over obstacles, and to master difficulties. It lightens toil, and facilitates attainment.— It gives to the energies of individual mind and will the comparative force of numbers. It enables man to achieve miracles of physical strength and moral power, not merely on the field of conflict, or under the gaze of admiration, but in the solitary grapple with physical obstacles, and the daring, unassisted encounter with the fury of the elements, when the lone adventurer hazards life on some far errand of scientific or humane exploration. In its higher relations, as a moral attribute, it inspires the individual to attack usurping or even approaching evil, in its most formidable shapes, and to encounter fearlessly opposition and opprobrium, and death itself, in the cause of truth and duty.

Courage may, it is true, degenerate into inconsiderate rashness or fool-hardy temerity, and prove itself but a blind animal impulse. It is the office of education to enlighten and elevate it, and render it a ministering spirit of good to humanity, inspiring it with intelligence, and hallowing it with the sanctity of benevolence; so that it may become worthy to fulfill its highest offices, and lead the van in noble endeavor for the advancement of human well being. Its moral power and value then become incalculable; and to cherish it is a peculiar duty of the educator.

(6.) *Fortitude.*—A virtue yet higher than even the noblest form of courage, is that *Firmness* to sustain, to bear, to withstand, to endure, or to resist every pressure of pain and of suffering which inevitable evil may call him to meet and to undergo. Along with this upholding power usually comes the *equanimity* which preserves from extremes of elation or depression, and maintains the moral identity of the individual, the *patience* which soothes and tranquilizes, and coöperating with the enduring firmness of its kindred virtue, contributes to that calm *self-possession* which leaves man master of himself, and equal, in his native greatness and acquired abilities, to resist the assaults of evil, and bear the double pressure of toil and pain with unshaken firmness.

These arduous virtues are, in no sense, innate, or constitutional merely: they are the fruits of diligent and persevering culture—the attainments of the trained and practiced spirit. They owe their power to that self-education which, although it may be wisely anticipated, must ever, in substance, be purchased at the peculiar price of personal experience and strenuous endeavor.

(7.) *Perseverance.*—Another quality of high rank as a moral power, and closely allied to the preceding group, is the persistent firmness of purpose which follows so worthily in the track of dauntless courage, and enables man, with the aid of time, to accomplish, in life-long battles with external nature, those wonders of triumphant human energy which inspire successive generations of the human race with mingled admiration and awe. It is the same trait of persistent resolution that has enabled communities to struggle, for successive years, for a foothold among the family of nations, and to endure, to the verge of extinction, for independence. The same element sustains the explorer of nature, in his years of solitary exposure and unmitigated hardship, through toil, and sickness, and peril. The same sustaining power cheers the secluded student onward through his labyrinths of exhausting investigation, pursued year after year, without aid or sympathy, yet never abandoned till some glorious discovery, duly verified, crowns his devoted loyalty to science. Indefatigable perseverance, in the face of opposition and accumulated difficulty, has been the condition of success in many a noble effort of philanthropy, in its devoted endeavors to alleviate the miseries of suffering humanity, by meliorating its outward conditions, enlightening its mental darkness, or inspiring it with the elements of a new moral and spiritual life.

Without the sustaining power of this attribute, no undertaking of moment has ever succeeded, in the experience of individuals or of communities. Yet it is a quality in which the young mind, in its eager desire of novelty, and its need of alternations of activity, is more deficient than it is in that which prompts to the most arduous attempts or heroic efforts. The vigor which manifests itself in firm adherence to plan or purpose, is usually acquired by degrees, under skillful training. But, when attained, it stamps the seal of certainty on whatever human endeavor is competent to effect.

(8.) *Self-government.*—This invaluable trait of cultivated character implies, in the individual who possesses it, the skill and the mastery acquired in the training schools of conscience, magnanimity, resolution, courage, patience, fortitude, and perseverance. It implies all these qualities turned inward for the control of self. Destitute of self-command, man, when brought to the test, is but as the infant, or the lower animal—the mere victim of passion and impulse. The main moral element of character, is, in such cases, wanting; and the individual sinks in the scale of being, not only in its moral, but its mental relations. The exigencies of life which try men's souls, and demand the perfect action of all their faculties, exhibit the inexpressible value of this trait of mental and moral power, by which man is enabled to call into activity the nobler elements of his being, and, by their authoritative mandate, control and restrain every lower tendency of his nature. He thus reigns in moral sovereignty over himself, and reveals the true majesty of manhood; while, in loyal subordination to Divine law, he manifests, not less impressively, the moral beauty of the spirit of filial obedience.

The power of *self-direction* and *self-guidance*, which that of self-government implies, enables man, as an intellectual agent, to concentrate the activity of his whole mental being, on whatever solicits his thoughtful attention, or tends to promote or enlarge his intelligence. In the moral relations of his being, it secures him against the allurements of evil, the eruptions of passion, the wreck of his peace of mind, or the moral ruin of degrading habits.

Education, in its common forms, it is true, can do little by mere external precautions, admonitions, or promptings, to confer the personal happiness which it is the peculiar office of self-government to bestow. Self-intelligence, self-experience, and self-culture, and the sanctity of religious principle, are, in this relation, the only sure reliance for human virtue. But when thus grounded and rooted, it becomes the firmest security for every trait of excellence.

(9.) *Self-reliance* is the moral reward which man becomes entitled to reap from the conscious power of self-government; and, within such limitation, it is the pledge of many of the distinguishing traits of manly virtue. It may, without the genial guidance of education, become over-weening confidence and presumption. But rightly developed, it is the proper result of faith in the attributes conferred on man's nature by the Source of his being, in virtue of which he is rendered competent for the station and the duties assigned him, as an intelligent, but responsible moral agent. The conscious feebleness which induces infancy and childhood to rely on the power on which they feel they are dependent, is a natural and appropriate influence. But in the history of the moral progress of the human being, there soon succeeds a stage, in which for the highest purposes of life and character, he is weaned from the helpless condition of dependence on others; and self-intelligence and self-respect consciously demand the independence of self-exertion and self-reliance. A manly spirit of just confidence in conscious ability, never inconsistent with the crowning grace of modesty, secures the sincere respect of all who themselves feel the dignity of manhood, whether in its dawn or its maturity. It is an indispensable element in personal character, as the pledge of courageous enterprise, and persevering application, of firmness of purpose, efficient exertion, and final success, in whatever the sense of duty, or a just ambition, prompts the aspirant to attempt.

14. THE SELF-RENOUNCING VIRTUES.—The dependent condition of childhood suggests the indispensable relation of habitual *obedience* to parental and guardian authority, and unquestioning *submission* to requirements which the young mind may not always be able to comprehend. The unity of plan and administration, and the perfect *subordination*, which even the imperfect vision of the human eye can distinctly trace in the arrangement of the visible creation, suggest to the reflective mind the universal prevalence of Law, as the prominent feature of Divine government. Order, and system, and gradation, which man sees inscribed on all things around him, and to which he is conscious that his own mind is an analogous agent, he feels to be indispensable in his own sphere of action. He recognizes them as prompters endued with a wisdom and authority above his own, and as the legitimate directors of his whole course of action. From the habit of early subordination, acquired under the guardian care of education, when rightly conducted in the sphere of home and school life, the self-intelligent mind, in its maturity of Christian growth,

learns to recognize the paramount claims of Divine authority to unhesitating obedience and cheerful submission, in the spirit of filial confidence and love, even when patient *resignation* to ordination not understood is the duty of the moment, and the utterance of the trusting spirit to its Author can only be, "not as I will, but as Thou wilt."

In the relations of human intercourse, the *Modesty* which feels what is due to others as exceeding the measure of merit in self, is no less surely an attribute of true nobility in man, than the self-reliance which forbids a feeble dependence on others or a weak, subservient compliance with their arbitrary wishes. A sincere *respect* for just superiority, indicates the open eye for excellence, as manifested in the attainments and actions of others, and a full recognition of the true worth and genuine merit embodied in their character or conduct. It is the rightful homage of the heart, which ennobles, and never degrades. It restrains presumptuous self-confidence and arrogant assumption, and accepts, in true nobleness of spirit, that lower relative position which conscious immaturity, or inexperience, or limited attainments justly assign. It constitutes the docility of childhood and youth, and not less that of the mature student of science, who loves to sit at the feet of a competent instructor, and treasure up his words of wisdom.

The true dignity of man, as an intelligent and moral being, while it secures his personal independence, and his equality, in the sight of God, with every individual of the race, is by no means inconsistent with that profound respect for man, as the offspring of the Father of spirits, which generates *humility* of spirit and deportment, between man and man, forbids all assumption as usurpation, arrogance as injury, and haughtiness as insult, and yet knows how to meet them with the gentle spirit of Christian meekness. True humility deems no office of kindness too low which can minister to the welfare of a fellow being, whether the beneficent act be gratefully or thoughtlessly received. The perfect model of this virtue exhibited by Him whose spirit was so lowly that he condescended to wash the feet of his followers, was nobly copied in the heroic explorer* who did not disdain to perform the lowest of menial offices for his suffering crew.

The spirit of *condescension* which shuns all parade and formality in intercourse with the young and the dependent, and easily and gently glides into sympathy and due familiarity with all worthy fellow beings—which skillfully breaks down every "middle wall of partition" between man and man, and knows how to "condescend to men of low

---

* Dr. Kane, in the scenes of his Arctic expedition.

estate," without the display of condescension—does homage to the Maker, in honoring the man, and recognizes the individual's own position as on the common level of membership in the great family which has but one Head and one Master.

In the management of the family and the school, the whole class of virtues on which we are now dwelling, requires particular attention in all communities in which there is a peculiar tendency, owing to the free spirit of their institutions, to place a high nominal value on those traits of character which indicate independence and self-reliance. The unreflective, unreasoning nature of childhood, early catches the spirit of the moral and social atmosphere in which it breathes, and in its natural tendency to exaggeration and excess, carries what might have been a positive excellence to a noxious vice. The absurd and culpable neglect of parental control, so prevalent in our day, often exhibits a spectacle of apparent insanity, in the boys and girls of our families and our schools abandoning the natural and beautiful character of their years, and ridiculously trying to play the part of self-responsible men and women.

15. EXAMPLE, *as a Moral Influence.*—Imitation—the power by which man is enabled to maintain his personal analogy to surrounding conditions of nature, life, and character, and thus to conform to the laws of being, in their requirements—lays him open, in the early stages of life, more particularly, to the influence of example in the actions of his fellow beings. The character of parents, teachers, companions, is, in this way, unconsciously transcribed in the daily life of childhood and youth, and, to a great extent, even in the habitual actions and expressions of maturer years. The law of sympathy, written on the human constitution, in its effects on the imitative tendency natural to man, is a most fruitful source of good or evil in every moral relation and, emphatically calls for the watchful care of the faithful educator.

16. PRUDENCE, *as a Moral Monitor.*—This virtue—if, in obedience to ancient classification, it may be so called—when it springs from just and honorable motives, is a negative but preventive wisdom, somewhat analogous in its conservative effects, to the modesty which reserves itself in communication with others. It is, indeed, but a preventive virtue, yet one which education properly inculcates as a protection against manifold evil to the individual himself as well as to others. It forbids hasty conclusions, rash resolves, injudicious communication, inconsiderate conduct, hazardous undertakings, foolish expenditures of time, strength, health, or other means of useful or beneficent action. It resembles thus the self-control which keeps man in possession of his powers, and enables him to use them at will. Its

moral value, therefore, though negative, is great, and great, obviously, in proportion to the inexperience and unconsciousness of the mind in its earlier stages of progress.

17. PERSONAL HABITS: *their Moral Value.*—(1.) *The observance of Order and Method* in the distribution of time and the succession of occupations, seems to be, in the sphere of daily life, what the regularity of alternation in day and night and the return of the seasons, is to the year. They form a security against a thoughless, random mode of life, destitute of steady aim and purpose, made up of loose scraps of time, unconsciously or idly passed in effecting nothing. Man's dignity and destination imperatively forbid such a life. Morality and religion equally condemn it. But from the multitude and variety of objects soliciting its attention, and of desires craving gratification, the young mind, unaided by education, is prone to lose itself in vague and abortive endeavor at the passing moment, instead of relying on that continuous and systematic industry to which nothing practicable is denied. As the bark of life floats down the ceaseless stream of time, the hand of diligence gathers into it, hour by hour, the rich and ever increasing freight of varied acquisition, in anticipation of another and yet happier voyage, in the great Hereafter.

Activity and energy, in any pursuit, are valuable or successful only as far as they have the continuity and sequence of *system.* It is this logical principle which gives unity and invaluable results to studies pursued under even the most limited opportunities of time, and which enables the student to weave the life of a day or of an hour into the continuous web of the week, the month, and the year.

(2.) *Industry.*—The love of work, and the habit of working—the steady pursuit of a practical purpose in practical forms, is man's first step in the efficiency which elevates him above the lower tribes of animal life, as a being endowed not with the mere sagacity—if it may be so called—of instinct, but with the intelligent forecast which foresees, and fore-ordains, and prepares; and which consciously shapes and sustains a definite purpose, and willingly and skillfully toils for its accomplishment. For the attainment of such results he is qualified by his original, native love of activity; and when this primary impelling power is directed by intelligence and benevolence, it gives efficiency and success to all his endeavors, whether in the toil which wins the treasures of knowledge and learning, in that which accumulates those of wealth, or in that which indefatigably works for human good, in the labors of beneficent philanthropy.

A judicious *apportionment of time and occupation,* however is indispensable to successful and continuous industry. By such a method only can the fatal evils of excessive close application be avoided, and the due alternation of intervals of entire rest and of renovating recreation afford opportunity of restoring and maintaining the energies of life and mind. He who does not bring to his work the powers of a whole man, is incompetent even to the task of the moment, and, in the long run, his exertions prove but a succession of failures. The jaded student or teacher, and the harassed man of business, are alike unfitted for the nobler moral purposes of their being. Habits of early-formed obedience to the Creator's laws which regulate the whole nature of man, are the only sure reliance for the possession of permanent vigor of body and mind, or the soundness of moral health in the dispositions and affections of the heart. Nothing short of this personal morality in planning and conducting the business of life, can secure the unity of life in the whole man, as an intelligent, efficient, responsible moral agent.

The hygiene of man's moral being demands the most faithful attention even to the minor details of corporal well-being; and in no respect can education more effectually subserve man's best interests, than by an enlightened and constant attention to these requisites of mental health, through the whole decisive period of childhood and youth, which so effectually determines the character of subsequent life.

The lengthened catalogue of virtues and of duties, which a distinct enumeration of the moral capabilities, of human nature, as the subject of educational culture, required, will not discourage the faithful teacher, in view of the manifold duties devolving on him as the guardian of the young mind; if, as we hope he does, he regards moral culture as the chief part of his work, and values intellectual attainment in his pupils only as it conduces to the higher ends of being and of character. Nor will the extent of detail in our suggestions be objected to by those who feel, from the daily experience of the teacher's life, how close must be the watchful observation of disposition and habit, and how thoroughly practical must be the meliorating methods of influence, in the management of the schoolroom as a scene of moral development.

If the preceding outline of classification serve no higher purpose than that of a convenient list for reference to prompt the memory of the teacher, in his endeavors to do some measure of justice to the numerous sources of moral influence on life and character, the purpose of the writer will have been effectually accomplished.

THOUGHTS ON RELIGION AND PUBLIC SCHOOLS.

BY RT. REV. GEORGE BURGESS, D. D.

If the Christian religion be from God, it ought to influence every thought and act of man, and to control every department of human life. If education be the school of character, it is least of all to be excepted from the sovereignty of that religion.

That Christian men, therefore, should view with indifference any attempt to establish an absolute separation between education and religion, is not to be expected from them till they renounce their faith. They can have no more idea that a child can be rightly educated without instruction in the laws of God and in the Gospel, than that a man can live without the same knowledge, and yet duly serve his Maker, and be prepared for the life to come.

Education, therefore, must be religious, and must include instruction in all necessary knowledge of the truths of divine revelation. In proportion as the dignity, the importance, and the efficacy of education are magnified, this necessity becomes but the more impressive and undeniable. If the educator could be content with defining his task as that of teaching to read and to write, or even to measure the earth and to number the stars, it might be allowed that this, like any other specific skill, could be imparted without saying a word concerning duty, or sin, or salvation. But we are accustomed to hear far higher praises of the work and of the men that are to form the youthful mind, and so to shape the character and the destinies of a people. Either undue and exaggerating honor is paid to the office of the teacher, or he must teach the most sacred truths, as well as those of inferior majesty and of only earthly interest.

The honest Christian must bid him take his choice. Be the teacher, he will say, of an art or any number of arts, if you will, and touch not moral things; or be a teacher of all which makes the man, and then you must teach the knowledge of God.

The honest teacher will answer, either that he is a Christian, and is ready, according to his ability, to teach religiously and to teach religion; or that he is content to leave to others the higher task, and to teach only the elements of secular science and art. In either event, there is no longer any confusion; and the question, whether there shall be a course of secular instruction, and a separate course of religious instruction, or whether one course shall mingle both, becomes a question of possibility or of expediency, and is transferred from the sphere of abstract principle and imperative conscience.

The clergy of most countries have adhered to the wider view of education in schools, and have insisted, as long as they could, that it should be distinctly Christian, and should even form a part of the ecclesiastical system. They are not to be blamed; and had union in religious belief been preserved, it is hard to prove that their plan would not have been altogether the best. But for this it is now too late. In all free nations the freedom of discussion, doubt, and denial has been practically asserted; and, for all purposes of religious education, the body of Christians is *one* no longer.

In education, viewed as a whole, the place to be occupied by religious truth has not lost, for this cause the smallest measure of its importance. Religion is still as sovereign there as ever. Somewhere in all true and sufficient education it must have its throne; and from that throne it must sway all the rest.

But the State can support no such throne; because the State is composed of an immense mass of men whose religion is not the same. When education becomes a matter of public provision, the very highest part of education is excepted. The public school, even if under that name we should embrace any more elevated institutions which the public funds might sustain, is not the seat of that portion of this moral work which has to do, most directly and most mightily, with the heart. That, however, it must forego, and be content with its own appropriate task and praise.

The higher task must be performed elsewhere; and the consecrated precincts of the church, and the equally hallowed walls of home, must be the scene of religious instruction. It has there, too, a fitter and a happier sphere than the State, with all its wealth or its universal care, can attempt to furnish.

All this is perfectly consistent with the undoubted fact that religion is the prompting motive from which public education has had its origin, and must have its best support. It sustains that education as it sustains every good design. It desires that all men should be trained in useful knowledge of every kind, because it desires their improvement and happiness. Ignorance, in its view, is weakness, is poverty, is exposure to moral disease, is the absence of many of the highest enjoyments, is the obstruction of the purposes for which the beneficent Creator made man in His own image. Therefore, ignorance is an enemy to godliness, and a hinderance of salvation, as well as, in itself, a positive and mighty evil; and religion must long and labor to remove it from the path of society. To suppose that a Christian can be indifferent to the intellectual cultivation of his fellow-men would simply imply that he had no appreciation of its value for himself; for he must wish to communicate all which he prizes.

It is perfectly true, also, that even in the teachers of all secular knowledge, religious men will desire and prefer a spirit and principles like their own. A father who merely commits his son to the instructions of a writing-master, would rejoice to find in him a man of Christian worth, and would feel that the boy was somewhat safer. It is not possible, in any department of life, to exclude or neutralize the beneficial influence of the steadfast fear of God and the sincere love of mankind. The religious man or woman will always be, all other things being equal, unspeakably the better teacher, even of arithmetic or of needlework. Under any system of public education, however remote from a sectarian or exclusive character, this preference will be felt, and cannot be changed into indifference.

Under these systems the introduction of religious instruction, in combination with secular instruction, is relinquished, not upon grounds of abstract excellence, but upon those of convenience or necessity. Accordingly, either the system is not extended over the youngest or the oldest of those who are to be educated; or if it be, it does not command a general acceptance. The public school offers no urgent invitation to the child just rising from infancy; it leaves him, not unwillingly, to the gentle hands of his mother or of some maternal preceptress. At the other end of the course, colleges and universities are commonly allied to the Church rather than to the State. From the latter they accept aid; to the former they accord welcome intervention and an active control. Not merely financial or political considerations fix the limits of public education on this side of the highest institutions of learning. For it is felt that all education must begin and end in religion; that the infant must learn the names of God and of the crucified Redeemer with his first accents; and that the young man should not go forth into the world of professional study, action, and influence, without a settled faith. But between these two periods lies the time which public education appropriates; appropriates, simply because the interests of the commonwealth require the instruction of all in useful knowledge, and because no other power can furnish the means of such instruction for all alike.

If the task of religious education be then declined by the public teacher, it is left in hands which certainly are better fitted to execute it with dignity, with diligence, with fidelity, and with tenderness. It is in the hands of special teachers, whose labors are voluntary; of pastors; and of parents.

The Sunday School has become one of the institutions of society, wherever the English tongue is spoken. It enlists a body of teachers whose intelligence is animated by no other impulse than that of Christian love. They receive no hire, and they wield no instruments of discipline. They come to their pupils on they day which is consecrated to all holy works of piety and charity. There is nothing to disturb the pure influence of their instruction; no other studies crowding in; no intermixture of heathen mythology or abstract science; no hurry to the playground; no dread of the rod or superadded task; and none of those hereditary associations, which, absurd, unjust, and pernicious as they are, yet do still, more or less, connect themselves with the relation between the boy and the professional teacher. Love is the bond between those who teach and those who learn on the Sabbath.

When the pastor is the teacher, love is united with reverence. His office inspires that reverence, and his intelligence in sacred things merits a confidence which might elsewhere be less readily bestowed. The duties of pastors to the young may be but imperfectly undertaken, especially where the ancient and most useful custom of catechising has fallen into neglect. But it would still be great injustice to compare their influence with that of teachers who sustain no sanctity of office, have devoted no special study to sacred letters, and are not, in virtue of their office, supposed to be persons of piety.

But no teachers have an appointment more holy or divine than fathers and mothers. The cannot but educate their children religiously or irreligiously. No separation can take place in the training of home; for that is purely for the heart and soul; and its first and supreme end is the goodness of the child. He learns his prayers on the knees of his mother; he is taught to examine himself at the close of each day; his conduct is, without ceasing, subjected to a watchful scrutiny; there is no vacation, no recess, no occasion when he is released from this supervision. These teachers have an authority, too, which, for him, is the direct interpretation of the will of his Maker. To the child, the voice of the parent is the voice of God; for so has God commanded. And all which he hears and learns from these sources comes to him as nourishment from the bosom of an exhaustless love, to which his childhood must cling as if it were to him the whole wide universe.

This is the provision which the Church and the family, with many collateral aids, assign for religious education. Piety in the public teachers, and religious truth in the common school, would be additional aids; but are they indispensable, or could their influence be weighed in the balance against all this? Whatever may be the excellence of many professional instructors, whatever their noble enthusiasm in their calling, it is not to be disputed, that, as a body, the teachers of public schools are governed, in the choice and pursuit of their occupation, by the same motives which incite persons of respectable and worthy characters in all departments of business. They engage in it for a remuneration; they abandon it when it becomes unprofitable; or they exchange it for positions which are more lucrative or more to their taste. They are not appointed, and cannot well be, for their personal devoutness. If they should teach religion, it would be as they teach grammar, not because the task is known to be enthroned in their affections, but because it is made a part of their business. We do not disparage the transcendent beneficence and exalted piety of many teachers; but it is an accident, so to speak, whether these mark the character of an individual teacher; they are not and cannot be the distinguishing properties of a class selected as teachers must always be under any public arrangements. Little will it avail, that a cold, dry, unfeeling, and perhaps unbelieving teacher, consent to teach catechism, or to open his school with prayers. A truly religious teacher, even without those exercises, will leave some impress of his own spirit on the minds which he has assisted in forming and replenishing. This can be attained even now; and if any would avoid this, they must make piety a ground of exclusion from the office. The most determined unbeliever would hardly desire such an issue; but neither can piety be made a condition of admission, if it were even in our power to enforce the rules, since the talents and acquisitions which make the successful teacher are dissociated from it; and since, precious as it is, it cannot, in this position, be deemed one of the chief instruments on which the cause of religion must rely.

What, then, is the power which Christianity *cannot*, and what is that which it *can*, exercise in the system of public schools of a land like our own?

It *cannot* teach all its doctrines and laws, as they are held by any body of Christian believers.

It *cannot* blend religious truth with secular instruction, to any degree which implies the attempt to communicate systematic religious knowledge.

It *cannot* attempt to inculcate a religious character, or, in other words, faith in the Lord Jesus Christ, by precept and exhortation.

It *can* take for granted a general acquaintance, in the pupils, with the facts of Christianity, united with reverence for it as a Divine revelation.

It *can* infuse into the teacher, so far as he obeys it, a spirit which attracts to his religion, and inspires the desire to resemble its faithful followers.

It *can* afford a Christian view of every science and every department of knowledge, and show their connection with revealed truth in its great outlines.

It *can* inculcate the whole moral code of the Gospel, by rule and example.

It *can* exclude and counteract every influence of infidelity.

It *can*, in many instances, with the universal consent of the community, affix a more decidedly religious character to the school duties of each day, by the observance of daily prayers.

It *can*, with the same consent, introduce the Bible, and promote, by daily reading, the familiar knowledge of its contents; not as if it were a mere reading-book, though the best, but as the generally acknowledged word of God.

It *can*, with the same consent, which may generally be assumed, impress, as occasion is offered, all that great and priceless mass of truth in which all Christians are substantially united.

☞ Orders for any of DR. BARNARD'S Publications can be addressed to
P. O. Box "U,"
Hartford,
CONN.

ENGLISH PEDAGOGY AND SCHOOLS.

TREATISES AND THOUGHTS—OLD AND NEW,
ON
EDUCATION, THE SCHOOL, AND THE TEACHER.

By HENRY BARNARD, LL. D.

ENGLISH PEDAGOGY. *First Series.* Ascham's *Schoolmaster;* Cecil's *Advice to his son;* Bacon on *Education and Studies,* with Annotations by Whately; Wotton's *Apothegms on Education;* Milton's *Tractate on Education;* Hartlib's *Plan of an Agricultural College;* Petty's *Trade School;* Locke's *Thoughts on Education;* Spencer's *Education;* Fuller's *Good Schoolmaster;* Shenstone's *Schoolmistress;* Cowper's *Review of Schools;* Crabbe's *Schools of the Borough;* Hood's *Irish Schoolmaster;* with *Index to Subjects.* 480 pp. Price, $2.50.

Second Series. William of Wykeham, Dean Colet, and the *Public Schools of Winchester, Eton, St. Pauls, Christ Church, Westminster, and Harrow,* with Report and Action of Royal Commission in 1866; Cardinal Wolsey's *Course for Ipswich Grammar School;* Elyot's *Governor;* Mulcaster's *Positions;* Hoole's *New Discovery of the Old Art of Teaching;* Cowley's *Plan of a Philosophical College;* South, Steele, and Pope on *Schools and Education;* Goldsmith's *Essay and Thoughts on Education;* Johnson's *Plan of Studies;* *Pedagogical Views of the 19th Century,* by Arnold, Carlyle, Faraday, Froude, Gladstone, Hamilton, Huxley, Lowe, Lyell, Masson, Mill, Russell, Southey, Temple, Tyndall, Whewell and others. 628 pp. $3.00.

PRIMARY AND ELEMENTARY INSTRUCTION IN GREAT BRITAIN: Object Teaching and Oral Lessons on Social Science and Common Things, with various Illustrations of the Principles and Practice of Education in the Model and Training Schools of England, Ireland and Scotland. *Second Edition.* 544 pp. $3.00.

SCIENTIFIC AND TECHNICAL SCHOOLS: Historical Development of the Department of Art and Science, and other Institutions of Special Instruction in Great Britain. 244 pp. $2.50.

EDUCATION, STUDIES AND CONDUCT: Letters and Advice to Studious Youth, by men eminent in literature and public service, on the Principles of Education, the Ordering of Studies, and the Conduct of Life, with Biographical Notes. 416 pp. $2.50.

NATIONAL EDUCATION: Systems of Public Instruction in England, Ireland, and Scotland. 800 pp. $4.50.

DR. HENRY BARNARD'S
STANDARD EDUCATIONAL PUBLICATIONS,
EMBRACING THE
HISTORY, ORGANIZATION, ADMINISTRATION, STUDIES, DISCIPLINE AND STATISTICS OF SCHOOLS OF EVERY GRADE AND FOR ALL CLASSES IN DIFFERENT COUNTRIES

Official Reports.

ANNUAL REPORTS AS SECRETARY OF THE BOARD OF COMMISSIONERS, AND SUPERINTENDENT OF COMMON SCHOOLS IN CONNECTICUT, 1 Vol. $4.00.

ANNUAL CIRCULARS AND REPORTS AS COMMISSIONER OF PUBLIC SCHOOLS IN RHODE ISLAND. $5.00.

REPORTS AND CIRCULARS AS NATIONAL COMMISSIONER OF EDUCATION.
Annual Report for 1867-8, 1 Vol. $5.00.
Special Report on the Educational Interests of the District of Columbia together with an account of systems and statistics of Public Instruction in American and European Cities, and of Schools for Freedmen and Colored children.
Special Report on National Education. $4.50.
Special Report on Technical Education. $4.50.

Educational Periodicals.

CONNECTICUT COMMON SCHOOL JOURNAL, 1838-42, 4 Vols. $4.00. Second Series, 1851-54.

JOURNAL OF R. I. INSTITUTE OF INSTRUCTION, 1845-48, 3 Vols. $3.75.

AMERICAN JOURNAL OF EDUCATION, 1856-71, 22 Vols.
Single Number, as issued, except 2º, 20, 33, $1.50.
Single Volume, in cloth, except IX, XIII, XIV, $4.50.
Single Volume, in Half Goat, $5.50.
Set of 22 Volumes, in Cloth. $93.50.
Set of 22 Volumes, in Half Goat, $110.00.

Biography, History, Organization, &c.

EDUCATIONAL BIOGRAPHY:—
1. AMERICAN TEACHERS AND EDUCATORS, $3.50. Second Series, $3.50.
2. PROMOTERS OF AMERICAN EDUCATION, $3.50.
3. ENGLISH TEACHERS AND EDUCATORS, $3.50.
4. FRENCH TEACHERS AND EDUCATORS, $3.50.
5. SWISS, ITALIAN, AND DUTCH TEACHERS, $3.50.

TRIBUTE TO GALLAUDET, with an account of the American Asylum for Deaf Mutes, &c., $2.00.

EDUCATIONAL CONVENTIONS, AND ASSOCIATIONS.
PART I. National Associations.
PART II. State Conventions and Associations.
PART III. European Educational Associations.
PART IV. Periodicals—American and European.

Public Instruction.

NATIONAL EDUCATION IN EUROPE (1854.) $2.00.

HISTORICAL DEVELOPMENT OF COMMON SCHOOLS, ENDOWED GRAMMAR SCHOOLS AND PUBLIC HIGH SCHOOLS IN CONNECTICUT. $3.00.

ELEMENTARY AND SECONDARY INSTRUCTION :
VOL. I. German States. 856 pages. $4.50.
VOL. II. Switzerland, France, Belgium, Holland, Denmark Norway, Sweden, Russia, Greece, Turkey, Italy, Portugal and Spain. $4.50.
VOL. III. Great Britain and American States.

UNIVERSITIES, and Superior Instruction :
PART I. German States, with an account of the Universities of the Middle Ages. $3.00.
PART II. France, Italy, Belgium, Holland, Scandinavia, Russia, Spain and Portugal.
PART III. Great Britain and American States.

PROFESSIONAL AND SPECIAL SCHOOLS:
1. SCIENCE AND NATIONAL INDUSTRIES. $4.50.
2. SEMINARIES FOR TEACHERS. $4.50.
3. MILITARY SCHOOLS, Part I and II. $4.50.
4. PREVENTIVE AND REFORMATORY SCHOOLS. $4.50.

Manuals of Organization and Method.

PAPERS FOR THE TEACHER AND SCHOOL OFFICER; or Library of Practical Education, gathered from the experience of different countries. REVISED EDITION. In uniform cloth binding. Sold in single volumes, or sets.

1. AMERICAN CONTRIBUTIONS TO THE PHILOSOPHY AND PRACTICE OF EDUCATION. First Series. $2.50.
Russell, Hill, Thayer, Burgess, Mann, Huntington, Hart, Page.

2. OBJECT TEACHING AND OTHER METHODS OF PRIMARY INSTRUCTION in the Model and Training Schools of Great Britain. $2.50.

3. MODERN GERMAN PEDAGOGY. $3.00.
Abbenrode, Beneke, Diesterweg, Fichte, Fröbel, Graser, Hentschel, Herbart, Raumer.

4. EDUCATIONAL APHORISMS AND SUGGESTIONS—Ancient and Modern. $2.00.

5. ENGLISH PEDAGOGY: or Treatises and Thoughts on Education, the School and the Teacher in English Literature. First Series. $2.50.
Ascham, Bacon, Wolton, Milton, Hartlib, Petty, Fuller, Locke, Shenstone, Cowper, Gray, Crabbe, Coleridge, Hood.

6. PESTALOZZI AND PESTALOZZIANISM. $3.00
Memoir, Leonard and Gertrude, Evening Hours of a Hermit, how Gertrude teaches her children, etc.

7. GERMAN EDUCATIONAL REFORMERS. $3.00.
Hieronymians, Erasmus, Trotzendorf, Sturm, Luther, Melancthon, Ratich, Comenius, Franke, Basedow, etc.

8. FRENCH SCHOOLS AND PEDAGOGY. $3.00.
Rabelais, La Salle, Fenelon, Montaigne, Rollin, Rousseau, Cousin, Guizot, Wilm, Marcel, etc.

9. DUTCH AND SCANDINAVIAN SCHOOLS. $3.00.
Van der Palm, Visser, Cuvier, Cousin, Bache, Arnold, Nissen, Siljeström and others.

10. GREEK AND ITALIAN SCHOOLS—Ancient and Modern.

11. ENGLISH PEDAGOGY: Second Series. $2.50.
Eylot, Colet, Mulcaster, Hoole, Cowley. Public Schools as they were and as they ARE, Faraday, Temple, Lowe, Mill and others.

12. AMERICAN PUBLIC SCHOOLS AND PEDAGOGY: a Digest of Rules and Regulations, and Courses of Instruction for graded Schools in American Cities, with an account of Public Schools in the Chief Cities of Europe. $3.00.

13. SECONDARY INSTRUCTION: Systems, Instructions, Subjects and Methods of Instruction, preparatory to Colleges and Universities, and to Special Schools of Practical Science, $3.00.

14. DRAWING IN IDEAL AND INDUSTRIAL ART: Programmes and Methods of the best European and American Schools. $3.00.

15. SCHOOL ARCHITECTURE. Revised Edition. $2.00.

16. SCHOOL CODES—Old and New. $3.00.

17. TRUE STUDENT LIFE: Hints respecting Studies and Conduct by men eminent in letters and affairs. $3.00.

18. EDUCATIONAL BIBLIOGRAPHY: Catalogue of Books relating to the History, Organization, Administration, Studies, Discipline, and Statistics of Schools and Education in different Countries. $3.00.

Orders will be received for any of the above Books by E. STEIGER, New York.

AMERICAN PEDAGOGY: Contributions to the Principles and Methods of Education, by Barnard, Burgess, Bushnell, Channing, Cowdery, Dickinson, Doane, Everett, Fairchild, Hart, Hopkins, Huntington, Mann, Page, Philbrick, Pierce, Potter, Sheldon, Wayland, and Wilbur. Selected from Barnard's American Journal of Education. First Series. *Third Ed.* 576 pages. $3.00.

CONTENTS.

                                                                                                     PAGE.

I.—EDUCATION AND SCHOOLS..1-4
    BUSHNELL—PAGE—POTTER—WOODBRIDGE—MANN........................ 5
II.—FACULTIES AND STUDIES—Their Order and Method of Treatment..5-268
    I. INTELLECTUAL AND MORAL EDUCATION. By William Russell.................5-156
        1. The Perceptive Faculties... 5
        2. The Expressive Faculties... 57
        3. The Reflective Faculties... 101
    II. MORAL EDUCATION. By William Russell................................ 157-186
        Health—Intellect—Taste—Sensibility—Instinctive Tendencies........... 160
        Primary Emotions—Benignant Affections—Generous Affections........... 165
        Religious Principles—The Will—Practical Virtues—Humane Virtues...... 175
        Personal Qualities—Self Renouncing Virtues—Example—Habits........... 179
    III. RELIGIOUS INSTRUCTION. By Rt. Rev. George Burgess.................... 187-192
        Intrinsic Importance—Limitations in Public Schools.................... 187
    IV. THE TRUE ORDER OF STUDY. By Thomas Hill, D.D........................ 193-254
        Mathesis—Physics—History—Psychology—Theology.................... 196
    V. THE POWERS TO BE EDUCATED. By Thomas Hill, D.D...................... 245-256
        The Senses—Inward Intuition—Memory—Reason—Sensibility—Will...... 245
    VI. MIND—OBJECTS AND METHODS OF ITS CULTURE. By Francis Wayland, D.D. 257-272
        1. Science of Education—To discover, apply, and obey God's Laws......... 259
        2. Methods of training the mind to these objects......................... 266
III.—THE TEACHER.. 273-304
    I. THE DIGNITY OF THE OFFICE, AND SPECIAL PREPARATION. By W. E. Channing.... 273
    II. THE TEACHER'S MOTIVES. By Horace Mann............................. 277
IV.—NATIONAL AND STATE RELATIONS TO EDUCATION........... 305-336
    I. EDUCATION A NATIONAL INTEREST. George Washington...................... 305
    II. THE DUTY OF THE STATE TO MAKE EDUCATION UNIVERSAL................... 31
        BISHOP DOANE—Address to the People of New Jersey....................... 313
        PENN—ADAMS—JEFFERSON—MADISON—JAY—RUSH—KENT................... 317
    III. THE RIGHT AND PRACTICE OF PROPERTY TAXATION FOR SCHOOL PURPOSES....... 323
        D. D. BARNARD—Report to the Legislature of New York..... 323
        DANIEL WEBSTER—The early School Policy of New England................ 327
        HORACE MANN—The principles underlying the Ordinance of 1647........... 828
        HENRY BARNARD—The Early School Codes of Connecticut and New Haven.... 332
                National Land Grants for Educational Purposes................... 334
V.—VARIOUS ASPECTS OF POPULAR AND HIGHER EDUCATION.... 337-400
    I. BISHOP ALONZO POTTER, D.D., of Penn................................. 337
        Consolidation and other Modifications of American Colleges.............. 337
    II. EDWARD EVERETT, President of Harvard College........................... 343
        Reminiscences of School and College Life—Conditions of a good school.... 344
        Popular Education and Sound Science—Moral Education.................. 350
        Generous Studies—Homeric Controversy—Education and Civilization...... 356
        Popular Education—Boston Public Library—Female Education............ 361
    III. F. A. P. BARNARD, D.D., LL.D., President of Columbia College................ 367
        College Contributions to the American Educated Mind.................... 367
        Sub-graduate and Post-graduate Collegiate Course—Oral Teaching 371
        Higher Scientific Instruction—Elective Studies......................... 375

AMERICAN PEDAGOGY.—FIRST SERIES.

	PAGE
IV. MARK HOPKINS, D.D., President of Williams College	378
Education—Self Education—Female Education—Academies	378
Medical Science—Theological Education—Colleges	381
V. JAMES E. FAIRCHILD, D.D., President of Oberlin College	385
Co-education of the Sexes	385
VI.—PROFESSIONAL OR NORMAL AIMS AND METHODS IN TEACHING	401
I. JOHN S. HART, Principal of State Normal School, Trenton	401
What is Special or Professional Preparation?—Teaching—Training	403
Recitations—Art of Questioning	417
II. CYRUS PIERCE, Principal of the first State Normal School	425
Aims and Methods in Training Pupil-Teachers	425
III. NICHOLAS TILLINGHAST, Principal of State Normal School at Bridgewater	431
Aims and Methods in Training Teachers	432
IV. J. W. DICKINSON, Principal of State Normal School at Westfield	433
The Philosophy and Method of Teaching at Westfield	433
V. D. P. PAGE, Principal of State Normal School, Albany	437
The Pouring-in Process—The Drawing-out Process—Waking up of Mind	437
DR. WAYLAND—THOMAS H. GRIMKE	447
Method of Recitation and Study	448
VI. E. A. SHELDON, Principal of State Training School, Oswego	449
Object Teaching as pursued at Oswego	449
VII. H. B. WILBUR, Superintendent of State School for Feeble Minded Youth	459
Object Teaching as pursued at Oswego	459
VIII. S. W. MASON, Principal of Hancock Grammar School, Boston	465
Physical Exercises in School	465
IX. M. F. COWDERY, Superintendent of Public Schools, Sandusky	473
Formation of Moral Character	473
VII.—WORK BEFORE THE AMERICAN TEACHER AND EDUCATOR	585–576
I. HENRY BARNARD	485
Magnitude and Modes of Advancing the Educational Interests of the United States	485
II. HORACE MANN	513
Addresses as President of the National Convention of the Friends of Common Schools, in Philadelphia, 1849	513
III. JOHN D. PHILBRICK, Superintendent of Public Schools, Boston	513
Address before the National Teachers' Association, 1862	510

SECOND SERIES.

[A Second Volume of Selections from Barnard's American Journal of Education on Topics in the wide field of American Pedagogy, will be issued in 1873, and will contain Reports, Essays, and Thoughts, by Adams, Bache, Barnard, Beecher, Boutwell, Brooks, Bushnell, Choate, Eaton, Emerson, Gregory, Harris, Huntington, Kiddle, Lewis, Lindsley, Mann, Sears, Smith, White, and others.]

I.—EDUCATION AND SCHOOLS	1–4
II.—LETTERS TO A YOUNG TEACHER. By Gideon F. Thayer	5–104
VII.—POWER OF CHARACTER AND EXAMPLE	385–416
I. HORACE BUSHNELL	385
Magnetism of Character—Unconscious Influence	387
II. RT. REV. F. D. HUNTINGTON	393
Unconscious Tuition	393

PRIMARY SCHOOLS AND ELEMENTARY INSTRUCTION: Object Teaching and Oral Lessons on Social Science and Common Things, with various illustrations of the Principles and Practice of Primary and Elementary Instruction in the Model and Training Schools of Great Britain. *Second Edition.* 544 pp. $3.00.

CONTENTS.

	PAGE.
I. METHODS OF INSTRUCTION. By Rev. William Ross............................	7
1. The Catechetical Method..	7
Conditions of a correct Question..	9
Conditions of a good Answer...	10
Counsels and Cautions...	13
2. Socratic Method applied to Religious Subjects..............................	15
3. Defense of the Catechetical Method.......................................	17
II. ORAL LESSONS ON REAL OBJECTS. By Thomas Morrison, Rector of the Free Church Training College, Glasgow,..	21
Science of Common Things,..	22
Oral Lessons—First Stage,...	23
" Second Stage,...	26
" Third Stage,..	26
Requisites for success in Oral Teaching,..	27
Materials,..	29
Methods,..	29
Notes of Lessons,...	30
First Stage. Example I. The Cow. II. A Fire. III. The Camel. IV. The Elephant,..	31
List of Subjects,..	35
Second Stage. Example I. Winnowing of Corn. II. The Spider's Web. III. The common Bat. IV. Reaping of Corn. V. Watering of Streets. VI. The Duck. VII. Nests of Birds. VIII. The making of Grain into Meal,.	36
List of Subjects,..	41
Third Stage. Example I. The Thermometer. II. The Barometer. III. Dew. IV. The Land and Sea Breeze. V. Why does Ice float. VI. Application of Lesson. VII. Locality often determines Custom. VIII. Rice. IX. The Cotton Plant. X. Oceanic Currents,..	42
List of Subjects—On Heat,...	47
Mechanics, Pneumatics, Optics, Daily life,.....................................	48
III. SPECIMEN NOTES OF LESSONS. Selected from various authors,................	49
The Palm Tree—Analysis of a Reading Lesson,.................................	49
Pens—1. Ancient Pens,..	49
2. Modern,..	50
Pens—differently treated—*First Lesson*,..	53
" " " *Second Lesson*,..	55
" " " *Third Lesson*,...	56
Roads,...	51
Weekly Expenditure of a Laboring Man—Food,..................................	52
" " Cooking of Food,....................	53
Climate,...	55
IV. GALLERY TRAINING LESSONS—ORALLY PRESENTED, ON NATURAL SCIENCE AND COMMON THINGS. By David Stow, Founder of the Glasgow Normal Training Seminary,...	57
Oral Training Lessons in Science,..	57
Objects of daily observation and experience,...................................	59

CONTENTS.

	PAGE.
Practical Examples,	63
I. *The Camel.* II. *The Mole.* III. *Air a Conductor of Sound,*	71
Selections of subjects for Oral Gallery Lessons,	74
I. Infant or Initiatory Department. II. Juvenile Department. III. Senior Department. IV. Miscellaneous Department. V. Human Body and Health,	87
Apparatus and Material required,	91
V. PRIZE SCHEMES FOR THE ENCOURAGEMENT OF A KNOWLEDGE OF COMMON THINGS AMONG TEACHERS. By Prof. Sullivan, and Lord Ashburton,	93
Special efforts to stimulate Teachers,	93
Prof. Sullivan's Prize Scheme,	97
Questions for the Ashburton Prizes,	101
VI. NECESSITY AND PROGRESS OF ELEMENTARY INSTRUCTION IN ECONOMICAL SCIENCE. By Charles Knight,	105
Objections to teaching Political Economy to the Laborer,	105
Objections answered by Dr. Chalmers, and Dr. Whately,	105
William Ellis, and the Birkbeck Schools,	106
Specimen Lessons by Mr. Shields at the Peckham School,	108
Lectures on Social Science, by Mr. Ellis,	110
Enlarged course at Mechanic's Institutes,	112
VII. SUBJECTS AND METHODS OF TEACHING IN REFERENCE TO THE PREVENTION OF MISERY AND CRIME. By Edward Campbell Tainsh,	116
Causes of Misery and Crime,	116
Idleness, Intemperance, Improvidence,	117
Extravagance, Dishonesty, Ungoverned Passions,	118
Correct Habits of feeling, thinking and acting,	119
Specimen Lesson—on Industry,	120
" " Economy, Forethought,	121
" " Drunkenness,	123
" " Honesty,	123
" " Envy, Jealousy, Cruelty, Revenge,	126
" " Morality,	127
" " Knowledge,	128
" " Social Relationship,	129
Objections to this kind of teaching answered,	131
VIII. PROGRESS OF ELEMENTARY EDUCATION IN IRELAND,	133
Varied educational experience,	133
Efforts of the English Government to establish Protestant Schools,	134
Parliamentary Commissioners of Inquiry,	135
Board of Commissioners of National Education,	136
Results—I. National system—as to creed and politics,	137
" II. Professional training of teachers,	138
" III. Schools of different grades,	143
" IV. School-houses,	147
" V. Cheap and uniform Text-books,	147
" VI. Inspection,	147
" VII. Liberal appropriations,	148
Testimony as to success in 1850,	150
IX. SUBJECTS AND METHODS OF PRIMARY EDUCATION, AS PRESENTED IN THE MODEL INFANT SCHOOL, DUBLIN. By Thomas Urry Young,	155
Necessity and nature of the Infant or Primary School,	155
Moral Education,	158
Intellectual Education,	162
Physical Education,	166
Hints to Teachers,	167
Qualifications of the Teacher,	169
Pestalozzi's opinion,	170
Wilderspin's,	170
School Rules and Regulations,	171
Rules for Parents,	171
Maxims to be observed by Teachers,	171

CONTENTS.

	PAGE.
School-room Rules,	172
Play-ground Rules,	172
Sanitary Regulations,	172
Time Table,	174
Daily Time Table,	175
Synopsis of a Weeks Lessons,	175
Developing Lessons—or the training of the Perceptive Faculties,	176
Form,	178
Lines,	180
Angles,	181
Plane Figures,	182
Solids—*Specimen Lesson*,	184
Color—*Specimen Lesson*,	186
Size—*Specimen Lesson*,	188

X. ORGANIZATION AND INSTRUCTION OF THE ORDINARY NATIONAL SCHOOLS, ... 205
  1. Circular of Commissioners in reference to the organization of National Schools, 205
  2. Remarks on the details of organization, ... 208
    (*a.*) Tripartite System, ... 210
    (*b.*) Bipartite System, ... 211
  3. Time Table for Boys' School, ... 212
  4. Time Table for Girls' School, ... 213
  5. Topics of Lectures on Methods of Teaching, ... 214

XI. PROGRESS OF ELEMENTARY EDUCATION IN SCOTLAND, ... 215
  Enactment of 1464, ... 215
  First Book of Discipline in 1560, ... 215
  Act of 1615, 1633, 1696, ... 216
  Results of the Parochial Schools, ... 217
  Act of 1829, ... 219
  Sessional Schools, ... 219
  Extension of the system, ... 220
  Lord Brougham and Dr. Chalmers, on the social character of the schools, ... 221
  Plan for improving the system, ... 223
  Statistics, ... 224

XII. SUBJECTS AND METHODS OF EARLY EDUCATION. By James Currie. Principal of the Church of Scotland Training College, Edinburgh, ... 229
  I. Introduction—General character of the Infant School, ... 229
  II. Physical circumstances, ... 233
  III. Intellectual instruction, ... 236
    1. Object-Lessons, ... 236
      List of Subjects for First Stage—(1.) *Natural History*. (2.) *Domestic Economy*. (3.) *Physiology*. (4.) *Industrial Economy*. (5.) *Common Things*. 6.) *Physical Appearance*, ... 239
      List of Subjects for Second Stage, ... 241
      " " Third Stage, ... 242
      Examples in Outline of Lessons for First Stage, ... 242
        I. The Sheep. II. A Bed. III. The Mouth. IV. The Baker's Shop. V. The Cart. VI. Rain, ... 244
      Examples of Lessons for Second Stage, ... 244
        I. The Elephant. II. The Sponge. III. The term "Porous," 245
      Example of Lessons for Analysis, ... 245
    2. Number, ... 247
    3. Color and Form, ... 258
    4. Singing, ... 267
    5. Geography, ... 269
    6. Reading to Children, ... 272
    7. Reading and Spelling, ... 277
    8. Grammar, ... 284
  IV. Religious Instruction, ... 284
    Example (1.) Narrative. (2.) Emblem. (3.) Precept. (4.) Prayer. (5.) Moral Lesson on Truth, ... 291

CONTENTS.

	PAGE.
Exercises of Devotion,	292

XIII. METHOD AND EXAMINATION. By James Morrison, Rector of Free Church Training College, Glasgow, ... 294
   1. Method in general, ... 294
   2. Synthesis and Analysis, ... 294
   3. Individual Instruction, ... 298
   4. Simultaneous Instruction, ... 299
   5. Mutual Instruction, ... 300
   6. Questioning, ... 301
   7. Ellipsis, ... 304
   8. Examination, ... 305

XIV. LESSON ON COLOR. By J. H. Hay, ... 321
   Diagram, ... 322

XV. PROGRESS OF ELEMENTARY EDUCATION IN ENGLAND, ... 323
   1. Early educational movements, ... 323
   2. Foundation of Grammar Schools and Free Schools, ... 324
   3. Origin of Sunday Schools, labors of Lancaster and Bell, ... 328
      Mechanic's Institutions—Ragged Schools, ... 332
   4. Parliamentary Action, from 1807 to 1854, ... 337
      Measures of the Committee of Council, ... 341
      Normal Schools, or Training Colleges, in England, ... 349
      Earliest efforts for the Professional Training of Teachers, ... 349
      Parliamentary Grant of 1835, ... 350
      System of Denominational Training Colleges, ... 351

XVI. BRITISH AND FOREIGN SCHOOL SOCIETY, ... 355
   History of Society, ... 355
    " Normal Establishment, ... 355

XVII. MANUAL OF THE SYSTEM OF PRIMARY INSTRUCTION IN THE MODEL SCHOOLS OF THE BRITISH AND FOREIGN SCHOOL SOCIETY, ... 381
   I. Fittings and Organization, ... 381
      1. School Fittings, ... 381
      2. Sections and Drafts, ... 383
      3. Classification for Reading, ... 383
      4.   " Writing, ... 384
      5.   " Arithmetic, ... 384
      6.   " for other Studies, ... 385
   II. Agency Employed, ... 385
      1. Pupil Teachers, ... 385
      2. Monitors, ... 387
   III. Methods of Instruction, ... 391
      1. General Principles, ... 391
      2. Preparatory Section, ... 393
      3. Collective Teaching, ... 395
      4. Class Teaching—Reading, ... 399
      5.   "   " Interrogation, ... 401
      6.   "   " Spelling, ... 409
      7.   "   " Writing, ... 410
      8.   "   " Arithmetic, ... 411
      9.   "   " Grammar and Composition, ... 415
      10. Class Teaching—Geography, ... 421
      11.   "   " Miscellaneous Lessons, ... 425
      12.   "   " Drawing, ... 426
      13.   "   " Vocal Music, ... 426
   IV. Scriptural Instruction, ... 427
   V. Girls' School—Needle-work, ... 432

XVIII. BRITISH AND FOREIGN SCHOOL SOCIETY—RELIGIOUS BASIS, &c. 435–448
XIX. HOME AND COLONIAL INFANT AND JUVENILE SCHOOL SOCIETY 449–486
XX. NATIONAL SOCIETY AND THE BELL OR MADRAS SYSTEM 487–500
XXI. MANUAL OF METHOD FOR NATIONAL SCHOOLS. By W. F. Richards ... 501–530

GERMAN PEDAGOGY:—Views of German Educators and Teachers on the Principles of Education, and Methods of Instruction for Schools of different Grades. *Republished from Barnard's American Journal of Education.* 3d Edition, 640 pages.

CONTENTS.

	Page.
INTRODUCTION,	9–22
SCHOOLS AND EDUCATION IN GERMAN LITERATURE,	11
FREDERICK FROEBEL,	23
SYSTEM OF INFANT GARDEN TRAINING AND INSTRUCTION,	23
FROEBEL,—HERBERT,—BENNEKE,	33–78
PEDAGOGIC VIEWS, IN REFERENCE TO THE REQUIREMENTS OF THE AGE. By PROF. J. H. VON FICHTE,	35
KARL VON RAUMER,	79–368
CONTRIBUTIONS TO PEDAGOGY,	81
I. EARLY CHILDHOOD AND YOUTH,	81
II. HISTORY,	101
III. GEOGRAPHY,	111
IV. NATURAL SCIENCE,	123
V. GEOMETRY,	153
VI. ARITHMETIC,	170
VII. PHYSICAL EDUCATION,	185
VIII. CHRISTIANITY IN PEDAGOGY,	218
IX. CLASSICAL INSTRUCTION,	229
X. METHODS OF TEACHING LATIN,	249
1. Old Grammatical Method,	249
2. Speaking as in the Native Tongue,	252
Montaigne,—Locke,—Maupertius,—Gesner,	252
3. Grammar evolved from Reading,—Interlinear,	253
Ratich,—Locke,—Hamilton,—Tafel,	253
4. Universal and other Methods,	254
Jacotot,—Ruthardt,—Meierotto,—Jacobs,	255
XI. SCIENCE AND ART,	283–294
XII. EDUCATION OF GIRLS,	295–368
RUDOLF RAUMER,	369–483
STUDY OF THE GERMAN LANGUAGE,	373
F. ADOLPH WILHELM DIESTERWEG,	439
I. CATECHISM OF METHODS OF TEACHING,	445
1. Intuitional Instruction. By *Diesterweg*,	445
2. Reading. By *Hencomp*,	447
3. Arithmetic. By *Diesterweg*,	449
4. Geometry. By *Diesterweg*	451
5. National History. By *Hentz*,	452
6. National Philosophy. By *Diesterweg*,	454
7. Astronomy. By *Diesterweg*,	455
8. Geography. By *Abbenrode*,	459
9. History. By *Abbenrode*,	464
II. GUIDE FOR GERMAN TEACHERS,	472
1. Intuitional and Speaking Exercises. By *Diesterweg*,	473
2. Drawing in Common Schools. By *Dr. E. Hentschel*,	491
3. Singing in Common Schools. By *Dr. E. Hentschel*,	513
4. Discipline in Schools. By *Diesterweg*,	541
G. A. RIECKE,	559–576
MAN AS THE SUBJECT OF EDUCATION,	559
JOHN BAPTIST GRASER, of Bayreuth,	577–582
SYSTEM OF INSTRUCTION FOR COMMON SCHOOLS,	577
JOHN HENRY WICHERN,	583–648
GERMAN REFORM SCHOOLS,	585
INDEX,	649–656
STEIGER'S LIST OF GERMAN PEDAGOGICAL WORKS,	1–32

NATIONAL EDUCATION.

EMINENT TEACHERS AND EDUCATORS OF THE SEVENTEENTH AND EIGHTEENTH CENTURIES: Supplement to Volume II., of Barnard's National Education, with Index. Pages 865–1264. Price, $2.00.

☞ VOLUME II. of Barnard's Comprehensive Survey of "*National Education in different countries*," is devoted to systems of Elementary and Secondary Instruction, with brief notices of Superior and Special Schools, in Switzerland, France, Belgium, Holland, Denmark, Norway, Sweden, Russia, Turkey, Greece, Italy, Spain and Portugal, in continuation of the account of the systems of the several German States as constituted in 1866, in Volume I.

CONTENTS.

SUPPLEMENT TO NATIONAL EDUCATION, VOLUME II.	865–1348
Progressive Development of Popular Education.	865
SWITZERLAND, POPULAR EDUCATION IN 1871.	865
Extracts from William Hepworth Dixon's *The Switzers*.	867
SCHOOL AND UNIVERSITY LIFE IN THE 15TH AND 16TH CENTURIES.	877
Autobiography of Thomas Platter, 1499–1582.	877
Bacchants, or Wandering Teachers, and School Life in Switzerland and Germany.	877
University Studies, Discipline and Customs.	889
Deposition—Pennalism—Landsmannschaften.	897
PROGRESSIVES OF THE 17TH AND 18TH CENTURIES.	919
Principles common to all.	923
Special Notice of the Great Educational Reformers.	927
RATICH—Memoir and Labors, 1571–1635.	927
COMENIUS—Memoir and Publications, 1592–1671.	955
LOCKE—Memoir and Thoughts on Education, 1632–1704.	997
FRANKE—Memoir and Orphan-House at Halle, 1063–1727.	1011
SEMLER, HECKER, HAHN, and other laborers for Real Schools, 1669–1778.	1029
Modern Gymnasium and Real School.	1039
ROUSSEAU—Memoir, and his Ideal Pupil, Emile, 1712–1778.	1045
BASEDOW—Memoir, and the Philanthropinum, 1723–1778.	1073
PESTALOZZI, FELLENBERG, KRUSI, and other founders of the modern Popular School.	1107
Principles and Methods applied in the Institutions at Burgdorf, Hofwyl, and other schools of Switzerland.	1107
DIESTERWEG, ABBENRODE, HINTZE, HONCAMP, and other prominent teachers, after the more advanced German Methodology.	1135
Methods and Discipline.	1134
Intuitional Instruction.	1137
Reading, Arithmetic, Geometry, Natural History.	1140
Natural Philosophy, Astronomy, Geography, History.	1146
Discipline, Principles, Rules, Plan of Work.	1207
RAUMER—Contributions to the History of Pedagogy.	1208
Arithmetic—old and new methods.	1163
Physical Culture, Health, Hardening the Body, Sharpening the Senses, Gymnastics.	1177
MONITORIAL SYSTEM—Bell, Lancaster, Spurzheim, &c.	1209
Historical Notice of the System.	1209
EDUCATION FOR LIFE.	1241
Graser's System and Schools.	1241
BURGHER, OR CITIZENS' SCHOOL.	1234
Dr. Vogel's School at Leipsic.	1234
INDEX TO VOLUME II. of Barnard's National Education.	1249
CONTENTS AND INDEX of other volumes of the Series.	1263
Volume I.—German States (912 pages).	1265
Superior Instruction in Europe (896 pages).	1279
Military System and Schools (960 pages).	1283
Technical Schools (800 pages).	1297
CLASSIFIED INDEX TO BARNARD'S AMERICAN JOURNAL OF EDUCATION, Volume I. to XVI.	1301

INDEX

TO

EDUCATIONAL APHORISMS.

Abelard, ... 168	Education, its nature and value, ... 38
Actual life, ... 129	Ehrenberg, ... 113
Æschylus, ... 14, 43, 99	Epidaurus, ... 167
Andromache, ... 96	Epicurus, ... 132
Anonymous, .. 17, 19, 20, 28, 30, 48, 53, 129, 169	Epictetus, ... 11, 43, 132, 168
Antoninus Pius, ... 14, 188	Everhard, ... 134
Appetite, ... 137	Evangel of Nature, ... 155
Aretinus, ... 26, 110	Euripides, ... 160
Aristotle, .. 40, 42, 43, 74, 75, 76, 79, 95, 96, 133,	Example, ... 194
145, 157, 162, 187, 194, 197	
Art, ... 165	Feelings, ... 128
Aurelius Antoninus, ... 44, 132	Fellenberg, ... 164
Aurelius Augustinus, ... 133	Female Education, ... 96
Augustine, ... 51	Fenelon, ... 105
	Fischer, (J. A.), 119, 120, 121, 125, 126, 130, 181
Bacon, ... 47, 144, 146, 147	Fichte, ... 29
Basedow, ... 78, 179	Forster, ... 87, 134, 135
Baur, ... 108, 112, 114, 192	Frederick (the Great,) 155
Bauer, (E.,) 34, 57, 58	French Encyclopedia, ... 62
Beday, ... 63	Froebel, ... 57, 118
Benda, ... 101	Fries, ... 25
Bhagavad-Gita, ... 10	Fundamental Impulses, ... 20
Bible,	
Genesis, ... 9, 24, 166	Galen, ... 76
Exodus, ... 92, 93	Garve, ... 56
Deuteronomy, ... 166	Geography, ... 150
Samuel, ... 187	Gizas, ... 73
Psalms, ... 9, 69, 147, 166, 167	Goethe, ... 20, 90, 100, 106, 113, 161, 175, 199
Son of Sirach, ... 65	Grafe, ... 57, 180
Ecclesiasticus, ... 93	Graser, ... 55, 58
Job, ... 147, 151	Grelling, ... 48
Proverbs, ... 93, 97, 187	Greszler, (F. G. L.,) 148
Wisdom of Solomon, ... 9	Greverus, ... 129
Apocrypha—Tobit, ... 93	
Matthew, ... 9, 166	Hanle, ... 6
Mark, ... 167	Harnisch, ... 58
Luke, ... 69, 93, 102	Hauter, ... 153
John, ... 10, 93	Hegel, ... 55, 171, 192
Paul, ... 10, 24, 93, 97, 147, 187	Helvetius, ... 87
Böhme, (J.,) 35, 197	Heinsterhnis, ... 17
Bouterwek, ... 17	Herder, .. 17, 19, 30, 33, 50, 124, 136, 143, 150, 175
Bolingbroke, ... 153	Hermannz, ... 192
Books, ... 158	Heydenreich, ... 21, 30, 49, 134
Bretschneider, ... 175	Hincking, ... 92
Bruno, ... 16	Hindoo Book, ... 10
Buchner, (Christian,) 70	Hippel, ... 72, 122
	Hitopadesa, ... 10
Callimachus, ... 162	Home Education, ... 75
Campe, ... 198	Huffel, ... 37
Chinese, ... 11, 65, 92, 169, 194	Humboldt, (W. Von) 20, 100
Charron, (P.,) 134	
Cicero, ... 13, 15, 43, 80, 94, 133, 151, 167,	Indian Tale, ... 40
188, 194, 195, 196	Imagination, ... 124
Channing, (W. E.,) 165	Impulses of Reason, ... 53
Character, ... 132	Intellectual Culture, ... 116
Chrysippus, ... 74	Iselin, ... 68
Comenius, ... 46, 76, 78, 84, 116, 146	
Confucius, ... 10, 11, 132, 167	Jacobi, (F.,) 37, 54, 56, 134, 135, 173, 199
Czour-Vedam, ... 10	John, ... 182, 186
	Juvenal, ... 194, 195
Democritus, ... 125, 139, 161, 163	
Diesterweg, ... 59	Kant, ... 48, 100, 135, 137, 191
Diodorus Siculus, ... 151	Knowing faculties, ... 116, 135
Dionysius of Halicarnassus, ... 153	Knowing *versus* Action 193
Dippolt, ... 143	Kohr, ... 47
Discipline, ... 187	Krause, ... 73
Doederlein, ... 50	Krug, ... 23, 60, 122, 123, 133
Early Training, ... 75, 173, 189	Language, ... 141

Lactantius, ... 168
Leibnitz, ... 57, 133, 134, 168
Livius, ... 151
Locke, ... 46, 161
Lucian, ... 59, 151
Luther, ... 16, 45, 67, 68, 78, 81, 84, 83, 85, 95, 98, 134, 137, 141, 147, 152, 163, 183, 188, 190, 191, 197.

Man, as the Subject of Education, ... 9
Mangelsdorf, ... 122
Marie Louise Wilhelmine, ... 18
Melancthon, ... 152
Memory, ... 126
Mencke, ... 103
Menu, Laws of, ... 10
Mendelssohn, ... 36, 48
Michaelis, ... 91
Milton, ... 164
Montaigne, ... 43, 46, 87, 152, 171
Moral Training, ... 166
Mors, ... 24
Moscherosch, ... 71, 84, 95, 99, 104, 190, 198
Moses Maimonides, ... 133
Music, ... 162
Musonius, ... 14

Nabbe, ... 37
Napoleon Bonaparte, ... 48
Nature, ... 165
Natural Science, ... 148
Niemeyer, ... 52, 56, 62, 67, 72, 109, 111, 117, 118, 119, 120, 121, 124, 126, 128, 130, 131, 132, 136, 138, 144, 149, 150, 156, 157, 158, 160, 161, 164, 173, 176, 184, 185, 197, 198, 199, 200.

Obedience, ... 92
Object Teaching, ... 117
Oezer, ... 106

Parents and Teachers, ... 65, 190
Perception, ... 116
Perictione, ... 94
Persius, ... 14
Pestalozzi, ... 50, 88, 150, 175, 182
Petrarch, ... 134
Physical Education, ... 75
Philosophy, Natural, ... 157
Philemon, ... 14
Philo, ... 51
Philosophie de la Nature ... 48
Plato, ... 12, 38, 43, 76, 78, 79, 94, 114, 139, 141, 157, 162, 167, 170, 194
Plautus, ... 65
Pliny, ... 151
Plutarch, ... 39, 40, 42, 66, 77, 81, 118, 127, 133, 159, 188, 194, 195
Poetry, ... 153, 161
Poleitz, ... 153
Pythagoras, ... 11, 12, 38, 42, 81, 96, 132, 162, 166

Quinctilian, ... 39, 42, 74, 75, 81, 85, 94, 127, 133, 151, 188, 195

Raumer, ... 104, 105, 107, 114, 115, 179
Reading, ... 160
Recreation, ... 189
Reason, ... 11, 132
Reinhard, ... 63
Religious Training, ... 131, 166
Richter, ... 27, 50, 97, 101, 104, 119, 127, 132, 154, 164, 177, 178, 179, 199
Ringwald, ... 95
Robbelen, ... 148
Rotteck, ... 61, 91

Rousseau, ... 68, 80, 90, 131, 19
Rudolphi, (Caroline.) ... 109
Rueckert, ... 11, 73, 110, 177, 178, 179, 199

Saadi, ... 166
Senses, ... 116
Sailer, ... 125
Schelling, ... 36, 49
Scherer, ... 63
Schlosser, ... 139
Schiller, ... 16, 26, 50, 98, 100, 102, 110, 123, 128, 136, 106, 153, 163
Schlenkert, (F. L.,) ... 17
Schleiermacher, ... 101, 112
Schmid, (C. C. E.,) ... 49, 56
Schneuber, ... 47
Schottin, ... 30
Schmid, (Karl,) ... 52
Schwabe, ... 73, 193
Schwarz, ... 35, 53, 165
Schroder, ... 90
Schrack, ... 156
Schubert, ... 27
Seneca, ... 13, 15, 39. 42, 61, 69, 81, 82, 94, 95, 133, 145, 151, 158, 159, 189, 194, 196
Siao Hio, ... 92
Simonides, ... 14, 158
Socrates, ... 77, 93, 168, 169, 187
Solon, ... 76, 94
Soldan, ... 100
State Lexicon, ... 61, 91
Starke, ... 34
Stoy, ... 50, 90, 181, 193
Stoics, ... 43
Sturm, ... 169
Subjects and Means of Instruction, ... 140

Tegner, ... 144, 179
Temperament, ... 138
Terentius, ... 14, 65
Tetens, ... 22
Tetzner, ... 88
Thenno, ... 44
Thomson, ... 153
Thibaut, ... 115
Thucydides, ... 96
Tischer, ... 58, 149, 171, 172, 176
Titteman, ... 155
Tschuchi, ... 10

Understanding, or thinking faculty, ... 121
Uz, ... 21

Valerius Maximus, ... 65
Von Ammon, ... 24, 54, 68, 140, 200
Von Dalberg, ... 36
Von Haller, ... 22
Von Gentz, ... 62
Voss, ... 25, 48
Virtue, ... 10, 132

Wagner, ... 137
Weikard, ... 50, 87
Wieland, ... 50
Will, ... 137
Wohlfarth, (J. F. T.,) ... 5

Young, ... 27

Zaleucus, ... 167
Zschokke, ... 21, 22, 32, 33, 51, 95, 102, 105, 108, 109, 112, 113, 142, 160, 169, 172, 173, 174, 177, 199.
Zenophon, ... 40
Zollikofer, ... 36
Zoroaster, ... 10, 11, 167, 179

PESTALOZZI AND HIS EDUCATIONAL SYSTEM.

PESTALOZZI AND PESTALOZZIANISM:—Memoir, and Educational Principles, Methods, and Influence of John Henry Pestalozzi, and Biographical Sketches of several of his Assistants and Disciples; together with Selections from his Publications. In Two Parts. By HENRY BARNARD, LL.D. New York: E. STEIGER.

CONTENTS.

PART I.
LIFE AND EDUCATIONAL SYSTEM OF PESTALOZZI.
Portrait of Pestalozzi, ... 1
Preface, ... 3
INTRODUCTION. Influence of Pestalozzi on the aims, principles, and methods of popular
  education, ... 11
  Influence on Reformatory Education. By Dr. Blochmann, ... 11
  Influence on the Sch'ls and Educational Methods of Germany. By Dr. Diesterweg, 16
  Summary of Pestalozzi's Principles of Education. By William C. Woodbridge, 29
  Influence on the Infant School System of England, ... 32
LIFE OF PESTALOZZI. By Karl von Raumer, ... 37
Preface, ... 41
  I. Childhood and Youth, 1746–1767, ... 49
  II. Agricultural and Educational Experiments at Neuhof, 1767, . . . 56
  III. The Evening Hour of a Hermit, 1780, ... 59
  IV. Leonard and Gertrude, 1781. 62
  V. Life and Writings between 1781 and 1798, ... 65
  VI. Experience at Stanz, 1798, ... 68
  VII. " Burgdorf, 1799–1804, ... 71
  VIII. " Buchsee, 1804, ... 87
  IX. " Yverdun, 1805, ... 87
  X. Last Years, 1815–1827, ... 115
  XI. Relations to Christianity, ... 116
  XII. Retrospect, ... 123
APPENDIX. By the American Editor, ... 127
  Celebration of Pestalozzi's Centennial Birth-day in Germany and Switzerland, 129
  List of Publications by Pestalozzi, ... 139
  List of Publications in different languages on Pestalozzi and his Educational Principles and Methods, ... 142
BIOGRAPHICAL SKETCHES of several of the assistants and disciples of Pestalozzi. 145
Preface, ... 149
  I. Johannes Niederer, ... 151
  II. Hermann Krüsi, ... 161
  III. Johannes Buss, ... 193
  IV. Joseph Schmid, ... 202
  V. John George Tobler, ... 205
  VI. John Ramsauer, ... 213
  VII. John Ernst Plamann, ... 217
  IX. Hans George Nägeli, ... 220
  X. Johannes Harnisch, ... 221
  XI. Karl Augustus Zeller, ... 223
  XII. Charles Christian Wilhelm von Türk, ... 155
  XIII. Bernhard Gottlieb Denzel, ... 227
  XIV. Friedrich Adolf Wilhelm Diesterweg, ... 229
    Gustavus Frederick Dibter, ... 232

PART II.
SELECTIONS FROM THE PUBLICATIONS OF PESTALOZZI. 515
Preface, ... 517
  I. Leonard and Gertrude,; a Book for the People. 519
  II. The School in Bonnal, ... 651
  III. Christopher and Alice, ... 665
  IV. How Gertrude Teaches her Children, ... 669
  V. Account of his own Educational Experience, ... 87
  VI. " " " Method of Instruction, ... 674
  VII. A Christmas Eve Discourse, December 24th, 1810, ... 703
  VIII. New-Year's Address, 1809, ... 712
  IX. Address on his Seventy-third Birthday, ... 715
  X. Paternal Instruction, ... 720
  XI. Evening Hour of a Hermit, ... 723

PART III.
PUBLIC INSTRUCTION IN SWITZERLAND, ... 313
Fellenberg, Vehrli, Kuratli and other Swiss Educators, ... 239

ENGLISH PEDAGOGY—OLD AND NEW: or, Treatises and Thoughts on Education, the School, and the Teacher in English Literature. *Second Series*. Republished from Barnard's American Journal of Education. 628 pages. $3.00. 1873.

CONTENTS.

	PAGE.
INTRODUCTION	1–16
CONTENTS AND INDEX OF FIRST SERIES	3
ART. I. WILLIAM OF WYKEHAM AND THE PUBLIC SCHOOLS	17–128
1. WILLIAM OF WYKEHAM, Bishop and Chancellor—1324–1404	19
2. PUBLIC OR ENDOWED SCHOOLS	23
3. ST. MARY'S COLLEGE, Winchester—1387–1865	49
4. REPORT OF ROYAL COMMISSIONERS ON THE GREAT PUBLIC SCHOOLS	81
5. ACTION OF PARLIAMENT AND COMMISSIONERS	118
II. DEAN COLET, AND ST. PAULS SCHOOL, London	129–160
III. CARDINAL WOLSEY.—1471–1530	161–164
PLAN OF STUDIES FOR IPSWICH GRAMMAR SCHOOL, 1528	161
IV. SIR THOMAS ELYOT.—1497–1535	165–178
THE GOVERNOR, or Training for the Public Weal, 1564	167
V. RICHARD MULCASTER.—1531–1611	179–190
POSITIONS respecting the Training of Children, 1581	179
VI. JOHN BRINSLY—WEBSTER—CHRISTOPHER WASE	185–190
VII. CHARLES HOOLE.—1616–1666	191–324
OBJECT TEACHING AND PICTORIAL ILLUSTRATIONS, 1661	192
THE NEW DISCOVERY OF THE OLD ART OF TEACHING, 1658	195
THE PETTY SCHOOL	195
THE GRAMMAR SCHOOL	223
SCHOLASTIC DISCIPLINE	293
VIII. ABRAHAM COWLEY.—1618–1677	325–336
PLAN OF A PHILOSOPHICAL COLLEGE, 1661	325
IX. ALEXANDER POPE—ROBERT SOUTH—SIR RICHARD STEELE	337–346
THOUGHTS ON EDUCATION	337
X. OLIVER GOLDSMITH.—1731–1774	347–358
ESSAY ON EDUCATION	347
XI. SAMUEL JOHNSON.—1708–1784	359–364
PLAN OF STUDIES AND DETACHED THOUGHTS	359
XII. SAMUEL PARR.—1747–1825	365–368
CHARITY SCHOOL SERMON	365
XIII. PEDAGOGY OF THE 19TH CENTURY	369–455
THOMAS K. ARNOLD.—1795–1842	369–410
MEMOIR AND EDUCATIONAL LABORS	369
DETACHED THOUGHTS ON STUDIES AND EDUCATION	417–544
1. TEMPLE—LOWE—GLADSTONE—DONALDSON—HODGSON	417
MARTINEAU—VAUGHAN—DE MORGAN—MULLER—SMITH	448
2. FARADAY—HERSCHEL—WHEWELL—HAMILTON	449
3. ACLAND—AIRY—HENFREY—HOOKER—HUXLEY	465
LYELL—OWEN—PAGET—TYNDALL—WILSON	481
4. MILL—FROUDE—CARLYLE, on University Studies	497
5. MACAULAY—NEWMAN, on the University of Books and Life	529
XIV. ART AND SCIENCE IN ENGLISH EDUCATION	545–592
XV. MECHANIC INSTITUTIONS AND POPULAR EDUCATION	593–628

GERMAN EDUCATIONAL REFORMERS; Memoirs of Eminent Teachers and Educators in Germany, from the Fourteenth to the Nineteenth Century, with contributions to the History of Education from the Revival of Classical Learning. From the "*Geschichte der Padagogik*" of Karl von Raumer. Republished from "*The American Journal of Education*," edited by HENRY BARNARD, LL. D. 586 pages. New York: E. STEIGER.

CONTENTS.

	PAGE.
Preface,	7
Memoir of Karl von Raumer,	0
I. INTRODUCTION. Revival of Classical Literature in Italy,	17—64
1. The Middle Ages—Condition of Studies, Teaching and the Arts,	17
2. Dante, Boccaccio, Petrarch,	28
3. Greek Scholars from Constantinople, John of Ravenna, Chrysoloras,	35
4. Italian Teachers—Guarino, Philelphus, Poggius, Valla, Landinus, Politianus, Picus,	49
5. Transition to Germany,	62
II. DEVELOPMENT OF EDUCATION IN THE NETHERLANDS AND NORTHERN GERMANY,	65—130
1. Gerard of Daventer—Rudewin—Gerard of Zutphen—The Hieronymians,	65
2. Wessel—Rudolph Agricola—Hegius—Lange—Busch,	72
3. Erasmus,	89
4. School of Schlettstadt—Dringenberg—Wimpheling—Reuchlin,	101
APPENDIX. Condition of Schools and Teachers in the Sixteenth Century,	113
Autobiography of John Platter; A-B-C-shooters and Bacchants,	125
III. THE PERIOD OF THE REFORMATION,	131—266
1. Martin Luther,	131
2. Philip Melancthon,	161
3. Valentine Friedland Trotzendorf,	185
4. John Sturm,	193
5. Michael Neander,	193
6. Ignatius Loyola and the Schools of the Jesuits,	229
7. The Early School Codes of Germany,	251
1. Dutchy of Wirtemberg; 2. Electorate of Saxony,	257
8. The Universities of the Sixteenth Century,	261
IV. REALISM,	267—334
1. Verbal Realism—Erasmus—Melancthon,	267
2. Real Realism—Influence of Lord Bacon's Philosophy,	273
3. Real Schools. Hecker, Halm, Semler; Modern Development of Realistic Instruction,	302
4. Michael Montaigne,	317
V. THE RENOVATORS, OR PROGRESSIVES,	335—520
1. New Ideas and Methods of Education,	335
2. Wolfgang Ratich,	343
3. John Amos Comenius,	371
4. Schools and Education in Periods of Peace and War,	413
1. The Thirty Years' War; 2. The Century after the Peace of Westphalia,	416
5. John Locke and Influence of his Pedagogy on German Education,	427
6. Augustus Hermann Franke, and the Pietists,	441
7. Jean Jaques Rousseau and his Influence on the Philanthropinists,	459
8. The Philanthropinum at Dessau,	487
John Bernhard Basedow,	487
VI. THE REFORMATORY PHILOLOGISTS,	521—574
1. Johann Mathias Gesner,	521
2. John August Ernesti,	530
3. Johann Georg Hamann,	533
3. Johann Gotfried Herder,	547
4. Friedrich August Wolf,	561
VII. PESTALOZZI AND THE COMMON, OR PEOPLE'S SCHOOLS,	575—586

NATIONAL EDUCATION.

AN ACCOUNT

OF THE

HISTORY, ORGANIZATION, ADMINISTRATION, STUDIES, DISCIPLINE AND STATISTICS OF PUBLIC SCHOOLS OF EVERY GRADE AND FOR ALL CLASSES IN DIFFERENT COUNTRIES.

By HENRY BARNARD, LL.D.

NOW READY.

Elementary and Secondary Instruction in the German States : Anhalt, Austria, Baden, Bavaria, Brunswick, Hanover, Hesse-Cassel, Hesse-Darmstadt, Liechtenstein, Lippe-Detmold, Lippe-Schaumburg, Luxemburg and Limberg, Mecklenburg-Schwerin, Mecklenburg-Strelitz, Nassau, Oldenburg, Prussia, Reuss, Saxony, Saxe-Altenburg, Saxe-Coburg, Saxe-Meiningen, Saxe-Weimar, Waldeck, Wurtemberg, and the Free Cities, with a general summary of the Educational Systems and Statistics for the whole of Germany. 856 pages. *Price,* $4.50. Sewed and in paper covers.

Elementary and Secondary Instruction in Switzerland (each of the 23 Cantons), France, Belgium, Holland, Denmark, Norway and Sweden, Russia, Turkey, Greece, Italy, Portugal and Spain. 800 Pages. *Price,* $4.50. Sewed and in paper covers.

Scientific and Industrial Education in Austria, Baden, Bavaria, Brunswick, Free Cities, Hanover, Nassau, Prussia, Saxony, Saxon-Principalities, Wurtemberg, France, Belgium, Holland, Denmark, Norway, Sweden, Russia, Switzerland, Italy. 800 Pages. *Price,* $4.50.

Special Instruction in Great Britain, with an Appendix containing selected Chapters from the Report on Scientific and Industrial Education in other European States with particular reference to Drawing, and Systems of Technical Schools. 500 Pages. *Price,* $3.00.

Superior Instruction in different countries: Universities of Germany, Past and Present; History of Higher Teaching in Athens, Rome, and Alexandria; Early Christian Schools; Universities of Bologna and Paris; Revival of Classical Studies in Italy, the Netherlands, &c.; Present Condition of Universities and Colleges in Europe and the United States. 1 Volume. 800 pages. $4.50.

Military Schools and Special Instruction in the Science and Art of War by Land and Sea, in France, Prussia, Austria, Bavaria, Italy, Switzerland, Russia, Great Britain, and the United States. 1 Vol. 900 pages. $4.50.

CLASSIFIED INDEX

TO

BARNARD'S AMERICAN JOURNAL OF EDUCATION.

VOLUMES I. TO XVI.

CLASSIFICATION OF SUBJECTS.

I. General Principles and History of Education.

II. Individual Views and Special Systems of Education.

III. Studies and Methods of Teaching; School Organization and Government.

IV. Teachers and their Training; Normal and Model Schools; Teachers' Institutes.

V. State and National Systems of Instruction.

VI. Secondary, Intermediate, Academical, and High Schools.

VII. University and Collegiate Education.

VIII. Special Schools and Departments of Science, Arts, Agriculture, Museums, &c.

IX. Military and Naval Education.

X. Preventive and Reformatory Education.

XI. Education of the Deaf and Dumb, Blind, Idiots, &c.

XII. Moral and Religious Education; Sectarian Schools and Instruction.

XIII. Female Education.

XIV. Physical Education.

XV. Supplementary, Self, and Home Education; Libraries.

XVI. Educational Societies and Teachers' Associations.

XVII. Philology and Bibliography; School-books and Periodicals, &c.

XVIII. School Architecture.

XIX. Educational Endowments and Benefactors.

XX. Miscellaneous.

XXI. Educational Biography and List of Portraits.

CHAPTER I. GENERAL PRINCIPLES AND HISTORY OF EDUCATION.

EDUCATION defined by Eminent Authorities; English, **XI**, 11-20; Greek, Roman, French, German, Scotch and American, **XIII**, 7-16.

Educational Aphorisms and Suggestions, from Two Hundred Authorities, Ancient and Modern.—Man, his Dignity and Destiny, **VIII**, 9. Nature and Value of Education, **VIII**, 38. Duties of Parents and Teachers, **VIII**, 65. Early Home Training, **VIII**, 75-80; **XIII**, 79-92. Female Education **XIII**, 232-242. Intellectual Culture in General, **X**, 116. Subjects and Means of Education, **X**, 141, Religious and Moral Instruction, **X**, 166. Discipline, **X**, 187. Example, **X**, 194-200. The State and Education, **XIII**, 717-624.

Education, Nature and Objects of—Prize Essay, by John Lalor, **XVI**, 33-64.

Education for the Times, by T. M. Clark, **II**, 375.

Education a State Duty, by D. B. Duffield, **III**, 81.

Education and the State; Aphorisms, **XIII**. 717-724. Views of Macaulay and Carlyle, **XIV**, 403. American Authorities, **XI**, 323; **XV**, 5.

Education Preventive of Crime and Misery, by E. C. Tainsch, **XI**, 77-93.

Home Education—Labors of W. Burton, **II**, 333.

Intellectual Education, by William Russell.—The Perceptive Faculties, **II**, 113-144, 317-332. The Expressive Faculties, **III**, 47-64, 321-345. The Reflective Faculties, **IV**, 199-218, 309-342.

Lectures on Education, by W. Knighton, **X**, 573.

Misdirected Education and Insanity, by E. Jarvis, **IV**, 591-612.

Moral and Mental Discipline, by Z. Richards, **I**, 107.

Objects and Methods of Intellectual Education, by Francis Wayland, **XIII**, 801-816.

Philosophy of Education, by Joseph Henry, **I**, 17-31.

Philosophical Survey of Education, by Sir Henry Wotton, **XV**, 131-143.

Problem of Education, by J. M. Gregory, **XIV**, 431.

Powers to be Educated, by Thomas Hill, **XIV**, 81-92.

Self-Education and College Education, by David Masson, **IV**, 262-271.

Thoughts on Education, by Locke; Physical, **XI**, 461; Moral, **XIII**, 548; Intellectual, **XIV**, 305.

Views and Plan of Education, by Krüsi, **V**, 187-197.

Unconscious Tuition, by F. D. Huntington, **I**, 141-163.

Schools as they were Sixty Years Ago in United States, **XIII**, 123, 837; **XVI**, 331, 738; **XVII**.

Progressive Development of Schools and Education in the United States, **XVII**.

History of Education, from the German of Karl von Raumer, **IV**, 149. History of Education in Italy. **VII**, 413-460. Eminent Teachers in Germany and the Netherlands prior to the Fifteenth Century, **IV**, 714. Schlettstadt School, **V**, 65. School Life in the Fifteenth Century, **V**, 79. Early School Codes of Germany, **VI**, 426. Jesuits and their Schools, **V**, 213; **VI**, 615. Universities in the Sixteenth Century, **V**, 536. Verbal Realism, **V**, 655. School Reformers at Beginning of Seventeenth Century, **VI**, 459. Thirty Years' War, and the Century Following, **VII**, 367. Real Schools, **V**, 689. Reformatory Philologists, **V**, 741. Home and Private Instruction, **VII**, 381. Religious Instruction, **VII**, 401. Methods of Teaching Latin, **VI**, 581. Methods of Classical Instruction, **VII**, 471. Methods of Teaching Real Branches, **VIII**, 101-228. German Universities, **VI**, 0-65; **VII**, 47-152. Student Societies, **VII**, 160.

Educational Development in Europe, by H. P. Tappan, **I**, 247-268.

Hebrews, and their Education, by M. J. Raphall, **I**, 243.

Greek Views of Education, Aristotle, **XIV**, 131; Lycurgus, and Spartan Education, **XIV**, 611; Plutarch, **XI**, 99.

Roman Views of Education, Quintilian, **XI**, 3.

Italian Views of Education and Schools, Acquaviva, **XIV**, 462; Boccaccio. **VII**, 422; Botta, **III**, 513; Dante and Petrarch, **VII**, 418; Picus, Politian, Valla, Vittorino, **VII**, 442; Rosmini, **IV**, 479.

Dutch Views of Education, Agricola, **IV**, 717; Busch and Lange, **IV**, 726; Erasmus, **IV**, 729; Hieronymians, **IV**, 622; Reuchlin, **V**, 65; Wessel, **IV**, 714.

French Views of Education and Schools, Fenelon, **XIII**, 477; Guizot, **XI**, 254, 357; Marcel, **XI**, 21; Montaigne, **IV**, 461; Rabelais, **XIV**, 147; Rousseau, **V**, 459; La Salle, **III**, 437.

German Views of Education, Abbenrode, **IV**, 505, 512; Basedow, **V**, 487; Comenius, **V**, 257; Diesterweg, **IV**, 235, 505; Dinter, **VII**, 153; Felbiger, **IX**, 600; Fliedner, **III**, 487; Frank6, **V**, 481; Graser, **VI**, 575; Gutsmuths, **VII**, 191; Hamann, **VI**, 247; Hentschel, **VIII**, 633; Herder, **VI**, 195; Jacobs, **VI**, 612; Jahn, **VIII**, 196; Luther, **IV**, 421; Meinotto, **VI**, 609; Melancthon, **IV**, 741; Neander, **V**, 509; Overberg, **XIII**, 365; Ratich, **V**, 229; Raumer, **VII**, 200, 381; **VIII**, 101; **X**, 227, 613; Ruthardt, **VI**, 600; Sturm, **IV**, 167, 401; Tobler, **V**, 205; Trotzendorf, **V**, 107; Von Turk, **V**, 155; Vogel, **IX**, 210; Wolf, **VI**, 260.

Swiss Views of Education, Fellenberg, **III**, 594; Krüsi, **V**, 189; Pestalozzi, **III**, 401; **VII**, 513; Vehrli, **III**, 389.

English Views of Education, Arnold, **IV**, 545; Ascham, **IV**, 155; Bacon, **XIII**, 103; Bell, **X**, 467; Colet, **XVI**, 657; Elyot, **XVI**, 485; Hale, **XVII**, Hartlib, **XI**, 191; Goldsmith, **XIII**, 347; Johnson, **XII**, 369; Lalor, **XVI**, 33; Lancaster and Bell, **X**, 355; Locke **VI**, 209; **XI**, 461; **XIII**, 548; Masson, **IV**, 262; **XIV**, 262; Milton, **II**, 61; Mulcaster, **XVII**, 177; Spencer, **XI**, 445; Sedgwick, **XVII**, ; Temple, F., **XVII**, ; Whewell, W., **XVII**.

Early Promoters of Realism in England, **XII**, 476. Bacon, **V**, 663; Cowley, **XII**, 651; Hoole, **XII**, 647; Petty, **XI**, 199.

II. INDIVIDUAL VIEWS AND SPECIAL SYSTEMS OF EDUCATION.

Abbenrode. On Teaching History and Geography, IV, 505, 512.
Abbot, G. D., and the Useful Knowledge Society, XV, 241. Educational Labors, XVI, 600.
Ackland, Henry W. Natural Science and Physical Exercise in Schools, XVII.
Acquaviva, and the Ratio Studiorum, XIV, 462.
Adams, John. Education and the State, XV, 12.
Adams, J. Q. On Normal Schools, I, 589. Education and the State, XV, 12. Educational Reform in Silesia, XVII.
Addison, Joseph. Education and Sculpture, XI, 16.
Adelung, J. C. Philological Labors, XI, 451.
Agassiz, L. Museum of Comparative Zöology, IX, 615.
Agricola, Rudolf. Life and Opinions, IV, 717.
Airy, G. B. Mathematics and Natural Science in Schools, XVII.
Akerly, S. Deaf-mute Training, III, 348.
Akroyd, E. Mode of Improving a Factory Population, VIII, 305.
Albert, Prince. On Science and Art, IV, 813.
Alcott, A. Bronson. School-days, XVI, 130.
Alcott, William A. Educational Views, IV, 629. Plan of Village School, IX, 540.
Allyn, Robert. Schools of Rhode Island, II, 544.
Anderson, H. J. Schools of Physical Science, I, 515.
Andrews, I. W. Educational Labors, XVI, 604.
Andrews, L. Educational Labors, XVI, 604.
Andrews, S. J. The Jesuits and their Schools, XIV, 455.
Anthony, H. On Competitive Examinations at West Point, XV, 51.
Aristotle, and his Educational Views, XIV, 131. Cited, III, 45; IV, 463; V, 673; VII, 415; VIII, 40-79; X, 132-195.
Arnold, Matthew. Tribute to Guizot, XI, 281. Schools of Holland, XIV, 712.
Arnold, Thomas, as a Teacher, IV, 545-581.
Ascham, Roger. Biographical Sketch, III, 23. Toxophilus; the Schoole of Shootinge, III, 41. The Schoolmaster, IV, 155; XI, 57.
Ashburton, Lord. Prize Scheme and Address on Teaching Common Things, I, 629.
Austin, Sarah. Ends of a Good Education, XI, 20.
Aventinus. Study of German, XI, 162.

Bache, A. D. On a National University, I, 477. Education in Europe, VIII, 435, 444, 455, 504, 609; IX, 167, 210, 569; XII, 337; XIII, 303, 307.
Bacon, Leonard. Life of James Hillhouse, VI, 325.
Bacon, Lord. His Philosophy and its Influence upon Education, V, 663. Essays on Education, and Studies, with Annotations by Whately, XIII, 103.
Bailey, Ebenezer. Memoir, XII, 429. Girls' High School in Boston in 1828, XIII, 252.
Baker, T. B. L. Reformatory Education, III, 789.
Baker, W. S. Itinerating School Agency, I, 729.
Barks, N. P. Museum of Zoölogy, IX, 619.

Bard, Samuel. Schools of Louisiana, II, 473.
Barnard, D. D. Right of State to establish Schools, XI, 323. Memoir of S. Van Rensellaer, VI, 223.
Barnard, F. A. P. Improvements in American Colleges, I, 269. Influence of Yale College, V, 723. Memoir, V, 753-780. Titles and Analysis of Publications, V, 763-769. Value of Classical Studies, V, 763. Open System of University Teaching, V, 765. Post-graduate Department, V, 775. Oral Teaching, V, 775.
Barnard, H. Educational Labors in Connecticut from 1837 to 1842, I, 669; Speech in Legislature in 1838, 678; Address to the People of Connecticut, 670; Analysis of First Report in 1839, 674; Expenditures for School Purposes, 679; Measures and Results, 685; Schedule of Inquiries, 686; Topics of School Lectures, 709; Plan of State Institute, 721. Labors in Rhode Island from 1843 to 1849, I, 723; XIV, 558; Institute of Instruction, 559; Series of Educational Tracts, 567; Educational Libraries, 568; Correspondence with Committee of Teachers, 579. Labors in Connecticut from 1850 to 1854, XV, 276; Plan of Public High School, 279; Public and Parental Interest and Coöperation, 285; Legal Organization of Schools, 289; School Attendance, 293; Agricultural Districts, 303; Manufacturing Districts, 305; Cities, 309; Gradation of Schools, 316; Private versus Public Schools, 323; Teachers' Institutes, 387. Arguments for, VIII, 672. Normal Schools, I, 753; X, 15. Plan of Society, and Journal and Library of Education, I, 15, 134. Principles and Plans of School Architecture, I, 740; IX, 487; X, 695; XII, 701; XIII, 818; XIV, 780; XV, 783; XVI, 781. National Education in Europe, I, 745; XV, 329. Reports and Documents on Common Schools in Connecticut, I, 754, 761. Reports and Journal of Public Schools in Rhode Island, I, 755. Tribute to Gallaudet, I, 417, 759. Memoir of Ezekiel Cheever, I, 297, 769. Reformatory Schools and Education, III, 551, 819. Military Schools and Education, XII, 3-400. Naval and Navigation Schools, XV, 17, 63. Competitive Examination, XI, 103. Educational Aphorisms, VIII, 7; XIII, 7, 717. German Universities, VI, 9; VII, 49, 201. Books for the Teacher, XIII, 447. German Educational Reformers, XIII, 448. American Text-books, XIII, 209, 401, 628; XIV, 753; XV, 539. English Pedagogy, XVI, 467; Object Teaching and Primary Instruction in Great Britain, 469. Pestalozzi and Pestalozzianism, VII, 284, 502. National and State Educational Associations, XVI, 311; American College Education, 339. Standard Publications, XVI, 797; Progressive Development of Education in the United States, XVII; Educational Land Grants, XVII.
Barnard, J. School-days in 1689, I, 307.
Barnard, J. G. Treatise on the Gyroscope, III, 537; IV, 529; V, 298.

Barney, H. H. Schools of Ohio, **II**, 531.
Barrow, Isaac. Education defined, **XI**, 13.
Basedow, and the Philanthropinum, **V**, 487-520.
Bateman, N. Educational Labors, **XVI**, 165.
Bates, S. P. On Liberal Education, **XV**, 155. Memoir, **XV**, 682.
Bates, W. G. On Training of Teachers, **XVI**, 453.
Becker, K. L. Study of Language, **XII**, 460.
Beecher, Miss C. E. Physical Training, **II**, 399. Western Education, **XV**, 274.
Beecher, Henry W. School Reminiscences, **XVI**, 135.
Bell, Andrew, and the Madras System, **X**, 467.
Benedict, St., and the Benedictines, **XVII**.
Beneke, F. E. Pedagogical Views, **XVII**.
Bernhardt. Teachers' Conferences, **XIII**, 277.
Berranger. Training of Orphan Children, **III**, 736.
Bingham, Caleb. Educational Labors, **V**, 325.
Bishop, Nathan. Public Schools of Boston, **I**, 458. Girls' High School of Boston, **XI**, 263. Plans of Providence School-houses, **XI**, 582. Memoir, **XVII**.
Blockman, Dr Pestalozzi's Poor School at Neuhoff, **III**, 585.
Boccaccio, and Educational Reform in Italy, **XII**, 418.
Bodleigh, Sir T. On Travel, **XV**, 380.
Bolingbroke. Genius and Experience, **XI**, 12.
Booth, Rev. J. Popular Education in England, **III**, 252, 265. Competitive Examination, **III**, 257.
Borgi, Jean, and Abandoned Orphans, **III**, 583.
Botta, V. Public Instruction in Sardinia. **III**, 513; **IV**, 37, 479.
Bowen, Francis. Life of Edmund Dwight, **IV**, 5.
Braidwood, J. Education of Deaf-mutes, **III**, 348.
Brainerd, T. Home and School Training in 1718, **XVI**, 331.
Braun, T. Education defined. **XIII**, 10.
Breckenridge, R. J. Schools of Kentucky, **II**, 488.
Brinsley, J. Consolations for Grammar Schools, **I**, 311.
Brockett, L. P. Idiots and their Training, **I**, 593. Institutions and Instruction for the Blind, **IV**, 127.
Brooks, Charles. Best Methods of Teaching Morals, **I**, 336. Education of Teachers, **I**, 587.
Brooks, K. Labors of Dr. Wayland, **XIII**, 771.
Brougham, Lord. Life and Educational Views, **VI**, 467. Education and the State, **XIII**, 722. Training of the Orator, and Value of Eloquence, **XVI**, 187.
Brown, Thomas. Education defined, **XIII**, 13.
Brownson, O. A. Education defined, **XIII**, 12.
Buckham, M. H. English Language in Society and School, **XIV**, 343. Plan of Study, **XVI**, 595.
Buckingham, J. T. Schools as they were, **XIII**, 129.
Bulkley, J. W. Teachers' Associations, **XV**, 185.
Burgess, George. Thoughts on Religion and Public Schools, **II**, 562.
Burke, Edmund. Education defined, **XI**, 17.
Burrowes, T. H. Reports on Pennsylvania Schools, **VI**, 114, 536. History of Normal Schools in Pennsylvania, **XVI**, 195.
Burton, W. District-school as it was, **III**, 456. Memoir, **XVI**, 330.

Bushnell, Horace. Early Training, **XIII**, 79. Pastimes, Plays, and Holidays, **XIII**, 93. Homespun Era of Common Schools, **XIII**, 142. The State and Education, **XIII**, 723.
Buss, J., and Pestalozzianism, **VI**, 293.
Byron, Lady. Girls' Reformatory School, **III**, 785.

Cady, L. F. Classical Instruction, **XII**, 561.
Caldwell, Charles. Education in North Carolina, **XVI**, 109.
Calhoun, W. B. Memorial on Nor. Sch., **XVI**, 86.
Calkins, N. A. Object Teaching, **XII**, 633.
Carlyle, T. Education defined, **XIII**, 13. The State and Education, **XIV**, 406. Reading, **XVI**, 191. University Studies, **XVII**.
Carpenter, Mary. Reformatory Education, **III**, 10, 785.
Carpenter, W. B. Physical Science and Modern Languages in Schools, **XVII**.
Carter, J. G. Life and Services, **V**, 409. Essay on Teachers' Seminaries, **XVI**, 71. Memorial, **XVI**, 80.
Cecil, Sir William. Advice to his Son, **IX**, 161.
Channing, W. E. Teachers and their Education, **XII**, 453. End of Education, **XIII**, 15.
Chauveau, P. J. O. Education in Lower Canada, **II**, 728.
Cheever, Ezekiel. Memoir and Educational Labors, **XII**, 531.
Cheke, Sir John. **III**, 24.
Chesterfield, Lord. Advice to his Son, **XVII**.
Choate, Rufus. The Peabody Institute, **I**, 239.
Christian Brothers, System of. **III**, 347.
Cicero. Cited, **VIII**, 13, 14, 43, 79; **X**, 133, 151, 167, 194-196; **XII**, 409.
Clajus, and the German Language. **XI**, 408.
Clark, H. G. On Ventilation, **XV**, 787.
Clark, T. M. Education for the Times, **II**, 376.
Claxton, T. First Manufacturer of School Apparatus, **VIII**, 253.
Clay, John. Juvenile Criminals, **III**, 773.
Clerc, Laurent. **III**, 349.
Clinton, DeWitt. Education of Teachers, **XIII**, 341.
Cocker, E. Methods of Arithmetic, **XVII**.
Coggeshall, W. J. Ohio System of Public Schools, **VI**, 81, 532.
Colburn, Dana P. Memoir and Educational Work **XI**, 289.
Colburn, Warren. Educational Work, **II**, 194.
Cole, David. On Classical Education, **I**, 67.
Coleridge, D. St. Marks' Normal College, **X**, 531.
Coleridge, S. T. The Teacher's Graces, **II**, 102.
Colet, John. Educational Views and Influence, **XVI**, 637.
Collis, J. D. Endowed Grammar Schools of England, **VIII**, 256.
Colman, Henry. Agricultural School at Grignon **VIII**, 555.
Comenius, Amos. Educational Labors, **V**, 257-298. Orbis Pictus, **VI**, 585.
Confucius. Cited, **VIII**, 10, 11; **X**, 132, 167.

Coote, Edward. The English Schoolmaster, **I.** 309.
Courteilles, Viscount de, and the Home Reformatory, **III.** 572, 647, 704.
Cousin, V. School System of Holland, **VIII.** 598. School Law of Prussia, **IX.** 382. Normal Schools, **XIII.** 282.
Coutts, Miss Burdett. Prize Scheme for Teaching Common Things, **II.** 708.
Cowdery, M. F. Moral Training, **XVI.** 323.
Cowley, A. Plan of Philosophical College, **XII.** 651.
Cowper, William. The Tirocinium, or Review of Schools, **VIII.** 469. Discipline, **VIII.** 489.
Crabbe, George. Schools of the Borough, **IV.** 582; **III.** 461.
Crosby, Alpheus. Massachusetts Schools, **II.** 508.
Currie, James. Methods of Early Education, **IX.** 239-293.
Curtin, A. G. Schools of Pennsylvania, **II.** 541.
Cuvier, Baron. Schools of Holland, **VIII.** 597, 607.

Dana, J. D. Science and Scientific Schools, **II.** 349.
Dante, and the Revival of Education in Italy, **VII.** 418.
Darlington, W. Schools as they were, **XIII.** 741.
Dawson, J. W. Natural History in its Educational Aspects, **III.** 428.
Day, Henry N. English Composition, **XVI.** 641.
Day, Jeremiah. On Schools as they were, **XVI.** 126.
Degerando, Baron. Monitorial Methods, **X.** 465.
De La Salle, Abbe. Memoir, and System of Christian Schools, **III.** 437.
De Laspe. Method und Motive of Instruction, **VIII.** 180.
Delille, James. The Village Schoolmaster, **III.** 153.
Demetz, M. Agricultural Colonies, **I.** 611; **III.** 572, 667.
De Morgan. Arithmetics and their Authors, **XVII.**
Dick. Bequest, **I.** 302.
Diesterweg. Methods of Teaching, **IV.** 233, 505. School Discipline and Plans of Instruction, **VIII.** 616. Intuitional and Speaking Exercises, **XII.** 411.
Dinter, G. F. Memoir and Educational Labors, **VII.** 153; **XIV.** 738. Defense of Catechetical Method, **IX.** 377.
D'Israeli, I. Influence of Books and Authors, **II.** 296.
Doane, G. W. The State and Education, **XV.** 5.
Dole, Isaiah. Requirements in an English Lexicographer, **III.** 161. Mary Lyon, **X.** 649.
Donaldson, J. W. University Teaching, **XVI.** Competition Tests, **XVII.** German and English Scholarship compared, **XVII.**
Ducpetiaux, M. Reports on Reform Schools, **III.** 677, 597, 599, 604, 716, 749.
Duffield, D. B. Education a State Duty, **III.** 81.
Dunn, H. Organization and Instruction of the Borough Road Schools, **X.** 381-459.
Dunnell, M. H. Report on the Schools of Maine, **II.** 495.
Dwight, Edmund. Memoir **IV.** 5.
Dwight, Francis. Educational Labors. **V.** 803

Dwight, Mary. Art Education, **II.** 409, 537; **III.** 467; **IV.** 171; **V.** 305.
Dwight, Timothy, as an Educator, **V.** 567.

Eaton, H. School-houses of Vermont, **XI.** 510.
Eberhard, J. J. Rural Reformatory School at Cann, **III.** 599.
Edgeworth, Maria. Extract from Practical Education, **XII.** 602.
Edson, T. Warren Colburn and his System of Arithmetic, **II.** 294.
Edwards, N. W. Report on Schools of Illinois, **II.** 479.
Edwards, Richard. Memoir of Tillinghast, **II.** 568. Normal Schools, **XVI.** 271.
Elgin, Lord. Education in the United States and Canada, **III.** 239.
Eliot, Samuel. Arnold as a Teacher, **IV.** 535.
Eliot, S. A. Educational Benefactions of Boston, **VIII.** 522; **IX.** 606. History of Harvard College, **IX.** 129.
Elyot, Sir Thomas. The Governour, **XVI.** 483.
Emerson, G. B. Educational Labors, **V.** 417. Memorial on State Superintendent, **V.** 652. Memorial on Normal Schools, **XVI.** 93. Life of Felton, **X.** 265. Plan of School-houses, **IX.** 542.
Epictetus. Cited, **VIII.** 11, 42; **X.** 132, 168.
Erasmus. Educational Views, **IV.** 729; **XVI.** 681.
Euclid, and the Method of Geometry, **VIII.** 155.
Everett, Alexander H. Normal Schools. **XVI.** 89.
Everett, Edward. Uses of Astronomy. **II.** 604. John Lowell and the Lowell Lectures, **V.** 437. Influence of Harvard, **V.** 531. Boston Library, **VII.** 266, 365. Female Education, **IX.** 635; **XII.** 721. Extracts from Addresses—Public Schools Fifty Years Ago—College Life—Common Schools and Colleges—Conditions of a Good School—Science and Popular Education—Moral Education—Popular Education—**VII.** 343; **XV.** 14. Life of Thomas Dowse, **IX.** 355.

Faraday, M. Claims of Natural Science in a Liberal Education. **XVII.**
Felbiger, J. I. Educational Labors in Austria, **IX.** 600.
Fellenberg. Principles of Education, **III.** 594; **X.** 81; **XIII.** 11, 523.
Felton, C. C. Characteristics of American Colleges, **IX.** 112. Memoir and Extracts, **X.** 265.
Fenelon. Memoir and Educational Views, **XIII.** 477.
Feuerbach, L. Intuition and Thinking in Education, **XII.** 422.
Fichte. On Learning by Heart, **XII.** 416. Physical Culture, **VIII.** 192. Cited, **VIII.** 29, 620.
Fletcher, J. Borough Road Normal School, **X.** 435-465.
Fliedner. Institution for Deaconesses at Kaiserswerth, **III.** 487.
Follenius, Karl. Relations to Karl Ludwig Sand, **VI.** 111, 125.
Forbes, E. Educational Uses of Museums. **IV.** 788

Fowle, W. B. Memoir and School Improvements, **X**, 600.
Francké, A. H. His Views and Labors, **V**, 441.
Franklin, B. His Interest in Higher Education, **VII**, 268; **VIII**, 251; **X**, 283.
Friesen, F., and the German Gymnastics, **VIII**, 197.
Froebel, and the Kindergarten System, **II**, 449; **IV**, 257, 793.
Fuller, Thomas. The Good Schoolmaster, **III**, 155.

Gallaudet, T. H. Life and Services, **I**, 425. Education of Teachers, **X**, 16.
Galloway, Samuel. Teachers' Institute, **XV**, 401. Memoir, **XVI**, 583.
Gammell, W. Memoir of Nicholas Brown, **III**, 291.
Gardner, Francis. Boston Latin School, **XII**, 553.
Garfield, J. A. Department of Education, **XVII**.
Gerard-Groote, and the Hieronymians, **IV**, 623.
Gesner, J. M. Educational Views, **V**, 741; **VI**, 583.
Gibbs, J. W. Philological Contributions, **II**, 198; **III**, 101–124.
Gilfillan. The Scotch School-dame, **III**, 456.
Gillespie, W. M. Mathemntical Methods of the Ecole Polytechnique, **I**, 533; **II**, 177.
Gilman, D. C. Scientific Schools of Europe, **I**, 315. Higher Special Schools of France, **II**, 93.
Gladstone, W. E. The Classics in a Liberal Education, **XVII**.
Goethe. Educational Views, **VIII**, 20, 619, 648; **X**, 51, 161, 199, 225, 617, 621.
Goldsmith. Essay on Education, **XIII**, 347. The Village Schoolmaster, **III**, 158.
Goodrich, S. G. Schools as they were, **XIII**, 134.
Goodwin, F. J. Norwich Free Academy, **III**, 195.
Gordon, John. Normal Schools of Scotland, **X**, 583.
Gottsched, J. C. German Grammar, **XI**, 447.
Gould, B. A. An American University, **II**, 265–293.
Graser. System of Instruction, **VI**, 575.
Gray, Thomas. Alliance of Education and Government, **VIII**, 287. Ode on Eton College, **VIII**, 285.
Green, L. W. Normal Schools for Kentucky, **III**, 217.
Green, S. S. Educational Duties of the Hour, **XVI**, 229. Object Teaching, **XVI**, 245.
Gregory, J. M. The Problem of Education, **XIV**, 431–5. Memoir, **XV**, 643.
Grimke, T. S. Plan of Study, **II**, 230.
Grimm, the Brothers. **XI**, 454.
Grimshhaw, A. H. Schools of Delaware, **II**, 474.
Griscom, John. Memoir and Educational Labors, **VIII**, 324.
Grote, J. Education defined, **XI**, 18.
Guilford, Nathan. Educational Labors, **VIII**, 289.
Guizot. Ministry of Public Instruction in France, **XI**, 254, 357. The State and Education, **XIII**, 718.
Gulliver, J. P. Norwich Free Academy, **II**, 665.
Guts-Muths. System of Physical Training, **VIII**, 191. Training of the Senses, **VIII**, 207.

Haddock, C. B. School-houses in New Hampshire, **IX**, 512.

Hale, R. Continental Reformatories, **III**, 642, 744.
Hale, Sir Matthew. Plan of Study, **XVII**.
Hall, E. E. Life of Edward Everett, **VII**, 325.
Hall, S. R. Educational Labors, **V**, 373. Teachers' Seminary at Andover **V**, 386.
Hall, W. On Schools as hey were, **XVI**, 127.
Halsey, L. J. Life of Philip Lindsley, **VII**, 9.
Hamann, J. G. Educational Views, **VI**, 247.
Hamilton, J., and the Hamiltonian Method, **VI**, 586.
Hamilton, Sir W. Education defined, **XI**, 18; **XIII**, 13. On Mathematics, **XVII**.
Hammill, S. M. School Government, **I**, 123.
Hammond, C. On N. England Academies, **XVI**, 403.
Harnisch. Cited, **VIII**, 58. Plan of Instruction for Annaberg Orphan House, **VIII**, 437.
Harris, James. Education a Growth, **XI**, 16.
Hart, J. S. Study of the Anglo-Saxon, **I**, 33–66. Memoir and Views, **V**, 91.
Hartlib. Plan of College of Husbandry in 1681, **XI**, 191, 649. Memoir, **XII**, 649.
Haskins, G. F. Reformatory School at Rome, **III**, 580.
Haupt. The Burschenschaften of the German Universities, **VII**, 161.
Haüy, V., and the Instruction of the Blind, **III**, 477; **IV**, 130.
Haven, Joseph. Mental Science as a Study, **III**, 125.
Hawley, Gideon. Memoir and Labors, **XI**, 94.
Hedge, N. On Schools as they were, **XVI**, 738.
Hedge. On University Reform, **XVII**.
Hegius. Educational Views, **IV**, 723.
Helps, Arthur. Learning and Doing, **XI**, 18.
Henfrey, A. Study of Botany, **XVII**.
Henry, Joseph. Philosophy of Education, **I**, 17.
Hentschel, E. Singing, **VIII**, 633; Drawing, **X**, 59.
Herbert, J. F. Pedagogical Views, **XVII**.
Herder. Life and Educational Views, **VI**, 195.
Herschel, Sir J. F. W. On Reading, **XVII**.
Heyder, W. Address at Jena in 1607, **VI**, 56.
Hickson, E. H. The State and Education, **XIII**, 718.
Hill, M. D. Preventive Treatment of Crime, **III**, 766.
Hill, Thomas. True Order of Studies, **VI**, 180, 449; **VII**, 273, 491. Powers to be Educated, **XIV**, 81. Didactics in Colleges, **XV**, 177.
Hillard, G. S. Public Library of Boston, **II**, 203. The State and Education, **XV**, 14.
Hillhouse, James A. Education and Literature in a Republic, **XVII**.
Hintz, E. Natural History, **IV**, 241.
Hobbs, Thomas. Knowledge and Experience, **XI**, 14.
Hodgins, J. G. Popular Education in Canada, **I**, 186.
Holbrook, Josiah. The Lyceum System, **XIV**, 535. Educational Labors, **VIII**, 229.
Holls, G. C. Family Reformatories, **IV**, 824.
Honcamp. Instruction in Reading, **IV**, 234; Language, **XII**, 482.
Hood, Thomas. The Irish Schoolmaster, **IV**, 183.
Hooker, J. Study of Botany in Schools, **XVI**, 403.
Hooker, Richard. Knowledge of and Obedience to Law, **XI**, 13.

CLASSIFIED INDEX OF BARNARD'S AMERICAN JOURNAL OF EDUCATION. 23

Hoole, C., and Object Teaching in 1658, XII. 647.
Old Art of Teaching, XVII.
Hopkins, Mark. Memoir and Educational Publications, XI. 225. Extracts—Education—Self-education—Female Education—Academies—Medical Science—Theological Education—Objections to Colleges—Taste and Morals—XI. 225-231.
Hornberg, T. Thoughts on the Education of Girls, VIII. 319.
Hovey, C. E. Memoir and Labors, VIII. 94.
Howe, S. G. Laura Bridgman's Education, IV. 383. Summary of Labors, XI. 389.
Hubbs, P. K. Schools of California, II. 467.
Hubbard, J. O. Normal Schools in New York, XIII. 345.
Humphrey, Heman. Normal Schools, XII. 655. Schools as they were, XIII. 125.
Huntington, F. D. Unconscious Tuition, I. 141. Public Prayers in Colleges, IV. 22.

Ickelsamer, V., and the German Language, XI. 402.
Ingraham, J. Plan of Primary School-house, X. 719.

Jackson, W. L. Schools of Virginia, II. 557.
Jacobs, F. Method of Teaching Latin, VI. 612.
Jacotot, I., and his Method, VI. 295; XII. 604.
Jahn, F. L. German Turning System and Physical Education, VII. 196; XV. 229.
Jameson, Mrs. Social Position and Occupations of Woman, III. 495.
Jarvis, E. Misdirected Education and Insanity, IV. 591.
Jay, John. Education and the State, XV. 13.
Jefferson, T. The State and Education, XV. 12.
Jerome, St. On Female Education, V. 593.
Jewell, F. S. Teaching as a Profession, XV. 579.
John of Ravenna. Educational Views, VII. 435.
Johnson, Samuel. Thoughts on Education and Conduct, XIII. 359.
Johnson, W. R. Educational Labors, V. 799.
Julius, Dr. Normal Schools in Prussia, XVI. 89.

Kant. Cited, V. 504; VIII. 28, 48; X. 135, 137, 191, 641; XIII. 13.
Kay, J. P. Training of Parochial Schoolmasters, IX. 170.
Kay, Joseph. Subjects and Methods of Primary Instruction, VIII. 416. Position of Prussian Teachers, XI. 169. Normal Schools in Saxony, XIII. 524.
Keenan, P. J. Monitorial System in Ireland, X. 462; XIII. 150. School Organization, XIII. 145.
Kepler. Estimate of Euclid, VIII. 159.
Kingsbury, John. Young Ladies' High School at Providence, V. 16.
Kingsley, J. L. Discourse on Yale College, V. 541.
Klüpfel. History of Tübingen University, IX. 57.
Knight, Charles. Economical Science, IX. 105.
Knighton, W. Educational Lectures, X. 573.
Krug. Cited, VIII. 23, 60; X. 122, 123, 133.

Krüsi. Life and Educational Labors, V. 161-186.
Kuratli, M. Reform School at Bachtelen, III. 596.

Lactantius. Cited, X. 108.
Lalor, J. Nature and Objects of Education, XVI. 33-64.
Lancaster, Joseph, and Monitorial Schools, X. 355.
Landor, W. S. Roger Ascham and Lady Jane Grey, III. 39.
Lange, R. Educational Labors, IV. 726.
Lathrop, J. Boston Association of Teachers, XV. 530.
Leach, Daniel. Public Schools of Providence, I. 468. Plan of School-houses, IX. 563.
Leibnitz. Cited, VIII. 57; X. 133, 134, 168.
Leigh, Lord. Reformatory Results of Mettray, III. 731.
Lewis, Dio. The New Gymnastics, XI. 531; XII. 665.
Lewis, Tayler. Methods of Teaching Greek and Latin, I. 285, 489.
Lieber, F. The Cooper Institute, I. 652. History of Atheneums, II. 735.
Lindsley, Philip. Memoir and Views of Education, VII. 26.
Ling, H., and the Swedish Gymnastics, XV. 236.
Lloyd, Robert. The School Usher, III. 160.
Locke, John. Views on Education, VI. 209. Thoughts on Education, XI. 461; XIII. 548; XIV. 305. School of Labor, III. 577.
Locke, W. Ragged Schools, III. 779.
Longstreet. School Scene in Georgia, XVI. 121.
Lord, A. D. Plan of School-house, IX. 502. Educational Labors, XVI. 607.
Lothrop, S. K. W. Lawrence and the Academies of New England, II. 33.
Lovell, John. Eulogy on Peter Faneuil, IX. 604.
Loyola, and his Society and System, V. 213; XIV. 455.
Lubinus. Grammatical Instruction, VI. 581.
Luther. Views on Education, IV. 421-449. Physical Culture, VIII. 190. Cited, VIII. 15, 78, 356; X. 137, 141, 151, 163, 183, 191.
Lycurgus, and Education among the Spartans, XIV. 611.
Lyell, Sir Charles. Physical Science in a Liberal Education, XVII.
Lyon, Mary. Principles of Mt. Holyoke Seminary, X. 670.
Lytton, Sir E. B. Address at School Festival, III. 259.

Macaulay, Lord T. B. The State and Education, XIII. 721; XIV. 403. Competitive Examinations for East India Service, XVII.
Madison, James. The State and Education, XV. 12.
Mansfield, E. D. The Military Academy at West Point, XIII. 17-48.
Marcel, C. Conversational Method, XI. 21, 330.
March, F. A. Study of English Language, XVI. 599.
Marion, General. On Free Schools, XVI. 119.

Mann, Horace. Teachers' Motives, **XIV**. 277. College Government, **III**. 65. Special Training a Prerequisite to Teaching, **XIII**. 507. Methods of Education in Germany, **VIII**. 382. Results of Normal Schools in Prussia, **VIII**. 361. Analysis of Reports, **V**. 623. Plan of District School-house, **IX**. 642. Estimate of S. G. Howe, **XI**. 389. Education defined, **XIII**. 16. The State and Education, **XIII**. 724; **XV**. 13. Normal Schools, **XVI**. 100.
Mason, S. W. Physical Exercise in Schools, **XIV**. 61.
Masson, D. College and Self-education, **IV**. 262. Milton's Home, School, and College Training, **XIV**. 159-190.
Mathews, J. D. Report on Schools of Kentucky, **II**. 493.
May, S. J. Life and Views of Cyrus Peirce, **IV**. 275. Educational Labors, **XVI**. 141.
Mayhew, Ira. School-houses of Michigan, **IX**. 515. Educational Labors, **XV**. 651.
McElligott, J. N. Debating as a Means of Educational Discipline, **I**. 495.
Meierotto. Method of Teaching Latin, **VI**. 609. Physical Culture, **VIII**. 191.
Meiring. On the Hamiltonian System, **VI**. 592.
Melancthon. Life and Educational Services, **IV**. 741-764.
Memminger, C. G. Schools of South Carolina, **II**. 553.
Mill, John Stuart. State and Education, **XIII**. 721. University Education, **XVII**.
Mills, Caleb. Report on Schools of Indiana, **II**. 480.
Milton. Treatise on Education, **II**. 61. Education defined, **XI**. 12. The State and College and Education, **XIII**. 719. His Home, School, and College Training, **XIV**. 159.
Molineux, E. L. Physical and Military Exercises in Schools a National Necessity, **XI**. 513.
Montaigne. On Learning and Education, **IV**. 461.
Montucla. Elements of Euclid, **VIII**. 156.
More, Sir Thomas. The State and Education, **XIII**. 719. Education of his Children, **XVII**.
Morrison, T. Manual of School Management, **IX**. 294. Oral Lessons, **IX**. 321.
Moscherosch. Cited, **VIII**. 71; **X**. 190, 198.
Moseley, Canon. Tripartite System of Instruction, **IX**. 316. English Training Colleges, **X**. 543-670.
Mulcaster, R. Positions, **XVII**.
Muller, Max. French and German in Public Schools, **XVII**.

Neander, Michel. Educational Labors, **V**. 599.
Niebuhr, B. S. Letter to a Student, **XVI**. 215.
Niebuhr, J., and Pestalozzi, **VII**. 289.
Niemeyer. Cited, **VIII**. 52, 56, 61, 67, 71; **X**. 118.
Nieuvenhuysen, and the Society for the Public Good in Holland, **XIV**. 641.
Nissen, H. Public Schools in Norway, **VIII**. 295.

Oberlin, John Friedrich. The Practical Educator, **V**. 505; **XVII**.
Oelinger, Albert, and the Study of German, **XI**. 406.

Olmsted, Dennison. Democratic Tendencies of Science, **I**. 164. Ideal of a Teacher; Timothy Dwight **V**. 567.
Osgood, S. G. Address at Dedication of School-house, **XIII**. 848.
Overberg, B. Educational Views, **XIII**. 365.
Owen, R. Natural History in Public Schools, **XVII**.
Page, D. P. Memoir and Processes of Teaching, **V**. 819. Education defined, **XIII**. 14.
Paget, J. Physiology, **XVII**. 119.
Paley, Dr. Education defined, **XI**. 15.
Palmerston, Lord. Popular Education, **II**. 712.
Park, Prof. The School of Locality, **XVI**. 331. Memoir of B. B. Edwards, **XIV**. 381.
Parr, Samuel. Principles of Education, **XI**. 17.
Partridge, Alden. Educational Views, **XIII**. 54, 683.
Pattison. On Prussian Normal Schools, **XVI**. 395.
Paulet. System of Monitorial Instruction, **X**. 464.
Payson, T. Boston Association of Teachers, **XV**. 533; **X**. 464.
Peabudy, George. Public Library of Baltimore, **III**. 226. Educational Benefactions, **XVII**.
Peel, Sir R. Study of Classics, **XVII**.
Peet, H. P. New York Institution for the Deaf and Dumb, **III**. 347. Memoir, **III**. 366.
Peirce, B. K. Reformatory for Girls, **XVI**. 652.
Peirce, Cyrus. Ideal of Education, **IV**. 285. Normal Schools, **IV**. 306.
Perkins, G. R. Labors in Normal Schools, **XIII**. 544.
Perry, Gardner. On School-houses, **IX**. 520.
Perry, W. F. Schools of Alabama, **II**. 465.
Pestalozzi. Life and Educational System, **III**. 401; **IV**. 65. Pestalozzi and the Schools of Germany, **IX**. 343. Pestalozzi, Fellenberg, and Wehrli, **X**. 81. Poor School at Neuhof, **III**. 585. His Assistants and Disciples, **VII**. 285. Hundredth Birthday, **V**. 503. Publications by and relating to, **VII**. 513. Selections from his Publications, **VII**. 519-722. Evening Hours of a Hermit, **V**. 169. Leonhard and Gertrude, **VII**. 519. Christopher and Alice, **VII**. 665. His Account of his Educational Experience and Methods, **VII**. 671.
Petrarch, and Education in Italy, **VII**. 424.
Petty, Sir W. Plan of a Trades School, 1647, **XI**. 199.
Peurbach, G. Method of Arithmetic, **VIII**. 170.
Phelps, W. F. Normal Schools, **III**. 417. Educational Labors, **V**. 7.
Philbrick, J. D. On the National Teachers' Association, **XIV**. 49. Extracts from Reports, **II**. 261. Report on Schools of Connecticut, **II**. 469. Plans of School-houses. **X**. 740; **XVI**. 701.
Phillips, J. H. Schools of New Jersey, **II**. 517.
Picket, A. Teachers' Association, **XV**. 493.
Pierce, Benjamin. On a National University, **II**. 88.
Pierpont, J. Public High School for Girls, **XIII**. 244.
Pitt, Earl of Chatham. Studies and Conduct, **XVII**.
Plato. Cited, **IV**. 166; **VIII**. 11, 43, 76-78; **X**. 141, 157, 162, 167, 170, 194; **XI**. 101, 105; **XII**. 409; **XIII**. 8.

CLASSIFIED INDEX OF BARNARD'S AMERICAN JOURNAL OF EDUCATION. 25

Plutarch. Views of Education, XI, 99–110. Cited, VIII, 77; X, 118-195.
Poggius, and Education in Italy, VII, 442.
Porter, J. A. Plan of an Agricultural School, I, 329.
Porter, Noah. Essay on Educational Reform in Connecticut, XIV, 244. Norwich Free Academy, III. 200.
Potter, Alonzo. Consolidation, &c., of American Colleges. I, 471. Moral and Religious Instruction, II, 169. School Houses in New York, IX, 507. Normal Schools, XIII, 344. What and How to Read, II, 215. Memoir, XVI, 509.
Pullicino, and Education in Italy, II, 721.
Pythagoras. Cited, VIII, 11, 12, 38, 43; X, 132, 162, 166; XI, 109; XIII, 8, 81.

Quincy, Josiah. Girls' High School in Boston, XIII, 297. Phillips' Academy in 1778, XIII, 740.
Quincy, Josiah, Jr. School Policy of Boston, XII, 706.
Quintilian. Views of Education, XI, 3.

Rabelais, and his Educational Views, XIV, 147.
Ramsauer. Memoir, VII, 301. Life at Hofwyl, IV, 84, 119.
Ramsden. The Heart of a Nation, XI, 17.
Rumusat. Circular to Teachers, adopted by Guizot, XI, 278.
Randall, S. S. On Francis Dwight, V, 809. Josiah Holbrook. Educational Labors, XIII, 227. New York Normal School, XIII, 532.
Raphall, H. L. Education among the Hebrews, I, 243.
Ratich. Life and Educational Methods, V, 229; XI, 418. On Teaching Latin, VI, 586.
Raumer, Karl von. History of Education, q. v. under SECTION I. German Universities, VI, 9; VII, 47, 160. Essays on University Reform, VII, 200.
Raumer, Rudolf. Instruction in the German Language, XI, 155, 419–429; XII, 460-527.
Ravaisson, F. Instruction in Drawing, II, 319.
Reid, D. B. College of Architecture, II, 629.
Reisch, Gregorius. Margarita Philosophica, XVII. Roman System of Measures, XVII.
Rendu, Eugen. Public Instruction in France and Prussia, II, 337.
Reuchlin, and German Educators of the Fifteenth Century, V, 65.
Rice, V. M. Schools of New York, II, 518.
Richard, W. F. Methods in the National Schools of England, X, 501-540.
Richards, Z. Discipline, I, 107. The Teacher an Artist, XIV, 69.
Richter, J. P. Cited, VIII, 27, 50, 618; X, 119-190.
Rickoff, A. J. National Bureau of Education, XVI, 299.
Rider, Captain. On System of Navigation Schools, XV, 67.
Rosenkrantz. Present Age to the Educator, XII, 425.
Rosmini, A. Philosophy of Pedagogy, IV, 491.

Ross, William. Cathechetical Method, IX, 368.
Ross, W. P. Education among the Cherokees, I, 120
Rousseau, and his Educational Views, V, 459–486
Education defined, XIII, 11.
Rush, Benjamin. The State and Education, XV, 13
Ruskin, John. Material of Education, XI, 19.
Russell, William. Principles and Methods of Intellectual Education, II, 113, 317; III, 47, 311; IV, 199. Moral Education, IX, 19–48. National Organization of Teachers, XIV, 7. Educational Labors of Lowell Mason, IV, 141. Recollections of Josiah Holbrook, VIII, 339. Legal Recognition of Teaching as a Profession, X, 297.
Russell, W. H. Plan of Gymnasium, IX, 534.
Ruthardt, J. C. Method of Teaching Latin and Greek, VI, 600.

Sarmiento, D. F. The Schoolmaster's Work, XVI, 65. Basis of U. S. prosperity, XVI, 533. Educational Labors, XVI, 593.
Schmid, Joseph, and Pestalozzi, VII, 297.
Schmidt. Definition of Education, XIII, 9.
Schottelius, J. G. Philological Labors, XI, 429.
Schwartz. Cited, VIII, 34, 53; X, 164.
Sears, Barnas. Schools of Massachusetts, II, 498.
Sears, E. I. Henry Lord Brougham, V, 467. Memoir.
Sedgwick, C. M. What and How to Read, II, 215.
Seguin, E. Treatment and Training of Idiots, II, 145.
Seneca. Cited, VIII, 12–68; X, 135-196; XII, 409.
Seton, S. S. Extracts from Manual, XIII, 858.
Shea, J. G. Catholic Institutions in the U. S., 435.
Shearman, F. W. Schools in Michigan, II, 510.
Sheldon, E. A. Object Teaching, XIV, 93.
Shenstone, William. The Schoolmistress, with Annotations, III, 449.
Shurtleff, N. B. Boston Latin School, XII, 559.
Shuttleworth, Sir J. K. Educational Progress in England, III, 245. Vehrli, III, 392. Training Schools, IX, 171-200.
Sidney, Sir H. On Conduct, XV, 378.
Simonson, L. Cadet System in Switzerland, XIII, 693.
Simpson, J. Education defined, XIII, 13.
Slade, William. Education at the West, XV, 274.
Smith, Adam. The State and Education, XIII, 720
Smith, B. B. Visit to Radleigh School, IV, 803.
Smith, Elbridge. Norwich Free Academy, III, 208.
Smith, Goldwin. History, XVII, 119.
Smith, H. D. The Dutch Universities, I, 327.
Smyth, Sidney. Objects of Education, XIII, 12
Snell, E. S. The Gyroscope, II, 701.
Socrates. Cited, IV, 156; VIII, 77; X, 167, 187; XI, 61, 62, 103, 107. Methods of Philosophy, X, 375.
South, R. Educational Views, XVII.
Southey, Robert. The State and Education, XIII, 719. Views of Home Education, XVI, 433. Conduct and Knowledge, XVI, 223.
Spencer, Herbert. Thoughts on Education, XI, 485–512; XIII, 372-400.
Spencer, J. C. Education of Teachers, XIII, 342

Sprague, W. B. Influence of Yale College, **X**, 681.
Spurzheim. Mutual Instruction, **X**, 611. Education defined, **XIII**, 11.
Stanley, Lord. Lyceums and Popular Edu., **III**, 241.
Stephens, L. Normal Schools of Prussia, **VIII**, 368.
Stewart, Dugald. Objects of Education, **XIII**, 13.
Stifler, Michael, and Algebraic Signs, **XVI**.
Stiles, W. H. Education in Georgia, **II**, 477.
Stow, David. Gallery Training Lessons, **IX**, 413.
Stowe, C. E. Life and Labors, **V**, 586. Educational Wants of Ohio, **V**, 588. Primary Instruction in Germany, **VIII**, 371. Teachers' Seminary, **XV**, 689.
Sturm, J. Life and Educational Labors, **IV**, 167, 401.
Sullivan, O. Teaching the Alphabet, **XII**, 601. Premiums for Knowledge in Com. Things, **X**, 93.
Swett, John. Educational Labors, **XVI**, 625, 790.
Swift, J. On Manners, **XVII**.

Tafel, L. The Hamiltonian System, **VI**, 591.
Tappan, H. P. Educational Development in Europe, **I**, 247-268. Educational Labors, **XIII**, 452.
Tarbox, I. N. Statistics of New England Colleges, **I**, 405. American Education Society, **XIV**, 367.
Tasso. Memoir and Educational Views, **XVII**.
Temple, F. Literature and Science, **XVII**.
Tenney, Jonathan. Schools of New Hampshire, **II**, 511. Memoir, **XVI**, 761.
Teutleben, K. von, and Society of Usefulness, **XI**, 424.
Thaer, August, and Gymnastics, **VIII**, 197.
Thayer, G. F. Letters to a Young Teacher, **I**, 357; **II**, 103, 391, 657; **III**, 71, 313; **IV**, 219, 450; **VI**, 435; **VIII**, 81. Chauncey Hall School, **XIII**, 851.
Thayer, S. Competitive Examination, **XV**, 58.
Thibaut. On Purity in Music, **X**, 635.
Thompson, A. Industrial School, **III**, 780.
Tice, J. H. Public Schools of St. Louis, **I**, 348.
Tillinghast, Nicholas. As an Educator, **II**, 568. On Normal Schools, **XVI**, 453.
Timbs, John. Endowed Schools of England, **VIII**, 261. The Hornbook, **XII**, 687.
Tixier, J. School Dialogues, **XVI**, 445.
Tobler, J. G. Methods of Teaching, **V**, 210.
Town, Salem. Schools as they were, **XIII**, 737.
Trask, A. B. Town School of Dorchester, **XVI**, 105.
Trench, R. English Language, **XVII**.
Trotzendorf, V. F. Educational Views, **V**, 107.
Turk, R. C. W. von. **V**, 155.
Turner, Sydney. Reformatory Schools, **III**, 772.
Tyndall. Study of Physics, **XVII**.

Vail, T. H. Methods of Using Books, **II**, 215.
Vassar, M. Plan of Vassar Female College, **XI**, 55.
Vehrli. Hofwyl and Kruitzlingen, **III**, 389; **X**, 81.
Verplanck, J. C. Memoir of D. H. Barnes, **XIV**, 513. Scientific Knowledge and Business, **V**, 116.
Vinci, Leonardo di. Drawing, **II**, 425.

Wadsworth, James. Labors of Education, **V**, 395.
Watts, Isaac. Improvement of the Mind, **II**, 215.
Webster, Daniel. Normal Schools, **I**, 590. Free Schools, **I**, 591. Education defined, **XIII**, 14.

Wayland, Francis. Objects and Methods of Intellectual Education, **XIII**, 801. Dedicatory Address at Pawtucket, **VIII**, 843. Educational Labors and Publications, **XIII**, 771. Extracts on Method of Recitation—System of University Education—System of Public Schools for a City—The Library in Popular Education—Theological Education—Moses Stuart—Dr. Nott—Thomas K. Arnold—**XIII**, 776.
Webster, Noah. Schools as they were, **XIII**, 123.
Weld, Theodore D., and Manual Labor, **XV**, 234.
Wells, W. H. Life and Educational Labors, **VIII**, 529. Teachers' Conferences, **XIII**, 272. Teaching English Grammar, **XV**, 241. Exercises on Retiring from Chicago High School, **XIV**, 811.
Wessel, John. Educational Views, **IV**, 714.
Whately, Archbishop. Annotations on Bacon, **XIII**, 103. Education defined, **XI**, 18.
Whewell, W. Education defined, **XI**, 11. School Studies and University Examinations, **XVII**.
White, E. E. National Bureau of Edu., **XVI**, 177.
White, H. R. The Village Matron, **III**, 460.
White, S. H. National Bureau of Edu., **XV**, 180.
Wichern, T. H. Reformatory Education, **III**, 5, 603.
Wickersham, J. P. Education as an Element of Reconstruction of the Union, **XVI**, 283.
Wilbur, H. B. On Object Teaching, **XV**, 189.
Wilderspin, S. Infant School, **IX**, 531; **XIII**, 163.
Wiley, C. H. Schools of North Carolina, **II**, 527.
Willard, Mrs. Emma. Female Education, **VI**, 125. Female Association, **XV**, 612.
Willm, J. The Monitorial System, **X**, 466. Teachers' Libraries, **XIII**, 293, 298.
Wimmer, M. Public Instruction in Saxony, **V**, 350; **IX**, 201. Educational Intelligence, **III**, 272; **IV**, 243, 793. On Real Schools of Austria, **III**, 275.
Winthrop, R. C. Free Schools, **I**, 645.
Wise, Henry A. Schools of Virginia, **II**, 557.
Wiseman, Cardinal. Education of the Poor, **XVII**.
Wohlfarth, J. F. F. Pedagogical Treasure Casket, **VIII**, 8-80; **X**, 116-290.
Wolf, T. A. Educational Views, **VI**, 260.
Wolsey, Cardinal. Plan for Grammar School, **VII**, 487.
Woodbridge, W. Suggestions on School Improvements, **XV**, 669. Reminiscences of Female Education prior to 1801, **XVI**, 137.
Woodbridge, W. C. Life and Educational Labors, **V**, 51. Education defined, **XIII**, 16.
Woolsey, T. D. Historical Discourse on Yale College, **V**, 546. Norwich Free Academy, **III**, 197.
Wordsworth, W. State and Education, **XIII**, 719.
Wotton, Sir Henry. Survey of Educa., **XV**, 123-143.
Wyatt, Sir T. On Conduct. **XV**, 376.
Wykeham, and Winchester College, **VIII**, 261.

Young, Samuel. Schools of New York, **IX**, 505.
Young, T. U. Infant School Teaching, **XII**, 155.

Zeller, C, H. Teachings of Experience for Christian Schools, **III**, 386. Memoir, **VII**, 305.
Zoroaster. Cited, **X**, 167.
Zschokke. Cited, **VIII**, 21, 30, 51; **X**, 142-198.

III. STUDIES AND METHODS; SCHOOL ORGANIZATION AND DISCIPLINE.

A B C-shooters, V, 90, 603; books, XII, 593.
Absence, II, 444, 504; V, 631; XV, 293.
Academy, plan for, XVI, 403.
Accuracy, XIII, 515.
Acquisition, XIII, 512.
Acting plays, IV, 175; VII, 503; XIV, 474.
Activity, independent, VIII, 617; XIII, 13, 376.
Adult education, I, 634; VIII, 230; XVI, 343.
Advice to Students on Studies and Conduct, XIII, 193; XV, 377; XVI, 186, 216, 223. Lord Bacon, XVI, 186; Sir Thomas Bodleigh, XV, 381; Lord Brougham, XVI, 186; Carlyle, XVI, 191; Sir Matthew Hale, XVII; Niebuhr, XVI, 216; Sir H. Sidney, XV, 370; Southey, XVI, 233; Vail, II, 215; Whately, XIII, 106; Wyatt, XV, 377.
Algebra, II, 177.
Alphabet, Modes of Teaching, XII, 593.
Amusements, III, 42; V, 449; X, 256; XIII, 93; XIV, 474.
Analysis and Analytic Method, II, 122, 133; IV, 505; VIII, 169; IX, 205.
Anger, XI, 482, 504.
Anglo-Saxon Lauguage, I, 33; XVI, 568.
Anthropology, XIII, 327.
Aphorisms on Studies and Conduct, XV, 376; Subjects of Instruction, X, 141; Discipline X, 187; Early Training, XIII, 79.
Appetites, X, 137; XIII, 512, 578; XVI, 53.
Aptness to teach, XIII, 762.
Archery, III, 41; XVI, 496.
Architectural Game, XI, 27.
Arithmetic, Currie, IX, 247; Hill, VI, 454; Gillespie, I, 539; Raumer, VIII, 170; Richards, X, 534.
Art—as a Study, by Miss A. M. Dwight, II, 409, 587; III, 467; IV, 191; V, 305.
Art and Science, by Dana, II, 349; Raumer, X, 218.
Attendance, Burnard, XV, 293.
Ball-frame, IX, 255; XI, 24.
Basedow's Methods, V, 487.
Beans in Arithmetic, VI, 454.
Beating of Children, IV, 156, 165; V, 509; XI, 479.
Bible, II, 613; Arnold, IV, 443; Locke, XII, 471; XIV, 308; Luther, IV, 443; Raumer, VII, 402; VIII, 104; Whately, XIII, 108.
Bifurcation, XII, 47.
Biographical Method in History, IV, 514, 577.
Biology, XIII, 392.
Bipartite Organization, XIII, 150.
Birch, III, 462; V, 509.
Blackboard or surface, V, 499; X, 600; XII, 648; XIII, 32.
Blocks in Geometry, VI, 451.
Books, Value of, II, 205, 215; X, 158; XIII, 788; XVI, 191.
Book-learning, II, 561; VII, 267, 366; XIII, 837.
Borough-road School Methods, X, 381.
Botany, VII, 296; VIII, 126; IX, 77, 109; X, 640; XI, 46.

Boy-tutors, XVI, 227.
Burgher, or Citizens' School, VIII, 414; IX, 210, 384; XI, 248; XII, 520.
Benschenschaff, VII, 80, 91, 165.
Calisthenics, II, 405.
Catechism on Methods, from Diesterweg, IV, 233, 505.
Catechetical Method, W. Ross, IX, 367.
Character, X, 129; XIII, 571.
Chemistry, V, 712; VII, 277; VIII, 665; XI, 210; XIII, 391.
Childhood, IV, 424; V, 467; VII, 382; XI, 483; XII, 629; XVI, 193.
Chiding, XIII, 559.
Church-cross-row, XVII, 195.
Christianity in Schools, I, 251; II, 567, 603; IV, 527, 572; V, 77; XIII, 118, 287, 325.
Christmas Festival, X, 260; XIII, 95.
Chronological Method, IV, 515.
City Influence, III, 323. VII, 33, 240; VIII, 143; XV, 309.
Classical Instruction, by Ascham, XI, 70; I. Cady, XII, 561; David Cole, I, 67: Erasmus, IV, 729; T. Lewis, I, 285; Raumer, VII, 471; Sturm, IV, 160; Woolsey, VII, 487.
Collective Teaching, X, 305.
Common Things, by Lord Ashburton, I, 629; Morrison, IX, 321; Stow, IX, 413; Specimen Lessons, X, 105, 575; IX, 349.
Competitive Examination, by Barnard, XIV, 108; Booth, III, 267.
Common Sense, V, 476; XIII, 599.
Composition, III, 331; VIII, 387; X, 415; XI, 122; XII, 494; XIV, 363; XVI, 641.
Compulsion in attendance, XI, 266; in study, VII, 213; XIII, 373.
Conduct, IV, 161; X, 141; XIII, 79; XV, 123, 378; XVI, 191.
Conversation, XI, 106, 339; XIII, 556; XIV, 360; XV, 152; XVI, 682.
Conversational Method, by Marcel, XI, 106, 339.
Constructive Method, by Abbenrode, IV, 507.
Corporal Punishment, Bell, X, 486; Diesterweg, XIII, 619; Erasmus, XVI, 680; Goldsmith, XIII, 352; Johnson, XIII, 363; Locke, XIII, 563; Austria, XVI, 614, 690; England, III, 157.
Country Training, III, 323: V, 472; X, 644; XIII, 141; XV, 303.
Counters, VIII, 182
Courage, IX, 41; X, 57; XIII, 584; XVI, 57.
Crime and Education, IV, 579; VI, 311, 494; XI, 77.
Curiosity, II, 118; V, 477; XIII, 112, 572.
Debating, by J. M. Elligott, I, 495.
Discipline, by Diesterweg, VIII, 619; Locke, XIII, 557; Hamill, I, 122; Spencer, XI, 498; Thayer, VI, 435; XIII, 831; Dorchester School in 1645, XVI, 106; Hopkins Grammar School, 1684, IV, 710.
Drawing, by Hentschel, X, 59; Ravaisson, II, 419.

English Language and Literature, by Buckham, **XIV.** 343; **XVI.** 556; Day, **XVI.** 641; Gibbs, **II.** 193; **III.** 101; Hart, **I.** 33; Felton, **X.** 284; March, **XVI.** 562; Wells, **XV.** 145.
Fagging in English Schools, **IV.** 569; **V.** 80; **XV.** 107.
French Language, **XV.** 772.
German Language, **XI.** 155, 400; **XII.** 460.
Geography—Methods of Teaching, by Abbenrode, **IV.** 505; Currie, **IX.** 269; Dunn, **X.** 421; Hill, **VII.** 275; Key, **IX.** 186; Mann, **VIII.** 390; Marcel, **XI.** 35; Pestalozzi, **X.** 150; Phelps, **IX.** 62; Raumer, **VIII.** 3; Thayer, **VIII.** 81.
Geometry, Basedow, **V.** 512; Diesterweg, **IV.** 239; Euclid. **VIII.** 155; Gillespie, **I.** 541; Hill, **VI.** 191, 449; Raumer, **VIII.** 155; Spencer, **XIII.** 383.
Geology **IV.** 785; **VI.** 238; **VII.** 71, 203; **VIII.** 241; **XI.** 46.
Graduation of Schools. **II.** 455.
Greek Language, **XII.** 561; **I.** 284, 482.
Grouping Method in History, **IV.** 515.
Gymnastics, Lewis' System, **XI.** 531; **XII.** 665.
History, Method in, by Abbenrode, **IV.** 512; **XII.** 665; Arnold, **IV.** 565; Basedow, **V.** 503; Hill, **VI.** 184; **VII.** 490; Marcel, **XI.** 41; Niemeyer, **X.** 156; Raumer, **VIII.** 101; **X.** 641; Richter, **X.** 154; Whately, **XIII.** 119.
Intellectual Training, by Eliot, **XVI.** 488; Fellenberg, **III.** 594; Goldsmith, **XIII.** 347; Hill, **VI.** 180; Krüsi, **V.** 187; Lalor, **XVI.** 40; Locke, **XIV.** 305; Milton, **II.** 79; Montaigne, **IV.** 161; Pestalozzi, **VII.** 512; Quintilian, **XI.** 3; Raumer, **VIII.** 81; Rousseau, **V.** 459; Russell, **II.** 112; Spencer, **XI.** 484; **XIII.** 372; Wayland, **XIII.** 801.
Infant Schools and Instruction, Currie, **IX.** 228; Froebel, **II.** 449; **IV.** 237; Home and Colonial Society, **XIII.** 78; Marcel, **XI.** 21; Prussian Schools, **VIII.** 371; Raumer, **VII.** 381; Young, **XIV.** 165.
Intuitional Instruction, **IV.** 233; **XII.** 411.
Italian Language, **VII.** 434, 459.
Itinerating Schools, **VIII.** 296.
Jesuit System of Schools, **V.** 212; **XIV.** 455.
Kindergarten, **IV.** 257.
Lacedamonian System, **III.** 85; **XIV.** 612.
Lancasterian System, **X.** 402.
Latin Language, by Acquaviva, **XIV.** 462; Arnold, **IV.** 564; Asham, **XI.** 70; Bates, **XV.** 155; Comenius, **VI.** 585; Erasmus, **IV.** 729; Gesner, **V.** 744; **VI.** 583; Hamilton, **VI.** 586; Herder, **VI.** 207; Hoole, **XVII.** 225; Jacotot, **VI.** 595; Jacobs, **VI.** 612: Locke, **XIV.** 311; Luther, **IV.** 44; Melancthon, **IV.** 755, 764; Meierotto, **VI.** 583, 609; Meiring, **VI.** 592; Milton, **II.** 79; Montaigne, **IV.** 473; **VI.** 584; Ratich, **V.** 234; **VI.** 586; Raumer, **VI.** 581; **VII.** 471; Rousseau, **V.** 473; Ruthardt, **VI.** 600; Sturm, **IV.** 169; **VI.** 581; Tafel, **VI.** 591; Textor, **XV.** 444; Trapp, **VI.** 261; Vossius, **VI.** 589; Wolf **VI.** 968; Woolsey, **VII.** 487.
Latin Pronunciation. **XV.** 171.
Lectures and University Teaching, Barnard, **V.** 775;

Johnson, **XIII.** 363; Masson, **IV.** 271; Raumer, **VII.** 201, 213; Vaughn, **IV.** 271; Wolf, **VII.** 487.
Liberal Education and Studies, Bates, **XV.** 155; Everett, **VIII.** 364; Felton, **X.** 281.
Madras System, **X.** 467.
Manners, Hopkins, **XI.** 930; Locke, **VI.** 213; **XIII.** 551; Montaigne, **IV.** 469; Thayer, **II.** 103; Plutarch, **XI.** 106.
Mathematics, French Polytechnic system, **I.** 533.
Memory, **II.** 385; **IV.** 171, 201, 721; **V.** 678; **VI.** 464, 602; **VII.** 279; **X.** 126; **XII.** 416; **XIV.** 87, 321, 469; **XVII.** 230.
Mental Arithmetic, **II.** 301; **VIII.** 385, 459.
Mental Science, by J. Haven, **III.** 125.
Methods, Essays on, by Currie, **IX.** 229: Diesterweg, **IV.** 233, 505; Dunn, **X.** 391; Morrison, **IX.** 204; Raumer, **VIII.** 101; Richards, **X.** 505; Ross, **IX.** 367; Spencer, **XIII.** 372; Thayer, **III.** 313; **IV.** 219, 450.
Military Exercises in School, by Molineux, **XI.** 513.
Monitorial System, English National Schools, **X.** 503; Irish National Schools, **XIII.** 150.
Moral Education, Brooks, **I.** 336; Cowdery, **XVI.** 323; Fellenberg, **III.** 595; Lalor, **XVI.** 48; Locke, **XI.** 473; **XIII.** 548; Russell, **IX.** 19; Spencer, **XI.** 496.
Music, or Singing, **VIII.** 633; **IX.** 267; **XVI.** 38.
Mutual Instruction, Bell, **X.** 491; De Gerando, **X.** 465; Fowle, **X.** 611; Keenan, **X.** 462; Lancaster, **X.** 402.
Mother Tongue, **III.** 327; **IV.** 473; **V.** 235, 246, 253; **VI.** 107, 201; **VII.** 375; **XI.** 458; **XII.** 464; **XIV.** 343; **XVI.** 340.
Motives to Study, Lyton, **III.** 295; Mann, **XIII.** 518; **XVI.** 279; Rousseau, **V.** 477; Spencer, **XIII.** 377; Thayer, **VI.** 435.
Natural Science, **IV.** 445; **VIII.** 123; **X.** 145; **XV.** 95; **XVI.** 528.
Number, Early Sessions In, **II.** 132; **V.** 188; **VII.** 698; **IX.** 247, 467; **XI.** 24.
Natural History, Dawson, **III.** 428.
Natural Consequences of Actions, the Law of Discipline, Spencer, **XI.** 498.
New Gymnastics, **XI.** 531; **XII.** 665.
Object Teaching, Bacon, **V.** 674. 680; Calkins, **XII.** 633; Comenius, **V.** 680; Halm, **V.** 696; Hecker, **V.** 693, 696; Henzky, **V.** 604; Hoole, **XII.** 647; Gesner, **V.** 748; Greene, **X.** 245; Locke, **VI.** 220; Marcel, **XI.** 21; Oswego System, **XII.** 604; **XIV.** 93; Pestalozzi, **V.** 76; Ratich, **V.** 689; Semler, **V.** 691; Sheldon, **XIV.** 93; Spencer, **XIII.** 378; Wilbur, **XV.** 180.
Oral Teaching, Barnard, **V.** 777; Currie, **IV.** 104; Masson, **V.** 270; Marcel, **XI.** 31, 330; Morrison, **IX.** 303, 321; Wolf, **VI.** 272; Vaugh, **IV.** 271.
Penmanship, Everett, **IV.** 452; **XII.** 556; Mulhausen, **X.** 524; Niebuhr, **XVI.** 207; Raumer, **X.** 620; Thayer, **IV.** 450.
Perception and Perceptive Faculties, Bacon, **XII.** 49; Hill, **XIV.** 96; Marcel, **XI.** 21; Raumer, **VIII.** 207; Russell, **II.** 113, 316; Spencer, **XIII.** 396.

CLASSIFIED INDEX OF BARNARD'S AMERICAN JOURNAL OF EDUCATION. 29

Physical Education, Aphorisms, **VIII.** 75; Aristotle, **XIV.** 140; Ascham, **III.** 41; Bandow, **V.** 510; Beecher, **II.** 399; Comenius, **V.** 281; Currie, **XI.** 233; Elyot, **XVI.** 490, Fellenberg, **III.** 596; Gutsmuths, **VIII.** 191; Jahn, **VIII.** 196; Lalor, **XVI.** 34; Locke, **XI.** 462; Lorinser, **VIII.** 187; Luther, **IV.** 448; **VIII.** 190; Lycurgus, **XIV.** 620; Mann, Mason, **XIV.** 61; Milton, **II.** 83; Montaigne, **IV.** 465; Pestalozzi, **VIII.** 192; Plutarch, **XI.** 105; Quintilian, **XI.** 118; Rubelais, **XIV.** 149; Raumer, **VIII.** 185; Rousseau, **V.** 475, **VIII.** 185; Spencer, **XI.** 485; Trotzendorf, **V.** 112; Vehrli, **III.** 390, 394; English Public Schools, **XV.** 105.
Pictures in School-books, **IV.** 509; **V.** 506, 512; **VI.** 585; **XII.** 647.
Picturing-out Method. **IX.** 413, 424.
Pleasure in Study and Work, **VI.** 464; **XIII.** 386, 488, 587.
Pleasure-grounds of Knowledge, **XIII.** 121; **XVI.** 438.
Play-state of Childhood, **XIII.** 93.
Physiology, **V.** 499, 512; **XI.** 49; **XVI.** 44.
Plays and Pastimes, **V.** 284; **X.** 259; **XI.** 490; **XIII.** 93, 539, 594; **XV.** 474.
Poetry, Study of, **II.** 82; **III.** 329; **VI.** 290, 226, 467, 517; **VIII.** 226; **X.** 161; **XI.** 509; **XIII.** 117; **XVI.** 47.
Political Science, **II.** 82; **III.** 82; **V.** 513; **IX.** 105; **XI.** 214; **XIV.** 135, 326.
Posture in Devotion, **IV.** 29; **VIII.** 631.
Pouring-in Method. **V.** 819.
Powers to be Educated, Hill, **XIV.** 84.
Practicality, **IV.** 477; **V.** 480; **X.** 129, 414; **XIII.** 13, 103, 812.
Praise, **VIII.** 618; **XVI.** 62.
Prayers in Colleges, **II.** 602; **IV.** 23; **V.** 515.
Precocity, **V.** 473, 749; **XI.** 492, 508.
Prize Schemes, **I.** 629; **II.** 708; **III.** 249, 255; **V.** 226; **VI.** 287.
Printing-press, uses of to Boys, **IX.** 636.
Private Schools, **II.** 719; **VI.** 213; **XIII.** 553.
Progression, **XVI.** 643.
Progressives of the 16th Century, **VI.** 463.
Promotion by merit, **XIII.** 667; **XV.** 92.
Pronunciation of English, **IV.** 226; **XIV.** 354; of Greek and Latin, **IV.** 226; **XV.** 171.
Public Schools in England, **VIII.** 257; **XV.** 81; **XVI.** 501, 567.
Public Schools and Private Schools, **XI.** 114; **XIII.** 361; **XV.** 323.
Punctuality, **II.** 659; **V.** 520.
Pupil-Teachers, **IV.** 191; **X.** 385, 504.
Puzzling Pupils, **XIV.** 313.
Quadriennium, **XIV.** 172.
Quadrivium, **I.** 254; **VI.** 21.
Quick-wits, **XI.** 58.
Questions for Examining a School, **I.** 686; **X.** 449.
Ratio Studiorum, of the Jesuits, **XIV.** 462.
Reaction, Law of, **XI.** 493, 502.
Real Schools, **VI.** 248; **V.** 661, 674, 691; **VIII.** 508; **IX.** 247; **XIV.** 425; **XV.** 440, 767.

Reading, Methods of Instruction, Currie, **IX.** 273, 277; Dunn, **X.** 399; Harwich, **VIII.** 436; Honcamp, **IV.** 234; Lloyd, **IV.** 225; Locke, **VI.** 219, **XIV.** 304; Morrison, **IX.** 307; Olivier, **V.** 508; Prinsen, **VIII.** 612; Quintilian, **XI.** 120; Raumer, **X.** 624; **XII.** 473; Thayer, **IV.** 218; Wilbur, **XV.** 201.
Reasoning with Children, **V.** 471; **XIII.** 562.
Reflection and Reflective Faculties, Marcel, **XI.** 33; Russell, **IV.** 198, 309.
Religion and Religious Instruction, Acquaviva, **XIV.** 471; Arnold, **IV.** 559; Bible, **X.** 167; Busedow, **V.** 501, 513; Brooks, **I.** 336; Burgess, **II.** 562; Currie, **IX.** 284; Cousin, **XIII.** 287; Comenius, **V.** 226; Cowdery, **XVI.** 323; Dunn, **X.** 427; Fellenberg, **XIII.** 325; Fisher, **X.** 180; Hegel, **X.** 171; Hoole, **XVII.** 238; Huntington, **IV.** 23; Krüsi, **V.** 195; Lalor, **XVI.** 49; Lindsley, **VII.** 35; Locke, **XIV.** 308; Luther, **X.** 183; Niemeyer, **X.** 132, 173, 177, 184; Plato, **X.** 170; Pestalozzi, **X.** 175, 182; Potter, **II.** 154, 162; Pythagoras, **X.** 167; Randall, **II.** 156; Raumer, **VII.** 401; **X.** 241; Richards, **X.** 512; Socrates, **X.** 169; Thayer, **III.** 71; Zchokke, **X.** 169, 176.
Religion in Public Schools of Baden, **X.** 206; Bavaria, **VI.** 281; **VIII.** 501; England, **IV.** 550, 573; **X.** 513; **XV.** 109; **XVI.** 670; Greece, **XII.** 574; Holland, **XIV.** 642, 693; Hanover, **XV.** 426, 769; Ireland, **XI.** 137, 152; Jesuit Schools, **XIV.** 471; Prussia, **VIII.** 420; Scotland, **IX.** 222.
Requisitions and Prohibitions, **XIII.** 851,
Rewards in School, **VI.** 212, 435; **XI.** 480.
Rote-learning, **V.** 247, 474; **VI.** 465; **VII.** 405; **XII.** 416; **XIII.** 113, 373.
Rules for School Attendance, **XIV.** 816; Good Behavior, **VIII.** 613; **X.** 438; **XIII.** 171, 549, 851; Hopkins' Grammar School, **IV.** 710; Dorchester School, **XVI.** 106.
Science in Schools, **I.** 164, 514; **II.** 66, 81, 349, 447; **III.** 147, 265; **IV.** 757; **V.** 671, 779; **VI.** 233, 448; **XIII.** 399.
Science and Art, **I.** 109, 315, 388; **II.** 715; **X.** 218.
Simultaneous Method, **IX.** 299.
Socratic Method, **IX.** 375; Currie, **IX.** 283.
Spelling, Dunn, **X.** 409; Richards, **X.** 517; Thayer, **III.** 312.
Studies, True Order of, Hill, **VI.** 180, 449; **VI.** 273, 491; Spencer, **XIII.** 374.
Synthetical Method, **IV.** 504.
Synchronistical Method in History, **IV.** 515.
Text-books, Catalogue of American, **XIII.** 208, 401, 627; **XIV.** 601, 753.
Topical Method in Geography, **VIII.** 82.
Tripartite Organization, **IX.** 316; **XIII.** 149.
Turners and Turning System, **VII.** 92; **VIII.** 189.
Unconscious Tuition, **I.** 141.
Utility of Studies, **II.** 386; **V.** 479; **XV.** 101.
Virtue, **V.** 494; **VIII.** 10; **X.** 167; **VIII.** 550.
Will, **V.** 511, 671; **IX.** 37; **V.** 137; **XIV.** 472, 617.
Writing and Reading, **IV.** 234; **VII.** 694; **XII.** 477.
Writing and Drawing, **VIII.** 388.

IV. TEACHERS; NORMAL AND MODEL SCHOOLS; TEACHERS' INSTITUTES.

The School and the Teacher in English Literature, III. 155, 449; IV. 183; VIII. 283; XVI. 432.
Legal Recognition of Teaching as a Profession; Memorial, X. 297-308.
The Teacher as an Artist, by Z. Richards, XIV. 69.
The Teacher's Motives, by Horace Mann, XIV. 277.
Essentials to Success in Teaching, I. 561.
Letters to a Young Teacher, by G. F. Thayer, I. 357; II. 103, 391, 657; III. 71, 313; IV. 219, 450; VI. 435; VIII. 81.
Lectures to Young Teachers; Intellectual Education, by W. Russell, II. 113, 317; III. 47, 321; IV. 199, 309. Moral Education, IX. 19.
Special Training a Pre-requisite to Teaching, by H. Mann, XIII. 507.
Teachers and their Education, by W. E. Channing, XII. 453.
Professional Training of Teachers, XIII. 269.
Didactics as a Department in Colleges, by T. Hill, XV. 177.
German Views upon Female Teachers, IV. 795.
Teachers' Conferences and other Modes of Professional Improvement, XIII. 273.
Teachers' Institutes in Wisconsin, VIII. 673. In Different States—Historical Development, XV. 387. Connecticut, 387; New York, 395; Ohio, 401; Rhode Island, 405; Massachusetts, 412.
School for Teachers, by W. R. Johnson, V. 799.
Teachers' Seminaries, by C. E. Stowe, XV. 688.
Relation of Normal Schools to other Institutions, by W. F. Phelps, III. 417.
Historical Development of Normal Schools in Europe and America, XIII. 753-770.
Germany and other European States—Number, Location and Results of Normal Schools, VIII. 360; Professional Training of Teachers in Anhalt, XV. 345; Austria, XVI. 345; Baden, X. 212; Bavaria, VI. 289; Belgium, VIII. 593; Brunswick, XV. 453; France, XIII. 281; Greece, XII. 579; Hanover, XV. 419; Hesse-Cassel, XV. 439; Hesse Darmstadt, XIV. 416; Holland, XIV. 501, 647; Lippe Detmold, XV. 475; Mecklenburg, XV. 464, 472; Nassau, II. 444; Prussia, XI. 165; Russia, XII. 727; Sardinia, III. 517; Saxony, V. 353; Switzerland, XIII. 313.
Great Britain. Training Colleges in England and Wales, X. 349. Normal Schools of the British and Foreign School Society, X. 435. Normal and Model Schools of the Home and Colonial Society, IX. 449. St. Mark's Training College for Masters of the National Society, X. 531. Battersea Training School for Parochial Schoolmasters, IX. 170. Chester Diocesan Training College, X. 553. Normal Schools for Training Schoolmistresses, X. 571; Normal Schools at Edinburgh and Glasgow, X. 583. Irish System of Training Teachers, XI. 136.
France. Normal Schools and Training, XIII. 281. Normal Schools of the Christian Brothers, III. 437.
Holland. Normal School at Haarlem, XIV. 501.
Prussia. Provisions for Education and Support of Teachers, XI. 165-190. System of Normal Schools, XIV. 191-240. Seminary School at Weissenfels, VIII. 455; XIV. 219. Dr. Julius on, XVI. 89. Regulations of 1854, XVI. 395.
Normal Schools in Switzerland, XIII. 313-440.
Normal and Model Schools of Upper Canada, XIV. 483.
United States—Documentary History of Normal Schools—Adams, I. 589; Bache, VIII. 360; Barnard, X. 24, 40; Bates, XVI. 453: Brooks, I. 587; Barrowes, XVI. 195; Calhoun, XVI. 86; Carter, XVI. 77; Channing, XII. 453; Clinton, XIII. 341; Dwight, IV. 16: Edwards, XVI. 271; Emerson, XVI. 93: Everett, XIII. 758; Gallaudet, X. 16; Hall, V. 386; XVI. 75; Humphrey, XII. 655; Julius, XVI. 89; Johnson, V. 798; Lindsley, VII. 35; Mann, V. 646; VIII. 360; Olmsted, V. 369; Peirce, IV. 305; Phelps, III. 417; Putnam, I. 588; Sears, XVI. 471; Stephens, VIII. 368; Stowe, XV. 688; Tillinghast, I. 67 ; Webster, I. 590; Wickersham, XV. 221.
Chapter in the History of Normal Schools in New England; Charles Brooks, I. 587.
California. State Normal School, XVI. 628.
Connecticut. History of State Normal School, X. 15-58. History of Teachers' Institutes, XV. 387.
Illinois. State Normal University at Bloomington, IV. 774.
Kentucky. State Normal School, III. 217.
Maine. State Normal School, XVII.
Maryland. State Normal School, XVII.
Massachusetts. State Normal School at Bridgewater, V. 646; XVI. 595. At Barre; Everett's Address, XIII. 758. At Westfield, XII. 652. Teachers' Seminary at Andover, V. 386. History of Teachers' Institutes, XV. 387.
New Jersey. State Normal School, III. 221. Its Aims, by D. Cole, V. 835. Farnum Preparatory School, III. 397.
New York. State Normal School at Albany, XIII. 341, 531. History of Teachers' Institutes, XV. 305. Training School at Oswego, XVI. 230. Normal School at Brockport, XVII.
Ohio. History of Teachers' Institutes, XV. 401. Normal Schools in, XVII.
Pennsylvania. Professional Training of Teachers, XIV. 721. Normal School at Millersville, XV. 221. Philadelphia Normal School for Female Teachers, XIV. 727. XVI. 195. Normal School at Mansfield, XVII.
Rhode Island. Education of Teachers, XI. 282. History of Teachers' Institutes, XV. 405.
Vermont. Teachers' Seminary in 1823, XVI. 146. State Normal Schools, XVII.
Wisconsin. Teachers' Institutes, VIII. 673. Normal Schools, XVII.

V. STATE AND NATIONAL SYSTEMS.

Educational Statistics, **I.** 640–651.
Anhalt. System of Public Instruction, **XV.** 344.
Austria. System of Public Instruction, **IX.** 589. Educational Statistics, **III.** 275; **IV.** 257; **XVI.** 5, 337, 609; **XVII.** 127.
Baden. System of Public Instruction; Primary, **X.** 201. Secondary, **XI.** 233. Seminary for Orphans at Beuggen, **III.** 383.
Bavaria. System of Public Instruction, **VI.** 273, 571; **VIII.** 491. Educational Statistics, **I.** 625.
Belgium. System of Public Instruction, **VIII.** 581.
Brunswick. System of Public Instruction, **XV.** 447.
Canada. History and System of Public Instruction in Upper Canada, by J. G. Hodgins, **I.** 186. Statistics of Education in Upper Canada, **XIII.** 649. Educational Institutions in U. and L. Canada, **II.** 728.
Denmark. System of Public Instruction, **XIV.** 625.
England. Historical Sketch of Elementary Instruction, **X.** 323. British and Foreign School Society and Borough Road Schools, **X.** 371–459. National Society for Promoting the Education of the Poor, **X.** 499–574. Home and Colonial Infant and Juvenile Society, **IX.** 449. Lord John Russell's Scheme of National Education, **I.** 638. Ashburton Prizes for Teaching Common Things, **I.** 629; **X.** 93. Miss Coutts' Prizes, **II.** 708. Public Endowed or Foundation Schools, **IV.** 807; **VIII.** 257; **XV.** 81–117. Appropriations to Education, Science, and Art, **I.** 385; **II.** 348; **X.** 347.
France. System of Public Instruction, **VI.** 293; **IX.** 481–412. Guizot's Ministry of Public Instruction, **XI.** 254, 357. Statistics of Education, **IV.** 257. Expenditures for Public Instruction, **II.** 337, 717.
Free Cities; Frankfort, Hamburg, Bremen, and Lübeck. System of Public Instruction, **XV.** 333.
Germany. History and Course of Primary Instruction, **VIII.** 348–402. Real Schools, **V.** 689–714. Educational Intelligence, **III.** 273; **IV.** 245.
Greece. System of Public Instruction, **XII.** 571–592. Statistics of Education, **I.** 628.
Hanover. System of Public Instruction, **IV.** 250; **XV.** 415, 752.
Hesse Cassel. System of Public Instruction, **XV.** 431.
Hesse Darmstadt. Public Instruction, **XIV.** 409–430.
Holland. System of Public Instruction, **IV.** 801; **VIII.** 595; **XIV.** 495, 641–720. Proposed Revision of System, **II.** 719. Statistics of Public Schools, **I.** 401. Scheme of Christian Education adopted at Dort, 1618, **V.** 77.
Honduras. Condition of Education, **II.** 236.
India. Progress of Education, **II.** 727.
Ireland. Elementary Education, **XI.** 133–154. System of National Education, **III.** 272; **IV.** 363. National Schools, **XIII.** 145. Educational Appropriations, **I.** 390; **II.** 348, 716. Endowed Grammar and English Schools, **XV.** 721.
Italy. Institutions for Public Instruction, **II.** 721. History of Education, **VII.** 413.
Lippe-Detmold and Schaumburg Lippe. System of Public Instruction, **XV.** 473, 576.
Luxemburg and Limberg. System of Public Instruction, **XIV.** 664.
Mecklenburg. System of Public Instruction, **XV.** 459. Ignorance in, **III.** 278.
Nassau. System of Public Instruction, **II.** 444.
New South Wales. Statistics of Education, **I.** 639.
Norway. System of Public Instruction, **VIII.** 295.
Portugal. System of Public Instruction, **XVII.**
Prussia. History and Statistics of Public Instruction, **IV.** 245; **VIII.** 403–434; **IX.** 569. Expenditures for Public Instruction in Prussia and France, **II.** 337. Public Schools of Berlin, **VIII.** 440. Frederic William Gymnasium and Real Schools of Berlin, **V.** 699. Burgher School at Halle, **VIII.** 434. Higher Burgher School of Potsdam, **VIII.** 457.
Russia. National Education, **XII.** 725
Sardinia. System of Public Instruction, **III.** 513; **IV.** 37, 479.
Saxony. System of Public Instruction, **V.** 350. Secondary Instruction, **IV.** 251. Burgher School, **IX.** 201. Early School Code, **VI.** 432.
Scotland. Elementary Education, **IX.** 215. Parochial School System, **II.** 716; **VII.** 319.
Spain. Public Instruction, **XVII.**
Sweden. Public Instruction, **II.** 720; **XVI.** 639.
Turkey. System of Education, **II.** 725.
Wurtemburg. Early School Code, **VI.** 426. System of Public Instruction, **XVII.**
UNITED STATES. Official Exposition of Common Schools, **II.** 257, 465–561. School Funds and Public Instruction in the several States, **I.** 371, 447. Statistics of Population, Area, and Education in 1850, **I.** 364. Statistics of Public Instruction in Cities and large Towns, **I.** 458. Educational Movements in the several States, **I.** 234, 641; **II.** 257, 452, 734; **IV.** 824. Plan of Central Agency for Advancement of Education, by H. Barnard, **I.** 134. National Bureau of Education, **XV.** 180. Lord Elgin on the American School System, **III.** 239. Education among the Cherokees, by W. P. Ross, **I.** 120. Schools as they were Sixty Years ago, **XIII.** 123, 737; **XVI.** National Department of Education, **XVII.** 49. Constitutional Provision, **XVII.** 81. Educational Land Policy, **XVII.** 65.
Alabama. School Statistics, **I.** 368, 371; **II.** 464. Constitutional Provision, **XVII.**
Arkansas. Statistics, **I.** 368, 371.
California. **XVI.** 625. Statistics, **I.** 372; **II.** 467.
Connecticut. History of Common Schools, by H Barnard, **IV.** 657; **V.** 114; **XIII.** 725; **XIV.** 244; **XV.** 275; **XVI.** 333. History of the School Fund, **VI.** 367–415. Henry Barnard's Labors, **I.** 669. Public Schools and other Educational Institutions, **XI.** 305. Free Academy and School Movements in Norwich, **II.** 665; **III.** 191. Statistics, **I.** 372; **II.** 469. Constitutional Provision, **XVII.**

Delaware. Statistics, **I**, 368, 373; **II**, 474.
Florida. Statistics, **I**, 367, 374.
Georgia. **I**, 368, 374; **II**, 477.
Illinois. **I**, 368, 375; **II**, 479.
Indiana. **I**, 368, 375; **II**, 480.
Iowa. **I**, 368, 374; **II**.
Kansas. **XVII**.
Kentucky. **I**, 368, 377; **II**, 488.
Louisiana. **I**, 368, 377; **II**, 473.
Maine. **I**, 368, 378; **II**, 495.
Maryland. **I**, 368, 378.
Massachusetts. Doctrine of Free Schools, **XV**, 15. Analysis of Horace Mann's Reports, **V**, 623. School Superintendence; Memorial of American Institute of Instruction, **V**, 653; Legal Recognition of Teaching as a Profession; Memorial of Worcester County Teachers' Association, **X**, 207. **I**, 368, 379; **II**, 409.
Michigan. **I**, 368, 447; **II**, 510.
Minnesota. **I**, 368.
Mississippi. **I**, 368, 447.
Missouri. **I**, 368, 448.
Nebraska. **XVII**.
Nevada. **XVII**.
New Hampshire. **I**, 368, 448; **II**, 510.
New Jersey. **I**, 368, 449; **II**, 517.
New York. **I**, 368, 449; **II**, 518
North Carolina. **I**, 368, 451; **II**, 527. Schools as they were in 1794, **XVI**, 1.
Ohio. System of Common Schools, by W. T. Coggeshall, **VI**, 81, 532; **I**, 368, 451; **II**, 531.

Oregon. **I**, 368; **XVII**.
Pennsylvania. History of Common Schools, **VI**, 107, 555; **I**, 368, 452; **II**, 541.
Rhode Island. **I**, 368, 454; **II**, 544. Labors of Henry Barnard, **I**, 723.
South Carolina. **I**, 368, 455; **II**, 553. Marion on Free Schools for, **XVI**, 119.
Tennessee. **I**, 368, 455.
Texas. **I**, 368, 445.
Vermont. **I**, 368, 466.
Virginia. **I**, 368, 457; Gov. Wise on Education, **II**, 557.
West Virginia. **XVII**.
Wisconsin. **I**, 368, 457.
District of Columbia. **XVII**.
Cities. Statistics of Population, **I**, 479. Gradation of Schools for, **XV**, 316, 309. Reports on, **I**, 458. Boston: Edward Everett and the Boston Schools, **I**, 642. Latin Grammar School of Boston, **XII**, 529. Girls in the Public Schools of Boston, **XIII**, 243. Dedication of the Everett School House, **IX**, 633. Report of N. Bishop, **I**, 458. School Houses in, **XVI**, 701.
Chicago High School, by W. H. Wells, **III**, 531. Retirement of Mr. Wells, **XIV**, 811.
Cincinnati; Woodward High School, **IV**, 520.
New York City. Public School Society, **XV**, 489.
Philadelphia High School, by J. S. Hart, **I**, 93. Report on Public Schools, **I**, 465.
Providence: Report on, **I**, 468.
St. Louis System of Public Instruction, **I**, 348.

VI. SECONDARY, INTERMEDIATE AND ACADEMICAL SCHOOLS.

Anhalt. Gymnasiums and Higher Schools, **XV**, 346.
Austria. System and Statistics of Secondary Instruction, **IX**, 598. **XVI**, 465. **XVII**, 127.
Baden. System of Sec. Instruction, **XI**, 233-253.
Bavaria. Secondary Schools, **VIII**, 491-521.
Belgium. Secondary Schools, **VIII**, 587.
Brunswick. Classical Schools, **XV**, 456.
Canada. Secondary Schools, **XIII**, 649.
Denmark. Outline of System and Statistics, **XIV**, 625.
England. Public or Foundation Schools, **VIII**, 257; **XV**, 81. Mr. Sewall's School at Radleigh, **IV**, 803. St. Mary's College at Winchester, **XVI**, 501. St. Paul's School in London, **XVI**, 667. Eton College, **XVII**.
France. Lyceums and Secondary Schools, **VI**, 294. Statistics of Secondary Education in 1843, **IX**, 400. Secondary Instruction under Guizot's Ministry, **XI**, 337. Schools of Preparation for the Polytechnic School, **XII**, 47.
Free Cities. Gymnasiums and Secondary Institutions, **XV**, 339.
Greece. Secondary Schools, Gymnasiums, &c., **XII**, 581.
Hanover. Real Schools and Girls' High School, **IV**, 250. Secondary Instruction, **XV**, 753-781.
Hesse-Cassel. Secondary Institutions, **XV**, 435.

Hesse-Darmstadt. Classical, Real, Trades, and Higher Female School Systems, **XIV**, 419.
Holland. Secondary Schools, **XIV**, 654.
Ireland. Endowed Grammar and English Schools, **XV**, 721.
Mecklenburg. Secondary Schools, **XV**, 465.
Nassau. Secondary Education, **II**, 445.
Norway. Burgher, Real, and Learned Schools, **VIII**, 301.
Prussia. Statistics of Secondary Instruction, **II**, 341; **IV**, 247. Higher Institutions of Berlin, **V**, 699. Secondary Education, **IX**, 569.
Sardinia. Secondary Instruction, **III**, 518; **IV**, 37.
Saxony. Real and Classical Schools, **V**, 354; **IV**, 251. Secondary Education, **IX**, 201.
United States. Historical Development of Incorporated Academies, **XVI**, 403. Statistics of Academies, &c. in 1850, **I**, 368; Lawrence Academy, Groton, Mass., **I**, 49. Williston Seminary, Easthampton, Mass., **II**, 173. Norwich Free Academy, Norwich, Conn., **II**, 665; **III**, 190. Public High School in Chicago, **III**, 531. Woodward High School in Cincinnati, **IV**, 520. Phillips Academy, Andover, Mass., **VI**, 73. Phillips Academy, Exeter, N. H., **VI**, 76. Boston Latin School, **XII**, 529. Public Grammar Schools of Philadelphia, **XIII**, 818.

VII. UNIVERSITY AND COLLEGE EDUCATION.

Signification of the term University, IX, 49-56.
University Honors, VIII, 313.
University Studies and Teaching, Raumer, VII. 201.
Classical Education. Erasmus' Views, IV, 729. David Cole upon, I, 67. Discussion before the American Association, I. 86. S. P. Bates, XV, 155. Speaking and Writing Latin, Raumer, VII, 471.
College Education and Self-Education, IV, 262.
Prayers in Colleges, by F. D. Huntington, IV, 23.
College Code of Honor, by Horace Mann, III, 65.
Authorities upon the History of Universities, and Academical Degrees, II, 747; VII, 49; IX, 56.
Canada. University and Colleges of Upper and Lower Canada, II, 728; VII, 188; XIII, 649.
England. Government Grants in 1856, II, 348. Oxford Commemoration, II, 234. Expenses in Eton College in 1560, IV, 259. University for Legal Education, I, 386. Working Men's College, I, 389.
France. University and Colleges, VI, 296.
Germany. German Universities in the Sixteenth Century, from Raumer, V, 535. History of German Universities, from Raumer, VI, 9-65; VII, 47-152. Student Societies in German Universities, VII, 160. Essays on the Improvement of German Universities, from Raumer, VII, 200-251. Statistics, I, 401.
Greece. The Otho University, XII, 591.
Holland. Condition of the Universities, I, 397.
Ireland. Queen's Colleges and University, IX, 579.
Prussia. Receipts and Expend. of Universities, II, 338.
Russia. Universities, I, 381.

Sardinia. University Education, IV, 43.
Saxony. University of Leipsic, V, 362.
Scotland. University of Edinburg, IV, 821.
Wurtemburg. University of Tübingen, IX, 57.
United States. Characteristics of American Colleges, by C. C. Felton, IX, 122.
Improvements Practicable in American Colleges, by F. A. P. Barnard, I, 175, 260.
Consolidation and other Modifications of American Colleges, by Alonzo Potter, I, 471.
An American University, by B. A. Gould. II, 265-293. By A. D. Bache, I, 477. By an Alabamian, III, 213. Discussion, I, 86.
Society for the Promotion of Collegiate and Theological Education at the West, I, 235; XV, 261.
Statistics of New England Colleges in 1855-6, I, 405.
Harvard University. History, IX, 129. Grants and Donations to, IX, 130-165. Progress under Pres. Felton, X, 293. Museum of Zoölogy, IX, 613.
Yale College. History, V, 541-566, Elihu Yale, V, 715. List of Deceased Benefactors, X, 693. Department of Philosophy and the Arts, I, 459. Influence of, by F. A. P. Barnard, V, 723; by W. B. Sprague, X, 681.
Illinois College. History, I, 225.
Transylvania University, Kentucky, III, 217.
Cumberland University, Tennessee; History, IV, 763.
University Convocation of New York, XV, 502.
St. John's College, Maryland, Charter, XVI, 549.
Report on Reorganization, XVI, 539.

VIII. SCHOOLS OF SCIENCE AND ARTS; MUSEUMS, &C.

Democratic Tendencies of Science, D. Olmsted, I, 164.
Progress of Science in the United States, I, 641.
Science and Scientific Schools, by J. D. Dana, II, 349.
Schools of Science and Art, X, 216.
Physical Science. By H. J. Anderson, I, 515-532.
Scientific Schools in Europe, by D. C. Gilman, I, 315.
Department of Science and Art, Eng., II, 233, 715.
Higher Special Schools of Science and Literature in France, by D. C. Gilman, II, 93.
Special Instruction in Science and Art in France, IX, 405.
Polytechnic Schools. At Paris, VIII, 661; XII, 51-130. Le Verrier's Report upon Mathematical Study preparatory to the Polytechnic School of Paris, I, 533-550; II, 177-192. Conditions for Admission, XIII, 678. Polytechnic Institute at Vienna, VIII, 670. Polytechnic School at Carlsruhe, XI, 209. Polytechnic School at Zürich, XI, 218. Polytechnic Schools of Bavaria, VIII, 510.
Russia. Schools of Special Instruction, I, 382.
Lawrence Scientific School at Cambridge, I, 216.
Scientific Department in Yale College, I, 359.
Cooper Scientific Union, New York, I, 652; IV, 526.
Industrial School at Chemnitz, III, 252; IV, 798.
School of Mines at Freyburg, Saxony, IX, 167.

Drawing; Report of a French Commission, II, 419.
Art Education, by Miss M. A. Dwight, II, 409-587; III, 467; IV, 191; V, 305.
On a College of Architecture, by D. B. Reid, II, 629.
Dudley Observatory, II, 593. Uses of Astronomy, by E. Everett, II, 605-628.
United States Coast Survey, I, 103.
Geological Hall and Agricultural Rooms of New York, IV, 785.
British Museum, VIII, 314. British Museum of Practical Geology, VI, 239. Museum of Comparative Zoölogy at Harvard, IX, 613. Educational Uses of Museums, by Prof. E. Forbes, IV, 785.
Institute of Agriculture and Forestry at Hohenheim, VIII, 564. At Tharand, Saxony, IV, 797.
Agricultural Education in France, VIII, 545-563. In Ireland, VIII, 567-580.
Plan of Agricultural School, by J. A. Porter, I, 329.
Hartlib's Plan of a College of Husbandry, XI, 191.
Mechanics' Institutes in England, I, 388; II, 712.
Plan of a Trade School, by Sir W. Pelty, 1647, XI, 199.
Industrial Training of Poor, X, 81. Industrial Schools in England, I, 653. Ireland, I, 545. Belgium, I, 384; VIII, 588. Bavaria, VIII, 510. Nassau, II, 446. Saxony, IV, 252, 798. Wurtemburg, IV, 799.

IX. MILITARY AND NAVAL EDUCATION.

Physical and Military Exercises in Public Schools a National Necessity, by E. L. Molineux, **XI.** 513.
Military Schools and Education in England, **IV.** 808; **XIV.** 523. France, **I.** 626; **XII.** 7-274. Holland, **XIV.** 241. Prussia, **XII.** 275-399; **VIII.** 437. Russia, **I.** 383; **XIV.** 503. Switzerland, **XIII.** 689-710. Sardinia, **XIII.** 455. Austria, **XIII.** 409-446, 711. Persia, **II.** 727.
United States; Military Academy at West Point, **XIII.** 17-48. Regulations for Admission, **XIII.**

659 Report of Visitors, 1863, **XIII.** 661; **XV.** 51. On the Conditions for Admission, by H. Barnard, **XIV.** 103-127. Military Academy at Norwich, Vt., **XIII.** 65. Englewood Military Academy, at Perth Amboy, N. J., **XIII.** 471.
Naval and Navigation Schools in England, **XIV.** 627; **XV.** 65.
French Naval School at Brest. **XII.** 263.
United States Naval Academy; Report of Visitors, 1864, **XV.** 17-50.

X. PREVENTIVE AND REFORMATORY EDUCATION.

Education a Preventive of Misery and Crime, by E. C. Tainsch, **XI.** 77.
Crimes of Children and their Prevention. **I.** 345.
Publications on Reformatory Education, **III.** 812.
Family Training and Agricultural Labor in Reformatory Education, **I.** 600-624.
Crime, Pauperism, and Education in G. Brit., **VI.** 311.
Preventive and Reformatory Education, **III.** 561-818. Reform Schools in England, **III.** 753. In Ireland, **III.** 807. In Scotland, **III.** 801. In France, **III.** 653. In Holland, **III.** 619. In Italy, **III.** 580. In Switzerland, **III.** 591.
Reformatory Establishment of Dusselthal Abbey, Prussia, **II.** 231.
Prison for Juvenile Criminals, Isle of Wight, **III.** 19.
Wichern and the Rauhe Haus, **III.** 5, 10, 603; **IV.** 824.

Agricultural Reform Schools in Belgium and France, **III.** 621-736.
Agricultural Colonies of France, particularly Mettray, **I.** 609; **III.** 653.
Reformatory Education in the United States, **IV.** 824; Statistics of State and City Reform Schools in the United States, **III.** 811; **VIII.** 339.
State Industrial School for Girls, at Lancaster, Mass., **IV.** 359; **XVI.** 652.
Mode of Improving Factory Population, **VIII.** 305.
Special Training of Women for Social Employments, **III.** 485.
International Philanthropic Congress at Brussels, **II.** 236; **III.** 231.
Industrial Training of the Poor, **I.** 384, 635; **II.** 446; **III.** 585; **IV.** 252, 798; **X.** 81.

XI. EDUCATION FOR DEAF-MUTES, BLIND AND IDIOTS.

Statistics of the Deaf, Dumb, Blind, Insane, and Idiotic in the U. S. in 1850, **I.** 650.
Statistics of the Deaf and Dumb Institutions in the United States, **I.** 444.
American Asylum for the Deaf and Dumb, **I.** 440.
N. Y. Institution for the Deaf and Dumb, **III.** 347.
Institutions and Instruction for the Blind, by L. P. Brockett, **IV.** 127.
Valentine Haüy and the Instruction of the Blind, **III.** 177; **IV.** 130.

Account of Laura Bridgman, by S. G. Howe, **IV.** 383.
Idiots and Institutions for their Training, by L. P. Brockett. **I.** 593.
Origin of Treatment and Training of Idiots, by E. Seguin. **II.** 145.
New York Asylum for Imbeciles at Syracuse. **IV.** 416.
Butler Hospital for the Insane, at Providence, R. I., **III.** 309.
Insanity as the Result of Misdirected Education, by E. Jarvis, **IV.** 591.

XII. MORAL AND RELIGIOUS EDUCATION; DENOMINATIONAL SCHOOLS.

Thoughts on Religion and Public Schools, by George Burgess, **II.** 562.
Christianity in Education, from Raumer, **VIII.** 216.
Religious Instruction, from Raumer, **VII.** 401.
Religious and Moral Instruction in Public Schools; Discussion by the American Association, **II.** 153.
Importance and Methods of Moral Training, by G. F. Thayer, **III.** 71.
Best Methods of Moral Teaching, by C. Brooks, **I.** 336.
Moral and Mental Discipline, by Z. Richards, **I.** 107.
Formation of Moral Character, the Main Object of Schools, by M. F. Cowdery, **XVI.** 353.

Moral Education, by W. Russell, **IX.** 19-48; Fellenberg, **III.** 595; Krüsi, **V.** 193; Lalor, **XVI.** 48; Locke, **XI.** 473; **XIII.** 548; Spencer, **XI.** 496.
Aphorisms on Religious and Moral Training, **X.** 166; **XII.** 407.
Prayers in Colleges, by F. D. Huntington. **IV.** 23.
Catholic Educational Establishments in the United States, **II.** 435.
The Hieronymians; from Raumer, **IV.** 622.
Jesuits and their Schools, **XIV.** 455-482. From Raumer, **V.** 213; **VI.** 615.
The Christian Brothers, (Freres Chrétiens,) **III.** 437.

XIII. EDUCATION AND SCHOOLS FOR FEMALES.

Aphorisms upon Female Education, **XIII.** 232.
Views of German Authorities, **XIII.** 495.
St. Jerome—Letter to Læta on the Education of her Daughter, **V.** 593.
E. Everett, Female Education, **IX.** 635; **XII.** 721.
Education of Girls, from Raumer, **X.** 227, 613.
Mental Education of Women, by C. McKeen, **I.** 567.
Training of Women for Social Employments, **III.** 485.
Sisters of Charity—Mrs. Jameson. **III.** 495.
Female Adult Education in Ireland, **I.** 634.
School for Girls in Paris, **I.** 394.

Girls in the Public Schools of Boston, **XIII.** 243.
Female Colleges in the State of Ohio, **XIII.** 267.
New York Grammar School for Girls, **I.** 408. Packer Collegiate Institute for Girls, **I.** 579. Young Ladies' High School, Providence, R. I., **V.** 14. Troy Female Seminary, **VI.** 145. Mt. Holyoke Female Seminary, **X.** 670. Bailey's Young Ladies' High School, Boston, **XII.** 435. Ohio Female College, College Hill, **XIII.** 503. Girls' High School, Charleston, S. C., **XIII.** 620. Vassar College, **XI.** 55. **XVII.**

XIV. PHYSICAL EDUCATION.

Aphorisms and Suggestions upon Physical Training, **VIII.** 75.
Physical Education; by Raumer, **VIII.** 185. By Locke, **XI.** 462. By Lalor, **XVI.** 34. By Spencer, **XI.** 485.
Health of Teachers, by Miss C. E. Beecher, **II.** 399.
Physical Exercises, by S. W. Mason, **XIV.** 61.
New Gymnastics, by Dio Lewis, **XI.** 531; **XII.** 665.

Physical and Military Exercises in Schools a National Necessity, by E. L. Molineux, **XI.** 513.
Plays, Pastimes, and Holidays of Children, by Horace Bushnell, **XIII.** 93.
Progressive Development of Physical Culture in the United States, **XV.** 231.
Military Gymnastic School at Vincennes, France, **XII.** 265.

XV. SUPPLEMENTARY, SELF AND HOME EDUCATION.

Hints on Reading; Selections from Authors, by T. H. Vail, **II.** 215.
Advice to Students and Young Men on Education, Studies, and Conduct, **XV.** 377; **XVI.** 187, 216, 223.
Pestalozzi—Address on Christmas Eve, **VII.** 701. On New Year's, **VII.** 712. Paternal Instructions, **VII.** 722.
Home Education; Labors of Rev. W. Burton, **II.** 333.
College and Self-education, by D. Masson, **IV.** 262.
Lowell Lectures, **V.** 439.
Mechanics' Institutes. **VIII.** 250.
Origin of Lyceums, **VIII.** 249. The American Lyceum, **XIV.** 535–558.

Lyceums, Mechanics' Institutes and Libraries in England, **I.** 388; **II.** 712; **III.** 241–272.
Statistics of Libraries in Europe, **I.** 370; **II.** 214. In the United States in 1850, **I.** 369.
Libraries for Teachers in France, **XIII.** 293. Economic Library, England, **III.** 271.
Astor Library, **I.** 648. Boston Public Library, **II.** 203; **VII.** 252. Baltimore Public Library, **III.** 226. Worcester Free Public Library, **XIII.** 606. Providence Atheneum, **III.** 308. Lawrence Library for Factory Operatives, **I.** 649.
Management of Libraries—Edward's Library Manual, **II.** 210.
Books of Reference, **VIII.** 315.

XVI. EDUCATIONAL ASSOCIATIONS.

Association for Educational Purposes, by H. Barnard, **XIV.** 366; **XV.** 819.
American Association for the Advancement of Education, **I.** 3–136, 234; **XV.** 267.
American Association for the Advancement of Science, **III.** 147.
American Association for the Supply of Teachers, **XV.** 237.
American Common School Society, **XV.** 247.
American Education Society, **XIV.** 367.
American Institute of Instruction, **II.** 19, 234. Index to Lecturers and Subjects, **II.** 241. Memorial on State School Superintendence, **V.** 653. Biographical Sketches of Presidents, **XV.** 211.
American Lyceum, **XIV.** 535.
American School Society, **XV.** 118.
American Social Science Association, **XVI.** 391.

American Sunday School Union, **XV.** 705
American Women's Educational Asso., **XV.** 273.
Baltimore County and City Association, **XVI.** 377.
Board of National Popular Education, **XV.** 271.
Boston Associated Instructors of Youth, **XV.** 527.
British and Foreign School Society, **X.** 371–459.
College Delegates (New England) Association, **XVII.** Guild of Schoolmasters, **XV.** 337.
Home and Colonial Infant and Juvenile Society, **IX.** 449–480.
Literary and Scientific Convention; New York, 1830, **XV.** 221.
National Associations, **XV.** 237, 823.
National Association (England) for Promotion of Social Science, **IV.** 818.
National Convention and Association of Superintendents of Schools, **XVI.** 389.

National Organization of Teachers, by W. Russell, **XIV**, 7.
National Teachers' Association; Proceedings, **XIV**, 5-92, 503. Its Nature and Objects, by J. D. Philbrick, **XIV**, 49.
National Society (England) for Promoting the Education of the Poor, **X**, 499-474.
National Society of Science, Literature, and Arts, **XV**, 61.
New York (City) Society of Teachers, **XIV**, 807; **XV**, 491. Teachers' Associations, **XV**, 495.
New York University Convocation, **XV**, 502.
North-Western Educational Society, **XV**, 275.
Public School Society of New York, **XV**, 489.
Society for the Diffusion of Useful Knowledge, **XV**, 239.
Society for Promoting Manual Labor in Literary Institutions, **XV**, 231.
Society for the Promotion of Collegiate and Theological Education at the West, **I**, 235; **XV**, 261.
State Convention of County Superintendents; New York, **XV**, 505.
TEACHERS' ASSOCIATIONS in France, **XIII**, 293.
General Assembly of German Teachers, **IV**, 258.
United Association of Schoolmasters, Eng., **III**, 262.

Teachers' Conferences and other Modes of Professional Improvement, **XIII**, 273.
Western Literary Institute and College of Professional Teachers, **XIV**, 739.
Middlesex County (Conn.) School Association, **XIV**, 397 : **XV**.
State Teachers' Associations, Educational Societies and Conventions—Alabama, **XVI**, 375. Arkansas, **XVI**, 381. California, **XVI**, 785. Connecticut, **XV**, 393. Delaware, **XVI**, 369. Florida, **XVI**, 381. Georgia, **XVI**, 358. Illinois, **XVI**, 149. Indiana, **XVI**, 765. Iowa, **XVI**, 745. Kansas, **XVI**, 385. Kentucky, **XVI**, 352. Louisiana, **XVI**, 382. Maine, **XVI**, 777. Maryland, **XVI**, 377. Massachusetts, **XV**, 507. Michigan, **XV**, 633. Minnesota, **XVII**, Mississippi, **XVI**, 381. Missouri, **XVI**, 365. New Hampshire, **XVI**, 751. New Jersey, **XVI**, 729. New York, **XVI**, 349, 477. North Carolina, **XVI**, 361. Ohio, **VI**, 532. Oregon, **XVI**, 383. Pennsylvania, **XV**, 647. Rhode Island, **XIV**, 559. South Carolina, **XVI**, 364. Tennessee, **XVI**, 357. Texas, **XVI**, 373. Vermont, **XV**, 617. Virginia, **XVI**. 172. Wisconsin, **XIV**, 583; **XVII**, District of Columbia, **XVI**, 380. West Virginia, **XVI**, 383.

XVII. PHILOLOGY AND BIBLIOGRAPHY.

Philological Contributions, by J. W. Gibbs, **II**, 198; **III**, 101-124.
English Language in Society and the School, by M. H. Buckham, **XIV**, 343.
Study of the Anglo-Saxon, or the Relation of the English to other Languages, by J. S. Hart, **I**, 33.
Dictionary of the English Language ; Requirements in a Lexicographer, by Isaiah Dole, **III**, 161.
Modern Greek Language, by S. G. Howe, **II**, 193.
Latin Language, from Raumer, **VII**, 471.
Early Illustrated School Books, **XIII**, 205. Primers and Hornbooks, **VIII**, 310. A B C Books and Primers, **XII**, 593.

Books of Reference, **VIII**, 315.
American Text Books—Catalogue of Authors and Books, **XIII**, 209, 401, 626; **XIV**, 601, 751; **XV**, 539.
Educational Literature—Book Notices, **I**, 415; **II**, 256, 737, 739; **IV**, 261, 272, 831 ; **V**, 318; **IX**, 351; **XI**, 319; **XIII**, 223, 652; **XIV**, 400.
Statistics of Newspapers and Periodicals in the United States in 1850, **I**, 651.
Educational Periodicals of America, **I**, 413, 656. Complete List, **XV**, 383.
English Educational Journals, **I**, 414. French, **I**, 413. German, **I**, 413. Italian, **IV**, 802.

XVIII. SCHOOL ARCHITECTURE.

Defects in School Constructions, **IX**, 487.
Principles and Practical Illustrations of School Architecture, by Henry Barnard, **IX**, 487; **X**, 695; **XI**, 563; **XII**, 701; **XIII**, 817; **XIV**, 778; **XV**, 782; **XVI**, 701.
District Schools, or for Children of every age. Plan by H. Mann, **IX**, 540; by G. B. Emerson, 542, 548; by H. Barnard, 550, 553, 555; by R. S. Burt, 556; by T. A. Teft, 559; by A. D. Lord, 562; by D. Leach, 563.
Primary and Infant Schools. General Principles, **X**, 695. Playground and Appliances, **X**, 697. Schoolroom, by Wilderspein, **X**, 699; by Chambers, 702; by British and Foreign School Society, 705; by National Society, 706; by Committee of Council on Education, 710; by Dr. Dick, 714 ; by J. Kendal, 715; by J. W. Ingraham, for Boston Primary

Schools, 718 ; by J. D. Philbrick, 740; by New York Public School Society, 750; in Providence, **XI**, 583.
Baltimore Female High School, **V**, 198 ; Cincinnati Hughes High School, **XIII**, 623; Boston Latin School, **XII**, 551; Woodward High School, **IV**, 522 ; Chicago High School, **III**, 537 ; High School, Hartford, **XI**, 606 ; Public High School, Middletown, **XI**, 612; New York Free Academy, **XIV**, 786 ; Providence Public High School, **XI**, 597; Norwich Free Academy, **II**, 696 ; St. Louis High School, **I**, 348.
Seminaries for Girls. Packer Collegiate Institute, Brooklyn, **I**, 581 ; Richmond Female College, **I**, 231 ; Public Grammar School for Girls in New York, **I**, 408 ; Providence Young Ladies' High School, **V**, 14 ; Vassar College, **XVII**.

Union and Graded Schools—Plans, Elevations, &c., X, 563-612; XII, 701. Union School, Ann Arbor, Mich., VIII, 91. Public Floating School, Baltimore, V, 201. Haven School Building, Chicago, XIII, 610. Newberry Public School, Chicago, VI, 515. Putnam Free School, Newburyport, Mass., XIII, 616. Public Schools No. 20 and No. 33, New York City, VI, 524. School Houses in Philadelphia, XIII, 817. Graded School, Simcoe, U. C., VIII, 679. Union Public School, Ypsilanti, Mich., IV, 780. Norwich Central School, II, 699. Grammar Schools—Plans. Lincoln Grammar School, Boston, VI, 518. Dwight Grammar School, Boston, IV, 709. Fifteenth Ward (N. Y.) Public Grammar School for Girls, I, 409. Central High School, Philadelphia, I, 92; XIII, 831. Grammar, Providence, XI, 588, 594. Prescott Grammar, XVI, 711.

Normal Schools—Plans, Elevations, &c. Illinois State Normal School, IV, 774. New Jersey State Normal School, III, 220. Massachusetts State Normal School at Westfield, XII, 653. New York State Normal School, XIII, 539. Philadelphia City Normal Schools, XIV, 737. Girls' High Normal School, Charleston, S. C., XIII, 620. Normal and Model Schools at Toronto, U. C., XIV, 488. Oswego Training School, XVI, 213. New Britain, X, 51. Bridgewater Normal School, XVI, 466. Framingham, XVI, 469. Salem, XVI, 470.

Public Library, Boston, VII, 252. Cooper Scientific Union, N. Y., I, 652. Dudley Observatory, Albany, I, 594. Yale College in 1764, V, 722. American Asylum for the Deaf and Dumb, Hartford, Ct., I, 440. New York Institution for the Deaf and Dumb, III, 346. New York Asylum for Imbeciles, Syracuse, IV, 416. N. Y. State Geological Hall, IV, 781. Harvard Hall, V, 530. Yale College, 1764, V, 722.

Apparatus for Physical Exercise, IX, 530; XI, 539; XII, 677; for illustration, XIV, 569. Blackboard and wall-surface, IX, 546, 563; X, 739; XVI, 575. Crayons, how made, XVI, 574. Declamatory Exercises and Addresses, III, 193; IX, 633; XIII, 836; V, 648; XII, 655; XIII, 532; XVI, 453; I, 645, 647. Drawing-room and Desks, X, 554; XIV, 705; XVI, 722. Furniture for Schools, IX, 551; X, 754; XII, 687; Defective Construction, IX, 492, 518; XI, 537; Chase's Adjustable Desk, XIII, 656; Mott's Revolving Seat, X, 563. Library of Reference, I, 739; IX, 545. Location and Playground, IX, 492, 503, 507, 510, 527, 542; X, 731. Privies and Facilities for Cleanliness, IX, 520, 539; X, 728; XI, 607; XIII, 853. Warming, IX, 546, 552; X, 705, 727; XI, 584, 598; XII, 832; XVI, 579, 713. Ventilation in American Dwellings, V, 35. In School Houses, IX, 563, 547, 568; X, 724; XIII, 612, 832, 858; XIV, 801; XV, 782; XVI, 716, 727. Ornamentation, X, 731; Mrs. Sigourney on, 732; Salem High School, XIV, 804; IX, 543. Specifications, Terms of, X, 733; XII, 708. Seats and Desks, Arrangement of, IX, 551; XI, 583; XIII, 656; Octagonal Plan, XVI, 728; Barnard's plan, with division, X, 760, 761. Size of building, XVI, 716. Stand, movable, for blackboard, XVI, 709. Furnaces, XVI, 579, 582; Hot-water apparatus, XVI, 713. Rules for Care of School-house, XIII, 851, 857; for use of Furnaces, XV, 803; setting furnace, XVI, 584.

XIX. EDUCATIONAL ENDOWMENTS AND BENEFACTORS.

Land Grants of the Federal Government for Educational Purposes, to 1854, I, 202; XVII, 65. List of Benefactions to Harvard University, IX, 139. List of Deceased Benefactors of Yale College, X, 693. Boston Educational Charities, VIII, 528; IX, 606. Individual Benefactors. Samuel Appleton, XII, 403. J. J. and W. B. Astor, I, 638. Joshua Bates, VII, 270. John Bromfield, V, 521. Nicholas Brown, III, 289. Peter Cooper, IV, 526. Thomas Dowse, III, 284; IX, 355. Mrs. Blandina Dudley, II, 593. Edmund Dwight, IV, 5. Peter Faneuil, IX, 603. Paul Furnum, III, 397. John Green, XIII, 606. John Harvard, V, 523. Edward Hopkins, IV, 668. John Hughes, IV, 520. William Lawrence, II, 33. John Lowell, V, 427. Theodore Lyman, X, 5. James McGill, VII, 188. S. J. North, IV, 104. George Peabody, I, 237; II, 642; III, 226. T. H. Perkins, I, 551. Miss Caroline Plummer, XIII, 73. John and Samuel Phillips, VI, 66. Henry Todd, IV, 711. Stephen Van Rensselaer, VI, 923. Matthew Vassar, XI, 53. James Wadsworth, V, 389. David Watkinson, II, 837. Samuel Williston, II, 173. William Woodward, IV, 520. Elihu Yale, V, 715.

XX. MISCELLANEOUS.

The Gyroscope, or Mechanical Paradox, II, 238. Explanation of the Gyroscope by E. S. Snell, II, 701. Treatise upon the Gyroscope, by Maj. J. G. Barnard, III, 537; IV, 529; V, 299. Lowe's Printing Press, IX, 636. Stereoscope. Educational Uses of, IX, 632. Museum of Zoölogy, IX, 61.

Indexes. Vol. I, ix.-xix.; II, 749; III, 819; IV, 839; V, 851; VI, 317, 623; VII, 723; VIII, 681; IX, 637; X, 763; XI, 613; XII, 731; XIII, 865; XIV, 817; XV, 829; XVI, 791. General Index to Vols. I. to V., V, 857. Classified Index to Vols. I. to XVI., XVII, 17-40.

XXI. EDUCATIONAL BIOGRAPHY AND LIST OF PORTRAITS.

BIOGRAPHICAL SKETCHES.

Abbot, Benjamin, **VI**, 80.
Abbott, Gorham D., **XVI**, 600.
Agricola, Rudolph, **IV**, 717.
Adelung, J. C., **XI**, 451.
Alcott, W. A., **IV**, 629.
Alcott, A. B., **XVI**, 130.
Allen, C. H., **XIV**, 306.
Allen, F. A., **XV**, 681.
Allen, W., **X**, 365.
Alexander, de Villa Dèi, **IV**, 726.
Andrews, I. W., **XVI**, 605.
Acquaviva, Claudius, **XIV**, 462.
Andrews, I., **XVI**, 604.
Appleton, Samuel, **XII**, 403.
Aristotle, **XIV**, 131.
Arey, Oliver, **XV**, 484.
Arnold, Thomas K., **IV**, 545.
Astley, J., **IV**, 165.
Ascham, Roger, **III**, 23.
Aventinus, **XI**, 163.
Bailey, Ebenezer, **XII**, 429.
Baker, W. M., **XVI**, 166.
Baker, W. S., **X**, 592.
Baldwin, Theron, **XV**, 261.
Barnard, F. A. P., **V**, 753.
Barnard, Henry, **I**, 650.
Barnard, John, **I**, 307.
Barnes, D. H., **XIV**, 513.
Basul, Marquise de, **III**, 510.
Basedow, T. B., **V**, 487.
Basedow, Emile, **V**, 491.
Bateman, Newton, **XVI**, 165.
Bates, J., **VII**, 270.
Bates, S. P., **XV**, 682.
Beck, T. Romeyn, **I**, 654.
Beecher, Miss C. E., **XV**, 250.
Benton, A. R., **XVI**, 775.
Bell, Andrew, **X**, 467.
Bild, **V**, 66.
Bingham, Caleb, **V**, 325.
Bishop, Nathan, **XVI**,
Blewett, B. T., **XVI**, 431.
Bodiker, J., **XI**, 437.
Boccaccio, **VII**, 422.
Boyd, E. J., **XV**, 645.
Braidwood, J, **III**, 348.
Bridgman, Laura, **IV**, 383
Brainerd, J., **XVI**, 331.
Borgi, Jean, **I**, 583.
Bromfield, John, **V**, 521.
Brooks, Charles, **I**, 581.
Brougham, Lord, **VI**, 467.
Brown, J. Horace, **XV**, 764.
Brown, Nicholas, **III**, 291.
Buckingham, J. T., **XIII**, 120.
Buckley, J. W., **XIV**, 28.
Burrowes, T. H., **VI**, 107, 555.

Burtt, Andrew, **XV**, 679.
Burton, Warren, **II**, 333.
Busch, **V**, 727.
Butler, Caleb, **II**, 54.
Butler, J. D., **XVII**,
Butler, Cyrus, **III**, 310.
Buss, Johannes, **V**, 293.
Caldwell, C., **XVI**, 109.
Calhoun, W. B., **XV**, 212.
Cæsarius, J., **IV**, 2 5.
Carlton, Oliver, **XV**, 523.
Carter, James, **V**, 337.
Carter, J. G., **V**, 407.
Cecil, Sir W., **IV**, 161.
Cheever, Ezekiel, **I**, 297; **XII**, 530.
Cheke, Sir John, **IV**, 163.
Chrysoloras, Emanuel, **VII**, 440.
Clajus, Johannes, **XI**, 412.
Claxton, Timothy, **VIII**, 253.
Clerc, Laurent, **IV**, 349.
Coburn, C. R., **XV**, 679.
Coclenius, C., **IV**, 2 5.
Coffin, J. H., **XVI**, 784.
Colburn, Dana P., **XI**, 289.
Colburn, Warren, **II**, 294.
Colet, John, **VIII**, 291; **XVI**, 405.
Comenius, **V**, 25.
Cosmo de Medici, **VII**, 445.
Conover, A. M., **XVI**, 393.
Cowley, A., **XII**, 151.
Courteilles, M. de, **III**, 704.
Corston, William, **X**, 363.
Corte, P. A., **IV**, 491.
Cowdrey, M. F., **XVI**, 589.
Craig, A. J., **XIV**, 394.
Crato, **V**,
Cross, M. K., **XVI**, 751.
Cruikshank, J. C., **XV**, 485.
Crozet, Claude, **XIII**, 31.
Curtis, Joseph, **I**, 655.
Curtis, T. W. T., **XV**, 607.
Dante, **VII**, 418.
Davies, Charles, **XV**, 479.
Davis, Wm. Van L., **XV**, 675.
Day, J., **XVI**, 126.
Denman, **XV**, 395.
Denzel, B. G., **VII**, 315.
Delillee, J., **III**, 158.
Dewey, Chester, **XV**, 477.
Dewitt, G. A., **V**, 17.
Diesterweg, **III**, 312.
Dick, James, **I**, 392.
Dinter, **VII**, 153.
Donatus, **XVII**,
Dowse, Thomas, **III**, 284; **IX**, 355.
Dringenberg, Louis, **V**, 65
Dudley, Mrs. E., **II**, 598.

Dunnell, M. H., **XVI**, 783.
Duncan, Alexander, **III**, 311.
Dwight, Edmund, **IV**, 5.
Dwight, F., **V**, 803.
Dwight, Theodore, **XIV**, 558.
Dwight, Timothy, **V**, 567.
Eaton, Theophilus, **I**, 298; **V**, 30.
Ebrardt, U., **XI**, 160.
Edson, H. K., **XVI**, 750.
Edwards, B. B., **XIV**, 381.
Edwards, Richard, **XVI**, 169.
Elyott, Sir Thomas, **XVI**, 483.
Emerson, G. B., **V**, 417.
Erasmus, **IV**, 729.
Ernesti, I. A., **V**, 750.
Everett, Edward, **VII**, 325.
Fanauil, P., **XI**, 603.
Farnum, Paul, **III**, 397.
Farnham, G. L., **XV**, 483.
Faville, O., **XVI**, 750.
Fellenberg, E., **III**, 591.
Felton, C. C., **X**, 265.
Fenelon, **XIII**, 477.
Fisk, Wilbur, **VI**, 297.
Fliedner, T., **I**.; **III**, 487.
Ford, Jonathan, **XIV**, 395.
Froebel, F., **IV**, 793
Fowle, **X**, 597.
Franklin, B., **I**, 45; **VIII**, 251.
Fuller, Thomas, **III**, 155.
Fox, **X**, 363.
Fry, Elizabeth, **III**, 508.
Frangk, Fabian, **XI**, 163.
Franke, V., 441.
Frisch, J. L., **XI**, 439.
Gall, James, **IV**,
Gallaudet, T. H., **I**, 417.
Gottsched, J. C., **XI**, 448.
Galloway, S., **XVI**, 601.
Geneintz, Christian, **XI**, 426.
George of Trebizond, **VII**, 440.
Gesner, J. M., **V**, 741.
Gerard, **IV**, 622.
Goodnow, I. T., **XVI**, 386.
Goodrich, S. G., **XIII**, 134.
Green, John, **XIII**, 606.
Grant, Miss, **X**, 656.
Gubert, John, **XI**, 42.
Greene, S. S., **XIV**, 600.
Grimm, J., **XI**, 454.
Gregory, J. M., **XV**,
Goswin, **IV**, 715.
Griscom, John, **VIII**, 325.
Gunrino, **VII**, 436.
Guilford, Nathan, **VIII**, 289.
Guizot, **XI**, 254.
Hagar, D. B., **XV**, 217.

CLASSIFIED INDEX OF BARNARD'S AMERICAN JOURNAL OF EDUCATION. 39

Hadden, **IV**. 164.
Hall, S. R., **V**, 373.
Hall, W., **XV**. 127.
Halm, **V**, 625.
Hamann. J. G., **VI**. 247.
Hancock, J., **XVI**, 602.
Harnisch, Wilhelm, **VII**. 317.
Hart, J. S., **V**, 91.
Harvard, John, **V**. 523.
Harvey, T. H., **XVI**. 608.
Hauberle, **V**. 509.
Haüy, V., **III**. 477.
Hawley, G, **XI**, 94.
Hazeltine, L., **XV**, 481.
Hecker, **V**. 695.
Hedges, Nathan, **XVI**. 737.
Hegius, Alexander, **IV**. 723.
Henkle, **XVI**.
Herder, **VI**. 195.
Higginson, John, **XIII**. 724.
Hillhouse, James, **VI**. 325.
Holbrook, J., **VIII**. 229; **XIV**. 558.
Hopkins, Mark, **XI**. 219
Hovey, C. E., **VIII**. 95.
Howe, S. G., **XI**, 389.
Hoole, C., **XII**. 647.
Hopkins, E., **IV**. 668.
Hoss, G. W., **XVI**. 775.
Hubbard, F., **XV**,
Hubbard, R., **V**, 316.
Huntington, **XV**. 606.
Hurty, J., **XVI**. 776.
Ickelsamer, **XI**. 402.
Ives, M. B., **V**, 311.
John of Ravenna, **VII**. 435.
Johnson, Samuel, **VII**. 461.
Johnson, Walter R., **V**, 781.
Jones, R. D., **XV**, 481.
Kelly, Robert, **I**. 655 ; **X**. 313.
Kempis, Thomas à, **IV**. 626.
Kingsbury, John, **V**, 9.
Kneeland, John, **XV**. 526.
Krachenberger, **V**. 79.
Krüsi, Hermann, **V**. 161.
Kyrle, John, the "Man of Ross," **II**. 654.
Ladd, J. J., **XIV**. 592.
Lancaster, Joseph, **X**. 355.
Lange, Rudolph, **IV**. 726.
Lawrence, Abbot, **I**. 205.
Leo X., **VII**. 454.
Lewis, Samuel, **V**. 727.
Lindsley, Philip, **VII**. 9.
Locke, John, **VI**. 209.
Long, W., **XVI**. 497.
Lord, A. D., **XVI**. 607.
Lowell, John, **V**. 427.
Loyola, Ignatius, **XIV**. 455.
Lycurgus, **XIV**. 611.
Lyman Theodore, **X**. 5.
Lyon, Mary, **X**. 649.

Lawrence, Amos, **XVII**.
Lawrence, William, **II**. 33.
May, Samuel J., **XVI**. 141.
McDonough, John, **II**. 736.
McGill, James, **VII**. 188.
McJilton, J. N., **XVII**.
McKeen, Joseph, **I**. 655.
McMynn, **XIV**, 391.
Mann, Horace, **V**. 611.
Marks, D., **V**. 64.
Marvin, J. G., **XVI**. 626.
Mason, Lowell, **IV**. 141.
Mayhew, Ira, **XV**. 641.
Medici, Lorenzo di, **VII**. 445.
Melancthon, Philip, **IV**. 741.
Micyllus, **IV**, 464.
Mildmay, Sir W., **IV**, 164.
Mirandola, Picus di, **VII**. 449.
Milton, John, **XIV**, 159.
Morhof, **XI**, 436.
Morse, Augustus, **XV**. 608.
Mowry, William A., **XIV**. 592.
Nagali, **VII**. 300.
Neander, **V**, 599.
Niederer, **VII**. 289.
North, Edward, **XV**, 486.
North, S. J., **VI**, 104.
Northend, C., **XV**, 220.
Oberlin, **XVII**.
Oelinger, **XI**, 406.
Olivier, **V**, 508.
Olmsted, Denison, **V**, 367.
Orbilius, **III**, 157.
Orcutt, **XV**, 630.
Overberg, **XIII**. 365.
Page, D. P., **V**, 811.
Parish, A., **XV**, 523.
Partridge, A., **XIII**, 49, 683.
Peabody, George, **I**. 328 ; **XVII**.
Peabody, S. H., **XIV**, 395.
Pease, Calvin, **XV**, 631.
Peckham, J., **XVI**, 743.
Peers, B. O., **XVI**. 147.
Peet, H. P., **III**. 365.
Peirce, C., **IV**, 275.
Pelton, J. C., **XVI**. 626.
Perkins, T. H., **I**. 551.
Pestalozzi, **III**, 401.
Phelps, W. F., **V**, 827.
Petrarch, **VII**, 424.
Philbrick, J. D., **XIV**, 32.
Philelphus, **VII**, 441.
Phillips, John, **VI**, 75.
Phillips, S., **VI**, 66.
● Pickard, J. L., **XIV**, 392.
Picket, Aaron, **XV**, 393.
Picket, Albert. **XVII**.
Picus, J, **VII**, 449.
Pierce, J. D., **XV**, 640.
Plamann, **VII**. 309.
Platter, Thomas, **V**, 79.

Plummer, Caroline, **XIII**, 73.
Poggius, **VII**. 442.
Politian, **VII**. 445.
Pomeroy, E. C., **XV**, 486.
Potter, Alonzo, **XVI**. 599.
Powell, W. H., **XVI**. 167.
Pradt, J. B., **XIV**. 394.
Putnam, D., **XV**. 646.
Radwin, Florentius, **IV**. 623.
Ramsauer, J., **VII**. 301.
Randall, S. S., **XIII**. 227.
Ratich, **V**. 229.
Ray, J., **XVI**. 603.
Raumer, **IV**. 149.
Redfield, W. C., **IV**. 833.
Reuchlin, **V**. 67.
Rice, V. M., **XV**. 391.
Richards, Z., **XIV**. 23.
Richard, C. S., **XVI**. 764.
Richardson, M., **XV**. 605.
Rickoff, A. J., **XIV**. 24.
Ripley, E. L., **XV**. 645.
Robbins, T., **III**. 279.
Rousseau, V, 459.
Russell, M., **III**. 139.
Rytwise, J., **XVI**. 682.
Sams, **XVI**. 602.
Sanborn, E. D., **XVI**. 762.
Sandinus, **VII**.
Sapidus, **V**, 66.
Sarmiento, **XVI**. 593.
Sargano, **VII**. 435.
Sawyer, H. E., **XVI**. 763.
Scheurl, C., **XI**. 161.
Schmidt, **VII**. 297.
Seymour, D., **X**, 321.
Sheldon, E. A., **XV**. 484.
Sheldon, W. E., **XV**, 525.
Sherwin, T., **VIII**. 461.
Shottelius, **XI**. 429.
Sill, D, M. B, **XV**. 645.
Slade, W., **XV**, 250.
Simler, **V**, 66.
Smith, Sir Thomas, **IV**, 165.
Spicer, A. C., **XIV**, 392.
Standish, J. V. N., **XVI**. 165.
Stearns, **XV**, 524.
Stieler, **XI**, 435.
Stoddard, J. V., **XV**, 480.
Stone, A. P., **XV**, 219.
Stowe, C. E., **V**, 586.
Strong, E. F., **XV**, 607.
Sturm, **IV**, 167.
Swett, J., **XVI**, 790.
Tappan, H. P., **XIII**, 451.
Taylor, J. O., **XV**, 248.
Thayer, G. F., **IV**, 613.
Tenney, J., **XVI**, 761.
Thayer, Sylvanus, **XVII**.
Thomasius, J., **V**, 742.
Thompson, J, B., **XV**, 487.

Thompson, Z., **I.** 654.
Tillinghast, N., **I.** 655.
Tobler, J. G., **V.** 205.
Todd, Henry, **IV.** 711.
Trotzendorf, **V.** 107.
Valentine, T. W., **XV.** 482.
Valla, **VII.** 443.
Van Rensselaer, **VI.** 223.
Vassar, M., **XI.** 53.
Vehrli, **III.** 389.
Vetrier, **XVI.** 665.
Vitellius, **XVI.** 669.
Vittorino, **VII.** 436.
Von Turk, **V.** 155

Wadsworth, J., **V.** 389.
Warton, J., **XVI.** 511.
Wayland, F., **XIII.** 771.
Watkinson, D., **IV.** 837.
Welch, A. S., **XV.** 642.
Weld, T., **XV.** 234.
Wells, F. D., **XVI.**
Wells, W. H., **VIII.** 529.
Werner, G., **IV.** 799.
Wessel, **IV.** 714.
Weston, E. P., **XVI.** 784.
White, E. E., **XVI.** 606.
Wickersham, J. P., **XVI.** 282.
Wichern, **III.** 5.

Willard, Mrs. Emma, **VI.** 125.
Wimpheling, **V.** 65.
Wines, E. C., **IX.** 9.
Wolf, F. A., **VI.** 200.
Woodbridge, W. C., **V.** 51.
Woodbridge, W., **XVI.** 136.
Woodman, J. S., **XVI.** 761.
Woolworth, S. B., **XV.** 498.
Wotton, Sir Henry, **XV.** 123.
Wright, L., **II.** 176.
Wykeham, William of, **XVI.** 497.
Yale, Elihu, **V.** 715.
Zeller, **VII.** 305.
Zerbolt, Gerard, **IV.** 625.

PORTRAITS.

Abbott, Gorham D., **XVI.** 600.
Alcott, W. A., **IV.** 629.
Allen, F. A., **XV.** 682.
Andrews, I. W., **XVI.** 605.
Appleton, Samuel, **XII.** 1.
Arnold, Thomas, **IV.** 545.
Bailey, Ebenezer, **XII.** 401.
Baker, W. S., **XIV.** 401.
Baldwin, Theron, **XV.** 269.
Barnard, F. A. P., **V.** 753.
Barnard, Henry, **I.** 1.
Bateman, N., **XVI.** 166.
Bates, S. P., **XV.** 1.
Bishop, N., **XVII.**
Blewett, B. G., **XVI.** 432.
Brooks, Charles, **I.** 587.
Brown, Nicholas, **III.** 291.
Bulkley, J. W., **XIV.** 28.
Burrowes, T. H., **VI.** 107.
Camp, D. N., **XV.** 605.
Carter, J. G., **V.** 407.
Coburn, C. R., **XV.** 679.
Colburn, D. P., **XI.** 289.
Colburn, Warren, **II.** 294.
Davies, Charles, **XV.** 479.
Dowse, Thomas, **IX.** 355.
Dwight, Edmund, **IV.** 1.
Dwight, Francis, **V.** 803.
Edwards, Richard, **XVI.** 167.
Emerson, G. B., **V.** 417.
Everett, E., **VII.** 325.
Farnum, Paul, **III.** 397.
Faville, O., **XVI.** 759.
Felton, C. C., **X.** 265.
Fisk, Wilbur, **VI.** 297.
Fowle, W. B., **X.** 597.
Gallaudet, T. H., **I.** 417.
Galloway, S., **XVI.** 601.
Garfield, James A., **XVII.** 1.
Goodnow, I. T., **XVI.** 387.
Green, John, **XIII.** 606.
Greene, S. S., **XIV.** 609.
Gregory, J. M., **XV.** 643.

Griscom, John, **VIII.** 325.
Hagar, D. B., **V.** 517.
Hall, S. R., **XV.** 5.
Hart, J. S., **V.** 91.
Hailly, V., **III.** 477.
Hazeltine, L., **XV.** 481.
Henkle, William D., **XVI.** 432
Hillhouse, James, **VI.** 325.
Holbrook, Josiah, **VIII.** 1.
Hopkins, Mark, **XI.** 219.
Hovey, C. E., **XIII.** 94.
Howe, S. G., **XI.** 321.
Johnson, W. R., **V.** 781.
Kelley, Robert, **X.** 313.
Kingsbury, John, **V.** 9.
Lawrence, Abbott, **I.** 137.
Lawrence, William, **II.** 1.
Lewis, Samuel, **V.** 727.
Lindsley, Philip, **VII.** 9.
Lord, A. D., **XV.** 607.
Lyman, Theodore, **X.** 1.
Lyon, Mary, **X.** 609.
McCarty, H. D., **XVI.** 388.
McGill, James, **VII.** 188.
McJilton, J. N., **XVI.**
McMynn, J. G., **XIV.** 391.
Mann, Horace, **V.** 611.
Mason, Lowell, **IV.** 141.
Mayhew, Ira, **XV.** 641.
North, E., **XVII.**
North, S. J., **VI.** 104.
Northend, Charles, **XVI.** 510.
Olmsted, Denison, **V.** 367.
Orcutt, Hiram, **XV.** 630.
Page, D. P., **V.** 811.
Parish, A., **XV.** 523.
Partridge, Alden, **XIII.** 657.
Peabody, George, **II.** 642.
Peckham, Isaiah, **XVI.** 743.
Peet, H. P., **III.** 366.
Peirce, Cyrus, **IV.** 275.
Perkins, T. H., **I.** 551.
Pestalozzi, **IV.** 65.

Phelps, Mrs. A. Lincoln, **XVII.**
Phelps, W. F., **V.** 827.
Philbrick, J. D., **XIV.** 32.
Phillips, Samuel, **VI.** 66.
Pickard, J. L., **XIV.** 129.
Potter, Alonzo, **XVI.** 1.
Randall, S. S., **XIII.** 227.
Ray, I., **XVI.** 603.
Richards, Z., **XIV.** 23.
Rickoff, A. J., **XIV.** 24.
Russell, William, **III.** 139.
Ryerson, E., **XVII.**
Sarmiento, D. F., **XVI.** 593.
Sawyer, H. E., **XVI.** 703.
Scammon, Jos. T., **XVII.**
Sears, B., **XVII.**
Sheldon, E. A., **XV.** 484.
Sheldon, W. E., **XV.** 525.
Sherwin, Thomas, **VIII.** 461.
Silliman, Benjamin, **XVII.**
Standish, J. V. N., **XVI.** 165.
Stoddard, J. F., **XV.** 675.
Stone, A. P., **XV.** 519.
Stowe, C. E., **V.** 586.
Swett, John, **XVI.** 790.
Tappan, H. P., **XIII.** 449.
Thayer, Sylvanus, **XVII.**
Thayer, G. F., **IV.** 613.
Tillinghast, N., **II.** 568.
Van Rensselaer, Stephen, **VI.** 223
Vassar, Matthew, **XI.** 1.
Wadsworth, James, **V.** 389.
Watkinson, David, **XVII.**
Wayland, Francis, **XIII.** 1.
Wells, D. F., **XVI.** 749.
Wells, W. H., **VIII.** 529.
Weston, E. P., **XVI.** 783.
Whitford, W. C., **XVII.**
Wichern, J. H., **III.** 1.
Wickersham, J. P., **XV.** 677.
Willard, Mrs. Emma, **VI.** 1.
Wines, E. C., **IX.** 9.
Woolworth, S. B., **XV.** 385.

True Student Life.

Studies and Conduct: Letters, Essays, and Thoughts, on the relative value of Studies and the right Ordering of Life by Men Eminent in Literature and Affairs: Edited by HENRY BARNARD, LL. D., 416 pages : *Special Edition*, 544 pages. 1873.

INDEX

TO

SPECIAL EDITION.

Abstract Thought, 149, 447, 457.
Abstract and Relative Truths, 457, 470.
Academy, equivalent to College, 154.
Accomplishments, 379, 392.
Accuracy, difficulty in reaching, 447, 501.
Action and Knowledge, 514.
ACKLAND, HENRY W., 479,
  Physiology, Physics, and Chemistry, 479.
Activity, self-determined, 15,
  Law of growth, 20.
ADDISON, JOSEPH, 16, 133, 184.
Advice, respecting studies and conduct, 67, 81, 123, 165, 193, 205, 231.
Adults, education, 193.
Æsthetics, science of the beautiful, 512.
Agriculture, 80, 155, 394.
Age for Study, 73, 77, 154, 158, 435.
Augustine, St., 384.
Affectation, 103.
AIKEN, JOHN, 239,
  Eyes or No Eyes—Art of Seeing, 239.
Air, pure, importance of, 35.
AIRY, GEORGE B., 448,
  Scientific Studies, 448.
Ambition, as a motive,
  Carlyle, 528.   Chesterfield, 124.
  Chatham, 142.
Amusements, from books, 121, 205.
  Children, 320
  Girls, 320, 324.
Analysis of a book, 112, 225, 230.
Anatomy, 79, 474.
Anaxageras, a teacher of Pericles, 135.
Anaxarchus, 100.
Ancient Geography, History, and Ideas, 426, 521.
Anger, 73, 137, 319.
Annotations by Whately, 103, 178.
Antipathies, 148, 315.
Appetites in children, 53, 321.
Aristotle, 78, 117, 502.
Aristippus, 100.
Arithmetic, 156, 460.
Argumentation, 128, 282.
Art, 512, 394,
  Open to women, 394.
Arts in the University curriculum, 153,
  Defective method of teaching, 153.
Ashburton, Lord, 442.
Ascham, R., 12,
  Lady Jane Grey, 377.
Associations, early, 40, 443.
Astronomy, 138, 156.
Athens, estimation of Teachers in, 64.
  University of, 529, 543.
Athletic Sports, 38, 159.
Attention, to business in hand, 126.
  Soul of memory, 126.
  Habits of, should be attained, 460.
Austin, Sarah, 20.
Authors, influence of, 205, 226.
Authority, method of, in teaching, 489.
Aversion to school text books, 444.

Bach, method on piano, 352.
BACON, FRANCIS, 71, 92,
  Essay on Discourse, 177.
  Essay on Riches, 255.
  Essay on Studies, 103.
  Essay on Travel, 235.
Bacon, Nathaniel, 140.
Basil, St., of Cappadocia, at Athens, 539, 543.
BARROW, ISAAC, 13, 93, 94.
Beauty, sense of, 47, 393,
  In age, 397.
Beguines, hospital Sisters, 403.
Behavior, in children, 316.
Benevolence in trifles, 186.
Bent, the Natural, 148, 107.
Bequeathing property, 263.
Beza, remarkable memory, 90.
BIBLE, Estimate of,
  Humbolt, 273.   Sedgwick, 228.
  Jerome, 293.   Southey, 101.
  Newman, 274.   Taylor, 286.
  Raumer, 309.   Whately, 108.
  Bible, influence on nations, 274.
Biblical History, 157, 361.
Biographies, 50, 229.
Biology, 470, 473.
Birth-day festivals, 331.
Boarding-schools for girls, 364.
BODLEIGH, SIR THOMAS, 71,
  Letter to Francis Bacon, 71.
Body, 14, 44.
Boethius, 372.
Bolingbroke, 12, 139.
Book and Voice, as a teacher, 22, 529, 544.
Books, value and use, 205.
  Bacon, 108, 110, 205.   Herschel, 205.
  Barrow, 94.   Hillhouse, 208.
  Burleigh, 74.   Locke, 222.
  Carlyle, 203.   Macaulay, 206.
  Channing, 207.   Masson, 27.
  Choate, 206.   Milton, 205, 223.
  Cicero, 209.   Moon, 208.
  Cowley, 208.   Newman, 530.
  DeQuincey, 193.   Potter, 215.
  Everett, 211.   Rice, 210.
  Fuller, 91.   Sedgwick, 228.
  Franklin, 213.   Verplanck, 219.
  Grimke, 230.   Watts, 216.
  Hall, 82, 84, 210.   Whately, 104.
  Heincius, 215.   Winthrop, 209.
Book education, 28.
Book-learning, 212.
Books, care of, 229.
Books, difficulty of recommending, 31, 208, 370
Botany, as a school study, 359, 491.
  Henfrey, 469.   Wilson, 49.
  Hooker, 472.
Boyle, Sir Robert, 227.
Boy-training, Greek idea of, 436.
Brothers and Sisters, 312.
BROUGHAM, HENRY, 163,
  Letter to Z. Macaulay, 161.

Training for public speaking, 162.
Appeal for human advancement, 164.
Teachers of mankind, 164.
Buffon, style, or manner, 302.
BURLEIGH, LORD, 74,
   Advice to his Son, 75.
BURNS, ROBERT, 95.
   Advice to a Friend, 95.
Burke, Edmund, 17, 162, 187,
   Model for English Student, in oratory, 162.
   Conversational Power, 187.
Burnet's History, 139.
Business of life, 104.
Business Men, Value of books to, 216.
Butler, Bishop, 16.
Byron, Aversion to school associations, 443.

Calling to a pursuit, 79.
Camelford, Lord, 129.
CARLYLE, THOMAS, 524.
   Letters to a Young Man, 203.
   Address as Rector of Edinburgh University, 524.
   Diligence and honesty in Study, 524.
   Books should be made more available, 524.
   Writers—the true Peers of nations, 526.
   Wisdom—Endowments—Silence, 527.
   Ambition avoided—Modesty—Wealth, 528.
Catechism, 309.
Catholic Church, 289, 399.
   Female Education, 289.
   Female Employments, 401.
   Sisterhoods, 402.
Cecil, Sir William, 74.
Ceremonial behavior, 245.
CHANNING, WILLIAM ELLERY, 207.
   Education and the Teacher, 22.
   Books and Reading, 207.
Charity, 94, 371.
Charity, Sisters of, 403.
CHATHAM, Earl of, 129.
   Letters to his Nephew, 130.
Chemistry, 470, 476, 490.
CHESTERFIELD, Earl of, 123.
   Letters to his Son, 125.
Choate, Rufus, books and reading, 206.
Christianity in education, 309.
Choice of books, 219, 388.
Choice of paths, 78, 88, 97.
Christmas holidays, 328.
Church festivals, 330.
Civilization, modern, 434.
Cicero, cited, 74, 209,
   Professional and oratorical training, 166, 538.
Clarendon, Lord, 140.
Classification of the sciences, 469.
Classical, origin of term, 200.
Classical studies, opinions respecting,
   Byron, 443.   Macaulay, 440.
   Chatham, 130.   Martineau, 445.
   Donaldson, 435.   Mill, 501.
   DeQuincey, 200.   Milton, 152.
   Froude, 520, 521.   Niebuhr, 171.
   Gladstone, 433.   Southey, 443.
   Herschel, 457.   Temple, 417.
   Hodgson, 444.   Tyndall, 481.
   Locke, 146.   Vaughan, 446.
   Lowe, 421.   Whewell, 458.
Class-reading of books, 223.
Cleanliness, 36, 70, 322.
Cleanthes at Rome, 537.
Clear and precise ideas of any subject, 454.
Clepsydra, water time-piece, 191.
Clothes, and dress, 323, 362.
Clulow, W. B., 16.
Coleridge, S. T. 189, 194.
College, or associated education, 23, 31.
Colleges, 31.
COLLINGWOOD, LORD ADMIRAL, 379,
   Letters on education of his daughter, 379.
Colored spectacles, reading with, 110.
Commands, should be few, 318.
Commentators, 145, 176.
Common-place book, 73, 90, 224.
Commencing Master of Art, 154.
Common-sense, 393.

Competition, 441.
Composition in ancient tongues, 152, 171, 425.
Composition in vernacular, 158, 173,
   Learned by translating from other languages, 165.
   Promoted by writing out notes of lectures, 495.
Conciliation, 397.
Condiments and dainties, 321.
Conduct, suggestions respecting points of
   Ambition, 124, 523.   Industry, 71.
   Attention, 126.   Inferiors, 76, 137, 327.
   Behavior, 124, 137, 243. Kindred, 76.
   Borrowing, 76, 353.   Law suits, 76.
   Charity, 94.   Lending, 237, 266.
   Companions, 75.   Manners, 243.
   Confidence, 76.   Marriage, 305.
   Conscience, 96.   Modesty, 70,293,322,370.
   Conversation, 76, 127,   Motives, 67, 96, 128, 370.
   Courtesy, 70.   [177.   Money, 249.
   Diet, 83.   Objects in life, 147.
   Discretion, 178.   Occupation, 79, 107.
   Diversions, 80.   Order, 90, 247.
   Dress, 81.   Profanity, 70.
   Drinking, 80.   Profession, 79, 97.
   Devotions, 69, 73, 82.   Profligacy, 134.
   Expenditures, 75, 86.   Quarreling, 236.
   Early rising, 397, 398. Religion, 74, 134, 370.
   Endorsing, 76.   Reverence, 67.
   Exercise, 37.   Sarcasm, 128.
   Familiarity, 182.   Self-control, 96.
   Filial duty, 75.   Sensuality, 95, 97.
   Friends, 76, 80.   Silence, 80, 134, 528.
   Gaiety, 70.   Sleep, 81.
   Health, 82, 528.   Sunday, 84.
   Honesty, 174, 525.   Superiors, 70, 76, 137.
   Hospitality, 76.   Travel, 71, 75, 231.
   Humility, 321, 456.   Truthfulness, 70, 318.
   Independent, 75.   Wife, 75.
Conference, with others, in reading, 112, 223, 225.
Confession of faults, 317.
Confirmation, 309.
Conscious manner, 179.
Consequences, pondered over, 285.
Contents and analysis of book read, 225, 230.
Conversation, value and method, 177.
   Addison, 184.   Steele, 184.
   Bacon, 177.   Swift, 179.
   Burleigh, 76.   Taylor, 88.
   Chesterfield, 127.   Temple, 184.
   DeQuincey, 185.   Whately, 178.
   Mackintosh, 368.
Conversation, common faults in, 180.
Conversation and reading, 103, 112, 150, 223, 229.
Conversers, examples of good, 187, 190.
Convent life for girls, 293.
Cotta, 168.
Country, education for children in, 363.
Courage, 37, 60.
Course or plan of life, 97, 339, 398.
Course of reading, 221.
Course of study, 133, 169, 195.
Courtesy, 70, 136, 189.
Court manners, 246.
Cowardice, 315.
Cowley, A., Value of a library, 208.
Cox, W., Scope of Education, 19.
Cramming, 480, 491.
Crates, cited, 100.
Crying and whining, 319.
Curiosity, 14, 112.
Custom, or habit, 16.
Cuvier, Logical advantages of Natural History, 477.

Dacier, Madame, 336.
Dainties, 321.
Dames Hospitalieres, 402.
Dancing, 136.
Dante, cited, 397,
   Value of morning hours, 397.
Darkness, fear of,
Day, the ordering of a, 81, 338, 396.
Death, 277, 311.
Debt, 236, 266.
Defoe, 227.
Demosthenes, 144, 163, 528.

DeMaistre, on education of Girls, 381, 398.
Denny, Letter to, 388.
DEMORGAN, 446.
 Thorough mastery of One Subject, 446.
DeQuincey, Thomas, 185,
 Conversation as an Art, 185.
 Letter to a person of neglected education, 193.
Descartes, Method of investigation, 469.
Devotional exercises, 73, 82, 83, 292.
Dialectics, 167.
Diary, 395.
Dictionaries, 228.
D'Israeli, 227.
Diet, 160, 321.
Diligence, 524.
Discovery, Pleasures of, 492.
Discretion, Age of, 87, 93.
Discretion in speech, 178.
Disputation, 145, 192.
Dissertations, 172.
Distrust, self, 149.
Diversions, 80, 86.
Docendo discimus, 342, 495.
Dolland and the Telescope, 218.
Dolls, for girls, 321.
Domestic life, 399.
DONALDSON, JOHN WILLIAM, 435,
 Classical Learning, and Competitive Tests, 435.
 Education, Information, Knowledge, Science, 456.
 English and German Scholarships, 437.
 Comparative value of Knowledge, 440.
Drawing, 358, 391.   Dress, 81.
Drudgery of details, 418.
DuBartas, 99, 101.
Dunces, will exist, can diminish, not extirpat, 154, 496.
DUPANLOUP, BISHOP OF ORLEANS, 381,
 Studious Women, 381.
Duty, 280, 284.

Earliest moral influence, 148.
Earliest reading, 117, 227.
Early impressions, 291.
Early rising, 81, 139, 376, 397.
Easter festival, 328.
Eating, 83, 321.
Economics, 156.
Edgeworth, Maria, 57, 118.
Edinburgh Review, 129.
Education, defined and described, 11.
 Addison, 16.   Jacobs, 437.
 Ascham, 12.   Johnson, 15.
 Austin, 20.   Lalor, 20, 34.
 Bacon, 12, 123.   Locke, 14, 145.
 Barrow, 13, 93.   Lowe, 121.
 Brown, 21.   Martineau, 445.
 Burke, 17.   Masson, 23.
 Butler, 16.   Mill, 497.
 Carlyle, 21, 204, 525. Milton, 12, 152.
 Channing, 22.   Newman, 529.
 Clulow, 16.   Paley, 15.
 Cox, 19.   Parr, 17.
 Doderlin, 436.   Pope, 11, 421.
 Donaldson, 435.   Raumer, 335.
 Faraday, 450.   Ramsden 17, 19.
 Froude, 515.   Ruskin, 19.
 Gladstone, 433.   Shakspeare, 11.
 Grote, 18.   Short, 13.
 Hamilton, 15,18, 21,441. Simpson, 20.
 Harris, 16.   South, 13, 92.
 Helps, 18.   Stewart, 21.
 Henfrey, 469.   Wayland, 22.
 Herschel, 457.   Whately, 18, 124.
 Hobbs, 14.   Whewell, 11, 458.
 Hooker, 13.   Whichote, 13.
 Huxley, 474.   Wotton, 12.
Educare, Educere, 11.
Education, designed, formal, 498,
 Accidental, of life, 497, 514.
 Mutual, 529.
Eloquence, 164, 168, 544.
Employments, 79, 399.
Emulation, generous ardor, 126, 155.
Encouragement, 78, 290.
Endorsing, surety, 76, 286.

Endowments, 430, 528.
English Bible, 274.
English Classical Scholarships, 437.
English Language, 208, 423, 429.
English Literature, 208.
English and Scotish Universities, 499, 516.
Ennui, 382.
Envy, and covetousness, 313.
Erasmus, 223, 373.
Esteem of others, 67, 125, 142, 370.
Ethics, 511.
Euclid, 198, 461,
 Repugnance to, 490.
Eunapius, at Athens, 538.
Evening reading, 365.
EVERETT, EDWARD, 211.
 Books, Libraries, Reading, 212.
Example, 53.
Excursions, 159.
Exercise, 37.
Experimental Sciences, 420, 469, 490, 507.
Experience and Knowledge, 14, 89.
Extempore speaking, 162, 165,
 Perfected into Oratory, 163.
Eyes or No Eyes, or Seeing, 239, 486.

Facts, the basis of scientific induction, 491.
Faculties, culture, 418, 421.
 Limitations, 150.
Fairness, 318.
Faith, 275.
Fagging, 37.
Familiarity, not accuracy, 501.
Family Government, 295.
Family Life, 295, 331.
Family Reading, 223.
Family, School of, 23, 295, 369.
FARADAY, MICHAEL, 449,
 Existing education does not train the judgment,
 Natural science develops laws, 452.   [450.
Fancies, 94.
Fasting, rule, 293.
Father, duty in education, 306, 342.
Fear of the Lord, 67, 101, 135, 283, 290.
Fear, or Cowardice, 59, 311.
Fear, as a Motive, 59, 96, 101.
Feltham, 223.
Female Education, 30, 289.
 Belongs to the Family, 307.
Female Employments, 399.
Fencing, 136, 158.
Fenelon, 297, 307, 328, 332, 340, 344.
Fiction, Works of, 229,
 Raumer, 304, 338.   Whately, 118.
Field Sports and Excursions, 158.
Flowers, studied with an artist's eye, 359, 491,
 Botanical or scientific aspect, 491.
Fliedner, Pastor, 399.
Fluency in speaking, 468.
Food, 35, 319, 321.
Foreign languages, important to a knowledge of na-
Foresight, 277, 286.   [tive, 501.
Forms, ignorance of, 247.
Foundations, 430, 527.
FRANKLIN, BENJAMIN, 212, 249,
 Poor Richard—or the Way to Wealth, 249.
 Indebtedness to Books, 213.
Fraternal feelings, 313.
Free services, 209.
French Language, 138.
Freshmen, at Athens University, 539.
Friendship, School of, 27.
Frivolity, and Ignorance, 884.
FROUDE, JAMES ANTHONY, 515,
 Address to Students of St. Andrews, 515.
 Ancient English and Scotch Universities, 516.
 Object of Modern Schools—High and Low, 518.
 Education should prepare for occupations, 519.
 Higher education should be less classical and or-
    namental, 521.
 Literature as a profession, 523.
Fry, Elizabeth, 411.
FULLER, THOMAS, 89,
 Memory—Books—Travel, 90.

Galleries of Art, 235, 513.
Games, of chance, 321,
  In-door, 321.
Gardening, 394.
General Culture, 161.
Genius, without wisdom, 284.
Geography, 487.
Geometry, scientific and practical, 459, 490.
Geology, 496.
German Language and Literature, 202, 480.
German Bible, 274.
German Scholarship, 437.
Girls, Education of, 289,
  General aims and defects, 297, 386.
  Music—French—Dancing, 298, 391.
  Multiplicity of studies—Superficialty, 303.
  Fiction—Romances—Frivolity, 304.
  Religious and moral culture, 309.
  Household duties and occupations, 332.
  Higher moral culture, 335.
  Home and school education compared, 341.
Globes, 43, 138, 155.
God, in Life and Education, 49, 81, 86, 281.
  Instruction respecting, 50, 380.
  Reverence of, 68, 75, 81, 243, 528.
  Old and New Testament teaching of, 274.
Goethe, 300, 308, 336, 340.
  Domestic work of Girls, 340.
Good-humor, 184.
Good-breeding, 185, 243, 247.
Good-manners, 185, 243, 247.
Government of Family, 75.
Grammar, 155.
Grafting, and Education, 18.
Gratitude, 135.
Gravitation, Law of, defied by Tableturners, 451.
Greediness, 321.
Gregory, of Nazianson, at Athens, 538.
Greece, the University of ancient, 541.
Greek Language and Literature, 465, 501.
  Historical development in school, 465.
  Pedagogical estimate, 501. Chatham, 133.
  CICERO, 167. Gladstone, 434.
  DeQuincey, 200. Lowe, 424.
  Froude, 520. Niebuhr, 174.
Grimke, Thomas, 230.
Grote, J., 15.
Grey, Lady Jane, 377.
  Conversation with Ascham, 376.
Grey Sisters, 402.
Growth, principle of, in education, 33.
Gymnastics, 88.

Habit of Mind, 446.
Habits, personal, 12, 16, 53.
HALE, SIR MATHEW, 77.
  Advice to his grandsons, 77.
HALL, JOSEPH, 81.
  Letter to Lord Denny—ordering of a Day, 81.
  Advice for all sorts of men, 86.
  Letter to Mr. Milman—Study and Meditation, 84.
HAMILTON, SIR WILLIAM, 461.
  Education defined, 15, 18, 21.
  Mathematics as mental discipline, 461.
Hand-writing, 380.
Hardwicke, Lord, 238.
Hardening the Body, 37.
Happiness, 102, 147, 277.
Harris, James, 16.
Health, 82, 147, 376, 528.
  Overtasked in school, 480.
Heart-knowledge, 113, 204.
Heart-wisdom, 102, 188, 285.
Heart-bearing, 480.
Heat, latent study of, 494.
Helps, Arthur, 19.
HENFREY, ARTHUR, 469.
  Claims of Botanical Science, 469.
Hercules, 53, 73, 77.
  Choice, 97.
Herode's Atticus, 543.
HERSCHEL, SIR JOHN F. W., 457.
  Mathematics in school curriculum, 457.
  Taste for reading, 205.

Hilda, 383.
Hillhouse, James, 208.
Hints on reading, 215.
History, subject of Reading and Study, 500.
  Bacon, 103.   Locke, 150.
  Carlyle, 525. Lalor, 43.
  Chatham, 143. Mill, 501.
  Dupanloup, 393. Raumer, 360.
  Johnson, 15, 543. Sedgwick, 228.
  Macaulay, 544. Whately, 113.
Hobbs, Thomas, 14.
HODGSON, W. B., 442.
  Classical Instruction: its Use and Abuse, 442.
Holidays for Children, 327.
Home Education for Girls, 340.
Home School of Sir Thomas More, 369.
Homer, 160.
Homes of Studious Women, 390.
Honesty, 67, 173.
HOOKER, JOHN, Study of Botany, 472.
Hooker, Richard, 13.
Hortensius, as an Orator, 168.
Horace, 131, 187, 139, 174, 538.
Hospital work for Women, 401, 408.
Houghton, Lord, use of Translations, 468.
Hotel-Dieu, 402.
House-keeping, 383.
Household Ordering and Expenses, 332.
HUXLEY, T. H., 473.
  Study of Zoology, 474.
Hufeland, Counsels for Mothers, 311.
Humanizing influence of Letters, 418, 521.
Humility, a lesson of science, 456.
Husbandry, 79, 155.
Hymns and Bible texts, 315.
Hypatia, 382.

Idleness, 132.
Ignorance, courage to own, 199.
  Knowledge of our own, 106.
Imagination, 48, 120, 422.
Impatience, 379.
Impulse, wisdom by, 284.
Independence, 95, 268.
Information, not education, 435.
Ingratitude, 134.
Instinctive opinions, 117.
Intellectual education, 40, 474.
Inclination and Incredulity, 453.
Industrial element, 79, 107, 362, 383, 399.
Investigation, faculty of, 489.

JAMESON, MRS., 399.
  Woman's Work, 399.
Jean, Paul, 297, 311.
JEROME, ST., 289.
  Letter to Laeta, 290.
Jest, subjects exempt from, 177.
Jester, in Society, 181.
Job, Book of, 286.
Johnson, Samuel, 15, 187, 202.
  Travel, History, Printing, 542.
  Conversational power, 187.
Joubert, common sense defined, 393.
Judgment, want of, in educated men, 450.
  Trained by natural science, 452, 456.
Jukes, Prof., accidental bias to Geology, 477.
Julian, Emperor at Athens, 543.
Juvenal, 175.

Kant, Emanuel, 25.
Knitting, and Needlework, 292, 362.
Knowledge, love of, 15.
Knowledge, is not science or education, 480.
Knowledge, and Wisdom, 15, 100, 279.
Kyrle, John, the Man of Ross, 256.

Labor, 80, 83, 204, 525.
Laboratory work, 496.
Laborissière, Hospital of, 407.
LaBruyère, 127.
Lady Jane Grey, 377.
Laeta, education of Daughter, 290.
LALOR, JOHN, 20, 33.

TRUE STUDENT LIFE. 549

Prize Essay—Nature of Education, 33.
LANDOR, WALTER S., 397.
Imaginary Conversation, 377.
Language, command of, how got, 124.
  Chatham, 144.   More, 372.
  Brougham, 163.   Niebuhr, 175.
  Pitt, 165.
Languages, 198, 445, 446.
  Ancient, 152, 461, 483.
  Modern, 201, 500.
  Labor of mastering, 153, 198.
  Faculties exercised, 198, 446.
  Latin Language and Literature, 501.
  Chatham, 500.   Milton, 154.
  DeQuincey, 201.   Niebuhr, 171.
  Hale, 77.   Parker, 465.
Lavater, 184.
Laughter, 136.
Laws of Nature, 450.
Law, Trade or Profession of, 153, 161.
Law, Universe of, 13.
Learn, by teaching, 342, 495.
Learner, object of education to make a good, 447.
Learning and Experience, 447.
Learning, 152, 370.
Learned Women, 336.
Lecture, and the Book, compared, 32, 193, 472.
  Value for accurate knowledge, 193, 497.
Lending, and suretyship, 263.
Lent, 372.
Lesson on Botany, 491.
Letter-writing, 141, 368, 372.
  Mackintosh, 368.
  Madame de Sevigne, 368.
  More, 372.
Levanna, 332.
Liberal education, different aspects, 103, 417.
  Bacon, 103.   Lowe, 421.
  Carlyle, 524.   Masson, 23.
  Chatham, 129.   Macaulay, 543.
  Doderlin, 436.   Mill, 499.
  Donaldson, 435.   Milton, 151.
  DeQuincey, 193.   Newman, 529.
  Gladstone, 433.   Niebuhr, 169.
  Faraday, 450.   Owen, 476.
  Froude, 515.   Temple, 417.
  Hamilton, 18.   Tyndall, 481.
  Hale, 77.   Whately, 105.
  Huxley, 473.   Whewell, 458.
  Jacobs, 437.   Wilson, 433.
  Locke, 145.
Libraries, origin of, 539.
Library, 205, 209, 215.
Lie, and Lying, 318.
Life, 147, 278, 396.
Literature, as a vocation, 194.
  Open to Woman, 394.
Literature, of knowledge and power, 199.
Literature, part of liberal culture, 419, 500.
Literary character, 227.
Listener, 134.
Locality, school of, 23, 535.
Logical Faculty, 488.
Logic, 195, 508.
Lord's Prayer, for children, 309.
Loving heart, 204.
Love, a motive to study, 000.
Lunatic Asylums, 410.
LYELL, SIR CHARLES, 475.
  Claims of physical science, 475.
LYTTON, LORD EDWARD BULWER, 272.
  Management of money, 265.

MACAULAY, THOMAS B., 206.
  Travel and History, 544.
  University of Athens, 543.
MACKINTOSH, SIR JAMES, Familiar Letters, 368.
Man of Ross, Pope's picture, 257.
  The original, 258.
Mandeville, 107.
Manly exercises, 87, 159.
Manners, defined and value, 136, 185, 243.
  Buffon, 802.   Newman, 531.
  Chatham, 136.   Raumer, 323.
  Chesterfield, 124.   Hale, 243.

Emerson, 243.   Swift, 244.
Landor, 243.
Maps, and map drawing, 43.
Marcus, Emperor of Rome, at Athens, 538.
Margaret More, 374.
Martha, Sisters of St., 403.
Martineau, James, 445.
Manual labor, 362.
Manufacturers, value of books to, 216.
Masson, David, 33.
  College and self-education, 23.
Mathematics, subject of study, 457, 486.
  Hamilton, 461.   Herschel, 457.
  DeQuincey, 197.   Whewell, 458.
  Hale, 78.   Mill, 506.
  Temple, 488.
Mathematics versus Philosophy, 461.
Mathematical reasoning, 114, 197, 463, 486.
  Dangers and difficulties, 464.
Marriage, 305.
Manual labor, 107, 292.
Mary, the Mother, 400.
Meals, 53, 83, 321.
Means and Ends, 229.
Measures, 43.
Mechanics, value of books to, 216.
Meditation, 83, 150.   Menippus, 167.
Memory, 89, 112.   Metropolitan City, 533.
Method of Studying, 110, 225, 226, 230.
Mental Science, 46.
Mensuration, 460.
Mental Training, 488, 498.
Mind, the basis of Academical polity, 542.
MILTON, JOHN, 151, 207.
  Letter to Samuel Hartlib, 151.
Military Art and Tactics, 154, 159.
MILL, JOHN STUART, 497.
  Education, in its larger and narrower senee, 497.
  Proper function of a University, 498.
  Scotch and English Universities compared, 499.
  General School Education, scientific and lib., 500.
  Modern languages, History, Geography, 500.
  Greek and Latin languages, and literature, 501.
  Limitations to classical studies—science, 504.
  Mathematics, pure and applied—experiments, 507.
  Logic, Physiology, and Psychology, 509.
  Politics, History, Economics, Jurisprudence, 510.
  International Law, Religion, Ethics, 511.
  Art and Æsthetic culture, Poetry, 513.
  Discipline of active life, 514.
Modesty, 70, 293, 322, 370.
Monologs, not conversation, 191.
Money, its acquisition and management, 249.
  Bacon, 255.   Lytton, 265.
  Burleigh, 75.   Pope, 357.
  Franklin, 249.   Taylor, 260.
Montesquieu, 126.
Moral Philosophy, 150.
Moral Science Tripos, 499.
Moon, G. W., 208.
Moral education, 22, 48.
Moral sense, 62.
More, Sir Thomas, 369.
  Letters on the education of his children, 370.
Morning hours, 398.
Mothers, 48, 341.
Motives for study, 78, 155.
Music, 39, 349, 351.
Music, in education, 159.
  Lalor, 39.   Raumer, 248, 298.
  Milton, 159.
Much, not Many, rule for reading, 230, 544.
Miscellaneous reading, 176.

Nations, University division at Athens, 542.
National Anniversaries, 331.
Nation, education of a, 17.
Nature, 274, 284, 450.
Naturalist, 473.
Natural History, 473, 476.
Natural Philosophy, 44, 78.
Natural Sciences, 359, 456, 484.
Natural Scenery, 351.
Needlework, 292, 302.
Necker, Madame, 297, 298, 340, 346.

Neglected education, remedies for, 193.
NEWMAN, JOHN H., 529.
　English Protestant Bible, 274.
　University of Life and Affairs, 529.
　University of Athens, 535, 545.
New Testament, 50, 273, 274.
NIEBUHR, GEORGE B., 169.
Letter on study of Philosophy, 170.
Non multa sed multum, 91, 521.
Note Book, 73, 90.
Number, 42.
Nuns for Hospital service, 401.
Nursery-maids, 325.

Oaths, vulgarity of, 70.
Obedience, 57, 318.
Object Teaching, 41.
Observation, habits of, 40.
Occupation, choice of, 77, 107.
　Education, training for, 436, 519.
　Manual, 362.
Old age, 170.
Old and the Young, 28.
Old Testament, 274.
One-sidedness of mind, 486.
Order and punctuality, 90, 322.
Oral method, 29, 31, 32, 529.
Ornamentation of home, 362.
Oratory, training for, 158, 161, 165.
　Reading, writing, and meditation, 167.
　Brougham, 161.　　　Cicero, 166.
　Pitt, 165.
Ovid, cited, 177.
Owen, Richard, 476.
　Claims of Natural History, 476.

Pagan views, 384.
PAGET, GEORGE E., 478.
　Physiology, 478.
Pain, Physical, 35.　　Painting, 394, 512.
Paley, William, 15.　　Pardon asking, 316.
Parr, Thomas, 17.　　Partiality of Parents, 313.
Patriotism, 32, 141.　　Patience of thought, 455.
Paula, 382, 401.
PARKER, CHARLES STUART, 465.
　Historical development of Greek and Latin, 465.
Peace and War, education for, 154, 158.
Pedantry, 18, 246.
Penmanship, 176, 369.　　Perseus, 135.
Pericles, 135, 541, 544.　　Perception, 469.
Perseverance, 279, 286.　　Pestalozzi, 295, 305.
Phidias, 544.
Philology and Philological studies, 170.
Philosophy, 99, 461, 489.
Philosophical Sciences, 461.
Physiology, 44, 478, 479, 496.
Phocion, Science of, 528.
Piano, abuse of, 391.　　Picture Bible, 309.
Piety, culture of, 70.
Pitt, Thomas, Letters to, 139.
Pitt, W., the Great Commoner, 129.
Pitt, William, training as an Orator, 165.
Pysical Education, 34.
Physics, how taught, 479, 481, 495.
Physical Geography, 472.
Physical Sciences, claims assented by,
　Ackland, 479.　　Faraday, 450.
　Airy, 448.　　Henfrey, 469.
　Cuvier, 577.　　Hooker, 472.
　Huxley, 473.　　Lyell, 475.
　Lowe, 429.　　Tyndall, 481.
　Owen, 476.　　Wilson, 483.
　Paget, 478.　　Vaughan, 445.
Plato, 503.
Pocket-money, 333.
Poetry, in higher education, 165, 174.
　Mill, 513.　　Milton, 157.　　Lalor, 47.
Politics and Political economy, 184, 510.
Politeness, 136, 243.
Poor Richard, or the Way to Wealth, 249.
POPE, ALEXANDER, 14, 104.
　Man of Ross, or the true Use of Wealth, 227.
POTTER, ALONZO, 215.
　Hand Book for Reading, 221.
　Advantages of Science, 215, 222.

Praise, 61, 128, 370.
Prayers, 113, 309.　　Preconceptions, 110.
Preface and Contents of a Book, 225.
Prejudices and Misconcertions, 149.
Pride, 62, 371.
Printing, civilization before, 543.
Priestly, 217.
Private or Home Education for Girls, 363.
Private tutor, 344, 369.
Prizes, 62.
Probabilities, Proximate judgment in, 452.
Proaeresius at Athens, 539.
Proairesis, 156.
Prodicus, 97.
　Choice of Hercules, 97.
Profanity, 70.
Professional Teaching, 32, 64.
Professors at Athens, 542.
　Endowed by the State, 542.
Pronunciation of Latin, 154, 290.
Proportionate Judgment, 455, 485.
Prytanes at Athens, 544.
Punctuality, 247.
Public School Commission, Report, 488.
Pursuits of Literature quoted, 199, 221.
Puzzled state of mind, 114, 148.
Pythagorean Letter, 291.
Pythagorean silence, 134.

Quantity, science of, 462.
Questions on a Book or Lesson, 112.
　Preliminary, or Socratic, 112.
Quarreling, 236, 314.
Quintilian, 155.

Raillery, 128, 182.　　Ramsden, 17, 19.
RAUMER, KARL VON, 295.
　Education of Girls, 295.
Reading, the art of, 343.
Reading, hints respecting, 215.
　Ascham, 377.　　Johnson, 203.
　Bacon, 103.　　Landor, 378.
　Carlyle, 203, 525.　　Potter, 220, 226.
　Collingwood, 320.　　Sedgwick, 227.
　DeQuincey, 193.　　Watts, 215.
　D'Israeli, 227.　　Whately, 104.
　Dupanloup, 383.　　Raumer, 337.
　Grimke, 230.　　Vail, 215.
Reading and Discourse or Conference, 150
Reading and Reflection, 150, 222, 230, 277.
Reading and Writing, 224.
Reading for Girls, 228, 388
Ready man, 103, 186.
Real objects, in early instruction, 41.
Reasoning, different kinds, 116, 485.
　Mathematical, 463.
　Problematical, 455, 464, 485.
　Philosophical, 464.
Receptive Faculty, 489.
Recreations of the Family, 365.
Reformatories, 414.
Reflection, 222, 229, 277.
Religion, 49, 134, 512.
Religious Culture and Work, 134, 309, 395.
Rewards and encouragements, 290.
Reverence, 67, 96, 135.
Reviews of lessons and books, 158, 176.
Rhetoric, 162.
RICE, A. H., 211.
Riches, uses and abuse, 257.
Riding, 136, 159.
Rivalry, 312.
Romance reading, 338.
Rote memory, 113.
Ruskin, 19.

Sainte-Beuve on Chesterfield's Letters, 125.
Sarcasm and severity, 76, 174, 177.
Schools, variety and office, 23, 230, 531.
Sculpture and education, 16.
Science in School Curriculum, 477, 532.
　General neglect, 476, 485.
Sciences, classification of, 469, 473, 476.
Scientific information, 487.
Scientific Training, 487, 497.

Science defined, 435, 490.
 Exactness and power, 485.
 Scheme, or plan of study, 150, 17.
 Scholarship, delights of, 85, 230.
Scotland, and education, 499.
Scott, Sir Walter, 443.
Scriptures, how to study, 108.
Sedgwick, Catharine M., 229.
 Reading for Girls, 227.
Seeing, art of, 239.
Self, and Selfishness, 95, 178, 180, 184.
Self-activity, 15, 233.
Self-education, helps to, 23, 28.
 Books, 28, 35, 215.   Work, 218.
 Examples, 29, 217.   Dangers of, 31.
Self-knowledge, 96, 128, 150, 286.
Self-love and Wisdom, 282.
Self-examination, 150, 452.
Seneca, 225.
Senses, Culture of, 40, 481.
Sevigne, Letters by, 368.
Sex, 55, 325, 370.
Sensuality, 97.
Shaftsbury, 225.
Shakspeare, 11, 92, 236, 380.
Shyness, 179.
Sherman, Roger, 219.
Short, Bishop, 13.
SIDNEY, SIR HENRY,
 Letter to his Son, 69.
SIDNEY, SIR PHILIP, 231.
 Letter on Travel, 232.
Silence, time for, 184, 528.
 Seldom repented of, 86.
Simpson, J., 21.
Simplicity, 90.
Singing, 89, 356.
Sisterhoods, 401.
 Beguines, 402.   St. Elizabeth, 403, 408.
 Grey Sisters, 402.   St. Martha, 403.
 Hospital, 402.   Charity, 406, 407.
Skill, Manuel, 292.
Site of a University typified at Athens, 538.
Sleep, 81, 147, 158, 397, 365.
Slow development, 41.
Smattering of knowledge, 104, 107, 392.
Smart, but ill natured words, 128.
Smith, Goldwin, 468.
Smith, Sidney, too much Latin and Greek, 442.
Smith, Southwood, Health, 45.
Socrates, 25, 97.
Social Reading, 228.
Social Sciences, 470.
Solitude, experience of, 185, 195, 276.
Songs of childhood, 40.
SOUTH, ROBERT, 13, 92.
SOUTHEY, ROBERT, 99, 443.
 Knowledge and Wisdom, 100.
Space and Time, 462.
Sparta, 158.
Species, 471.
Speaking, fluency in, how acquired, 162.
Speculations, useless, 147.
Sports and Pastimes, 38.
ST. JEROME, 289.
 Letter to Laeta, 290.
Steele, Sir Richard, 184.
Story-tellers in society, 133.
Statesmanship, school of, 532.
Stanhope, Son of Earl Chesterfield, 125.
Stewart, Dugald, 21.
Staupitius, 90.
STRAFFORD, LORD,
 Letters to his Son, 73.
Studium Generale, defined, 529.
Study, Objects, Limits, and Methods, 145.
Student Life at Athens, 537.
Studies, Characteristic of different, 103.
STUDIES, ELEMENTARY, LIBERAL, AND SPECIAL,
 Agriculture, 80, 155.   Mensuration, 459.
 Anatomy, 474.   Modern Languages, 476,
 Arithmetic, 45, 334, 348.   500.
 Art, or æsthetics, 512.   Military tactics, 159.
 Astronomy, 380, 484.   Moral Duty, 156.
 Biology, 470, 471.   Moral Philosophy, 150.

Book-keeping, 448.
Botany, 469.
Chemistry, 476, 479.
Classical, 445.
Civil economy, 510.
Economics, 156.
Ethics, 103, 155, 511.
Experimental Sciences,
 494, 507.
Drawing, 356.
French, 346, 138, 202.
German, 480.
Greek, 133, 200, 465.
Geometry, 460, 490.
Geography, 138, 500.
Geology, 477, 484, 496.
Grammar, 154.
Globes, 43, 138, 155.
Hebrew, 157.
Hydrostatics, 494.
History, 103, 176, 345,
 500, 510.
Humanities, 418.
Hand-writing, 176, 380.
International Law, 510.
Italian, 156.
Jurisprudence, 510.
Language, 198, 445, 446,
 500.
Logic, 103, 153, 157, 197,
 508.
Latin, 152, 201, 466, 502.
Mathematics, Pure, 103,
 153, 156, 198, 506.
Mathematics, Mixed, 156,
 457, 507.
Mechanics, 494.
Studious manner, 369, 381.
Style, 146, 173, 178.
Sunday, 83.
Subjects, Reading by, 221.
Swetchine, Madame, 398.
Swimming, 38.
SWIFT, JONATHAN, 179,
 Conversation, 179,   Manners, 244.
Sword, use of, 136.

Table-turning, 451.
Taxonomy, 471.
TAYLOR, HENRY, 281, 286,
 Money, its management, 291.
 Wisdom in conduct, 281.
TAYLOR, JEREMY, 87,
 Manly Element in Education, 87.
Teaching, 495, 500.
Teachers, special training, 64, 170.
Teachers of Mankind, 164, 170.
Telescope, 218.
Temper, 56, 137.
Temple, Sir William, 184.
TEMPLE, FRED., 417,
 Languages, Mathematics, Science, 418.
Tenderness,
Tonnelé on Female Culture, 389.
Tennyson, 401.
Terror, Impulse of, 59, 315.
Text-book, 495.
Tents and Hymns, 315.
Theresia, 382.
Things, Knowledge of, 41, 422.
Thinking, Faculty of, 186, 447, 485.
Theophrastus, at Athens, 542.
Theology, 157.
Thibaut, on Purity in Music, 354.
Time, 250, 462.
Timidity, 315.
Timing speakers, in conversation, 191.
Tractate on Education, by Milton, 151.
Translations, oral and written, 165, 175.
Training, 17, 488.
Training to Think, 495.
Travel, Advice respecting, 235,
 Aiken, 239.   Littleton, 237.
 Bacon, 27, 235.   Macaulay, 239.
 Bodleigh, 71.   Masson, 37.

Medicine, 156.
Music, 159, 356.
Natural History, 476,
 456.
Natural Philosophy, 103,
 135, 156.
Natural Sciences, 359,
 456, 477.
Oratory, 151, 157, 161,
 168.
Painting, 394, 512.
Penmanship, 176, 379.
Physical Sciences, 445,
 467, 480.
Philosophy, 78, 461.
Philosophical Sciences,
 461.
Physical Geography, 472,
 487.
Pneumatics, 494.
Philology, 170, 176.
Physiology, 156, 479,
 508.
Physics, 256, 479, 481,
 Piano, 351.   [494.
Psychology, 509.
Politics, 157, 510.
Political Economy, 510.
Poetry, 157, 513.
Rhetoric, 103.
Reading, 343.
Religion, 51.
Science generally, 487.
Singing, 348.
Theology, 157.
Trigonometry, 156.
Zoology, 473.

Fuller, 91.
Hardwicke, 238.
Johnson, 238.
Milton, 160, 237.
Shakspeare, 236.
Travel, Objects of Attention, 231.
 Administration of Cities and States, 71, 233.
 Art, 235, 238, 512.
 Church Affairs, 71, 235.
 Government, 72, 233.
 Geography, 72.
 Judiciary, 72, 235.
 Trade and Traffic, 72, 234.
 Languages, 91, 235.
 Comparative estimate, 232.
Travel, how made profitable, 73, 91, 232.
 Maturity of Mind and Character, 237.
 Previous knowledge from books, 91, 235.
 Access to best society, 234, 236, 237.
 Separate from countrymen, 236.
 Remove prejudices, 73, 237, 239.
 Avoid foreign vices, 71, 91, 236.
Travels, Books of, 119.
Trifles, in Training, 308.
Truth, Law of Education and Science, 51, 148, 173.
 Love of, 128, 168.
Truths, Classification of, 470.
TYNDALL, JOHN, 481,
 Physics, 481.
 Physics, 481.
Tutor, 77, 344.
Type and Voice, in teaching, 32, 529.

Ulysses' bow, 160.
University, lectures, not for uneducated men, 193.
Unconscious manner, 323.
Uneducated mind, 488.
University, defined, 529, 534,
 Site, 535.
 Student life at Athens, 537, 543.
 Proper function, 498, 529.
 English and Scotish, 499, 516.
University studies,
Carlyle, 524.
Froude, 515.
Lowe, 421.
Milton, 151.
Mill, 495.
Newman, 528.
University, and the great Public Schools, 458.
University Men, deficiencies in, 428.
Unlearning, necessity for, 113.

VAIL, THOMAS H., 215,
 Hints respecting Books and Reading, 215.
Valor, 204.
Vanity, 61, 371, 389.
VAUGHAN, H., 11, 32,
 Oral Teaching, 32.
 Exclusion of physical science, 446.
 Relative value of languages 446.
Veracity, in dealing with children, 52.
Ventilation, 35.
Verplanck, Gulian C., Reading, 219.
Versification in a dead language, 152, 440, 425.
Vincent de Paul, 405.
Virgil, 131.
Virtue in Education, 14, 97.
 Address to Hercules, 98.
Voice, Power of the living, 32, 39, 187.
 Universal cultivation, 39.
 Cicero's culture, 167.

War, too much in education, 75, 146, 152.
Warrior, The Happy, 97.
Watching children, 390.
Watt, James, 218.
Watts, Isaac, 215, 223.
Wedgewood, Josiah, 218.
Weights and Measures, 43.
WHATELY, RICHARD, 18, 178,
 Annotations on Bacon's Studies, 104.
WHEWELL, WILLIAM, 11, 458,
 Mathematics in Liberal Education, 458.
Whitaker, Rules in reading, 230.
Whitheote, 13.
Whickliff, Huss, and Luther, 226.
Whittier, Treatment of the Insane, 410.
Wife, Choice of, 69, 75, 270.
Will, Force and control of, 57.
Will, Coffee House, 181.
WILSON, J. M., Rugby School, 483,
 Natural Science in Schools, 483.
 Failure of Latin and Greek in discipline, 483.
 Intrinsic Dignity and Power of Science, 485.
 Subjects and Methods, 487.
 Specimen Lesson—Botany, 491.
 Experimental Physics, 494.
Winemon, 223.
WINTHROP, ROBERT C., 209.
 Books and Reading, 209.
Wisdom, in Conduct, 93, 281,
Barrow, 93.
Bible, 101, 102.
Carlyle, 279.
Humboldt, 237.
Southey, 99.
Taylor, 281.
Wordsworth, 279.
Wise men, in word and deed, 279, 282.
Wise men of Greece, characteristics, 99.
Wits, proffered in company, 141.
Woman, her Aim and Merit, 281,
 Pagan and Christian view, 384.
 Dangers of mental culture, 388.
 Home of studious women, 389.
 Pursuits open to, 373, 401.
 Necessity of method to—Morning hours, 398.
 Exclusion from society, influence of, 183.
Words, Study of, 153, 423.
WORDSWORTH, WILLIAM, 279,
 The Happy Warrior, 279.
Work, cure of all maladies, 204, 525.
Working-day World, 399.
World, Knowledge of, 94, 204.
Wrestling, and other athletic sports, 158.
Wotton, Sir Henry, 12.
Writing, or Penmanship, 176, 379.
Writing and Speaking, 112, 163, 165, 168.
Writing with Reading, 112, 224, 225.
WYATT, SIR THOMAS, 67,
 Letter to his son at school, 67.
 Honesty, Reverence, Goodness, 68.
Wyttenbach, on daily reading, 225.

Y. Pythagorean Symbol, 291.
Yorke Philip, 238.
Young Children, 33, 299.
Young Ladies, 382.

Zenophon, Prodicus' choice of Hercules, 97.
Zoology, Study in Schools, 473.

Barnard's National Education.

INDEX

TO

ELEMENTARY AND SECONDARY EDUCATION IN GERMANY.

A. B. C. Tablets, 528, 541.
Abecedarians, 780, 865.
Abroad, scholars from, 506.
Absence from School, valid excuses for, 687, 887.
 How dealt with, 128. *See Attendance.*
Academic (university) study, preparation for, 242.
Account-book, Teachers in Brunswick, 213.
Agricola, George, 535.
Administrative authorities, 755.
 See State, Provincial, Municipal, Authorities.
Adults, schools and classes for, 56, 419, 434, 807.
Æpinus. John, in 1525, 372.
Æsop's fables, 536, 537.
Age for school attendance,
 Austria, 55, 887.　　Hesse-Darmstadt, 281.
 Baden, 128.　　　　Mecklenberg, 312, 319.
 Bavaria, 160.　　　Prussia, 434.
 Brunswick, 210.　　Saxe-Coburg, 895.
 Hanover, 227.　　　Saxony, 550.
 Hesse-Cassel, 267.　Wurtemberg, 361.
Agriculture, in common schools, 50, 590.
Agriculture, special schools of, 196, 851.
Aira, church and school, 531, 539.
Altenzelle, convent school, 533.
Aix-la-Chapelle, 859.
Albert, of Brandenburg, 449.
Altenberg, Teachers' Seminary, 569.
Altenstein, minister of public in, 411, 441.
 Letter to Pestalozzi in 1808, 363.
 Letter to Plamann in 1822, 413.
 Normal school system for Gymnasia, 441.
Altona, school system, 647.
Amelia Institute, 567.
ANHALT, Principality, 17, 744, 845.
Dessau-Cothen, 17.
 1. Primary Schools, 17.
 2. Secondary, 19.
 3. Special schools, 19.
Bernberg, 20.
Public schools, 20, 744.
Anthropology, 115, 443, 896.
Apparatus, 52, 201, 610.
Apprentices, schools for, 105.
Appointment of teachers,
 Provisional, 174, 602. 612, 897.
 Definitive, 593, 888, 897.
 Revocable, 696, 889.
Aquaviva, author of Jesuit plan of studies, 67.
Architecture, special schools of, 599, 850.
Arch-Gymnasium, 109.
Arithmetic, extent and methods of teaching.
 Austria, 54, 103.　　Nassau, 324.
 Baden, 130, 144.　　Prussia, 419, 781.
 Bavaria, 169, 189.　　Saxe-Weimar, 628.
 Hanover, 255.　　　Wurtemberg, 685.
Assistant teachers, 83.
Associate teachers, 83.
Association of teachers, 214, 695, 702.
Astronomy, rudiments in 1580, 547.

Attendance, law respecting in
 Anhalt, 18.　　　　Nassau, 324.
 Austria, 55, 42, 63, 887.　Oldenburg, 327.
 Baden, 123.　　　　Prussia, 380, 433, 339.
 Bavaria, 161.　　　Saxony, 555.
 Hanover, 227.　　　Saxe-Coburg, 592, 895.
 Hesse-Cassel, 267.　Saxe-Meiningen, 609.
 Hesse-Darmstadt, 281.　Wurtemberg, 661.
 Mecklenburg, 312.
Augsburg, school organization, 168, 859.
 Institute of English Ladies, 176.
Augustines, 522, 531.
Augustus, of Brunswick, 208.
Augustus I., of Saxony, 549.
Order for Schools, in 1580, 540.
AUSTRIA, Empire, 9.
 Area, population, religion, 23, 120.
 Public instruction—historical, 26.
 1. Elementary schools, 26.
 Organization, administration, studies, 40.
 Statistics, 61, 68, 120, 744.
 2. Secondary schools—classical, 67.
 Historical development in detail, 67.
 Present organization, studies, 82.
 Statistics, 78, 120, 845.
 3. Real schools, 98.
 History and organization, 101.
 Statistics, 101, 105, 120, 845.
 4. Superior Schools or Universities, 120.
 Faculties, Professors, Students, 120, 846.
 5. Special Schools, 120.
 6. Hungary, Croatia, Slavonia,, 107.
 General view of Educational institutions, 120.
 School code of Maria Theresa, 1774,879.
 School code of 1869, 885.
 School ordinance abrogating Concordat, 892.

Bache, A. D. cited, 801.
BADEN, Duchy of, 121, 156.
 Area. Population, History, 121, 744.
 1. Elementary schools, 122.
 Summary of laws and regulations, 127.
 Statistics, 134, 744.
 2. Secondary instruction, 135.
 Classical schools, organization, studies, 135, 845.
 3. Real schools, 149, 845.
 4. Higher institutions, pupils, 152, 846.
 5. Orphan and Rescue institutions, 153.
 Universities, 846.
 Law of 1864, 155.
Baden-Durlach, 121, 153.
Bathing, 718.
Barefooted schools, 735.
Barnard, Henry, National Education, 3.
 German Pedagogy and Schools, 905.
 German Educational Reformers, 903.
 German Universities, 904.
Barth, town school in 1305, 373.
Basedow, 117.

Basle, university, 846.
Bassewitz, cited, 352, 357.
BAVARIA, kingdom of, 157, 206.
 Area, population, religion, 157.
 1. Primary or common schools, 158, 744.
 History, law of 1802, 1808, 1811, 1836, 1848, 158.
 Attendance, parishes, inspection, 160.
 Schools, studies, methods, 166.
 Teachers, school apprentices, seminaries, 172.
 2. Secondary schools, 176, 845.
 High school for girls, Classical schools, 176.
 Latin school, gymnasium, 185.
 Real schools, Technical schools, Polytec. schools, 195.
 3. Rescue and Supplementary schools, 204.
 General view of schools and their distribution, 156.
Benefactors of Education, early.
 Saxony, 535.
Beck, A., Life of Ernest the Pious, 582.
Beck, Christian Daniel, 551.
Beckedorf, L. 387, 413, 345.
Bee raising in Silesia, 50.
Behavior, or Manners in school, 581.
Bensheim, Catholic seminary at, 286, 589.
Bergen, in 1862, Pomerania, 373.
Berlin, school system, 363.
 Institute for girls, 359.   Seminary, 848, 864.
 Private schools, 427.   University, 524, 526, 846.
 Statistics, 420, 586, 859.
Berner, instruction in music, 364.
Bernhardi, plan for gymnasium, 492.
Bible as a reading-book, 803, 806.
Bible History, treatment of, 418, 791.
Bible in schools, 418, 440, 682, 803.
Blocks in school, 781.
Blackboard, 376, 541, 865.
Boarding, Gymnasiums, 562.
Blind, schools for, 206, 850.
Boarding round, 225, 294, 607, 802.
Bockh, Pedagogical seminary, 488.
Bodily Culture, 591.
Bohemia, 23, 41, 95, 99.
Bonitz, Hermann, in Vienna, 79.
Bonn, University, 459, 524, 846.
Book publication in Austria, 60.
Branch schools, 40.
Brandenberg, mark and electorate, 335, 336.
Brandenberg, Province of Prussia, 425.
 Elementary schools, 425.
 Secondary schools, 459, 515.
Braun, 416.
Breslau, 345, 846, 859.
Bremen, school system, 739, 859.
Bromberg, 301, 397, 411.
Brotherhood of Christian Instruction, 26.
Brotherhood of Common Life, 235.
Bruggmann, Catholic gymnasium councilor, 447.
Brunn, school system, 859.
BRUNSWICK, Duchy of, 207.
 Historical development of schools, 207.
 1. Primary schools, 209.
 2. Orphan and Rescue institutions, 216.
 3. Classical schools, 216.
Brunswick, city, 208, 217, 859.
Buildings for school purposes, 44, 160.
Büdingen, gymnasium, 289, 859.
Bugenhagen, John, school reforms, 372 734.
Burgher schools in
 Austria, 64, 100, 886.,   Mecklen-Strelitz, 321.
 Baden, 149, 150, 845.   Oldenburg, 329.
 Bavaria, 150, 845.   Prussia, 501, 845.
 Brunswick, 850.   Reuss. 528.
 Bremen, 719, 859.   Saxony, 556.
 Frankfort, 737.   Saxe-Altenburg, 568.
 Hamburg, 740.   Saxe-Coburg ,568.
 Hanover, 850.   Saxe-Meineugen, 600.
 Hesse-Cassel, 859.   Saxe Weimar, 632.
 Hesse-Darmstadt, 296.   Thuringian States, 815.
 Lippe-Detmold, 306.   Schleswig-Holstein, ,647.
 Lippe-Schaumburg, 307.   Swarzburg, 650.
 Lubeck, 740.   Waldeck, 632, 845.
 Mecklenberg-Sch., 313.   Wurtemberg, 721.

Bückeburg, Burgher schools, 307.
 Gymnasium, 307.
 Teachers' Seminary, 307.
Busch, Herman, 534.
Catholic and Protestant school attendance.
 Bavaria, 300.   Wurtemburg, 726.
Catholic Church and schools,
 Austria, 26, 39.   Prussia, 347, 423, 869.
 Bavaria, 165.   Wurtemberg, 657.
 Silesia, 869.
Calendar and Catechism, memorizing, 654.
Callenberg, Female Teachers' Seminary, 558.
Calligraphy, 103, 109, 151.
Cameralisten, 847.
Campe, school books, 375.
Canisius, Catechism, 121.
Canton, 531.
Carinthia, 23, 61.
Carlsruhe, school statistics, 859.
Carlsbad, gymnasium, 121.
Carniola, 23, 66.
Cassel, school statistics, 278, 859.
Catechisms, Carnisius, 23, 66.
 Heidelberg, 121.   Luther's, 541, 804.
 Josephine, 121.   Dinter, 802.
Catechists in Austria, 85.
Catechism, instruction in
 Austria, 89.   Wurtemberg, 547.
 Baden, 121, 130.   Hanover, 229.
 Bavaria, 168.
 Prussia, 341, 439, 791, 798, 804, 865.
Cathedral schools, 531, 732.
 Mecklenberg, 315.   Hanover, 234.
Chain-rule in Arithmetic, 169.
Charlemange, 235, 531.
Charles I., of Brunswick, 209.
Charles V., Interim, 237.
Chemnitz, 859.
Chemnitz, Martin, 216.
Cato, early school-book, 536.
Chemistry, 103, 197.
Church attendance of pupils on Sunday 867.
Chorister, 215.
Church and State in school, 227, 802.
Church in relation to school, 159, 165.
 Austria, 802.   Prussia, 798, 800.
 Baden, 125.   Saxe-Coburg, 902.
 Bavaria, 165.   Wurtemberg, 654.
 Brunswick, 209.
Church Convention, Wurtemberg, 724.
Chronological development of higher schools, 503,
Circle School Board in Austria, 32.
Ciphering, 807.
Cities, school system and statistics, 859.
 Berlin, 427.   Neustrelitz City, 321.
 Dresden, 958.   Newbrandenburg, 321.
 Friedland, 32.   Schoningen, 212.
City Constitution of Frederick II., 362, 461, 755.
Civil status of teachers, 240,
 Baden, 147.   Lippe-Detmold, 305.
 Bavaria, 160.   Prussia, 472.
 Hanover, 240.   Wurtemberg, 695, 723.
Classification of knowledge, 590.
Classification, 168, 757, 778,
Class and department organization, 146.
Class-book in discipline, 91.
Class Professors, 469.
Class-record, 258.
Class system of organization, 212.
Class-teaching, 76, 292, 810.
Classes in Elementary school, 21, 51, 62.
Classes in Secondary schools, 146.
Classical studies, 135, 149, 564.
Clergy and public schools, 528, 708, 875.
Cloister schools, 208, 712.
Coburg, city schools, 896.
Cosurg duchy, 896.
Code for schools,
 Austria, 8, 881, 887.   Saxony, 540.
 Baden, 255.   Saxe-Gotha, 591, 897.

ELEMENTARY AND SECONDARY INSTRUCTION IN GERMANY. 907

Code for Schools,
  Prussia, 861, 564.   Wurtemberg, 654, 659.
Colleague Teacher, 470, 564.
Comenius, cited, 230, 239. 579.
Commerce, schools of, 857,
Commerce, ministry of, 158.
Commercial Academy in, 1770, 98.
Common objects and phenomena, 579, 768.
Common School, origin of, 798.
  Aim and objects, 158, 885.
Common Science, 304.
Commune, 24.
Communal school, 123, 801, 890, 894.
Concordat of 1855, in Austria, 30, 802.
Conduct-List, 472.
Conferences of Teachers,
  Austria, 51. 889.   Prussia, 468, 836.
  Baden, 132.   Saxe-Coburg, 901.
  Hanover, 174.   Wurtemberg, 695.
Confessional schools, 41, 135, 553, 797.
Consistory, 226, 304.
Competitive Examination, 34, 710.
Composition, exercises in, 777, 783.
Compulsory attendance, 703. (*See* Attendance.)
  Prussia, 381.
Concentration of teaching, 806.
Confirmation, 161, 554.
Convent schools, 531, 533.
Corporal punishment, 211, 320, 609.
Conversational method, 767, 780, 784.
Country Schools, 170 669.
Council of studies, 136.
Cousin, on Prussian schools, 444.
Crime and Schools, 167.
Croatia and Slavonia, 23, 105, 107.
Crusius, Martin, Greek Grammar, 544.
Criminal Children, school for, 676.
Curriculum vitæ, 242, 478.
Custodian, 861.

Daily Routine, 767.
  Austria, 52.   Prussia, 767, 864.
  Baden, 131.   Saxe-Gotha, 588.
  Bavaria, 167 203.   Wurtemberg, 767.
Dalmatia, 23, 35.
  Gymnasiums, 95.
Dammau, on teachers' wages. 383.
Darmstadt, Gymnasium, 239.
Deaf-Mutes, 314, 850.
Decuria, or Section Master, 541, 542.
Definitely appointed teachers, 897.
Denominational character of schools, 552, 664, 798.
  Wurtemberg, 664.   Saxony, 552.
Department system of teaching, 77.
Deportment of pupils, 134.
Design, schools of, 671.
Dessau, Basedow's Philanthropinum, 17.
  Female schools, 19.   Real-classes, 19.
  Gymnasium, 19.   Trades-school, 19.
Detention after school, 506.
Detmold, 303.
  Gymnasium, 306,
  Higher Trade Seminary, 306.
  Teachers' Seminary, 305.
Diary, school,
  Baden, 133.   Wurtemberg, 686.
  Bavaria, 171.   Hesse-Cassel, 269.
Dialectics and Rhetoric, 544.
Diaspora, 799.
Diesterweg, 387, 416.
  Dismissal from Berlin Normal school, 415.
  Guide for German teachers, 588.
Dietsch, Dr. R., author of article on Saxony, 530, 554.
Dinner, teachers' right to, 374.
Dinter, 360, 833.
  Private training school at Dresden, 550.
  Catechism, 802.
Director, 79, 84, 466.
Discipline, general principles,
  Baden, 134.   Hesse-Darmstadt, 292.
  Bavaria, 171.   Prussia, 506, 866.

Discipline, general principles.
  Hesse-Cassel, 276.   Wurtemberg, 717.
Discipline out of school
  Baden, 146.   Saxony in 1580, 546.
Dissenters in Germany, 425, 799.
Dissenters in Prussia, 799.
District in Austria defined, 25.
Doctrinale of Alexander, 235.
Domestic economy in schools, 222, 492.
Domestic training, 796.
Donatus, Latin Grammar, 536.
Dortmund petition, on Prussian Regulative, 416.
Drawing, instruction in
  Austria, 54, 103.   Hanover, 556.
  Baden, 151.   Prussia. 784.
  Bavaria, 170.   Wurtemberg, 685.
Dresden, schools, 859.
  Holy Cross gymnasium, 535.
  Poor-school, 550.
  Burgher-school, 551.
  Fletcher seminary, 551.
Du and sic, in school language, 191, 258.
Due to the school, children of certain age, 41, 555.
Duke, Christopher, of Wurtemberg, 709.
  Grand Ecclesiastical order of 1559, 654, 709.
Duke Ernest, the Pious, 581.
Dwelling-house for teachers, 610, 697, 821.

Ecclesiastical authorities, and the public school.
  Austria, 44.   Hanover, 226.
  Baden, 126.   Hesse-Cassel, 266.
  Bavaria, 163.   Prussia, 756.
  Brunswick, 210.   Wurtemberg, 709.
Ecclesiastics as teachers, 84, 95.
Educational Fund of Austria, 69.
Eichorn, J. A. F., ministry of, 414, 444.
  Decree concerning æsthetic culture, 415.
Eilers, Dr., assistant of Eichorn, 414, 446.
Elberfeld, 859.
Elementary schools, 801. (*See* Primary schools.)
Elementary studies, limits of 805.
  Concentration of teaching, 805.
Emerited schools, 176, 410, 613.
Endowed Schools, 247, 759.
Ephori, in school administration, 136, 591, 617, 628.
Eppingen, Higher Burgher school, 151.
Equipment of schoolhouse, 779.
Erfurt, Normal school, 371.
Erlangen, university, 846.
Ernest, the Pious, of Saxe-Coburg, 572, 576.
Ernesti, John A . 548, 550.
Esslingen, Normal school, 691.
Evangelical schools, 530.
Ernest, Duke of Saxe-Coburg-Gotha, 894.
Evening schools, 105, 131.
Examination of Elementary schools, 55.
  Austria, 54.   Mecklenberg, 311, 320.
  Baden, 125.   Nassau, 325.
  Bavaria, 164.   Prussia, 754.
  Hanover, 230.   Saxe-Meiningen, 618.
  Hesse, 286.   Wurtemberg, 694.
Examination of Secondary schools,
  Austria, 91.   Prussia, 474.
  Baden, 141.   Saxe-Meiningen, 624.
  Hanover, 242.   Wurtemberg, 722.
Examination of Elementary Teachers,
  Austria, 47, 888.   Hesse-Darmstadt, 287.
  Bavaria, 174.   Prussia, 835.
  Brunswick, 213.   Saxe-Coburg, 896,
  Hanover, 231.   Wurtemberg, 692, 721.
Examination of Secondary Teachers in
  Austria, 93.   Hesse, 276, 287.
  Baden, 147.   Mecklenburg, 316.
  Bavaria, 173,   Prussia, 474.
  Brunswick, 217.   Saxe-Meiningen. 634.
  Hanover, 242.   Wurtemberg, 785.
Example. teaching by, 585, 863.
Examination on leaving Gymnasium, 92, 724, 843.
Examen pro facultate docendi, 476,
Exclusion from school, 506, 593.
Exner, 78, 100.

Fabricius, Historiæ Sacræ, 545.
Faber, compendium Musical, 544.
Factory children and schools,
  Austria, 43, 105, 55, 886, 890.
  Baden, 131.   Prussia, 434, 750.
  Bavaria, 167.   Saxony, 553.
  Hanover, 229.   Wurtemberg, 671.
Facultas docendi, 478.
Faculties, in universities, 535.
  Cameralisten, 747.
  Jurisprudence, 846.
  Medicine, 849, 846.
  Pedagogy and Philosophy, 848.
  Theology, Catholic, 848, 846.
  Theology, Protestant, 848.
Family life of the peasant, 362.
Feeble-minded children, 233, 677.
Fees, rates of. (*See* Tuition.)
  Difficulties in collecting obviated, 729.
  Influence on attendance, 729.
Felbiger, John Ignaz Von, 347.
Female Education, 177, 540.
Female Industries, 64, 131.
Female teachers,   Hesse, 288.
  Baden, 127, 133.   Saxony, 558,
  Bavaria, 176.   Saxe-Coburg, 599, 897.
  Frankfort, 736.   Wurtemberg, 701.
Feuchtersleben, Baron Von, 36, 78.
  Real and Burgher schools, 99.
Fichte, cited, 647, 657.
Finance, faculty, 847.
Fines on Parents, 134, 283, 592.
Firmian, Count, memorial of, 27.
Forest-culture, 621, 852.
Fort-bildungsschulen, or Supplementary schools, 434.
  Austria, 56.   Bavaria, 205.
  Baden, 123.   Wurtemberg, 671.
Formula Concordiæ, 546.
Francis Joseph, Emperor of Austria, 73.
  School code of 1869, 885.
  Inspection of schools and the church of 1868, 892.
Franke at Halle, 338, 309.
Frankfort, area, population, schools, 731, 737.
  Collegiate Church schools, 732.
  Gymnasium, Model school, 737.
  Burgher High school, 737.
Fraternity of poor scholars, 733.
Frederick I., of Prussia, 338.
  School regulation of 1715, 339.
Frederick II., 342, 861.
  Regulations for village schools in 1760, 342.
  General regulation for country schools, 343 861.
  Reform of Secondary schools, 436.
  Letter on Education, 437.
  Regulations for Catholic schools, 869.
  Normal schools in Silesia, 1869.
Frederick William I., 436.
Frederick William III., 353, 362.
  Abolition of serfdom, 363.
  School-section in Ministry of Interior, 361, 440.
  Educational policy, 360, 438.
  Letter to Wollner, 439.
Frederick William IV., 364.
  Tribute to Pestalozzi, 304.
FREE HANSEATIC cities, 731, 845, 859.
  Bremen, 732, 739.   Hamburg, 731, 740.
  Frankfort, 731, 737.   Lubeck, 732, 740.
Free, or Gratuitous instruction, 798.
Free lodgings for teachers, 897.
Frieburg, university, 846.
French language in
  Austria, 86, 104.   Hanover, 253.
  Baden, 142.   Prussia, 496.
  Bavaria, 185.   Wurtemberg, 720.
French System in Rhenish Provinces, 456.
Fruit-culture, 50.
Fulda, 234, 275.
Funds, for school expenses, 61, 63, 249.
Furstenberg, Count Bishop, 368.
  Austria, 58, 887.
  Prussia, 425.

Galicia, 23, 29, 41, 61.
Gall, J. A., labors in Austria, 30.
  Socratic system, 31.
Gang-schools, in Pomerania, 351.
Gardens attached to schools, 226.
Garden-culture, for teachers, 226, 415.
Gedike, 358.
  Schools for Girls, 359.
  Burgher school, 551.
Gelehrtenschulen, 135.
Gemund, Catholic Seminary for teachers, 691.
Geography in Elementary schools,
  Austria, 52.   Bavaria, 169.
  Baden, 16.   Prussia, 420.
Geography in Gymnasia.
  Austria, 79, 88.   Hanover, 189.
  Baden, 143.   Prussia, 786, 807.
  Bavaria, 160.   Wurtemberg, 715.
Geography in Real School in
  Austria, 103.   Prussia, 502.
  Hanover, 255, 256.   Wurtemberg, 720.
Geometry, 419.
Gera, public schools, 528.
  Rutheneum Gymnasium, 528.
German language and literature.
  Austria, 87.   Prussia, 783, 806, 839.
  Baden, 143.   Wurtemberg, 683.
  Hanover, 253.
German Pedagogy, Schools, and Teachers, 903, 904.
  Barnard's publications respecting, 904.
  Steiger's Contents of catalogue, 920.
German schools, why so called, 31, 653, 715, 798.
  Saxony in 1580, 547.   Hanover, 235.
  Brunswick, 208.   Prussia, 798, 801.
  Bavaria, 159.   Wurtemberg, 653.
  Free Cities, 71.
German work Day schools, 150.
Germany, in 1815, general view, 15.
  Organization area, population, 1867, 743.
  Public instruction, summary and statistics, 743.
  1. Elementary schools, 744.
    Teachers' seminaries, 813.
  2. Secondary schools, 845.
  3. Superior schools or universities, 846.
  4. Special schools, 850.
  5. Higher instruction in 30 cities, 859.
  6. School Codes—old and new, 861.
Gertsner, plan for Real school, 99.
Gesner, 239, 549.
Gewerbeschulen, 151, 850.
Geissen, Gymnasium, 280.
  University, 846.
Gingst, German school at, 375.
Girls, Special and Higher schools for
  Anhalt, 19.   Lippe-Detmold, 306.
  Austria, 122.   Saxony, 560.
  Baden, 152.   Saxe-Altenberg, 571.
  Bavaria, 176.   Saxe-Coburg, 597.
  Brunswick, 215.   Saxe-Meiningen, 621.
  Hanover, 232.   Saxe-Weimar, 633.
  Hesse-Cassel, 274.   Wurtemberg, 669.
  Hesse-Darmstadt, 298.
Glatz, in Silesia Regulations, 870.
Gotha, city schools, 572, 506.
  Normal school, 385, 508, 806.
  Technical school, 599.
  Gymnasium, 595.
  Sunday school, 509.
Gottingen, Latin school, 237.
  Seminary for Secondary teachers, 238, 245.
  Mathematical and Physical Seminary, 246.
  Scientific Committee of Examination, 245.
  University, 238, 846.
Governesses, first school for, 359.
Gratz, university, 846.
Grammar, methods of teaching, 783, 806.
Greek language,
  Austria, 87.   Saxony, 543, 652.
  Baden, 142.   Prussia, 497.
  Bavaria, 185.   Wurtemberg, 709, 715.
  Hanover, 187, 230, 252.

ELEMENTARY AND SECONDARY INSTRUCTION IN GERMANY.

Greiz, city schools, 528.
Griefswalde, normal school, 381.
  University, 524, 846.
Guild, of teachers, 735.
Gustrow, school statistics, 315, 318.
  Cathedral School, 316.
Gymnasium, details of organization, &c.,
  Grades and classification, 82.
  Administration and supervision, 82, 135, 714.
  Teachers, grades, duties, 83, 136, 713, 148.
  Training and appointment, 93, 721.
  Salaries and pensions, 85.
  Scholars, admission, promotion, 91, 138, 496.
  Fees, 85, 94, 138, 714.
  Discipline, 717.
  Lesson tables, 715, 495, 496.
  Hygiene, 717.
  Gymnastics, 718, 500.
  Leaving—examination, 92, 317, 724, 843.
  Confessional, 135.
Gymnasium, specimens of,
  Brunswick, 217,   Lippe-Detmold, 306.
  Cassel, 275.   Tübingen, 715.
  Cöthen, 19.   Neustrelitz, 321.
  Dessau, 19.   Mayence, 290.
  Hanover, 256.   Schwerin, 315.
  Gymnastics,   Hanover, 256.
  Austria, 54.   Prussia, 422, 500.
  Baden, 145.   Wurtemberg, 685, 718.
  Bavaria, 190.

Halberstadt, teachers' seminary, 368.
Haluander, founder of Comments on Justinian, 635.
Half-day instruction. 62, 229, 284, 646, 862.
Halle, university, 846,
  Franke's labors, 369.
  Pedagogic seminary, 479.
Hamilton, Sir William, 745.
Hamburg, city schools, 731, 740, 859.
  Gymnasial academy, 740.
Hanau, 274.
Handel, labors in Neisse, 368.
Hanover, city school statistics, 858.
  Real school, 157.
HANOVER, Kingdom, 219.
  Area, population, 219.
  1. Primary schools, 321, 228, 744.
  2. Secondary schools, 234.
    Classical, 242, 250.
    Realistic, 257.
  3. Superior, 846.
  4. Special, 850.
  Teachers' seminaries, 815.
  Girls' school, Blind Mutes, 233.
Harnisch, cited, 366, 368, 371.
Haynau, Baron, gift to schools, 113.
Head-master, *Oberlehrer*, 886.
Health of pupils in
  Elementary schools, 767.
  Gymnasiums, 494, 717.
Hebrew, in Gymnasium, 252, 270, 290, 547.
Hecker, J. Julius, 343, 501, 799.
Hedge-schools, 227.
Hegel, Prof. of Philosophy at Berlin, 441.
Heinicke, Samuel, institution for deaf-mutes, 550.
Heidelberg, Catechism, 304.
  University, 846.
Helmstadt University, 211, 237.
Helfert, Von, 40.
Herder, John Gottfried, 307.
Hermann, Geo., Philosophical seminary, Leipsic, 551.
Hess, Prof., gymnasial reform, 70.
HESSE CASSEL, Electorate, 263.
  Area, population, government, 263.
  1. Elementary schools, 265, 744.
  2. Higher schools, 282, 845.
    Real schools, 272, 845.
    Gymnasiums, 274, 945.
  3. Special schools, 277, 866.
HESSE DARMSTADT, Grand Duchy, 279.
  Area, population, government, 279.

HESSE DARMSTADT,
  1. Primary or lower schools, 281, 744.
  2. Classical school system, 289, 855.
  3 Real and trade schools, 295, 850.
  4. Female schools, 298.
Heyne, Christian G., schools in Gottingen., 240.
Higher Burgher schools, 503, 845, 859.
High school, 33, 41.
High Consistory, 345.
Hilburghausen, Teachers' seminary, 607, 611.
Hildesheim, 228.
Historical development of schools, (*See* Austria, Baden, etc.)
History in Gymnasium. 38, 139, 143, 188, 496.
Höch, Æpinus, 372.
Hochegger, 81.
Hohenzollern, 425, 453, 518.
Holidays in,
  Austria, 147.   Hesse, 269, 286.
  Baden, 128.   Saxony, 556.
  Bavaria, 168.   Saxe-Altenburg, 570.
  Brunswick, 210.   Saxe-Meiningen, 609.
  Hanover, 229, 259.   Wurtemberg, 686.
Hollweg, minister of public instruction, 417.
  Normal school regulation, 417.
  Memorial on school regulations, 421.
HOLSTEIN, School system and statistics, 643.
Home and its surroundings, lessons in Geography, 707.
Home preparation of lessons, 171, 685.
Horn-book, 581.
History in common schools, 842.
HUNGARY, 23, 107, 113, 120.
  Catholic, Jewish, Lutheran schools, 111.
  Protestant schools and influence, 108.
  Hygienic condition of schools, 492, 707, 717.
  Hymns, to be memorized, 304, 418, 423.
  School movement of 1848, 113.
  Statistics of schools, 115, 121.
  Part of religious instruction, 204, 683.
  Regulations of Frederick II., 1763, 866.

Idiotic children, 676, 677.
Ilfeld gymnasium, 237.
Illiteracy,
  Austria, 65.   Prussia, 792.
  Baden, 127.   Wurtemberg, 679.
  Bavaria, 167.
Incarceration, 146, 506.
Industrial Schools, 131, 192, 550, 560.
Industrial Schools in
  Baden, 154.   Prussia, 526,
  Bavaria, 196, 205.   Saxony, 560.
  Brunswick, 215.   Saxe-Altenburg, 571.
  Hanover, 233.   Saxe-Gotha, 599.
  Hesse, 270, 277, 297.   Saxe-Weimar, 633.
  Lippe-Schaumburg, 307. Saxe-Meiningen, 620.
  Oldenburg, 331.   Wurtemberg, 671.
Industrial element in common schools.
  Austria, 54.   Bavaria, 170, 196.
  Baden, 131.   Hesse-Cassel, 277.
Inspruck, University, 846.
Infant Schools and Kindergarten, 671, 648.
Informing of pupils, by each other, 687.
Inspectors and Inspection.
  Austria, 44.   Saxony, 553.
  Baden, 127.   Saxe-Gotha, 594, 899.
  Bavaria, 162.   Saxe-Weimar. 626.
  Hanover, 228.   Wurtemberg, 664.
  Prussia, 753, 876.
Intermediate Schools, 135, 229, 669.
Itinerating students and teachers, 533.

Janitor in Gymnasium, 473.
Jena, university, 846.
Jesuits in Austria, 28, 67, 69.
  Bavaria, 179.   Prussia, 348.
  Hungary, 107.
Jewish Schools in,
  Austria, 29, 31.   Hesse-Cassel, 371.
  Baden, 124.   Lippe-Detmold, 304.
  Bavaria, 166.   Prussia, 348, 403, 425.

Jewish Schools, in
 Hungary, 114. Wurtemberg, 667, 726.
Jeziorowsky, Joseph, 356.
Joachimsthal gymnasium, 400.
Journey, expense of school, 472.
Joseph I, of Austria, 68.
Joseph II, of Austria, 71.
 Educational work in Hungary, 109.
Josephine Catechism in Baden, 121.
Julius, Duke of Brunswick, 208, 237.
Julius, Dr., on Prussian schools as they were, 833.
Junker school, 735.
Jurisprudence, faculty and practice, 847.
Juliana, Princess of Lippe-Schaumburg, 307.
Jus Patronatus, 863.

Kamptz, Von, 442.
 Mandate of 1824, 443.
Kay, Primary Schools in Germany, 748, 792.
Kellner, on Catholic Schools, 423.
Kiel, Public Schools, 646.
 University, 846.
Kindergarten, 434.
 Attached to Seminaries for female teachers, 887.
 Teachers must be acquainted with system, 888.
 Kohler's in Gotha, 598.
Kochly, gymnasial reform, 564.
Kindermann, 29.
Kleemann, 80.
Klumpp, F. W., and Real school, 718.
Koningsberg, university, 846.
 Professorship and Seminary of History, 486.
Kortum, 446.
Krause, Private Gymnasium, 563.
Krunitz, Village School, 302.
Kreise, or Circle government, 25.
Kurmark, neglect of schools, 345, 438.
 Normal school in 1748, 342.
Krassow, Count, School of Pomerania, 378.
 Change produced by Prussia, 380.

Lancasterian system in Germany, 760.
Land proprietors, duty to schools, 760.
Lang, J. F. Plan of reform, 73.
Language and Grammar, 774, 806.
 Prussian Regulation, 806.
Language used in instruction, 53.
 Austria, 53, 77, 81, 88, 101, 885.
Languages, time and method, to,
 English, 253, 256, 717.
 German, 87, 102, 185, 253, 290, 496, 502.
 French, 139, 142, 150, 253, 496, 715.
 Greek, 86, 139, 183, 252, 497, 715.
 Hebrew, 252, 291, 715.
 Latin, 86, 139, 185, 261, 281, 486, 502, 715.
 Latin conversation, 236.
Latin Grammar *versus* literature, 77.
Latin in Gymnasiums,
 Austria, 86. Baden, 140.
 Bavaria, 186. Hanover, 239.
 Wurtemburg, 709, 715. Prussia, 496.
Latin in Real Schools,
 Austria, 107. Prussia, 502.
Latin Schools, of the 16th Century, 236, 709.
 Wurtemberg, 709, 711. Bavaria, 181.
 Hanover, 236.
LAUENBURG, Duchy of, 645.
Law and Jurisprudence, 820.
Leibnitz, 548.
LEICHTENSTEIN, Principality, 301.
Leipsic, 533, 540, 846, 859.
 St. Thomas Singing School, 532.
 University 1409, 533, 547, 846.
 Professorship of Pedagogy in 1815, 551.
 First Real School in Saxony, 551, 559.
Lemgo, Gymnasium, 306.
Leopold II. and School Reform, 73.
Lesson, plans of Classical Gymnasium, 54, 96, 185 256, 270, 496, 552, 306, 643, 715.
Lesson, plans of Real School and Real Gymnasiums 196, 257, 295, 502, 644, 720.

Liberty of Instruction, 892.
Liberty of religious training, 30.
Libraries in Gymnasiums, 145, 716.
Life-insurance for teachers, 319.
LIMBURG, Duchy of, 308.
LIPPE-DETMOLD, Principality of, 303, 306.
 Area, Population, 303.
 1. Primary Schools, 303.
 2. Secondary Schools, 306.
LIPPE-SCHAUMBURG.
 Primary schools, teachers' seminary, 307.
 Gymnasium and Latin school, 307.
 Burgher school—Female High school, 307.
Littorale, Statistics and schools, 23, 62.
Limitation of subjects in Common Schools, 808.
Liturgies for Schools, 164, 802, 890.
Local authorities in school administration.
 Austria, 892. Mecklenburg, 311.
 Baden, 127. Nassau, 325.
 Bavaria, 161. Oldenburg, 327.
 Hanover, 223. Prussia, 752.
 Hesse-Darmstadt, 283. Saxe-Gotha, 587, 890.
 Hesse-Cassel, 266. Wurtemberg, 665.
Lombardy, 35, 61, 95.
Lorinzer, Health in Gymnasia, 494.
Louisa, Queen of Prussia, 300.
Lubeck, School System, 732, 740.
 Catharineum Gymnasium and Real School, 740.
Ludwigslust, Deaf-mute School, 314.
Luther, Martin, 575, 621, 625.
Luther's Catechism, 541, 791, 804, 866.
 Influence on Schools, 236, 535, 709.
Lutheran High Consistory, 342.
LUXEMBURG, Duchy of, 308.
 Public Instruction, 308.
Lyceum, 137, 181.

Madebach, Jacob, in Frankfort, 735.
Madgeburg, 369, 859.
 Influence on School Reform, 368.
 Order of Visitation, 463.
Magyars, 107, 110.
Major, George, Epitome, 544.
Management of Schools, 439, 577.
Mann, Horace, 756.
 Account of Schools of Prussia, 778.
 Prussian teachers and their training, 823.
Mannheim, Higher Burgher Schools, 150.
Manorial Schools, 319.
Marburg, University, 846.
Maria Institute at Gotha, 597.
Maria Theresa, 26, 30, 69.
 General Law of Schools of Austria, 879.
Marine Schools, 526.
Marks, system of, in examination, 692, 165.
Martini, Gymnasium reform in Austria, 32, 72.
Marx, Gratian, System for Austria, 71.
Massow, Minister of Education, 354, 356.
 Plan of School Reform, 355.
 Schools of Pomerania, 350.
Maturity examination, 495, 724, 843.
 Austria, 92. Prussia, 843.
 Mecklenburg, 317. Wurtemberg, 724.
Mathematics in Gymnasium.
 Austria, 88.
 Baden, 144.
 Bavaria, 185.
 Prussia, 497.
Mathematics, professors of, 246, 848.
 Early introduction, 534.
Maurice, Elector of Saxony, 539.
Mayence, 296.
Mechanics School in 1751, 98.
MECKLENBURG, Duchy of, 309.
 1. Schwerin, 309, 310.
 2. Strelitz, 318.
Medicine, Faculty of, 846, 849.
Meierotto, 437.
Meiningen, city Schools, 634, 855.
 Gymnasium, of 1544, 633.
Meissen, Cathedral and Royal School, 531, 551.

Melanchthon,
 Book of Visitations, 535.
 Plan of Schools in 1528, 536.
 Grammar and other text-books, 541.
Memorizing Psalms and Scripture, 417, 421.
 Bavaria, 169.
 Prussia, 804.
 Wurtemberg, 655.
Memory, overburdening, 418.
Mensam cursoriam, 376.
Messmer, Joseph, 27.
Methods of Instruction, 439, 557, 577, 588, 716.
Micyllus, 735.
Mileage, for teachers on School visits, 473.
Middle Schools, 329, 359.
Migatzzi, Archbishop, 69.
Military Frontier in Austria, 23, 35. 46, 68.
Military system and schools, 583, 586, 834.
Mining, schools of, 858.
Ministries charged with supervision of schools,
 Commerce and public works, 156.
 Education and medical affairs, 411.
 Interior, 127, 267.
 Ecclesiastical affairs, 162.
 Worship, 82, 228.
 Public instruction, 162, 244.
 Distribution of schools in Austria, 22.
 Diagram of arrangement in Bavaria, 156.
Ministry of Public Instruction,
 Austria, 32.   Wurtemberg, 664, 704.
 Baden, 127.   Bavaria, 162, 184.
 Hesse-Darmstadt, 283.   Hanover, 244.
 Prussia, 350, 361, 411.   Saxony, 551.
Minors, punishment of, 688.
 Policeman, 688.
 Teacher, 688.
 Parent, 688.
Mirabeau, cited, 331.
Mirow, teachers' Seminary, 322.
Mixed Schools as to confessions, 109, 122, 400, 753.
 Experience in Silesia, 800.
Mixed Schools as to Sex, 40.
Model or Normal Schools in Austria, 28, 41, 887.
Modern Language, 886.
Monitors in Prussian schools, 761.
Mother Tongue, see Native Language.
Monthly record book, 213, 230.
Morality in Austrian Schools, 71.
Moravia, 23, 61, 95.
Moravian brethren, 550, 597.
Morus, Samuel F., 551.
Mountain-blessing in Saxony. 531.
Motives to study and work, 589.
Munich, Schools, 859.
 University, 846.
Munster, Schools, 859.
 University, 846.
Mühler, Ministry of Public Instruction, 447.
Music, Instruction in Elementary Schools,
 Austria, 34.   Baden, 130.
 Bavaria, 170.   Hanover, 239, 256.
 Prussia, 792, 808. Saxony, 544.
 Wurtemberg, 685.
Music in Normal School, 694, 808.
Music in Gymnasia, 694.
Music in Real School, 720.
Myconius, F., 574, 595, 715.
 Gymnasium, at Gotha, 595.

Nageli, Method of teaching singing, 657, 685.
Nassau, Duchy of, 323.
 Public Instruction—historical, 323.
 Obligatory attendance in 1624, 323.
 Teachers' Seminary in 1734, 324.
 1. Elementary Schools, 324.
 Parental and communal obligations, 324.
 2. Secondary Education, 325.
 Pedagogium—Gymnasium, 326.
Nations, division of students into, 535.
 Merged in Faculties, 535.

Native Language, how taught, 177.
 Austria, 87.
 Baden, 130, 139, 143, 150.
 Bavaria, 169, 177, 185, 188, 196.
 Hanover, 253, 256.
 Hesse, 575, 292.
 Mecklenburg, 321.
 Oldenburg, 328.
 Prussia, 364, 434, 495, 772.
 Saxony, 547, 552.
National holidays observed, 449.
Nationality, Austria, 25, 42, 95.
Nationality of Germany, 361.
 Austria, 25, 42, 95.   Prussia, 365.
Nature, common phenomena, 789.
Natural History.
 Austria, 89.   Baden, 144.
 Prussia, 789.   Saxony, 551.
Naval Schools.
 Mecklenburg, 314.
Navigation Schools, 314, 331, 857.
Neander, 237.
Needle work, 229.   Austria, 54, 886.
 Prussia, 422.   Baden, 131.
Saxe-Gotha, 589.
Neglected Children, School for,
 Saxe-Meiningen 620.   Baden, 153.
Neukloster, Teachers' Seminary, 314.
Neumark, 344.
Newspapers, 26.
Niavis (Schneevogel), 534.
Nicolovius, 440, 442.
Niemeyer, 369, 437.
Nitzsch, Prof. 639.
Nonne, Dr. Ludwick, 606.
 Labors in Hildburghausen, 606.
 Extraordinary, or Special course for teachers, 607.
Normal, meaning of, in Austria, 41, 880.
 Established by Frederick II, 869.
Normal Schools, for elementary teachers,
 Number and Statistics, 814.
 Historical, 108, 338, 339, 869.
 Authorities in administration, 173.
 Condition and mode of Admission, 165, 693.
 Subjects, course of studies, 887.
 Examinations, 165, 693.
 Model School, 692.
 Teachers, 691.
 Practice School, 887.
Normal School System in Prussia, 819.
Notaries, 435.
Nurlingen, Normal School, 691.
Nuremberg, School system, 170, 859.
 Agricultural department, 196.

Official Position of Teachers, 147.
Object Lessons, 579, 590.
Object Teaching, 54.
Observation, habit of, 590, 762.
Observatores morum, or Street Monitors, 546.
Obligatory school attendance, 609, 656, 662, 703.
 Date of introduction, 209, 222, 281, 319, 861, 882.
 Results in Prussia, 381.
 Legal limit, 661, 703.
OLDENBURG, Grand Duchy of, 327.
 Public Instruction, 327.
 1. Elementary Schools, 327, 744.
 Supreme School Board, 327.
 Parental Communal Duties, 327.
 Programme of School of one and two classes, 328.
 Middle Schools, Higher, Burgher, Private, Infant, 329
 2. Secondary Schools, 330, 845.
 Gymnasium of Oldenburg, Vechta, 330.
 3. Professional and Special Schools 331, 850.
 Navigation School, Teachers' Seminary, 331.
Olivier of Dessau, 359.
Optional Studies, 104.
Opening School with Prayer, 633, 864.
 Discussion respecting, 862.
Oral Examination, 479.

Orchards, care of, taught, 54.
Ordinarius, or class teacher, 246, 563.
Osnabruck, Cathedral School, 228.
Oral exercises in language, 87, 130.
Organ playing for teachers, 696.
Organists, as teachers, 391.
Orphans of teachers,
  Austria, 51, 85.   Mecklenburg, 317.
  Baden, 135.   Prussia, 432.
  Bavaria, 175.   Schleswig. 642.
  Brunswick, 215.   Saxon-Principalities, 560,
  Hanover, 232.   616, 620, 630.
  Hesse, 264, 288.   Wurtemberg, 701.
  Lippe-Detmold, 335,
Orphans' Asylums, 216, 233, 567, 599, 620, 633, 674.
  Special Judges for, 153, 206.
Out of School hours and premises, pupils, 129, 140, 171, 236, 683.
Outside Occupation for the Teacher, 232, 699, 821.
Overberg, Normal School at Munster, 385.
Over-governing in Germany, 810.

Pädagogik, 837, 841.
Parental rights and duties, 381, 749, 887, 895.
  Law of Saxe-Coburg-Gotha, 895.
  Fined for neglect as to attendance, 895.
  Laws of Austria, 887.
Parental rights and duties as to
  Attendance of children at school, 42, 128, 227, 887, 895.
  Religious instruction of children, 895.
  Private, or family instruction, 896.
  Interference with, or abuse of teachers, 896.
  Labor of children, 131, 887.
  Appeal to committees, 696.
  Payment of fees, 890, 896.
  Behavior and offenses out of school, 688.
  Text-books and aids of instruction, 37, 887.
Parish in School organization,
  Austria, 25, 42.   Oldenburg, 328.
  Baden, 124, 135.   Prussia, 752, 799.
  Bavaria, 161.   Saxony, 551.
  Hesse-Darmstadt, 282.   Saxon Principalities, 623.
  Hanover, 236.   Wurtemberg, 708.
  Mecklenburg, 311, 319.
Particular Schools, 546.
Pasturage for cow of teacher, 320, 372.
Pattison, Mark, Report on German Schools, 798.
  Substance of Prussian Regulations, 827.
Payments in kind, 272, 697.
Pedagogical Seminaries and Professors, 848.
  Berlin, 487.   Breslau, 488.
  Gottingen, 245.   Halle, 489.
  Magdeburg, 489.   Stettin, 488.
  Vienna, 75, 93.
Pedagogium, 137, 325, 489.
Penmanship, 207, 784, 841.
  Frederick II, regulations, 872.
Pensions for teacher,
  Anhalt, 20.   Mecklenburg, 317.
  Austria, 51.   Prussia, 410, 431, 474.
  Baden, 133.   Saxony, 554.
  Bavaria, 175.   Saxe-Altenburg, 569.
  Hanover, 232.   Saxe-Coburg, 898.
  Brunswick, 215.   Saxe-Meiningen, 615.
  Hesse-Cassel, 264.   Saxe-Weimar, 630.
  Hesse-Darmstadt, 285.   Wurtemberg, 711.
  Lippe-Detmold, 305.
Perceptive faculties, end and measure of infant culture, 591.
Periodicals, School, 660, 830.
Pestalozzi, 367, 370.
  Royal tribute to his principles, 364.
  Official reaction against, 367, 637.
  Religious teaching, 802.
Pestalozzianism in Germany, 356, 360, 804.
  Wurtemberg, 657
Peter Von Dresden, 533.
Philology, instruction in, 479 848.
Philological Seminaries, 848.
  Berlin, 484.   Koningsberg, 485.

Philological Seminaries.
  Heidelberg, 149.   Tübingen, 721.
Philosophy, in Gymnasium.
  Austria, 89.   Bavaria, 189.
  Baden. 145.   Prussia, 408.
Philosophical classes and schools.
  Austria, 75, 77, 78, 111.
  Baden, 145.
Physics in Gymnasiums, Austria, 89.
Piarists, 26, 68, 71, 109.
Plan of Sessions, 130.
Playground to School, 758.
Plutarch, Instruction of Boys, read in 1580, 547.
Poland, Schools in, 449, 870.
  Language in schools, 450.
Polytechnic Schools, 197, 853.
Pomerania, 371, 452.
Pusen, Province. 390. 449.
Potsdam, Schools, 859.
Practice, School of, 887.
Prayer in School,
  Austria, 130.   Prussia, 802, 864.
  Baden, 130.   Hanover, 186.
  Bavaria. 171.   Wurtemberg, 683.
Praparanden, 160, 213, 841.
Poor parents, to be helped, 862.
Poor children, separate school, 166.
  How supplied with books, 874.
Poor students, 540, 660.
Prague, school, 859.
  University, 846.
Preceptor, 721.
  Temporarily employed teacher in Thuringia, 607.
Prepariti, 34.
Primary Instruction, limits to, 706, 808.
Primary Schools in Anhalt, 17, 20, 744.
  Austria, 26, 74.
  Baden, 122, 744.
  Bavaria, 158, 744.
  Brunswick, 219. 744.
  Free Cities, 744.
  Hanover, 221, 744.
  Hesse-Cassel, 265, 744.
  Hesse-Darmstadt, 281. 744.
  Leichtenstein, 302, 744.
  Lippe-Detmold, 303, 744.
  Lippe-Shaumburg, 307, 744.
  Luxemburg and Limburg. 308, 744.
  Mecklenburg Schwerin, 310, 744.
  Mecklenburg Strelitz, 318, 744.
  Nassau, 324. 744.
  Oldenburg, 327, 744.
  Prussia, 335, 744, 798.
  Reuss, 527, 744.
  Saxony, 554, 744.
  Saxon-Principalities, 565, 744.
  Saxe-Altenburg, 567, 744.
  Saxe-Coburg-Gotha, 573, 744.
  Saxe-Meiningen, 608, 744,
  Saxe-Weimar, 627, 744,
  Schleswig-Holstein, 640, 744.
  Schwarzburg-Rudolstadt, 649, 744.
  Shwarz-Sonderhausen, 650, 744.
  Waldeck, 651, 744.
  Wurtemberg, 653, 744.
Principia Regulativa, 340.
  Provisions respecting schools, 340.
Printing, 534.
Printzen, 436.
Privileges of gymnasial students, 506.
Professor, title of, 471.
Prussia, Duchy of, 333.
PRUSSIA, Kingdom of,
  Area, Population, History, 333.
  Public Instruction, 335, 402, 744.
  1. Primary Schools, 335.
  Historical development by reigns, 335.
  Development by Provinces, 368.
  Schools as they were, 362, 833.
  Statistical, Results in 1819, 1861, 424, 744.
  2. Secondary Schools, 435.

RUSSIA,
Development of Administration, 435.
Provincial Progress, 447.
Local Administration, 460.
Summary of School Organization, 462.
Teachers, Appointment, director, 463, 522.
Professions, Title, Grades, Salaries, 420.
Examination of Teachers, 474.
Seminaries for secondary school teachers, 484.
Studies, course, methods, 492.
Real Schools, and Higher Burgher Schools, 501, 522.
Review, chronological and provincial, , 508.
3. Subjects, courses and methods of Primary Schools, 745.
4. Teachers and their training, 819.
5. Universities, 525, 846.
6. Special schools, 526, 856.
Private Instruction and Schools in,
  Austria, 92, 56, 891. Saxony, 552.
  Baden, 145. Saxe-Coburg, 896.
  Bavaria, 181. Wurtemberg, 724.
  Prussia, 507, 757.
Prizes, 171, 191, 717, 203.
Programmes, gymnasial, exchange of, 508.
Programme for schools in Saxe-Gotha, 583.
Promotion from class, 91.
Progymnasium, 247, 516, 816, 845.
Protestant basis of Schools. 65, 76. 110, 798.
Protestant School Authorities, 166.
Provincial or District School Authorities,
  Austria, 45, 83, 97, 892. Prussia, 753.
  Baden, 127. Saxony, 564.
  Bavaria, 163. Saxe-Coburg, 901.
  Hesse, 267, 283. Wurtemburg. 665.
Public Schools defined, 209, 425, 885, 892.
Puffendorf, Samuel, 548.
Punishment, mode of,
  Austria, 56. Prussia, 505.
  Baden, 129, 146. Saxe-Gotha, 580.
  Bavaria, 171. Wurtemberg, 687.
Punishment, barbarous, prohibited, 171, 506, 546, 609.
Corporal, restrained, 129, 258, 320, 609.

Quadrivium, 531.
Qualities, inherent of a good teacher, 309, 383.
Qualifications of teachers acquired, 383.
Quintilian, text-book in Pedagogy in 1580, 546.

Rahstein, plan of mechanics' school 1751, 98.
Rank of Teachers in civil service, 723.
Rank in class, 506, 717.
Ratich, 578.
Ratio Educationis, 109.
Ratio Studiorum, 67.
Ratzeburg, Principality of, 320.
Raumer, minister of education, 446.
Regulations of 1854, 416.
Reader in Prussian Schools, 419, 806.
  Wurtemberg, 683.
Reading, method of teaching, 590, 769, 779.
Real Commercial Adademy at Vienna, 98.
Real Schools, System of,
  Anhalt, 19. Nassau, 326.
  Austria, 98. Oldenburg, 329.
  Baden, 149. Prussia, 501, 522.
  Bavaria, 193. Reuss, 528.
  Brunswick, 217. Saxony, 551, 558.
  Free Cities, 740. Saxe-Altenburg.
  Hanover, 247, 257. Saxe-Coburg, 596.
  Hesse-Cassel, 272. Saxe-Meiningen. 625.
  Hesse-Darmstadt, 295. Saxe-Weimar, 632.
  Lippe-Detmold, 306. Schleswig-Hol., 644, 647.
  Luxemburg, 306. Schwarzburg, 650.
  Mecklnb'g-Shwerin, 318. Waldeck, 652.
  Mecklenb'g-Stielitz, 845. Wurtemberg, 718.
Real Schools, features of,
  Grades, 101, 149.
  Administration, 101, 150, 718.
  Teachers, grades, duties, 102, 719.
  Studies, 102, 104, 149, 150, 502, 719.
  Admission, 104, 150, 559.

Real Schools, features of,
  Discipline, 104.
  Examination, 104.
  Graduation, 104, 724.
  Expenses, 105, 149, 728.
  Statistics, 101, 726, 845.
  Libraries, 104.
  Practical work, 105.
  Directors, 150.
  Central Study, 719.
  Rank of teachers, 724.
Rector, or director, 84, 148, 224, 326, 466, ...
Rector Schools, 20, 229, 305.
Referee, in Austrian School Board, 34.
Reformation of 16th Century, and Schools, 663, 709.
Regencies in Prussian Organization, 515.
Register, or official list of children, 863, 873.
Regularity of attendance, 55, 380.
Regulativ, Prussian, of 1854, 802.
Real Gymnasium, Examples of,
  Coburg, 600. Saalfield, 625.
  Gotha, 596. Schleswig, 644.
  Leipsic, 559. Stuttgard, 720.
  Manheim, 151. Tübingen, 720.
  Meiningen, 625. Weimar, 634.
Religious Instruction,
  Austria, 34, 39, 80, 89, Oldenburg, 328.
    102, 885. Prussia, 498, 770, 791, 79t,
  Baden, 130, 139. 803.
  Bavaria, 68, 171. Saxe-Altenburg, 591.
  Brunswick, 209. Saxe-Coburg, 602.
  Free Cities, 737. Saxe Meiningen, 612.
  Hanover, 250. Saxony. 545, 552.
  Hesse-Cassel, 270. Saxe-Weimar, 631.
  Hesse-Darmstadt, 291. Schleswig-Holstein, 643.
  Mecklenb'g-Strelitz, 338. Schwazburg, 650.
  Nassau, 325. Wurtemberg, 682, 770.
Religious life and the School, 167.
Repetition School, 66, 648, 670, 672, 882.
Rescue Institutions, 203, 216, 223, 277.
Retirement of teachers of Gymnasium, 85, 473.
REUSS, Principality of, area, population, 528.
Public Instruction, 528.
Reviews of lessons, 767.
Reyher, Andrew, 577.
Rhenish Provinces, 384, 425, 459.
Rich and poor educated together, 166.
Riese, Adam, 540.
Ritter Academy, 238.
Rochow, 657, 865.
  Children's Friend, 655.
  Examples of improved schools, 350.
Rod, in discipline, 287, 580.
Roman Catholics, 107, 424, 892.
  Relations to Schools in Prussin, 346, 389, 800.
Romer, Martin, 535.
Rostock, Schools, 859.
  University, 846.
Rote learning, 209, 809.
Rottenhann, Count, 32, 109.
  Board of Educational Reform, 33.
  Gymnasium Reform, 73.
  Real Schools and Instruction, 98.
Royal Schools in Saxony, 546.
Rural Districts, 363, 604, 680.

Saalfield, Lyceum and real schools, 621, 625.
Sacristan, relations to schools, 378, 575, 698, 861.
Sagau, Normal School of Felbiger, 347. 869, 874.
Seat of Catholic School reform, 347.
Salzburg, 23, 61.
Salaries in,
  Baden, 133. Prussia, 429.
  Bavaria, 175. Saxe-Coburg, 593.
  Hanover, 229, Wurtemberg, 628.
Salaries, insufficient, 362.
Salzman Institute at Schepfenthal, 597.
Saturday, half or entire holiday, 146.
  Catechism-day, 545.
SAXONY, Kingdom, 531, 564.
  Area, population, history, 530.

SAXONY,
  Historical development of Education, 530.
  Convent and Cathedral schools, 531.
  School plan of 1528, 536.
  School Order of the Electorate 1580, 540.
  Studies, discipline, books, 546.
    1. Common Schools, 554, 744.
    2. Secondary schools, 562, 843.
    3. Superior school, 562, 846.
    4. Special school, 850.
SAXON PRINCIPALITIES, statistics, 565.
ALTENBURG, area, population, 567.
  Historical development, 567.
    1. Schools for young children, 568.
    2. Common schools and teachers, 569.
    3. Classical gymnasium, 572.
    4. Supplementary, 571.
COBURG-GOTHA, area, population, 572.
    1. Elementary schools, 573, 588, 600, 894.
    Historical, Myconius, Duke Ernest, 575, 600.
    2. Higher schools, 595.
    Gymnasium, Ernestinum, 596.
    Real school—Schnepfenthal—Dietendorfer, 597.
    Maria Institute—Girls' High School, 599.
    3. Special school for teachers, architects, etc., 599
MEININGEN, area, etc., 605.
    1. Elementary system, 605, 608.
    2. High schools, 621.
WEIMAR, area, population, 627.
    1. Elementary schools, 626.
    2. Higher schools, 632.
Schirmer, in Frankfort, 736.
SCHLESWIG, Duchy of, 635.
Schleiz, early school in, 527.
  Rutheneum Gymnasium, 528.
  Teachers' Seminary, 528.
SCHLESWIG-HOLSTEIN, Province of Prussia, 635.
  Historical development of Schools, 636.
  Organization and condition of system, 640.
    1. Elementary schools, 640.
    2. Secondary Schools, 642.
    3. Real School, 644.
Schmid's method of drawing, 364, 777.
Schmid's Pädagogich Encyclopädie, 3.
  Articles based on, 17, 135, 159, 207, 219, 264, 231, 310, 327, 333, 567, 731.
Schnepfenthal, Salzmann Institute, 597.
Scholasticus, 531, 734.
Scholars to a teacher, 51, 129, 166, 248, 595.
Schoningen, public schools, 212.
School Apprentices, 160.
School Architecture, 46, 160, 610, 796.
School Attendance. (See Attendance.)
School Committee, 125, 752.
School Codes, 891. (See Codes.)
School Collegium, 443, 641.
School Diary, 171, 269.
School Discourses, 862.
School Government, 54, 134, 171, 609, 704.
School Libraries, 53.
School-house, laws respecting,
  Expenditures on, 380.
  Frederick II, 393, 870.
  Maria Theresa, 879.
School Management, 837.
School Manual of Ernest, 581.
School Methods, 577.
School Order for Chemnitz, 1547, 540.
School Plan, 536. (See Plan of Studies.)
School Register, 863.
Schubert, Ferdinand, 40.
Schulpforta, 502.
Schuckmann, 441.
Schulze, Dr. John, 441, 477.
Schulze, G. of Saxony, 554.
SCHWARZBURG, Principality, 649.
  Area, population, division, 649.
  Public Instruction, 649.
    1. Rudolstadt, 649.
    2. Sondershausen, 650.
Schwerin, gymnasium, 315.

Scripture, Selections from, to be memorized, 418.
Secondary Instruction, defined, 135, 709.
Secondary schools in Germany, 843.
  Statistics, 846. (See Austria, &c.)
Sectarian Schools. (See Confessional.)
Sectarian Instruction, 791, 800.
Secular Schools, 800, 801.
Semler, Charles, and Real Schools, 501.
Senses, training of, 778.
Serfdom, and Schools, 25, 368.
Sexes, separation of, 229, 304, 386.
Seven Years War, 549.
Seebeck, Prof., plan of gymnasium, 623.
Sewing and knitting school, 305.
Schrötter, 356.
Shepherd Schools, in Lippe-Detmold, 304.
Sickness of Teacher, 473.
Siber, Adam, Nomenclature, 541.
Silk Culture, 353.
Silesia, in Austria, 23, 61.
Silesia, in Prussia, 398, 428.
  Regulations for Catholic Schools, 869.
Simultaneous method, 810.
Singing in Common Schools.
  Austria, 31, 54.   Hanover, 256.
  Bavaria, 170.   Prussia, 375, 808.
  Baden, 130, 145.   Saxe-Gotha, 591.
  Wurtemberg, 685.
Singing Associations, 364, 696.
Sisters, teaching orders of, 176, 233.
Slavonia, 23, 61.
Slate and Pencil, early uses of, 779.
Schneider, founder of Rescue House, 620.
Spelling, 169, 683, 806.
  Prussian Regulations of 1763, 871.
Special Schools in Germany, 850.
Spendou, in Austria, 34.
Spener, Jacob, 548.
St. Michaels Sunday, Discourse, 862.
  Collections to be taken up, 862.
Stralsund, early schools in, 372.
  Regulations for, 372, 376.
State and Schools, 27, 743, 790, 892.
State authorities, in Public Instruction.
  Austria, 892.   Hesse Darmstadt, 283.
  Baden, 126.   Prussia, 411, 799.
  Bavaria, 162.   Saxony, 551.
  Brunswick, 298.   Saxe-Coburg, 901.
  Hanover, 208.   Wurtemburg, 664, 705.
Statistics of Schools generally, 744, 846, 850.
Steiger, E., German Pedagogy, 904.
Stein, School Policy for Prussia, 361.
Steinmetz, 338, 362.
  Labors in behalf of Normal School, 339.
Stenography, regular study in Gymnasium, 500.
Real schools, 104.
Stephens, Prof. L., on Normal schools, 836.
Stettin, School policy, 361, 859.
Stiehl, Frederick, 416, 422.
  Needlework in girls' schools, 422.
  Author of Prussian Regulations of 1854, 416.
Stowe, Calvin E., 745.
Strehl, John, 40.
Sturm, John, 237.
Stuttgardt schools, 850.
  Burgher School, 721.
  Pedagogium, 710.
  Real Gymnasium, 720.
Styria, 23, 61.
Subjects of Elementary Instruction, 745, 767.
  Too many and too diffuse, 158, 766.
  Necessity of limitation and concentration, 808.
Subjects of Secondary Instruction, 85, 139, 185, 249, 492, 715.
Subjects of Real School Instruction, 273, 501, 720.
Summer Schools, 269, 285.
Sunday Schools and Lessons, 161, 670, 802.
  Austria, 105.   Hanover, 220.
  Baden, 131.   Hesse-Cassel, 270.
  Bavaria, 161.   Prussia, 357, 802.
Superannuated Teachers, 232, 305, 899.

ELEMENTARY AND SECONDARY INSTRUCTION IN GERMANY. 915

Superintendence,
(See State Authorities, *Provincial, Municipal*.)
Superintendents of Church, 867.
Supplementary Schools and Instruction, 633.
Support of Schools,
  Austria, 43.   Prussia, 528, 520, 758.
  Baden, 134.   Saxony, 552.
  Bavaria, 166, 183.   Saxon Principalities, 595,
  Brunswick, 210.   630.
  Hanover, 226, 229.   Wurtemberg, 563, 727.
Suvern, School-Counsellor, 440.
Superior Primary school, 758.
Surgery, schools of, 526, 850.
Swedish influence in Pomerania, 380.

Tacitus, on Germany, cited, 375.
Tatel, or Blackboard, 865.
Taxation, teachers' exemption from, 133, 232.
Taxation for School purposes, 663.
Teacher, particulars respecting office of,
  Absence, leave of, 288, 472.
  Account-book, 213.
  Appointment, 174, 465, 690.
  Appointment document, 465.
  As they were, 374, 833.
  Associations, 695.
  Certificates, grades of, 164.
  Civil Status, 160, 696.
  Commons, 320, 822.
  Conferences, 174, 695.
  Curriculum Vitæ, 470.
  Degrees, 481.
  Designation, 192.
  Dwelling, 320, 821.
  Examination, 470.
  Garden, 821.
  House of Instruction, 471.
  Installation, 231, 464.
  Journey for School Inspection, 822.
  Legal ideal, 173, 382, 464, 705, 819.
  Library, 888.
  Life Insurance, 215.
  Military Service, 464.
  Misdemeanors, 472.
  Moral Power, 464, 405, 613.
  Oath, 231, 465.
  Oath formula, 465.
  Orphans, 432.
  Outside occupations, 353, 699.
  Pasturage, 632, 822.
  Pensions, 51, 474.
  Permanent, 697.
  Periodicals, 888.
  Prize Essay, 696.
  Qualifications, 813.
  Rank, 471, 613, 723.
  Salaries, 473, 697, 888.
  Substitutes, 468, 889.
  Title, 470.
  Trial year, 489.
  Widows, 432.
Teachers' Associations, 30, 174, 695, 836.
Teachers' classification and designation.
  Adjuncti, 564.
  Apprentice, 236.
  Assistants, 95, 175, 613.
  Associates, 713.
  Cantor, 172, 215.
  Catechist, 47.
  Choir-rector, 172.
  Chorister, 215.
  Colleague, 564, 470.
  Custodian, 861.
  Director, 47, 465.
  German Teachers, 172.
  Head master, 470.
  Parish Clerk, 375.
  Parish School Teacher, 215.
  Practitioners, 274.
  Professor, 47, 471, 552, 564.
  Rector, 564, 470.

Teachers' classification and designation,
  School-Teachers, 172.
Universities of Germany,
  Oberlehrer, 470.
  Ordinarius, 83, 471, 563.
  Preceptor, 713.
  Principal, 713.
  Superior and Inferior, 470.
  Under Teacher, 47, 470.
Teachers' Elementary, how trained, in
  Anhalt, 18, 20.   Nassau, 324.
  Austria, 58, 61, 887.   Oldenburg, 331.
  Baden, 514.   Prussia, 433, 862,
  Bavaria, 173.   Saxony, 557.
  Brunswick, 213.   Saxe-Altenburg, 569.
  Hanover, 223.   Saxe-Coburg, 598.
  Hesse-Cassel, 271.   Saxe-Meiningen, 611.
  Hesse-Darmstadt, 286. Saxe-Weimar, 630, 818.
  Lippe-Detmold, 305.   Schleswig-Holstein, 641.
  Lippe-Schaumburg, 307. Schwazburg, 650.
  Mecklenburg, 313, 322. Wurtemberg, 691.
Teachers' Secondary, how trained, 484, 843.
Teachers' Seminaries, 382, 814. (*See Normal School*.)
Technical Schools and Instruction, 195, 599, 853.
  Frederick II regulation, 872.
Terence, as a Text-book, 542.
Terms and Vacation, 91.
Text-books.
  Austria, 52, 60, 74, 886.   Hanover, 252.
  Bavaria, 201.   Prussia, 504, 866.
Theology, faculties of, 840.
  Course of Studies, 848.
  Students, in School matters, 216, 240, 870.
Theresa Maria, 26, 69, 100.
Theresian Institutions, 100.
Thiersch, Professor, on Prussian Schools, 444.
Thilo, Professor, Author of Article, 335, 423.
Thinking Exercises, 788, 809.
Thirty Years' War, 322, 549.
Thou, in school parlance, 238, 293.
Thun Count, 37, 79.
Time Table.
  Burgher Schools, 57, 150, 737.
  Gymnasium, 90, 130, 185, 256, 290, 495, 406, 506,
     715.
  Primary Schools, 52, 128, 328.
  Real Schools, 99, 257, 296, 502, 644.
Toga Monastica, 712.
Toleration Act in Austria, 30.
Town Schools, 372, 575, 755.
Trade Schools, 167, 270, 295, 853.
Training Schools for Teachers, 896.
Transylvania, 23, 66, 119.
Trapp, Professor of Pedagogics, 437.
Traveling Students, 533.
Traveling Teachers, 472, 719, 822.
Trieste, Schools, 859.
Trivial Schools in Austria, 28, 32, 40, 61.
Trial year, 94, 489.
Trotzendorf, at Goldberg, 451.
Tübingen University, 846.
  Gymnasium, 715.   Real school, 720.
  Philological Seminary, 721.
Tuition in—Elementary—Gymnasial—Real School,

Austria,	55	90	104
Baden,	127	138	150
Bavaria,	175	183	200
Brunswick,	209	217	
Hanover,	227	249	
Hesse-Cassel,	268	275	273
Hesse-D'mst,	282	290	297
Prussia,	428	473	502
Saxe-Coburg,	592	596	
Wurtemberg,	729	720	720

Turnanstalten, 364, 483, 500.

Understanding of lessons, 130, 589.
Upper Austria, 62, 66, 95.
  University of, 846.
Universities of Germany, 847
  Foundation, faculties, professors, students, 846.

Vacations in schools.
Austria, 52.
Baden, 128.
Bavaria, 168.
Brunswick, 269.
Hanover, 229, 259.
Saxony, 558.
Saxe-Altenberg, 371.
Wurtemberg, 686.
Vechta, Normal school, 332.
Venice, 35, 75.
Vernacular, how taught in, 101, 131, 177.
Versification, Latin in 1580, 547.
Veterinary Schools, 853.
Village schools, 378.
Prussia, 403, 494, 809.   Brunswick, 212.
Vienna, Statistics of schools, 37, 859.
Diagram of schools, and studies, 22.
Salaries of teachers, 50.
Seminary for secondary teachers, 75, 93.
Commercial Academy and Real school, 98, 857.
Physical Institute, 93.
University, 846.
Vine Culture, school for, 851.
Vitzhum, gymnasium, 563.
Vogel, Dr., 557.
Vocalization, 769.
Volksschulen, 554, 798.
Voluntary principle in education, 703.
Vor Pomerania, 371.
Von Massow, 354.
Voss, visit to Pestalozzi, 356.

Wagner, Gymnasial Programmes, 179.
Waiblinger, training school for rescue teaching, 671.
WALDECK, Principality, 651-2.
Area, population, history, 651.
Public instruction, 651.
War, influence on the virtues, as well as vices, 442.
Walther, system of school management, 21.
Weber, Tobias, 323.
Weldemann, 634.
Weimar, Schools in, 632.
Sophia Foundation, 633.
Weingarten, Orphan Home, 675.
Wiesbaden, Schools, 859.
Westphalia, Province, 454.
Weissenfels, Normal school at, 371.
Wimmer, Dr. H. on Schools of Saxony, 554.
Schools of Waldeck, 651.
Wendler, bequest for free school, 550.
Wettin, House of, 531.
Widows of teachers, provision for.
Austria, 51, 85.
Baden, 135.
Bavaria, 175, 193.
Brunswick, 215.
Hanover, 232, 261.
Lippe-Detmold, 305.
Lippe-Shaumberg, 307.
Mecklenburg, 317.
Nassau, 325.
Prussia. 410, 431, 474.
Saxony, 554.
Saxe-Altenburg, 569.
Saxe-Coburg, 594, 898.
Wurtemberg, 658, 700, 711.

Wiese, Dr. L., Prussia High school, 446. 501, 844.
Gymnasial counsellor, 446, 552.
William I., 606.
Winter schools, 862.
Wismar, higher city school, 316.
Wittenberg, University, 535.
Winrich von Kniprode, in 1351 449.
Wolf, Commercial academy, 98.
Wolf, F. A., 475, 484.
Wöllner, 438, 799.
Religious edict, of 1788, 439.
Worship, Ministry of, 551.
Written examinations, 478.
Writing Schools, 208, 735.
Written Exercises, 87.
Writing, in schools of,
Austria, 59, 103.
Baden, 131, 139.
Bavaria, 169, 185.
Brunswick, 208.
Prussia, 770, 777. 807.
Wurtemberg, 770.
Writing, ornamental, 777.
WURTEMBERG, Kingdom of, 653.
Public instruction, historical, 654.
1. Elementary schools, 654.
School code of 1559, 654.
Teachers, salaries, training, 658, 690.
Statistics, 677, 744.
2. Secondary schools, 709.
Latin schools, Cloister schools, 709, 845.
3. Special and Technical schools, 730, 850.
Wurtzburg, university, 846.

Yard to Schoolhouse, 760.
Year, school in,
Austria, 103.
Baden, 147.
Bavaria, 191.
Prussia, 503.
Saxony, 557.
Wurtemberg, 686.
Young Children, methods of teaching, 768, 778.
Arithmetic, 781.
Common Things, 789.
Drawing, 779, 784.
Geography, 786.
Language, 778.
Natural Sciences, 789.
Observation, 778.
Reading, 781.
Religion, 771, 791, 802.
Thinking, 788.

Zedlitz. 351, 437.
Supreme School Board in 1787, 437.
Zeller, on Pestalozzi's method, 657.
Zerbst, school for Girls, 19.
Gymnasium, 19.
Pedagium, 19.
Zerrener, 369.
Views of Pestalozzi, 370.
Westphalia Children's Friend, 369.
Zurich, university, 846.

SUPERIOR INSTRUCTION: Contributions to the History of the Universities of Germany, with an account of the Systems and Institutions of Superior Instruction in other countries. 912 pages. $5.50. Republished from Barnard's American Journal of Education, with additions.

CONTENTS.

1. GERMAN STATES.

	PAGE.
INTRODUCTION	3
I. THE GERMAN UNIVERSITIES. From the German of Karl von Raumer	9
I. Historical	9
1. Introduction. Universities of Salerno, Bologna, and Paris	9
2. List of German Universities, with date of their foundation	10
3. The German Universities in the Fourteenth and Fifteenth centuries	11
A. Charters, or Letters of Foundation	11
B. The Pope and the Universities	12
C. The Emperor and the Universities	16
D. Organization of the earliest German Universities	17
a. The Four Nations. Four Faculties. Rector. Chancellor. Endowments	18
b. The Four Faculties	20
1. Faculty of Arts	20
2. Faculty of Theology	21
3. Faculty of Canon and Civil Law	24
4. Faculty of Medicine	26
c. Customs and Discipline	27
4. University of Wittenberg and its relations to the earlier Universities	30
5. History of the Customs of the Universities in the Seventeenth Century	37
A. The Deposition	42
B. Pennalism	52
6. History of the Universities in the Eighteenth Century	52
A. Nationalism. National Societies	52
B. Students' orders	56
7. History of the Universities in the Nineteenth Century	58
Introduction; the author's academical experience	59
A. Entrance at Halle, 1799; a preliminary view	59
B. Göttingen; Easter 1801 to Easter 1803	59
C. Halle; Easter 1803 to Sept. 1805	68
D. Breslau; 1810 to 1817	76
a. Establishment of the Jena Burschenschaft, July 18, 1816. Wartburg Festival, Oct. 18, 1817	80
b. Establishment of the general Burschenschaft, in 1818	91
E. Breslau, 1817 to 1819	92
a. Sand	102
b. The consequences of Sand's crime. Investigations. Breaking up of the societies. Destruction of the Burschenschaft	124
F. Halle, 1819 to 1823	136
Conclusion	153
II. APPENDIX	155
I. Bull of Pius II., creating University of Ingoldstadt	157
II. List of Lectures in the Faculty of Arts in 1366	159
III. Bursaries	160
IV. The "Comment" of the National Societies	161
V. Statutes	165
A. Constitution of the General German Burschenschaft	165
B. The Jena Burschenschaft	168
VI. The Wartburg Letters	183
VII. Bahrdt with the iron forehead	186
VIII. Substance of Tubingen Statutes for organizing a students' committee	187

		PAGE
IX.	Extract from an Address of Prof. Heyder, at Jena, in 1607	189
X.	Synonyms of "*Beanus*"	191
XI.	Meyfart's "*Aretinus*" or Student Life in the Sixteenth Century	191
XII.	Grant of Privileges by Leopold 1. to the University of Halle	192
XIII.	Works referred to	253
XIV.	The Universities in the summer of 1853	198

III. ACADEMICAL TREATISES 201
   1. Lecture system. Dialogic instruction 201
   2. Examinations 206
   3. Obligatory lectures. Optional attendance. Lyceums. Relations of the philosophical faculty and their lectures, to those of the professional studies 213
   4. Personal relations of the professors and students 229
   5. Small and large universities. Academies 236
   6. University instruction in elementary natural history 241
   7. Student songs 245
   Conclusion 049
INDEX 255

II. THE GERMAN UNIVERSITIES COMPARED WITH THOSE OF FRANCE AND ENGLAND.
   By Prof. H. Von Sybel, Bonn 259
   French idea of Superior Instruction. Renan 260
   Isolated courses and Lectures. College of France 260
   English idea of Superior Instruction 260
   Continuation of Subjects and Methods of Grammar Schools 260
   German union of original Research and thorough Instruction 262
   Relations of Universities to Gymnasia 262
   Defects of German Universities 266

III. UNIVERSITIES OF THE MIDDLE AGES. By Prof. Charles Savigny, Berlin ...... 271—330
   INTRODUCTION. Influence on the civilization of Europe 273
   1. UNIVERSITIES OF ITALY. Origin and Peculiarities 275
      (1.) Bologna. Earliest Statutes. Rector. Faculties. Nations. Degrees 275
      (2.) Padua. (3.) Pisa. (4.) Vicenza. (5.) Vicelli. (6.) Arezzo 275
      (7.) Ferrara. (8.) Rome. (9.) Naples. (10.) Perugia. (11.) Modena, Pavia, 296
   2. UNIVERSITIES OF FRANCE 309
      (1.) Paris. Oldest Documents. Peculiarities. Teachers. Colleges 309
      (2.) Montpellier. (3.) Orleans. (4.) Other French Universities 316
   3. Universities of England, Scotland, Spain, Portugal 324
   Remarks on the older universities 325
      Name. Relations to the Church and State. Chancellor 327
      Law Lectures. Subjects. Relation of Students to Teachers 327

IV. UNIVERSITIES—PAST AND PRESENT, by Dr. Döllinger, Munich 331
   Meaning and origin of the University 333
   Characteristic features of the ancient Schools of Italy and France 334
   Late development of the German High School 335
   Rapid Multiplication. Religious Agitation. Thirty Years' War 337
   New University without territorial circumspection 343
   Reorganization of the University of Vienna 345
   Common bond of all Faculties and Sciences 347
   University organization and Teaching in other European States 348
      France—Great Britain—United States—Italy 349
      Spain—Holland—Scandinavia—Russia 350
   Universities—the seed-beds and workshops of German thought 351
      German Faculty of Historical Research 353
      Quadruple Task of German High Schools 355
   Contributions to Scientific and Literary Production 357
   Chief acquisition of University Training in the Historical Sense . 359

V. STATISTICS—FACULTIES, PROFESSORS, STUDENTS 361

VI. HISTORICAL DEVELOPMENT OF PARTICULAR INSTITUTIONS 385

SUPERIOR INSTRUCTION.

II. ITALY.

I. HISTORICAL DEVELOPMENT OF SUPERIOR INSTRUCTION........................... 453
  1. Higher Education in Ancient Greece... 453
    State policy—The Sophists—Public Life—Attic Oratory...................... 456
    Schools of Athens—Plato, Socrates, Aristotle................................. 462
    Museum of Alexandria—its Rector, Professors, Students..................... 464
    Rhodes—Antioch—Tarsus.. 466
  2. Higher Education among the Romans... 467
    Teachers of Rhetoric and Grammar. Study of Greek....................... 469
    Personal Influence. Unconscious Tuition of Eminent Men. Etruria......... 474
    Athenæum of the Capital. University of Athens............................ 475
    Professors, appointment, salaries and assistants................................ 477
    Sophists of the later Roman Empire. Mode of Instruction.................. 481
  3. Effects of Christianity on Academic study...................................... 486
    Octagon or Tetradision of Constantine... 487
    Theological Seminaries—Alexandria—Constantinople......................... 488
    Roman Law at Rome and Berytus... 489
    Rule of the Ostrogoths—German element...................................... 490
  4. Differences between Ancient and Modern Academic Institutions............. 492
    Corporate privileges—Academic degrees....................................... 463
    Faculty of Arts, associated with Theology and Law.......................... 495
    Special Sciences—Canon Law—Medicine—Roman Law..................... 500
    Influence of Byzantine Greeks—Platonic element—Arabic culture......... 505
    Internal Economy of Ancient and Modern Academic life................... 506
    Emancipation of the Faculty of Arts—Classical Learning................... 507
    Notes—Museum of Alexandria—Literary Clubs, or Symposia............. 510
II. CHRISTIAN SCHOOLS—as distinguished from Pagan........................... 513
  St. Basil and St. Gregory of Nazianzus at Athens............................. 515
  Cassiodorus at Vivaria... 517
  St. Benedict and the Benedictines... 519
  Monte Cassino—Summary of the Rule of St. Benedict....................... 521
  Confirmation of Rule—Guarantees and Exemptions of Pope Gregory VII.... 524
  Monasteries as Schools, and Repositories and Disseminators of Learning.... 525
  Cathedral Schools—Training of Theological Students.......................... 527
  Order of St. Dominic—Society of Jesus—Council of Trent.................. 529
III. REVIVAL OF THE LANGUAGES AND LITERATURES OF GREECE AND ROME.......... 541
  1. Literary studies of the Middle Ages—Intellectual Life...................... 545
    Trivium, Quadrivium, Mathematics, Astronomy, Natural History........... 548
    Roger Bacon—Lay of Nibelungen... 549
  2. Dante and Boccaccio—Use of the Vernacular.................................. 550
    Petrarch—precursor of Philological Poetry—aversion to scholasticism...... 556
  3. Growth of Classical Learning—Florence....................................... 565
    John of Ravenna and Chrysoloras—Guarino and Vittorino di Feltre........ 567
    Cosmo di Medici—Lorenzo—Pope Nicholas V.—First printed books...... 570
    Platonic Academy at Florence—Marsilius, Ficinus, George of Trebezond... 572
    Francis Philelphus—Poggius—Laurentius Valla—Bessarion—Gaza........ 573
    Lorenzo di Medici—Landinus—Politianus—Picus, Count of Mirandola.... 577
    Leo X.—the dark side of his Pontificate—Machiavelli and Ariosto........ 586
    Retrospect—Influence on Germany, France, and England................... 592
IV. SUPERIOR INSTRUCTION IN THE KINGDOM OF ITALY............................. 595
  I. HISTORICAL NOTICE OF EXISTING UNIVERSITIES.............................. 597
    1. State Universities... 598
      Bologna, Cagliari, Catania, Genoa, Maceralta, Messina, Modena, Naples, 603
      Palermo, Parma, Padua, Pavia, Pisa, Sassari, Siena, Turin................ 609
    2. Non-government Universities... 616
      Camerino, Ferrara, Perugia, Urbino... 616
    3. Superior Institutes... 619
    4. Higher Learning in the city of Rome....................................... 622
  II. ADMINISTRATION, FACULTIES, PROFESSORS, STUDENTS, AND STATISTICS........ 621
  III. TEACHING ORDERS OF THE CATHOLIC CHURCH............................... 641

III. THE NETHERLANDS.

- I. Historical Development... 673
  - 1. Schools and Institutions of the Church... 677
  - 2. Instruction of Eminent Teachers.. 685
  - 3. Universities.. 705
- II. Superior and Professional Instruction... 713
  - I. Holland.—II. Belgium.. 713

IV. FRANCE.

- I. Historical Development... 723
  - 1. Schools and Institutions of the Church... 723
  - 2. Universities and Colleges.. 729
  - 3. Imperial University.. 737
- II. Superior and Professional Instruction... 745
  - 1. Faculties—(1.) Literature and Science. (2.) Theology. (3.) Law. (4.) Medicine. 745
  - 2. Institutions outside of the Faculties. (1) College of France. (2.) Oriental Languages, &c.. 747
  - 3. Practical School of Higher Studies.. 749
- III. Statistics of Institutions and Expenditures... 757
  - Guizot's Ministry of Superior Instruction.. 767

V. SWITZERLAND.

- I. Historical Development... 803
- II. Cantonal Institutions of Superior Instruction.. 805

VI. DENMARK, NORWAY, SWEDEN.

- I. Historical Development... 811
- II. Institutions of Superior Instruction.. 812
  - I. Denmark.—II. Norway.—III. Sweden... 812

VII. RUSSIA.

- I. Historical Development... 819
- II. Institutions and Statistics of Superior Instruction.................................... 825

VIII. GREECE AND TURKEY.

- I. Historical Development... 835
- II. Institutions and Statistics of Superior Instruction.................................... 835
  - I. Greece.—II. Turkey... 837

IX. SPAIN AND PORTUGAL.

- I. Historical Development... 843
  - 1. Institutions of the Church... 843
  - 2. Arabic Culture... 845
  - 3. Universities.. 849
- II. Institutions and Statistics of Superior Instruction.................................... 853
  - I. Spain.—II. Portugal... 850

X. GREAT BRITAIN.

- I. Historical Development... 867
- II. Institutions of Superior Instruction.. 871
  - I. England.—II. Scotland.—III. Ireland.. 871

XI. AMERICAN STATES.

- I. Historical Notice.. 883
- II. Institutions of Superior and Professional Instruction................................. 885
  - I. United States.—II. British Dominion.—III. Other American States.... 885